Warman's
Antiques& Collectibles
2017

50

FIFTIETH EDITION

NOAH FLEISHER

Published by

Krause Publications, a division of F+W Media, Inc.
700 East State Street • Iola, WI 54990-0001
715-445-2214 • 888-457-2873
www.krausebooks.com

To order books or other products call toll-free 1-800-258-0929
or visit us online at www.krausebooks.com

ISBN-13: 9781440246296
ISBN-10: 1440246297

Cover Design by Nicole MacMartin
Designed by Nicole MacMartin
Edited by Mary Sieber

Printed in China

10 9 8 7 6 5 4 3 2 1

BACK COVER: Bird chair and ottoman by Harry Bertoia, design date 1952, Knoll International, circa 1974, blue upholstery on steel rod frame, chair 40 1/4" high x 33" deep x 38 1/4" wide, ottoman 14 1/2" high x 17 1/4" deep x 23 1/2" wide. $984 *(Courtesy of Skinner, Inc., www.skinnerinc.com)*

Contents

Introduction 4

The Mid-1960s Special Section...................16

Advertising 54

Art 63

    American Art.............................64

    Contemporary Art 82

    Fine Art 94

    Illustration Art.........................102

Asian..112

Autographs 122

Banks...126

Books...132

Bottles 140

Ceramics 147

    American

        Fiesta 148

        Fulper..............................155

        Grueby 162

        Rookwood 170

        Roseville Pottery 182

        Weller Pottery 192

    European

        Select Makers...................200

        KPM 219

        Limoges 232

        Majolica 237

        Meissen 246

        Sèvres 258

        Wedgwood 267

Children's Books 276

Civil War Collectibles 290

Clocks..298

Coca-Cola...306

Coin-Operated Devices 314

Comics 322

Cookie Jars 336

Disneyana 342

Folk Art & Americana 358

Furniture 365

Glass 397

    Art Glass 398

    Carnival Glass.........................402

    Daum Nancy 409

    Depression Glass 420

    Fenton Art Glass 438

    Lalique 444

    Quezal 454

Halloween 459

Jewelry..469

Lamps & Lighting..................................492

Mantiques 506

Maps & Globes......................................516

Maritime Art & Artifacts........................522

Movie Posters..532

Music Memorabilia 542

North American Indian Artifacts..............552

Perfume Bottles......................................559

Petroliana..566

Photography...574

Political Memorabilia..............................586

Porcelain Signs.......................................598

Quilts..612

Records 620

Science & Technology.............................634

Silver..640

Sports 652

Tiffany Studios 658

Toys 676

Vintage Fashion Accessories....................686

World War II 696

Index 702

Introduction

Warman's 50ᵗʰ Edition – *Going Back to Our Roots*

By Noah Fleisher

NOAH FLEISHER received his Bachelor of Fine Arts degree from New York University and brings more than a decade of newspaper, magazine, book, antiques and art experience to his position as Public Relations Director of Heritage Auctions, one of the country's foremost auction houses. He is the former editor of *Antique Trader, New England Antiques Journal* and *Northeast Antiques Journal*, is the author of *Warman's Modern Furniture* and co-author of *Collecting Children's Books*, and has been a longtime contributor to *Warman's Antiques & Collectibles*.

Thumbing through the 2017 edition of *Warman's*, you have to admit it looks pretty spectacular for something turning 50. Can it really have been that long? The truth is, it's been even longer than that. While this is the 50th *edition,* the first year this venerable guide was published was actually 1948.

Edwin G. Warman of Uniontown, Pennsylvania, was an avid antiquer. So much so, he published price listings in response to requests from friends and seekers alike. In 1948 he decided to take it a step further and formalize it into a book, which he continued doing until his death in 1979.

It was a transformative moment.

Suddenly everyone – via a modest little book called *Warman's Antiques and Their Current Prices* – had access to information that was once the sole purview of dealers, shops, and auctions. Before the guide was published, buyers were on their own. Now, with *Warman's* on their side, the playing field was leveled, baseline values were established, and the balance of power was now equalized.

What I have always loved about *Warman's* – and one of the things that makes it humbling to occupy this seat – is that it is a living, breathing model, a fluid document that reflects the ebb and flow of tastes and sensibilities across the spectrum. The prices, the subjects, and the perspectives reflected herein are meant to change as the years pass, just as the occupant of the seat that I now command will someday – hopefully not too soon, though – change.

This is not lost on me. There will, at some point, be someone after me who will continue to steward this lovely book. This anniversary is a chance to celebrate, just as it is chance to be philosophic: It is the nature of all things to pass. I have been lucky to follow immense talents in the field here at *Warman's*, editors who will forget more about antiques in a day than I will ever know in my lifetime. Fortunately for all of us who love this business, we are able to achieve a little continuity via our shared love and custodianship of the varied, marvelous pieces of material culture we choose to oversee. In this way we all achieve a little immortality.

To ring in this 50th edition, let's go back to my predecessors at *Warman's*: Harry Rinker and Ellen Schroy, two legendary names in the business who have left an indelible mark both on this book and on how we all buy, sell, and trade antiques. I should be so lucky to spend even half the time that they did on this book, and I humbly thank them for their time, energy, and graciousness. The best part about their enlightening and entertaining answers is how accurately they reflect both the personalities of these wonderful editors as well as their philosophies and their deep and abiding love for antiques and collectibles.

Also, as a bonus, former *Warman's* publisher Stanley Greene, who took up the mantle in 1981 following Warman's death in 1979, adds his perspective on this milestone edition.

WARMAN'S: What year did you join Warman's as editor? What year was your last edition?

HARRY RINKER (HR): Following the death of Edwin G. Warman, the estate decided to sell Warman Publishing. In 1981, Stanley and Katherine Greene asked Lita Solis-Cohen to recommend an editor for the non-pattern glass listings. She recommended me; at the time I was working as the executive director of the Montgomery Country [Pennsylvania] Federation of Historical Societies.

The 16th edition, copyrighted in 1982, was the first edition of *Warman's Antiques and Their Prices* I edited. The cover notes that Warman Publishing was in its 33rd year, publishing every two years beginning in 1948. Starting with that edition, Stanley and Katherine Greene made *Warman's* an annual publication. My editorship ended with the 30th edition.

ELLEN SCHROY (ES): I started as associate editor in 1982, on the 16th edition, and took over as editor in 1998 with the 32nd edition. I retired after the 42nd edition, in 2009.

WARMAN'S: What was the book like back then?

ES: It was pocket-sized (or bible-sized), hence the nickname "Antiques Bible" to collectors. I always thought its name could have been *Antiques A to Z* – every edition went all the way from ABC Plates on down to Zsolnay porcelain.

HR: Glass – especially pattern glass – was the focus of the first 14 editions of *Warman's*. The antiques categories were the traditional collecting categories dating back to the early 20th century. There were a few "collectible" categories such as Depression glass, mechanical banks, and toys.

My initial impression was that the title needed a major overhaul. The pattern glass content needed to be greatly reduced and the number of collecting categories and background material needed to be expanded. The primary need was to create an identity for *Warman's* that challenged its chief rival. This was accomplished in part by using an expanded listing format and making the listing methodology reflective of what was important in the collecting mindset for each separate category. Hence, the listing format changed from category to category. By the 22nd edition of *Warman's Antiques and Their Prices*, the background histories had been completely rewritten and the heads also included a list of key reference books relating to that specific collecting category.

WARMAN'S: What was your first impressions of the book?

HR: The collecting categories reflected those of greatest interest to E. G. Warman and his dealer friends, not what was happening in the field. The early 1980s was a period when 20th century collectibles were gaining acceptance. Antiques still dominated, but collectibles were

Courtesy of Heritage Auctions, ha.com

"Marilyn Monroe, Sleeping" gelatin print, Bert Stern, circa 1962, signed in ink lower right margin recto, small ripple in center left edge, matted and framed under acrylic, 27 1/2" high x 37" wide. **$10,625**

the hot spot for the young collector. Antiques from the post-Civil War period were gaining in popularity, due in part to the rise in cost of 18th and early 19th century pieces.

ES: I thought to myself, "Oh my. Who knows about all this stuff?"

WARMAN'S: *What areas of the market were the hottest when you took over?*

ES: By the 32nd edition, Barbie was hot, as were toys in general. We were also seeing militaria gaining in popularity. Advertising was also quite strong at the time.

HR: In 1981, the antique mall was in its infancy and the Internet did not exist. The secondary sales market was all traditional venues: shops, shows, and flea markets. Strong regional auction houses were minimal. The simple answer is that "hot" was whatever the price guides reported as hot, primarily by showing a continuing rise in value. The antiques and collectibles boom market continued until the late 1980s recession.

WARMAN'S: *When you took over, did you have a vision for the book?*

HR: My vision was basic: Be better than our main competitors. Although Stanley Greene made it clear that he would be happy if *Warman's* retained its No. 2 position, I wanted the top slot. I recognized that *Warman's* would not be able to incorporate the growing number of new categories, so I envisioned splitting off the collectibles categories into a separate book. *Warman's Americana and Collectibles,* copyrighted in 1984, eventually became the flagship publication for the *Warman's Encyclopedia of Antiques and Collectibles* for which I served as series editor.

ES: My vision was simple: to make *Warman's* the most thoroughly researched price guide available on the market to collectors, appraisers, and dealers alike.

WARMAN'S: *Looking back, what did you bring to Warman's that you think is your*

greatest lasting contribution?

ES: My greatest contribution was one of the spin-off books I wrote, *Warman's Depression Glass* [now in its 6th Edition]. This book was conceived about the time that Chilton Books, who purchased the title from the Greenes, was selling the *Warman's* line to Krause Publications. The line drawings included in the volume, and a few other features, were new to the industry at the time and have turned into a valuable asset, in and of themselves, to collectors and dealers.

HR: My greatest contribution to *Warman's* was the concept that a general antiques and collectibles price guide is an educational tool rather than just a listing of objects and prices. It's the initial starting point for the appraiser, auctioneer, collector, or dealer. The category introductions contained information that allowed an individual to take their learning to the next level.

WARMAN'S: What is the biggest or most startling change in the business of antiques and collectibles since you started?

HR: *Warman's* contained 200-250 collecting categories. Warman's *Americana* added another 250-300 categories. When eBay closed its collectibles division in 2005, it identified more than 30,000 separate collecting categories. It is now impossible for any general antiques and collectibles resource to accurately reflect the market. Perhaps the most startling change is change itself. When I assumed the editorship of *Warman's*, the book reflected the market as it existed through the first two-thirds of the 20th century. As the 1980s progressed, the traditional market faced challenges. By 2000, the stability of the traditional market had vanished. Now change is the order of the day, many traditional collecting categories are endangered, and the cyclical market no longer exists.

ES: The Internet was just emerging as a viable source when I took over as editor of *Warman's*. Before the web, most of the research in the business was done by humans via auctions, antique shows, dealer lists, and advertisements in *Antique Trader Weekly*.

WARMAN'S: What is the one thing you wish more collectors knew?

ES: That they should truly love and *use* their collections.

HR: That antiques and collectibles are not liquid assets. The introduction to every *Warman's* book title contained a note indicating the book was a price guide and not a price *absolute*. Yet individuals saw the pricing information as gospel. There are no fixed prices in the field. The guarantee that antiques and collectibles will increase in value over time is a myth. The secondary antiques and collectibles market is manipulated and speculative.

WARMAN'S: If you could look back and choose the one collectible or collecting category that got away, what would it be?

HR: When I became editor of *Warman's*, I created Rinker Enterprises, Inc., an antiques and collectibles research and education center devoted to tracking and analyzing developments within the trade. Thanks to the staff of Rinker Enterprises and the *Warman's* Board of Directors, there were no missed categories. Categories came and went as a reflection of market movement. During my editorship, the cage door was closed – no categories got away.

ES: For me it would be political memorabilia such as jugate buttons, bumper stickers, etc., now that those things are all being replaced by sound bites and social media. You can't put those things in a display case to enjoy later.

WARMAN'S: What advice would you give newer collectors today?

ES: Buy what you love because you want to own it. Don't assume that everything will continue to go up in value.

HR: Collecting should be about the stories inherent in an object, not about the potential for long-term investment. Research the objects you are collecting; follow the leads wherever they go. Do not listen to old-time collectors. Their collecting philosophy and methodology is archaic. Collecting is more individually driven than ever before.

WARMAN'S: What do you think people will be collecting 10-20 years from now?

HR: Objects from the 20th century will be antiques. Interest in pre-2000 objects will not be strong. Current generations are much more "me" focused. The hot decades will be the 2000s and 2010s. Look around. Visit Crate & Barrel, Pottery Barn, Target, and Wal-Mart. Pay attention. The objects on the shelves [there] are tomorrow's collectibles and 2050's antiques.

ES: Collecting good-quality handmade items will always be the best investment. Artwork, jewelry, folk art, quilts, and glasswares that are hand-crafted will be treasured in future generations, just as we treasure antiques hand-crafted by former generations today.

Special Thanks

There have been so many talented and insightful people who have worked on *Warman's* over the years that it would take up

A few words from Stanley Greene, *former owner of Warman's Publishing Co.*

My wife Katherine and I purchased the rights to *Warman's Antiques & Collectibles* from the estate of E. G. Warman in 1981, sadly after antique lover and entrepreneur Edwin G. Warman passed away while on safari in 1979. His third wife, Pat Warman, remained in Uniontown, Pennsylvania, where she was working on the 15th edition.

Our background was publishing, not the antique business, so we hired Harry L. Rinker as editor. He developed the staff, which included Doris Ford and Ellen Schroy. Later associate editors included Terese Oswald, Diane Sterner, and Dana Moryakan as well as Harry Rinker, Jr. By the time we sold the publishing company to Chilton Books in 1989, Harry and the staff had developed several new titles under the Warman's banner, which became standards in the field, such as *Warman's Americana & Collectibles, Warman's Pattern Glass* and *Warman's Country.* They also guided other authors, such as Susan and Al Bagdade, to create the new *Warman's Pottery and Porcelain Price Guide.*

During this period we saw the publishing industry change from professional typesetters to inputting material directly into computers. I doubt the staff will ever forget sitting in the offices of the typesetters and, literally, taking a scissors to the galleys of the first edition of *Warman's Americana* because it was too long to fit the pages allotted. Scooping up those strips of leftover material was the basis of the second edition of that book.

Both the antiques business and book publishing have taken dramatic leaps in the intervening years, and I wish to congratulate those responsible for meeting the challenge and maintaining *Warman's* as one of the leading references in the field.

— Stanley A. Greene

far too much space to thank them all here. They know who they are and I hope they accept these heartfelt thanks from me on behalf of Krause Publications for all the work and effort they have put into this title over the years. I am honored to follow in their footsteps.

For the 2017 edition in particular I would be remiss in not thanking Paul Kennedy, editorial director of this book, for his continued guidance and friendship. I would also like to thank all the contributors whose brilliant work makes up these pages. Last, but certainly not least, I would like to thank the great loves of my life, my wife and daughter, Lauren Zittle and Fiona Fleisher. As always, their patience and love guide my every action.

In the Beginning

Edwin G. Warman was an entrepreneur in Uniontown, Pennsylvania. He dabbled in several ventures, including ownership of a radio station. He was also an avid antiques collector who published his price listings in response to requests from friends and fellow collectors. The first modest price guide was published in 1948 as *Warman's Antiques and Their Current Prices*. It was a bold move. Until then, antiques were sold primarily through dealers, antiques shops, and at auctions. The buyers and sellers negotiated prices and were forced to do their own research to determine fair values. Under Warman's care, the price guide changed all that forever. Warman also published some specialized price guides for pattern glass and milk glass, as well as his "Oddities and Curiosities" editions, under the banner of the E.G. Warman Publishing Co.

Although the name varied slightly over the years, *Warman's Antiques and Their Current Prices* covered such collectible areas as mechanical banks, furniture, and silver, just like the Warman's of today. His pages consisted of a brief statement about the topic, either relating to the history or perhaps the "collectibility" of the category. A listing of current prices was included, often containing a black and white photograph.

E.G. Warman died in 1979. His widow, Pat Warman, continued the tradition and completed work on the 15th edition after his death. The estate sold the E.G. Warman Publishing Co. to Stanley and Katherine Greene of Elkins Park, Pennsylvania, in 1981. Chilton Books bought the Warman Publishing Co. in the fall of 1989. With the 24th edition, Warman's was published under the Wallace-Homestead imprint. Krause Publications purchased both the Warman's and Wallace-Homestead imprints in 1997.

We are proud to continue the rich tradition started nearly 70 years ago by Mr. Warman, a man driven by his love of antiques and collectibles and by a thirst for sharing his knowledge.

The Warman's Advantage

The Warman's Advantage manifests itself in several important ways in the 2017 edition. As we reviewed past volumes, we wanted to make this book as easy to use as possible. To that end, we've consolidated and reorganized how we present several key categories. Our new mantra is, "What is it first?"

For instance, an antique clock may also have an advertising component, an ethnic element (like black memorabilia), reflect a specific design theme (like Art Deco), and be made of cast iron. But first and foremost, it's a clock, and that's where you'll find it listed, even though there are other collecting areas involved.

There are a few categories that remain iconic in the collecting world. Coca-Cola collectibles cross many interests, as do folk art, Asian antiques, and Tiffany designs, to name just a few. These still have their own broad sections.

In honor of the 50th edition of *Warman's*, a special retrospective essay on the 1960s was added to the book, complete with images of iconic items of the era and their current values. Please see "The Mid-1960s" following this "Introduction."

Courtesy of James D. Julia Auctioneers, Fairfield, Maine,
www.jamesdjulia.com

Monumental Moser vase with amethyst glass
body with large gilded panels of platinum and
gilded flowers and scrolls with center white
enameled stylized flower, amethyst glass with
platinum gilded stylized flowers and leaves and
applied gold enamel beading, unsigned, very
good to excellent condition, 22 1/4" high. **$1,235**

Prices

The prices in this book have been
established using the results of auction
sales across the country, and by tapping
the resources of knowledgeable dealers and
collectors. These values reflect not only
current collector trends, but also the wider
economy. The adage that "an antique (or
collectible) is worth what someone will pay for
it" still holds. A price guide measures value,
but it also captures a moment in time, and
sometimes that moment can pass very quickly.

Beginners should follow the same advice
that all seasoned collectors share: Make
mistakes and learn from them; talk with
other collectors and dealers; find reputable
resources (including books and websites);
and learn to invest wisely, buying the best
examples you can afford.

Words of Thanks

This 50th edition of the *Warman's* guide
would not be possible without the help of
countless others. Dozens of auction houses
have generously shared their resources, but
a few deserve special recognition: Heritage
Auctions, Dallas; Backstage Auctions,
Houston; Woody Auction, Douglass, Kansas;
Greg Belhorn, Belhorn Auction Services LLC,
Columbus, Ohio; Andrew Truman, James D.
Julia Auctioneers, Fairfield, Maine; Anthony
Barnes at Rago Arts and Auction Center,
Lambertville, New Jersey; Karen Skinner
at Skinner, Inc., Boston; Morphy Auctions,
Denver, Pennsylvania; Susan Pinnell at Jeffrey
S. Evans & Associates, Mount Crawford,
Virginia; Rebecca Weiss at Swann Auction
Galleries, New York; and Leslie Hindman
Auctioneers, Chicago. And, as always, special
thanks to Catherine Saunders-Watson for her
many contributions and continued support.

Read All About It

There are many fine publications that
collectors and dealers may consult about
antiques and collectibles in general. Space

does not permit listing all of the national and regional publications in the antiques and collectibles field; this is a sampling:

- *Antique Trader,* published by Krause Publications, 700 E. State St., Iola, WI, 54990 – *www.antiquetrader.com*

- *Antique & The Arts Weekly,* 5 Church Hill Road, Newton, CT 06470 – *www.antiquesandthearts.com*

- *AntiqueWeek,* P.O. Box 90, Knightstown, IN 46148 – *www.antiqueweek.com*

- *Maine Antique Digest,* P.O. Box 358, Waldoboro, ME 04572 – *www.maineantiquedigest.com*

- *New England Antiques Journal,* 24 Water St., Palmer, MA 01069 – *www.antiquesjournal.com*

- *The Journal of Antiques and Collectibles,* P.O. Box 950, Sturbridge, MA 01566 – *www.journalofantiques.com*

- *Southeastern Antiquing & Collecting Magazine,* P.O. Box 510, Acworth, GA 30101 – *www.go-star.com/antiquing*

Visit an Antiques Show

One of the best ways to enjoy the world of antiques and collectibles is to take the time to really explore an antiques show. Some areas, like Brimfield, Massachusetts, and Manchester, New Hampshire, turn into antiques meccas for a few days each summer when dealers and collectors come for both specialized and general antiques shows, plus auctions.

Here are a few of our favorites:

- *Brimfield, Massachusetts, shows,* held three times a year in May, July, and September, *www.brimfield.com*

- *Round Top, Texas, antique shows,* held spring, fall, and winter, *www.roundtoptexasantiques.com*

- *Antiques Week* in and around Manchester, New Hampshire, held every August, *www.antiquesweeknh.com*

- *Christine Palmer & Associates antiques and collectibles shows,* including the Portland, Oregon, Expos, *http://christinepalmer.net*

- *The Original Miami Beach Antique Show,* www.originalmiamibeachantiqueshow.com

- *Merchandise Mart International Antiques Fair,* Chicago, *www.merchandisemartantiques.com*

- *High Noon Western Americana Show and Auction,* Phoenix, *www.highnoon.com*

LET US KNOW WHAT YOU THINK

We're always eager to hear what you think about this book and how we can improve it.

Contact:
Paul Kennedy
Editorial Director
Antiques & Collectibles Books
Krause Publications
700 E. State St.
Iola, WI 54990-0001
715-318-0372
Paul.Kennedy@fwcommunity.com

Contributors

John Adams-Graf
Tom Bartsch
Eric Bradley
Brent Frankenhoff
Kyle Husfloen
Paul Kennedy
Karen Knapstein
Mark B. Ledenbach
Kristine Manty
Michael Polak
Antoinette Rahn
Ellen T. Schroy
Mary Sieber
Maggie Thompson
David Wagner
Martin Willis

Auction Houses

Sanford Alderfer Auction & Appraisal
501 Fairgrounds Rd.
Hatfield, PA 19440
215-393-3000
www.alderferauction.com
Full service

American Bottle Auctions
915 28th St.
Sacramento, CA 95816
800-806-7722
www.americanbottle.com
Antique bottles, jars

American Pottery Auction
Waasdorp Inc.
P.O. Box 434
Clarence, NY 14031
716-983-2361
www.antiques-stoneware.com
Stoneware, redware

American Sampler
P.O. 371
Barnesville, MD 20838
301-972-6250
www.castirononline.com
Cast-iron bookends, doorstops

Antiques and Estate Auctioneers
861 W. Bagley Rd.
Berea, OH 44017
440-647-4007
Fax: 440-647-4006
www.estateauctioneers.com
Full service

ATM Antiques & Auctions LLC
811 SE US Hwy 19.
Crystal River, FL 34429
800-542-3877
www.charliefudge.com
Full service

Auctions Neapolitan
1100 First Ave. S.
Naples, FL 34102
239-262-7333
www.auctionsneapolitan.com
Full service

Belhorn Auction Services, LLC
P.O. Box 20211
Columbus, Ohio 43220
614-921-9441
www.belhorn.com
Full service, American art pottery

Backstage Auctions
448 West 19th St., Suite 163
Houston, TX 77008
713-862-1200
www.backstageauctions.com
Rock 'n' roll collectibles and memorabilia

Bertoia Auctions
2141 DeMarco Dr.
Vineland, NJ 08360
856-692-1881
www.bertoiaauctions.com
Toys, banks, holiday, doorstops

Bonhams
101 New Bond St.
London, England W1S 1SR
44-20-7447-7447
www.bonhams.com
Fine art and antiques

Brian Lebel's Old West Auction
3201 Zafarano Dr., Suite C585
Santa Fe, NM 87507
480-779-9378
www.codyoldwest.com
Western collectibles and memorabilia

Brunk Auctions
P.O. Box 2135
Asheville, NC 28802
828-254-6846
www.brunkauctions.com
Full service

Caroline Ashleigh Associates, LLC
1000 S. Old Woodward, Suite 201
Birmingham, MI 48009-6734
248-792-2929
www.auctionyourart.com
Full service, vintage clothing, couture and accessories, textiles, western wear

Cedarburg Auction Co., Inc.
227 N. Main St.
Thiensville, WI 53092
262-238-5555
www.cedarburgauction.com
Full service

Christie's New York
20 Rockefeller Plaza
New York, NY 10020
www.christies.com
Full service

Clars Auction Gallery
5644 Telegraph Ave.
Oakland, CA 94609
510-428-0100
www.clars.com
Full service

Coeur d'Alene Art Auction
8836 Hess St., Suite B
Hayden Lake, ID 83835
208-772-9009
www.cdaartauction.com
19th and 20th century Western and American art

Cowan's
6270 Este Ave.
Cincinnati, OH 45232
513-871-1670
www.cowanauctions.com
Full service, historic Americana, Native American objects

Doyle New York
175 E. 87th St.
New York, NY 10128
212-427-2730
www.doylenewyork.com
Fine art, jewelry, furniture

DuMouchelles Art Gallery
409 E. Jefferson Ave.
Detroit, MI 48226
313-963-6255
www.dumouchelle.com
Fine art and antiques, art glass

Early Auction Co., LLC.
123 Main St.
Milford, OH 45150
513-831-4833
www.earlyauctionco.com
Art glass

Elder's Antiques
901 Tamiami Trail (US 41) S.
Nokomis, FL 34275
941-488-1005
www.eldersantiques.com
Full service

Elite Decorative Arts
1034 Gateway Blvd. #106
Boynton Beach, FL 33426
561-200-0893
www.eliteauction.com
Full service, decorative arts

Greg Martin Auctions
660 Third St., Suite 100
San Francisco, CA 94107
415-777-4867
Firearms, edged weapons, armor,
Native American objects

Great Gatsby's Antiques and Auctions
P.O. Box 660488
Atlanta, GA 30366
770-457-1903
www.greatgatsbys.com
Fine art, fine furnishings, lighting,
musical instruments

Grey Flannel
13 Buttercup Ln.
Westhampton Beach, NY 11977
631-288-7800
www.greyflannel.com
Sports jerseys, memorabilia

Guernsey's
65 E 93rd St.
New York, NY 10128
212-794-2280
www.guernseys.com
Art, historical items, pop culture

Guyette Schmidt & Deeter
24718 Beverly Road
P.O. Box 1170
St. Michaels, MD 21663
410-745-0487
www.guyetteandschmidt.com
Antique decoys

Hake's Americana &
Collectibles Auctions
P.O. Box 12001
York, PA 17402
717-434-1600
www.hakes.com
Character collectibles, pop culture

Heritage Auctions
3500 Maple Ave., 17th Floor
Dallas, TX 75219-3941
800-872-6467
ha.com
Full service, coins, pop culture

Humler & Nolan
225 E. Sixth St., 4th Floor
Cincinnati, OH 45202
513-381-2041 or 513-381-2015
www.humlernolan.com
Antique American and European art
pottery and art glass

iGavel, Inc.
229 E. 120th St.
New York, NY 10035
866-iGavel6 or 212-289-5588
igavelauctions.com
Online auction, arts, antiques and
collectibles

Jackson's International
Auctioneers and Appraisers
2229 Lincoln St.
Cedar Falls, IA 50613
319-277-2256
www.jacksonsauction.com
Full service, religious and Russian
objects, postcards

James D. Julia, Inc.
203 Skowhegan Rd.
Fairfield, ME 04937
207-453-7125
www.juliaauctions.net
Full service, glass, lighting, firearms

Jeffrey S. Evans & Associates
2177 Green Valley Ln.
Mount Crawford, VA 22841
540-434-3939
www.jeffreysevans.com
Full service, glass, lighting, Americana

John Moran Auctioneers, Inc.
735 W. Woodbury Rd.
Altadena, CA 91001
626-793-1833
www.johnmoran.com
Full service, California art

Keno Auctions
127 E. 69th St.
New York, NY 10021
212-734-2381
www.kenoauctions.com
Fine antiques, decorative arts

Lang's Sporting Collectibles
663 Pleasant Valley Rd.
Waterville, NY 13480
315-841-4623
www.langsauction.com
Antique fishing tackle and memorabilia

Leland Little Auctions &
Estate Sales, Ltd.
620 Cornerstone Ct.
Hillsborough, NC 27278
919-644-1243
www.llauctions.com
Full service

Leslie Hindman Auctioneers
1338 W. Lake St.
Chicago, Il 60607
312-280-1212
www.lesliehindman.com
Full service

Litchfield County Auctions, Inc.
425 Bantam Road (Route 202)
Litchfield, CT 06759
860-567-4661
212-724-0156
www.litchfieldcountyauctions.com
Full service

McMasters Harris Auction Co.
1625 W. Church St.
Newark, OH 43055
800-842-3526
www.mcmastersharris.com
Dolls and accessories

Michaan's Auctions
2751 Todd St.
Alameda, CA 94501
800-380-9822
www.michaans.com
Antiques, fine art

Michael Ivankovich Auction Co.
P.O. Box 1536
Doylestown, PA 18901
215-345-6094
www.wnutting.com
Wallace Nutting objects

Morphy Auctions
2000 N. Reading Rd.
Denver, PA 17517
717-335-3435
www.morphyauctions.com
Toys, banks, advertising, pop culture

Morphy Auctions, Las Vegas
4520 Arville St. # 1
Las Vegas, NV 89103
702-382-2466
www.morphyauctions.com

Mosby & Co. Auctions
5714-A Industry Ln.
Frederick, MD 21704
240-629-8139
www.mosbyauctions.com
Mail, phone, Internet sales

Neal Auction Co.
4038 Magazine St.
New Orleans, LA 70115
504-899-5329
800-467-5329
www.nealauction.com
Art, furniture, pottery, silver,
decorative arts

New Orleans Auction Gallery
801 Magazine St.
New Orleans, LA 70130
800-501-0277
www.neworleansauction.com
Full service, Victorian

Noel Barrett Vintage Toys @ Auction
P.O. Box 300
Carversville, PA 18913
215-297-5109
www.noelbarrett.com
Toys, banks, holiday, advertising

Old Town Auctions
11 St. Paul St.
Boonsboro, MD 21713
240-291-0114
301-416-2854
Toys, advertising, Americana; no Internet sales

Old Toy Soldier Auctions USA
P.O. Box 13324
Pittsburgh, PA 15243
Ray Haradin
412-343-8733
800-349-8009
www.oldtoysoldierauctions.com
Toy soldiers

Old World Auctions
4325 Cox Rd.
Glen Allen, VA 23060
804-290-8090
www.oldworldauctions.com
Maps, documents

Past Tyme Pleasures
5424 Sunol Blv., #10-242
Pleasanton, CA 94566
925-484-6442
www.pasttyme1.com
Internet catalog auctions

Philip Weiss Auctions
74 Morrick Rd.
Lynbrook, NY 11563
516-594-0731
www.prwauctions.com
Full service, comic art

Pook & Pook, Inc.
463 E. Lancaster Ave.
Downingtown, PA 19335
610-629-4040
www.pookandpook.com
Full service, Americana

Quinn's Auction Galleries & Waverly Auctions
360 S. Washington St.
Falls Church, VA 22046
703-532-5632
www.quinnsauction.com
www.waverlyauctions.com
Full service, rare books and prints

Rago Arts and Auction Center
333 N. Main St.
Lambertville, NJ 08530
609-397-9374
www.ragoarts.com
Arts & Crafts, modernism, fine art

Red Baron's Antiques, Inc.
8655 Roswell Rd.
Atlanta, GA 30350
770-640-4604
www.rbantiques.com
Full service, Victorian, architectural objects

Rich Penn Auctions
P.O. Box 1355
Waterloo, IA 50704
319-291-6688
www.richpennauctions.com
Advertising and country-store objects

Richard D. Hatch & Associates
913 Upward Rd.
Flat Rock, NC 28731
828-696-3440
www.richardhatchauctions.com
Full service

Robert Edward Auctions, LLC
P.O. Box 7256
Watchung, NJ 07069
908-226-9900
www.robertedwardauctions.com
Baseball, sports memorabilia

Rock Island Auction Co.
7819 42nd St. West
Rock Island, IL 61201
800-238-8022
www.rockislandauction.com
Firearms, edged weapons and accessories

St. Charles Gallery, Inc.
1330 St. Charles Ave.
New Orleans, LA 70130
504-586-8733
Full service, Victorian

Samuel T. Freeman & Co.
1808 Chestnut St.
Philadelphia, PA 19103
215-563-9275
www.freemansauction.com
Full service, Americana

Seeck Auctions
P.O. Box 377
Mason City, IA 50402
641-424-1116
www.seeckauction.com
Full service, carnival glass

Skinner, Inc.
63 Park Plaza
Boston, MA 02116
617-350-5400
www.skinnerinc.com
Full service, Americana

Sloans & Kenyon
7034 Wisconsin Ave.
Chevy Chase, MD 20815
301-634-2330
www.sloansandkenyon.com
Full service

Slotin Folk Art
Folk Fest Inc.
5619 Ridgetop Dr.
Gainesville, GA 30504
770-532-1115
www.slotinfolkart.com
Naïve and outsider art

Sotheby's New York
1334 York Ave.
New York, NY 10021
212-606-7000
www.sothebys.com
Fine art, jewelry, historical items

Strawser Auctioneers & Appraisers
P.O. Box 332, 200 N. Main
Wolcottville, IN 46795
260-854-2859
www.strawserauctions.com
Full service, majolica, Fiestaware

Susanin's Auctions
900 S. Clinton St.
Chicago, IL 60607
312-832-9800
www.susanins.com
Fine art, Asian, fine furnishings, silver, jewelry

Swann Galleries, Inc.
104 E. 25th St., #6
New York, NY 10010-2999
212-254-4710
www.swanngalleries.com
Rare books, prints, photographs, posters

Ted Owen and Co. Auctions/ The Fame Bureau
Suite 71
2 Old Brompton Rd.
SW7 3DQ London, United Kingdom
http://famebureau.com

Theriault's
P.O. Box 151
Annapolis, MD 21404
800-638-0422
www.theriaults.com
Dolls and accessories

Tom Harris Auction Center
203 S. 18th Ave.
Marshalltown, IA 50158
641-754-4890
www.tomharrisauctions.com
Full service, clocks, watches

John Toomey Gallery
818 North Blvd.
Oak Park, IL 60301
708-383-5234
www.treadwaygallery.com
Arts & Crafts, modernism, fine art

Tradewinds Antiques & Auctions
P.O. Box 249
24 Magnolia Ave.
Manchester-By-The-Sea, MA
01944-0249
978-526-4085
www.tradewindsantiques.com
Canes

Treadway Gallery
2029 Madison Rd.
Cincinnati, OH 45208
513-321-6742
www.treadwaygallery.com

Turkey Creek Auctions, Inc.
13939 N. Highway 441
Citra, FL 32113
352-622-4611
800-648-7523
antiqueauctionsfl.com

Waverly Auctions
360 S. Washington St.
Falls Church, VA 22046
703-532-5632
www.quinnsauction.com
www.waverlyauctions.com
Full service, rare books and prints

Woody Auction
P.O. Box 618
317 S. Forrest
Douglass, KS 67039
316-747-2694
www.woodyauction.com
Glass

Ask an Expert

Many contributors have proved invaluable in sharing their expertise during the compilation of the 50th edition of the *Warman's* guide. For more information on their specialties, call or visit their websites.

Caroline Ashleigh
Caroline Ashleigh Associates, LLC
1000 S. Old Woodward, Suite 201
Birmingham, MI 48009-6734
248-792-2929
www.auctionyourart.com
Vintage clothing, couture and accessories, textiles, western wear

Tim Chambers
Missouri Plain Folk
501 Hunter Ave.
Sikeston, MO 63801-2115
573-620-5500
E-mail: moplainfolk@gmail.com
Folk art

Noah Fleisher
E-mail: noah.fleisher@yahoo.com
Modernism

Reyne Haines
Reyne Gallery
2311 Westheimer Rd.
Houston, TX 77098
513-504-8159
www.reyne.com
E-mail: reyne@reyne.com
20th century decorative arts, lighting, fine jewelry, wristwatches

Ted Hake
Hake's Americana & Collectibles Auctions
P.O. Box 12001
York, PA 17402
717-434-1600
E-mail: hakes@hakes.com
Pop culture, Disneyana, political

Mary P. Manion
Landmarks Gallery & Restoration Studio
231 N. 76th St.
Milwaukee, WI 53213
800-352-8892
www.landmarksgallery.com
Fine art and restoration

Suzanne Perrault
Perrault Rago Gallery
333 N. Main St.
Lambertville, NJ 08530
609-397-9374
www.ragoarts.com
E-mail: suzanne@ragoarts.com

David Rago
Rago Arts and Auction Center
333 N. Main St.
Lambertville, NJ 08530
609-397-9374
www.ragoarts.com
Art pottery, Arts & Crafts

Dennis Raleigh Antiques & Folk Art
P.O. Box 745
Wiscasset, ME 04578
734-604-0898
www.dennisraleighantiques.com
E-mail: dgraleigh@myfairpoint.net
Decoys, silhouettes, portrait miniatures

Henry A. Taron
Tradewinds Antiques
P.O. Box 249
Manchester-By-The-Sea, MA
01944-0249
(978) 526-4085
www.tradewindsantiques.com
Canes

James D. Julia, Inc.
203 Skowhegan Rd.
Fairfield, ME 04937
207-453-7125
www.juliaauctions.net
Toys, dolls, advertising

The Mid-1960s

総天然色

ラドン キングギドラ・謎のX星、全宇宙をゆるがす大激闘！

怪獣大戦争

佐々木孝丸
千石規子
清水元
村上冬樹
田島謙三
田崎潤
土屋嘉男

久保明
沢井桂子
水野久美
ニック・アダムス

特技・円谷英二
監督・本多猪四郎
製作・田中友幸
脚本・関沢新一
東宝株式会社製作・配給

INVASION OF
ASTRO-MONSTER

By Noah Fleisher

The mid-1960s were, arguably, the cultural peak of the 20th century; it was a time of rapid shifts in social morés, in attitudes about race, religion, sexuality, and the American place in the world. The grand hegemony of the 1950s, arising from the vanquishing of the totalitarian threats of the 1940s via World War II, had begun to split. The upheaval was intense as inter-

generational relationships fractured. The Allied victory in World War II resulted in great spoils for Western society, but it also led to greater introspection, an examination of our ways of seeing and thinking and, ultimately, a questioning of our very way of being.

The result? It can only be summed up as "the 1960s."

Those great societal shifts, as echoed in American pop culture – music, sports, film, television, comic books, and cartoons, etc. – are fascinating to examine, making the mid-1960s, the heart of the era (defined for our purposes in this section as roughly 1964-1967), an incredibly rich resource for both collectors and historians. Between you and me, I don't see a lot of difference in the two.

We're visiting the era in honor of the 50th edition of *Warman's Antiques & Collectibles*. While the beginning of the book itself dates back further, the 50th edition makes examining the mid-1960s a natural step. The number 50 is what has inspired us here, and we choose to apply it by looking at this most pivotal of American moments.

There is no one in the business of antiques and collectibles more qualified to speak on the era than Gary Sohmers, of Wex Rex Collectibles, rightfully known as "The King of Pop Culture."

Sohmers is one of the most well-known figures in the business. He produces and hosts the syndicated talk radio show "Calling All Collectors" and famously appeared on PBS' "Antiques Roadshow" for 13 seasons as an appraiser of toys, collectibles, and memorabilia. He's been a guest on dozens of other TV and radio programs and is regularly consulted by national media for his expert knowledge of the value and history of collectibles.

He gives us some gems of wisdom from his prolific career, reveals some insights into his process, and introduces us to his concept of a "nostalgia curve," a brilliant way to gauge the rising and falling popularity and prices of collectibles.

WARMAN'S: *You're quite well known in the business, with features and television appearances aplenty. Can you tell me a bit about how you developed your expertise and your key experiences in becoming an expert?*

SOHMERS: I learned values by buying and selling, by making mistakes, by selling too low and by sometimes holding on to items too long. Over

Courtesy of Heritage Auctions, ha.com

▶ Acrylic painting of TV stars of late 1950s to mid-1960s era with 33 celebrities, excellent condition overall, illustration board with edge and corner wear, image area 18" x 27 1/2". Provenance: From the Cracked Vault Collection. **$1,912**

time, however, the wins and losses all average out. What matters is that I always bought and sold what I liked, so if I was stuck with it, at least I liked it. Also, selling in numerous venues and marketplaces helped me build a more realistic opinion of value.

I started selling at my first yard sale when I was about eight years old. I sold my old toys so I could buy new ones (Roko Mini Tanks and Airfix HO figures). I then learned from my father about collecting and dealing in campaign buttons. I went from toys to history and into music, where I sold all things musical before I finally settled on all things pop culture. I've lived through the Golden Age of pop culture, experienced the rise of television, radio, pop music, electronics, technology, art, fashion, advertising, style, film, animation, literature, and comics and believe that the culture of this era will forever influence all that comes after it.

WARMAN'S: *Can you tell me what kind of collectible defines this era?*

SOHMERS: In my world, anything that was created during the mid-20th century Modern era defines it. This era is framed by everything I mention above: television, radio, music, electronics, technology, art, fashion, advertising, style, film, animation, literature, and comics.

Courtesy of Brunk Auctions,
www.brunkauctions.com

Glass-top dining table, circa 1960s/1970s, round top on round Lucite stepped pedestal base, good condition overall, 28 1/2" x 54". **$310**

WARMAN'S: *If you had to choose the three favorite areas from the era, what would they be?*

SOHMERS: Psychedelic concert posters, record albums, and every toy in the Sears Christmas catalog.

WARMAN'S: *Who is buying mid-1960s right now?*

SOHMERS: As generations age, certain aspects of pop culture fall off the "nostalgia curve" [a term Sohmers created to define popularity to a buying public]. Shirley Temple, Howdy Doody, and Davy Crockett lost their sizzle in the past 10 years, [and] it's because the generation that is traditionally nostalgic for those characters are aging and de-accessioning their collections at the same time as less and less people are buying in those niches. The 1960s winners are those that have crossed over and been discovered and desired by new generations due to the Internet: The Beatles, Mid-Century Modern style, psychedelia, and hipster-chic fashion all have evolved to be popular with younger generations.

WARMAN'S: *Is there a particular mid-1960s market that looks stronger than others?*

SOHMERS: In every category there are desirable and undesirable items. In records, heavy metal, punk, psychedelic, and other niches sell well, while popular million record-selling acts sell for low dough. Concert posters are a favorite of mine as they're like any fine art produced during a key historical time period, in small quantities, as advertising for a singular event, which makes it exclusive to its niche. Like Picasso, Peter Max, and Keith Herring, the concert poster artists of the 1960s – Rick Griffin, Stanley Mouse, and Wes Wilson – are great investments.

WARMAN'S: *Is there a particular mid-1960s market to watch right now?*

SOHMERS: I'd suggest concert posters of the 1960s, as mentioned above, original comic art, and action figures.

WARMAN'S: *How are collectors of mid-1960s buying these days, particularly at places like Brimfield?*

SOHMERS: Stuff in this niche is plentiful at yard sales, on Craigslist, Facebook, Fleabay, and at collectors shows. ComicCons have surfaced as the new generation's source for buying products; a lot of it is handmade art and products featuring their favorite pop culture characters, interspersed with vintage toys, comic books, and posters. The Collectibles Extravaganza with the Northeast ComicCon is a great place to see many items from this era. Personally, I've been selling to people from all over the world looking for pop culture and 1960s artifacts at Brimfield for 31 years.

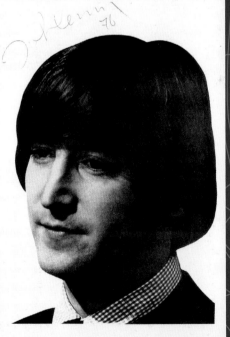

Courtesy of Heritage Auctions, ha.com

The Beatles John Lennon and Paul McCartney signed poster, undated but likely from mid-1960s, separated by horizontal and vertical center folds, very good condition with clear tape over tear in top center fold, 20 1/2" x 13 1/2", with certificate of authenticity from Heritage Auctions. More than three decades separate these two signatures: Lennon signed in blue ink with the date "76." McCartney's signature was added in 2012 in blue marker. $1,500

WARMAN'S: *What is the best piece of advice you were ever given when it comes to the business?*

SOHMERS: Buy what you like first, buy what you can afford, buy the best condition you can find, and do your research, then find a market that pleases you and study it.

WARMAN'S: *What piece of advice do you give when asked?*

SOHMERS: Surround yourself with the things of your youth and you'll always feel young.

WARMAN'S: *Where can people find you in 2017?*

SOHMERS: I appear at about 40 shows per year, coast to coast. I also do written appraisals for insurance, probate, or knowledge, and I always buy items for resale and sell items on consignment.

Gary Sohmers can also be found at his business website, www.AllCollectors.com, as well as at www.NortheastComicCon.net and www.facebook.com/GarySohmers.

Rayon "shirt jac," early 1960s, black rayon with inserts of white, red, and gray stripes down center front, spread collar, long sleeves with banded buttoned cuffs, 2" wide self-fabric waistband, white plastic buttons down center front, labeled "Clubman – L – Shirt Jac," mint condition. **$150**

Walnut table, circa 1960s, manufactured by Virginia Maid (Lane trademark), rectangular upper tier over projecting rectangular tabletop, both cross-banded with corners inlaid with "butterflies," turned and tapered supports on black-painted caps, marked to underside of top "Virginia Maid, Style no 984-07, Serial no 265121," 21" high x 27 3/4" wide x 20 3/4" deep. **$300-$500**

▲ Often regarded by automotive enthusiasts as the first true muscle car – a midsize car with a big-block V-8 engine – the original Pontiac GTO was not really a separate model at all. An ad man named Jim Wangers snuck the GTO into existence as an extra-cost package for the Tempest LeMans. Late in October 1963, the Grand Turismo Omologato package was announced for the LeMans coupe, hardtop, and convertible as a $295 option. Performance car buffs loved the hot GTO, and by year's end Pontiac could barely keep up with demand. They are still considered among the most collectible and desirable of the muscle cars from that period. **$60,000 for excellent condition, $50,000-plus for excellent condition coupes, $40,000-$50,000 for very good condition**

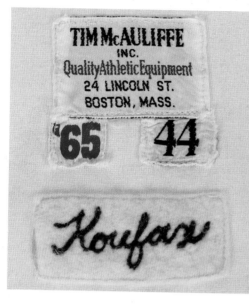

Courtesy of Heritage Auctions, ha.com

1965 Sandy Koufax game-worn Los Angeles Dodgers jersey from his final world championship season, MEARS A10 rated, white flannel with blue scripted "Dodgers" over red number 32, number repeated in larger blue digits on reverse, lower left front tail with "Tim McAuliffe Inc." manufacturer's label, "65" year and "44" size designator below, embroidered white felt swatch with "Koufax" in blue, 100% original and unaltered condition, no staining or moth damage, with letters of authenticity from MEARS and Heritage Auctions. Koufax spent five consecutive seasons atop the "earned run average" leader board and won three Cy Young Awards and an MVP. **$262,900**

Courtesy of Heritage Auctions, ha.com

1965 Mickey Mantle game-used bat from former New York Yankees batboy, MEARS A8.5 rated, Hillerich & Bradsby signature model M110 cracked by Mantle during July 1965 series in Bronx against Detroit Tigers, with photocopy of batboy's notarized letter. The bat was the fulfillment of a promise made by Mantle to the batboy, who told Mantle his younger brother was his greatest fan. Mantle assured the boy that the next bat he cracked belonged to him. **$18,523**

Courtesy of Heritage Auctions, ha.com

Three Topps baseball card issues display boxes, mid-1960s, rare, one each from 1962, 1963, and 1967, expected wear. $96

St. Louis Cardinals bobbing head doll, 1965-1967, NFL issue with round gold-toned base, cracks in front and back of helmet. $34

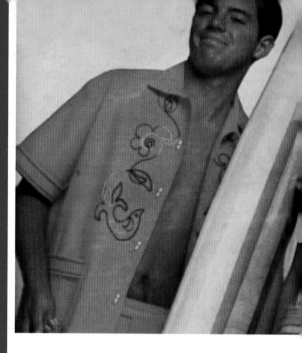

◀ Green Bay Packers vs. Cleveland Browns original game program from 1965 NFL World Championship Game played on Jan. 2, 1966, complete and intact, moderate water damage and wear throughout. **$66**

Jim Brown game-worn Cleveland Browns Jersey, virca 1965, MEARS A10 rated, thin "tear-away" brown fabric with number 32 on chest, back, and shoulders, rings of white and orange on each sleeve, "King O' Shea [size] 48" tag in buttoned crotch piece, 9+/10 black Sharpie signature on front numerals, excellent condition, sweat-staining at interior armpits, with MEARS letter of authenticity stating potential range of 1961-1965, 1988 letter of provenance from son of fellow team member Lou "The Toe" Groza, who often begged for souvenirs from team equipment manager Maurie Kono. Brown claimed the NFL rushing title in eight of nine seasons in the league, and his 1,863 rushing yards in 1963 remains a Cleveland Browns franchise record, oldest franchise rushing record of all 32 teams. **$95,600**

Hank Aaron game-worn jersey as baseball player for Milwaukee Braves, 1965, possibly the last jersey Aaron wore as a Brave before the team moved to Atlanta, gifted by him to young star Bill Madlock in mid-1970s. $59,750

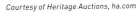

Courtesy of Heritage Auctions, ha.com

Wilt Chamberlain Philadelphia 76ers shorts, 1965-1966, worn by superstar center during his first full season with the team, tackle twill "76" ringed by 13 white stars at each hip on blue satin body and red, white and blue ring drawstring waistband, hip padding at interior, "Pearson [size] 36" manufacturer's label, embroidered swatch with "13-36 HR 65" denoting jersey number, waist size, increased/high rise and year, respectively. **$21,510**

They said it couldn't be done. It couldn't.

We tried. Lord knows we tried. But no amount of pivoting or faking could squeeze the Philadelphia 76ers' Wilt Chamberlain into the front seat of a Volkswagen.

So if you're 7'1" tall like Wilt, our car is not for you. But maybe you're a mere 6'7".

In that case, you'd be small enough to appreciate what a big thing we've made of the Volkswagen.

There's more headroom than you'd expect ... er 37½" from seat to roof.)

... re's more legroom in front than in a limousine. Because the en-

gine's tucked over the rear wh it's out of the way (and where the most traction).

You can put 2 medium-sized front (where the engine isn't), sized kids in the back seat. A sleep an enormous infant in back seat.

Actually, there's only one p that you can't put much into The gas tank.

But you can get about 2 miles per gallon out of it.

© VOLKSWAG

YANKEES

Courtesy of Heritage Auctions, ha.com

1964 Topps Mickey Mantle #50, SGC 40 VG 3, mid-1960s, right-handed batting pose illustration, rounding at corners, mild printing marks above word "outfield" on front of card. **$90**

MICKEY MANTLE outfield

Help! (United Artists, 1965) three-sheet poster, second film with The Beatles; Ringo Starr is pursued by a cult that marks him for human sacrifice due to his inadvertent possession of a sacred ring. Music includes "Help!," "Ticket to Ride," "You're Going to Lose That Girl," and "You've Got to Hide Your Love Away"; very fine condition on linen, crossfold separation and surface paper loss in bottom right, professional restoration, 41" x 81". **$777**

Mid-1960s Mosrite Ventures red electric bass guitar, #5185, all original and lightly played with minimal weather checking, good condition, little fret wear, no changed parts or modifications, pot dates are early '65, original hard case included. $2,271

ISNT IT A PITY   (words + music)

Isn't it a pity - Isn't it a shame
How we break each others hearts - and
cause each other pain - how we take
each others love - without thinking
anymore - forgetting to give back - oh
isn't it a ~~_____~~ Pity .

Somethings take so long - but how
do I explain - when not too many
~~♥~~ people, can see were all the same
and because of all their tears -
their eyes cant hope to see -
the beauty that surrounds them
isn't it a pity .
          repeat ① ~~instrumental~~

Courtesy of Heritage Auctions, ha.com

George Harrison original handwritten lyrics for "Isn't It a Pity," black ink on white 8 1/4" x 10" sheet, trimmed at top truncating "P" in title and just touching "T" in "It," another word above "words + music" missing, writing bold and clear with three places where text is crossed out, George wrote at bottom "Repeat 1," minor wear, fine condition, certificate of authenticity from Perry Cox. This song was released on Harrison's landmark "All Things Must Pass" album and as a double "A" side with "My Sweet Lord," both in 1970; originally written by him in mid-1960s. **$87,500**

Johnny Cash owned and worn jacket, circa 1960s, size large black faux leather with knit sleeves, worn by Cash during his UK tour in mid-1960s, given to his friend Richard McGibony when Cash was a houseguest in 1967, label reads "Exclusive Sportswear of California," excellent condition, missing one of three front buttons, letter of authenticity from Richard McGibony. **$1,375**

▶ **Elvis Presley owned and worn motorcycle belt, 1960s, ornate black leather with five colored plastic reflectors, dozens of metal studs, and two zippered pockets, fine condition, wear around edges and at front straps and buckles, 7" wide at widest, 5 1/2" wide in front, 32" waist. Belt was given by Presley to his longtime personal hairdresser, Homer M. Gilleland, with letter of authenticity from Gilleland. $4,375**

Courtesy of Heritage Auctions, ha.com

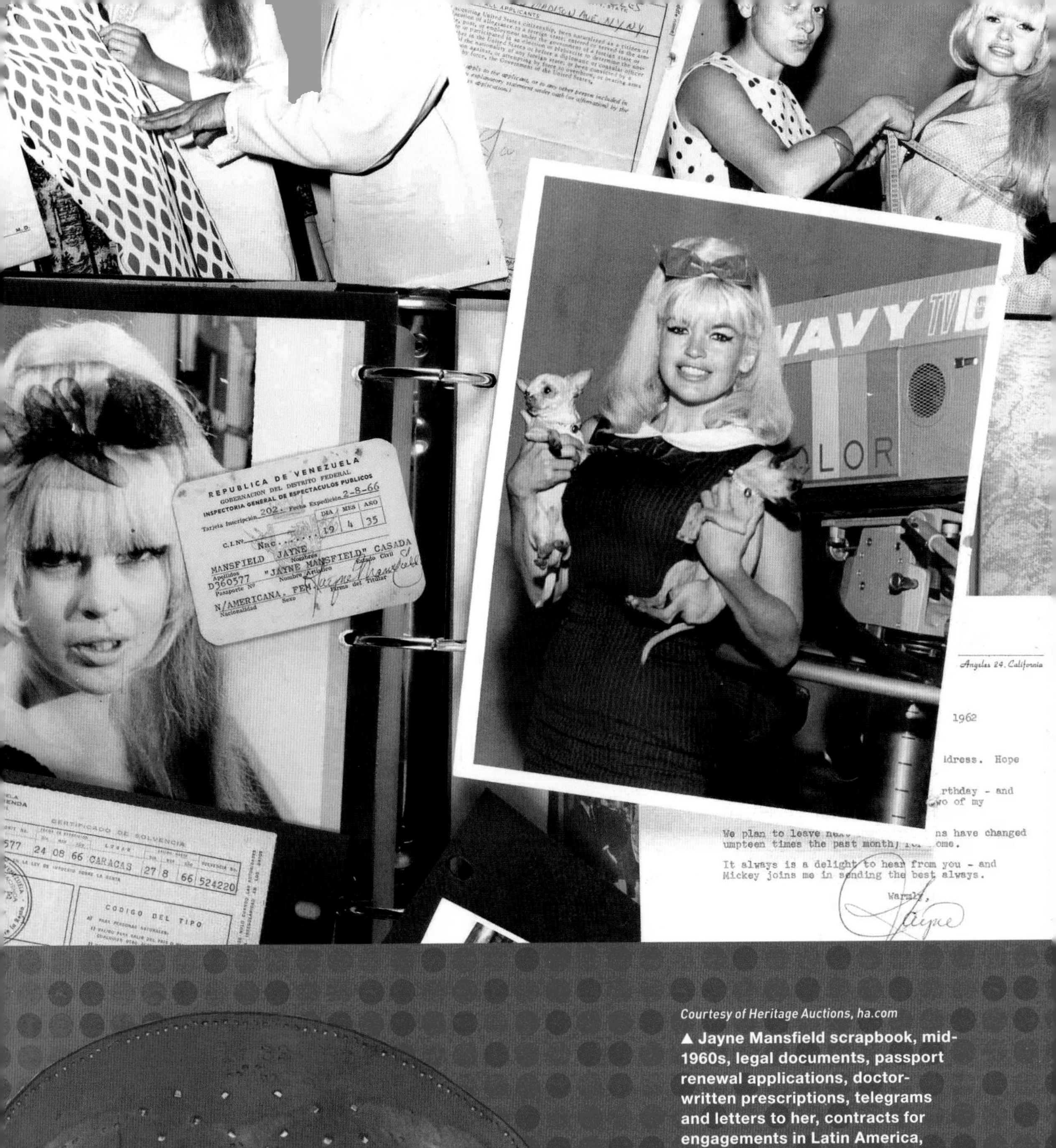

▲ Jayne Mansfield scrapbook, mid-1960s, legal documents, passport renewal applications, doctor-written prescriptions, telegrams and letters to her, contracts for engagements in Latin America, foreign and American ID cards including ones from Automobile Club of Southern California and Venezuelan government signed by her in blue ballpoint ink, newspaper and magazine clippings including many related to her death, and approximately 50 black and white original print photographs (8" x 10" and smaller) of star with her Chihuahuas as she traveled in South American countries, with cards and letters star-signed and sent to owner of scrapbook, scrapbook 12" x 11" x 3". $1,625

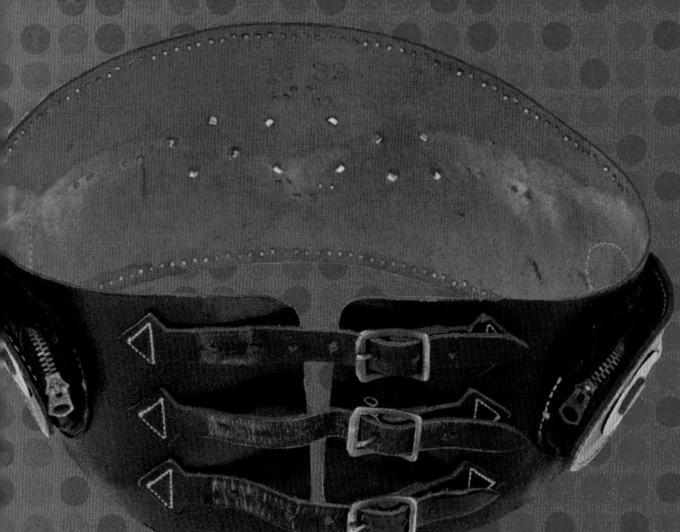

Car and Driver magazine called the debut Mustang "easily the best thing to come out of Dearborn since the 1932 V-8 Model B [Ford] roadster." Lee Iacocca, at the time vice president and general manager of Ford Division, had a vision of a sporty family car with four seats, two doors, a low price, and lots of versatility that would appeal to a wide cross section of America. He hit a home run with the Mustang, which was a runaway success in its first year, 1965. Ford cranked out 121,000 of the first-year cars and changed the auto industry for good. Competitors were sent scrambling, and before long Chrysler and GM were fighting back with models like the Camaro, Firebird, Barracuda, Challenger, and Charger. The Mustang spawned the "pony car" class of American automobiles – sporty coupes and convertibles with long hoods and short rear decks. Convertibles are valued slightly higher than coupes. **$50,000 in excellent condition, $35,000-$45,000 for very good condition**

Courtesy of Quinn's Auction Galleries & Waverly Auctions, www.quinnsauction.com, www.waverlyauctions.com

Pair of rosewood end tables, mid-20th century, designed by Rasmus Solberg, cabinetmaker, Norway, for Westnofa, Norway, each with open shelf underneath tabletop, underside of tabletop on each with Westnofa label, Furniture Control Mobelfakta Norway label, and Rasmus Solberg Cabinetmaker Norway label, 20 1/2" high x 29" wide x 19" deep. **$665**

America has fallen in love with the
new *Princess* phone

In white, beige, pink, blue and turquoise—attractively priced

it's little !... it's lovely !... it lights !

...of many reasons why the ...opular. It fits in where ...oom for a telephone be-...sion on a kitchen coun-...lesk or a bedside table.

Graceful styling is another reason why everyone is so charmed by this phone. You can put the Princess anywhere and be sure that its lines and the color you choose will blend in beautifully.

Lighted dial. It glows in the dark, so it's easy to find, and lights brightly when you lift the receiver, so it's easy to dial. To order the Princess, just call our Business Office or ask your telephone man.

BELL TELEPHONE SYSTEM

JACK KIRBY '66

Silver Age ink and watercolor masterwork that appeared on cover of *Jack Kirby Collector* #38 (Spring, 2003), excellent condition, 14 1/2" x 20" overall. Editor John Morrow wrote, "The front cover is another of those mid-1960s concept pieces Jack did (this one from 1966). It looks to have been inked by Don Heck, and then watercolored by Jack. Who this enchanting lady was meant to be is anybody's guess, but 'E' on her belt makes me want to simply call her 'Enchantra,' so I guess that's as good a name as any to use when referring to her in future." **$8,050**

Courtesy of Heritage Auctions, ha.com
"Bent Figure with Ghosts / KKK, 1965," John Biggers (American, 1924-2001), mixed media on board, dated verso "65," 11 5/8" x 18 3/8". **$6,573**

Courtesy of Ahlers & Ogletree Auction Gallery, www.aandoauctions.com
Modernist steel frame bench, Lewittes Furniture (American, Taylorsville, North Carolina), mid-20th century, seat upholstered in tufted white vinyl, chrome-plated steel frame, chrome-plated steel legs, chrome-plated steel side rails, paper label reads "Made by Lewittes Furn. Ent. Inc. / Taylorsville, NC," 21 1/4" high x 41" long x 17" wide. **$434**

Courtesy of Los Angeles Modern Auctions, lamodern.com
Alexander Girard ottoman, designed in 1967, manufactured by Herman Miller, 13" x 35" diameter. **$5,440**

Courtesy of Heritage Auctions, ha.com

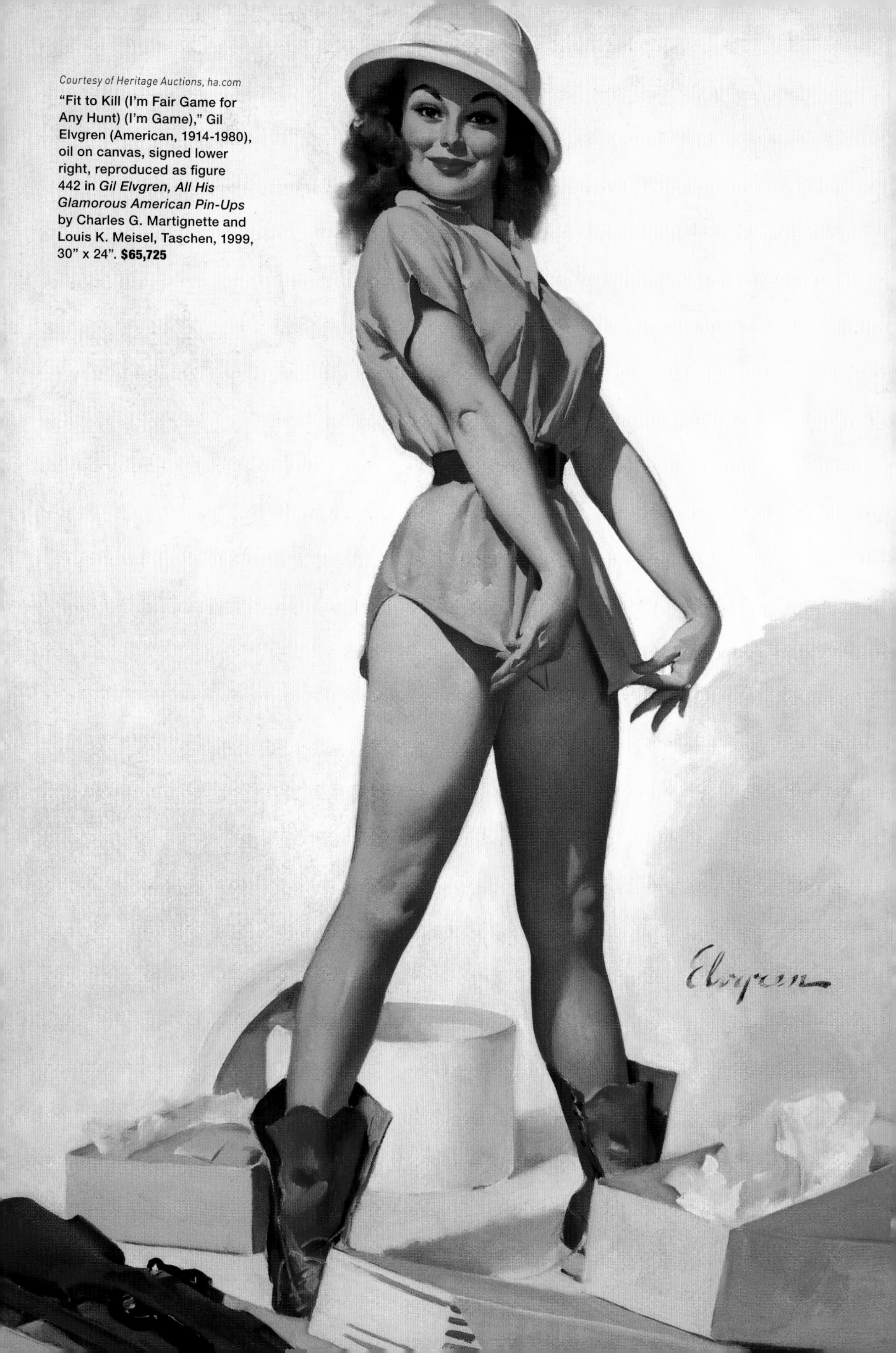

"Fit to Kill (I'm Fair Game for Any Hunt) (I'm Game)," Gil Elvgren (American, 1914-1980), oil on canvas, signed lower right, reproduced as figure 442 in *Gil Elvgren, All His Glamorous American Pin-Ups* by Charles G. Martignette and Louis K. Meisel, Taschen, 1999, 30" x 24". **$65,725**

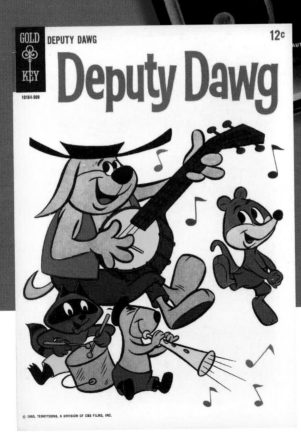

"Man From U.N.C.L.E." spy attache case toy (Ideal, 1965), heavily used with gun, clip, and dart, cigarette lighter/case with hidden gun and controls, several badges and cards, THRUSH cloth patch, billfolds, passport, and spy pen, good to very good condition. $263

Deputy Dawg #1 file copy (Gold Key, 1965), CGC NM 9.4, off-white pages, mid-1960s, highest CGC-graded example to date, Overstreet 2003 NM 9.4. **$236**

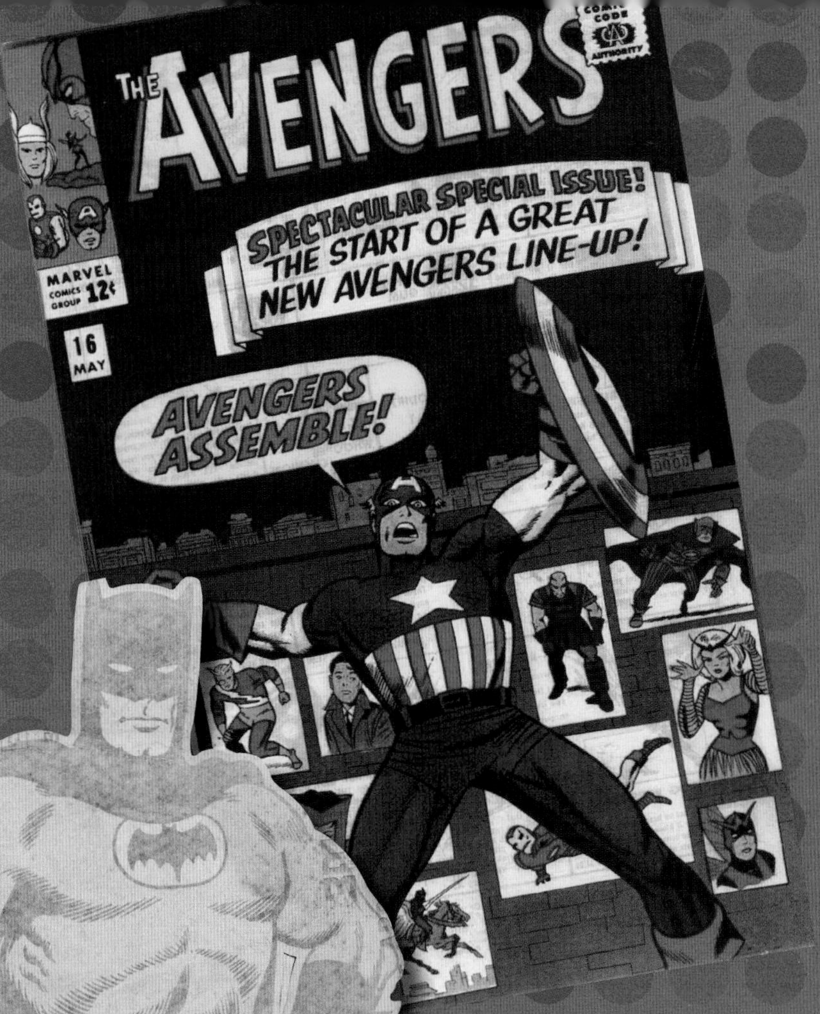

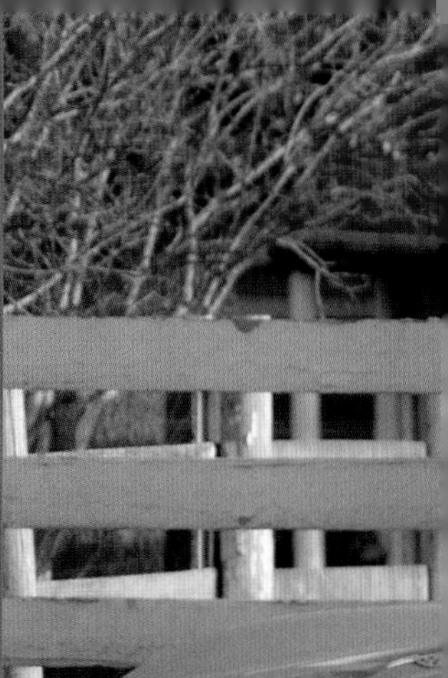

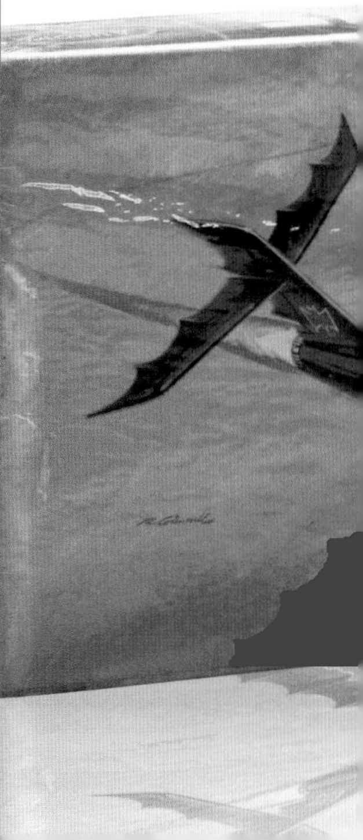

▲ *The Avengers* #16 Pacific Coast pedigree (Marvel, 1965), CGC NM-9.2, white pages, mid-1960s, cover of Captain America in front of images of Avengers by Jack Kirby and Don Heck, new team assembled in this issue, adding Hawkeye, Quicksilver, and Scarlet Witch, Overstreet 2002 NM 9.4. **$575**

◄ Batman and logo vinyl sticker group, All Star Dairy Association/DC Comics, circa 1966, overall good condition, faded and worn with folds and foxing, Batman 31" high, oval 15" wide. During the Batmania craze of the mid-1960s, All Star Dairy Association licensed Batman and Robin for dairy-based promotional campaigns, and stickers were produced to adorn the delivery vehicles. Some of the oval stickers were used on the 1963 Batmobile when it was originally repainted black and used as an official Batmobile to promote Batman and Robin ice cream sales in three northeastern states. **$956**

▲ 1963 Corvette "split-window" was the first Corvette coupe ever built with a hard top. All previous versions were roadsters. The car was an instant smash with all-new styling, including a distinctive tapering rear deck and a one-year-only split rear window. The Sting Ray featured hidden headlamps, non-functional hood vents, and an independent rear suspension. Corvette chief engineer Zora Arkus-Duntov was not a fan of the split window because it blocked rear vision, but collectors and car buffs have been smitten with the unusual Corvettes and made them among the most coveted of all American sports cars. **$80,000-plus in excellent condition, $50,000-$75,000 in very good condition**

Courtesy of Heritage Auctions, ha.com
◄ Batplane model kit in original shrink wrap (Aurora, 1966), excellent condition. **$489**

Courtesy of Heritage Auctions, ha.com

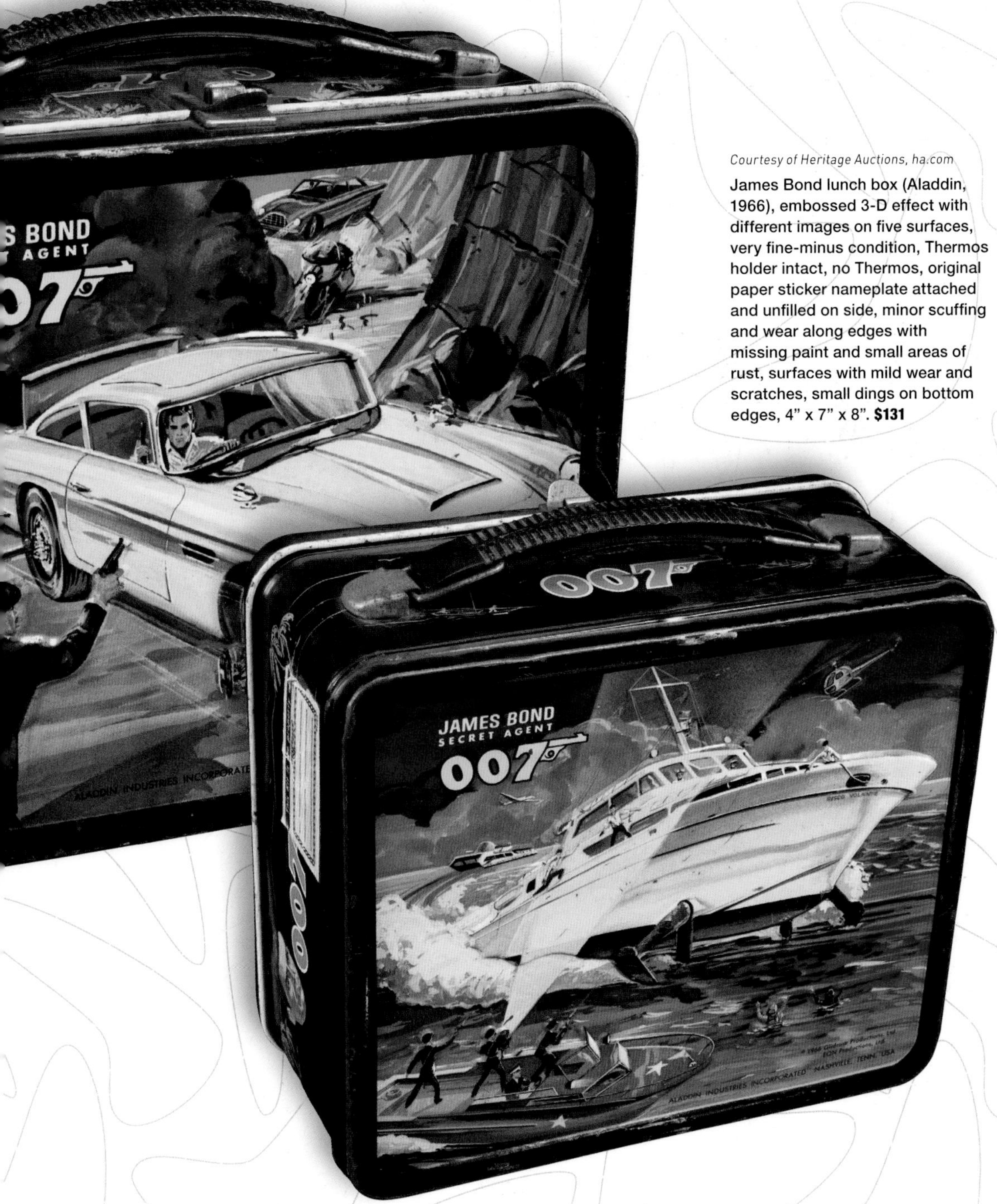

James Bond lunch box (Aladdin, 1966), embossed 3-D effect with different images on five surfaces, very fine-minus condition, Thermos holder intact, no Thermos, original paper sticker nameplate attached and unfilled on side, minor scuffing and wear along edges with missing paint and small areas of rust, surfaces with mild wear and scratches, small dings on bottom edges, 4" x 7" x 8". **$131**

Courtesy of Heritage Auctions, ha.com

▲ Two Cochiti silver jewelry items attributed to Joseph H. Quintana, circa 1965, necklace of graduated silver beads interspersed with 15 finger-like pendants and hair ornament in shape of fan, each with small silver tag attached, inscribed JHQ, each accompanied by statement of authenticity from estate of Irma Bailey, who employed Joe H. Quintana in her Old Town, Albuquerque store in late 1960s-early 1970s; necklace 10 1/2" long. **$1,063**

Courtesy of Sotheby's, www.sothebys.com

Turquoise and diamond brooch, Cartier, circa 1960, designed as turtle set with polished turquoise and brilliant-cut diamonds, signed Cartier, numbered, French assay and maker's marks. **$42,532**

At breakfast... between meals... or night!
Drink this much Florida Orange Juice every day!
A FULL BIG GLASS
Start the day right . . . end the day bright! A full big glass of healthful Florida Orange Juice gives you plenty of Vitamin C—one vitamin your body doesn't store up. And don't take "half-measures" with old-fashioned half-portion juice glasses. For a full measure of health, drink a full, big glass of Florida Orange Juice at least once during the day!
FLORIDA CANNED
Always ready to serve at a moment's notice. Natural full strength. Try blended Florida Orange-Grapefruit juice in cans, too. Delicious, different, refreshing!
FLORIDA FRESH-FROZEN CONCENTRATE
Tree-fresh flavor in new hand
Add three parts water, stir, p
full, big glasses. Pure juice—
no sugar added.
FLORIDA FRESH
They're the sweetest—for finer flavor, more energy. Save money, too—Florida Oranges have thin skins and they're juicier!
FLORIDA
THEY'RE THE SWEETEST
ORANGES
FLORIDA CITRUS COMMISSION, LAKELAND, FLORIDA

Courtesy of Treadway Gallery, www.treadwaygallery.com

Bubble wall lamp, George Nelson for Howard Miller, 1960s, walnut, brass, enameled steel, sprayed plastic over wire, signed with Howard Miller clear decal, shade 9 1/2" high, 14" diameter. **$563**

Courtesy of Midwest Auction Galleries, www.midwestauctioninc.com

Circular table with drop leaves, white Formica top with gold glitter, vinyl chairs with kitchen and floral designs, table 29 1/2" high, 41" diameter, chairs 32" high x 16" wide x 20 1/2" deep. **$35**

Courtesy of Rago Arts and Auctions, www.ragoarts.com

Walnut bedroom suite: tall chest, long chest with mirror, full-sized bookcase headboard and frame, and book trough, circa 1960s, branded Ramseur Furniture Co., tall chest 38 1/2" x 40" x 19", long chest with mirror 68" x 60" x 19", headboard 38" x 58" x 10". **$192**

Pepsi-Cola shift-style dress, 1960s, yellow cotton sleeveless design with Pepsi-Cola slogans and large bottle printed design, round neckline, darts at bustline, center back zipper, labeled "Regatta by Mill Fabrics Corporation – Penney's – 18," mint condition with original tags. **$350**

Courtesy of Heritage Auctions, ha.com

Space Ghost production cel and drawing of animation art group (Hanna-Barbera, 1965), hand-painted, with Jan, Jace, and Blip the monkey, with original similar but non-matching clean-up drawing, art in very good condition, ink loss on cel, edge wear on drawing, upper two corners missing, both 12 1/2" x 10 1/2". **$287**

▲ "Peanuts" daily comic strip original art dated 1-12-65 by Charles Schulz (United Feature Syndicate, 1965) of Schroeder's concerto interrupted by a nose, ink on Bristol board, excellent condition, paper tanning, mainly on mat, image area 27" x 5 1/2", matted overall 30 3/4" x 9 3/4". **$20,315**

▶ Suite of floriform jewels, Van Cleef & Arpels, circa 1960: necklace, bracelet, ring, and pair of pendant-earclips, set throughout with numerous round diamonds weighing approximately 36.40 carats, round sapphires, and emeralds; necklace signed Van Cleef & Arpels, numbered 79138, with French assay and workshop marks; bracelet signed Van Cleef & Arpels, numbered 76647, with French assay and workshop marks; pendant-earrings with French workshop and assay marks, pendants detachable; ring signed Van Cleef & Arpels, numbered 5768 C.S., with French assay mark; necklace 14 1/2" long, bracelet 6 1/2" long, ring size 3. **$60,000-$80,000**

Courtesy of Heritage Auctions, ha.com

Flintstone Circus (Kohner, 1965), "Action acrobats you snap together yourself... unlimited combinations," complete and in original packaging, very fine condition, minor wear on box corners, tape pulls on box lid and small tear at corner of lower die-cut box lid window. **$49**

Courtesy of Heritage Auctions, ha.com

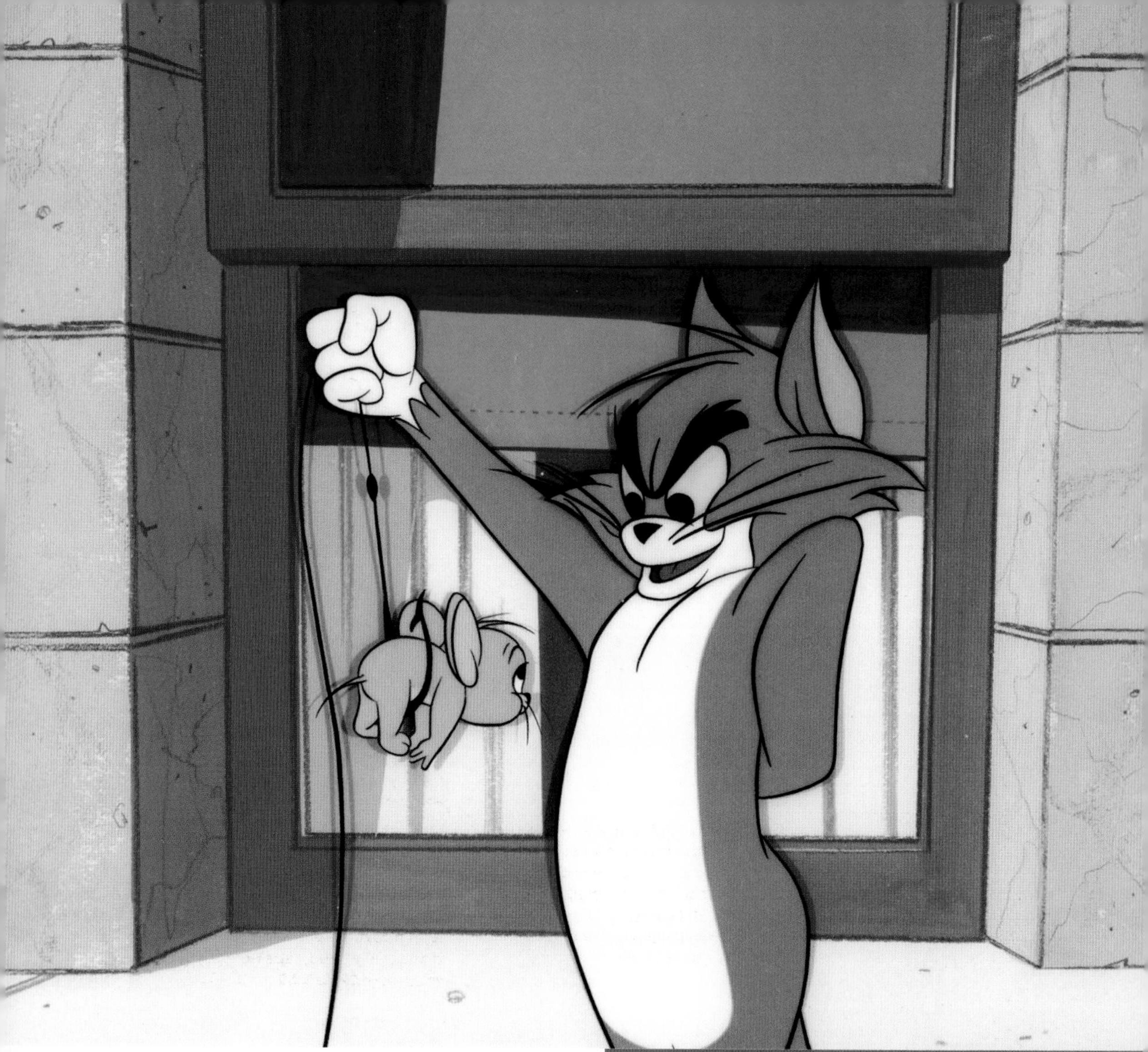

"Ah Sweet Mouse-story of Life" Tom and Jerry production cel over hand-painted MGM production background (MGM, 1965), original hand-inked and hand-painted cel of Tom and Jerry together for MGM theatrical short directed by Chuck Jones, mat inscribed "All the best to Irvine Barber from Tom and Jerry," matted and framed 22" x 18 1/2", image 12" x 8 1/2". **$1,105**

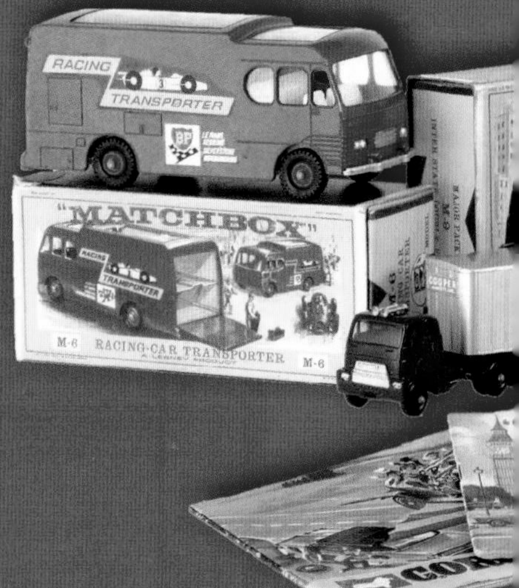

Courtesy of Charles A. Whitaker Auction Co.,
www.whitakerauction.com

Lime green knit high-neck A-line
dress, upper bodice with scalloped
cutout joined by intertwined self
bands, topstitched details, label
reads "Rudi Gernreich Design
For Harmon Knitwear," very good
condition. **$200-$300**

Courtesy of Charles A. Whitaker Auction Co.,
www.whitakerauction.com

Navy blue short-sleeve tunic with
U-shaped patch pockets with button,
scalloped hem, and back belt
with buttons, topstitched details,
matching straight-leg pants with
topstitched waistband and front
zipper, fully lined, labeled, very good
condition. **$300-$400**

Courtesy of Heritage Auctions, ha.com

**Twenty-six cars and trucks in
original boxes with five Corgi
catalogs from 1965-1970 in
German, including James
Bond's Aston Martin D.B.5 (261)
secret agent car with working
"secret" features, Land-rover
with Ferrari racing car on trailer
(gift set 17), Land-rover with
trailer and pony (gift set 2),
Lesney Matchbox racing-car
transporter (M-6), interstate
double freighter (M-9), combine
harvester (M-5), king-size car
transporter (K-8), king-size
ready-mix concrete truck (K-13),
Lord Neilson Ice Cream Shop
(47), Honda motorcycle and
trailer (38), Budgie Leyland
Hippo truck (206), and others.
$956**

Advertising

By Noah Fleisher

NOAH FLEISHER received his Bachelor of Fine Arts degree from New York University and brings more than a decade of newspaper, magazine, book, antiques and art experience to his position as Public Relations Director of Heritage Auctions, one of the country's foremost auction houses. He is the former editor of *Antique Trader, New England Antiques Journal* and *Northeast Antiques Journal,* is the author of *Warman's Modern Furniture* and co-author of *Collecting Children's Books,* and has been a longtime contributor to *Warman's Antiques & Collectibles.*

The enduring appeal of antique advertising is not hard to understand. The graphics are great; they hearken back to a simpler time and a distinct American identity, and – perhaps best of all – are available across all price levels. That means buyers from all tax brackets and walks of life.

"It's like anything in collectibles and antiques," said Dan Matthews, former president and owner of Matthews Auction in Moline, Illinois, and the author of *The Fine Art of Collecting and Displaying Petroliana*. "The best stuff, the very top, sells no matter what. Right now the medium market is doing OK and the lower continues to drag a bit behind."

The most reliable value in Matthews' market continues to be top-of-the-line petroliana – names like Harbo Petrolium, Keller Springs, Quiver, or Must-go can command tens of thousands of dollars – but there is a definite hierarchy at play and, if you are thinking of expanding your collecting horizons to include antique signage, you would do well to know the market.

Seasoned collectors will warn, with good reason, that money should not be the motivating factor in the hobby, so it may be somewhat deceptive to start this discussion with the idea of monetary value. The true value of antique advertising signs, from gas stations to country stores to soda pop, lies in the context of their production and the nostalgia they evoke of that time.

The best antique advertising evokes the meat of the first half of the 20th century, when signs were the most effective ways to catch the eyes of car culture consumers. The signs and symbols evolved to reflect the values and styles of the regions where they were posted and the products they reflected. A sign with bold color, great graphics, and a catchy slogan can transport a collector back decades in an instant. Collectors feel a rapport with a piece; they don't see dollar signs.

"Buy it because you like it," said Matthews, "because you can live it with it and it means something to you. Never get into something because you think you'll make money."

Look at the market for one of the most collectible and popular markets: Coca-Cola. Fifteen years ago the best Coke pieces in the

**Rare Anheuser-Busch sign
manufactured by Kaufmann
& Strauss Co., very good/
excellent condition, light
wear, original condition,
12" wide x 8" high. $2,280**

middle market could reliably command several thousand dollars. Coca-Cola manufactured hundreds of thousands of signs and related ephemera, millions even, and they began to come out of the woodwork. There is little more evocative of classic Americana than the red and white of Coke, but as everybody sold their pieces and everybody acquired their bit of nostalgia, the market cooled and prices went down significantly. Pieces that had routinely brought $500-$1,000 could suddenly be had for significantly less, and people stopped selling.

Now, however, with several years of very quiet action in the books, the cycle seems to be turning around. New collectors have entered the market and older collectors are leaving. Those collections are finding new owners at a decent price.

"Coca-Cola does seem to be coming back," said Matthews. "It's been stagnant for the past five years, but good clean signs are finding good homes at good prices."

As with any category, the very best antique advertising will bring top dollar no matter what, as a look through the recent advertising sales database of prices realized at an auction house like Morphy's will attest. In those sales it can be seen that the rarest of Coca-Cola paper and tin routinely bring tens of thousands of dollars.

That said, then, let's talk money. Antique advertising provides a tangible place for collectors to put real money. Looking through recent prices realized at the top auction venues – like Matthews, Morphy Auctions, and William Morford – it's obvious that top dollar can be

had for the true rarities in the business and that the middle market provides a solid outlet for design-minded collectors as opposed to those who collect to amass a sizable grouping.

There are opportunities everywhere for the educated collector – from the country auction to the flea market. Going head to head, out of the blocks, with the top collectors in the business at the top auctions can result in frustration. Rather, if you're just getting your feet wet, research online, email experts and ask for resources, do your due diligence in seeing what the market is bringing and, then, take those skills to unlikely places and see what turns up.

"All the fields we deal in seem to be doing quite well right now," said Matthews. "Gas and oil, which there's more of than anything else, keeps going up more and more. The best thing to do is buy from reputable auction houses and dealers, from people who guarantee your product."

Barring the finds you can make at small antiques shows, shops and markets, expect to go into an auction ready to spend an average of $500 for a quality piece of petroliana, for pieces like rare oil and gas cans. A sharp and patient buyer can grab a steal for $10 or a masterpiece for $1,000. As with anything else, a seasoned and practical eye comes with practice. The prices broaden greatly when the market is expanded to include country store advertising and specific brand advertising, like Campbell's Soup.

"Like most kinds of collectibles, everybody starts out buying middle grade stuff and graduates to the higher stuff," said Matthews. "Collectors in this hobby are very dedicated; prices on the best stuff haven't peaked yet, that's for sure."

A lot of the steadiness in the market is coming from the exposure antique advertising is getting in places like cable television, via shows like "American Pickers" and "Pawn Stars," where a premium is placed on supreme objects.

"These kinds of shows are only helping the hobby get

Courtesy of Heritage Auctions, ha.com

Chief Red Jacket cigar store tobacconist's Indian trade figure in style of Julius Melchers, polychrome paint on wood, two eye hooks for attaching sign to building, paint touch-up and over-painting, carved area of cape with cracks to wood along folds, pitting and abrasions on back, back of headdress over-painted in gray, signs of restoration to base and feet, 75" high including 22" x 23" base. Figure is identified by experts as Chief Red Jacket, legendary Seneca orator who negotiated with the United States after the Revolutionary War and signed the Treaty of Canandaigua. In most of the paintings and statues of Red Jacket, he is shown wearing the Peace Medal given to him by George Washington. $45,000

Kellogg's Pep cereal premium buttons display sign, die-cut cardboard with easel back designed to fit around cereal box, "Free! A COMIC BUTTON IN EVERY PACKAGE OF PEP! Get the whole set of 18 / Save 'em! Trade 'em! Copyright1946," 10 button designs: Dick Tracy, Little Orphan Annie, Perry Winkle, Superman, Harold Teen, Winnie Winkle, Nina, Kayo, Smokey Stover, and Uncle Walt, excellent overall condition, unused with blank pricing area at lower left, some aging, faint crease to die-cut edge of Nina button design, rare, 10 1/2" x 12". **$1,844**

◄ Coca-Cola large round sign commonly known as button sign, 1950s, painted pressed steel, large bottle image at center behind large Coca-Cola name, heavy wire connected to two holes at top as intended for display, fine/very fine overall condition, scattered wear, small nicks/scratches with some aging to red areas across center and at bottom, 36" diameter. **$413**

bigger," Matthews added. "Take Ford Oil cans, for instance. Before these shows, the market was dominated by a handful of players. The prices ran way up. Those guys all got out, cans went down to $500 or so from $1,000 or more. Then these shows premiered, oil cans got some attention, and now a lot more collectors are back in at $1,000."

Factor in the pop culture value, as blue collar treasures are increasingly regarded as art , and the horizon is bright for this working-man's collectible.

"I see younger generations continuing to get into this hobby more and more," said Matthews. "As long as we have to put gas in our cars and food in our mouths, people will collect this stuff."

Courtesy of Heritage Auctions, ha.com

Cigar store tobacconist's smoking Indian with tomahawk, restored with filling and repaint, some touch-ups to unfilled cracks, applied carved lettering added to base, "S" missing top curve to tip, significant crack in front from neck through hand and down skirt, recent touch-up on feathers and nose, 92 1/2" high including 31" x 33" base. **$42,500**

Courtesy of Heritage Auctions, ha.com

Pocahontas cigar store tobacconist's Indian maid trade figure, carver unidentified, draped in dark-colored robe and holding round of cigars in left hand, exhibited at University of Pennsylvania's Museum of Cigar Store Indians in 1966, overall surface cracks and some pitting, filling and touchup down center back of cape, tops of feathers on headdress touched up, hair with some areas of over-paint, 72" high with 20" x 18" base. **$25,000**

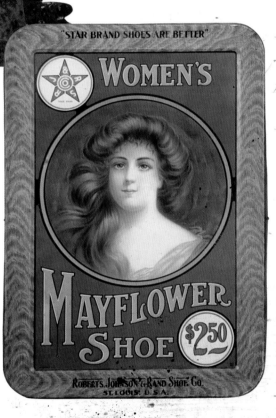

Beeman's Pepsin Chewing Gum
giraffe tin sign with tin easel back,
very good condition, some scratches
and areas of loss, 10" high. **$510**

▲ Mayflower Shoe tin sign with woman with long brown
hair, near mint condition, 26" x 18". **$1,680**

◄ McGregor Happy Foot socks molded composition store
display with anthropomorphic sock atop base, 1930s, 8"
scratch on reverse of sock, light wear to painted "Happy
Foot" text, rare gold variety (most are blue), 6" x 10" x
16 1/2" high overall. **$569**

Munyon's countertop display cabinet, late 19th/early 20th century, oak case with single hinged door concealing fitted interior, embossed tin panel with "Price List of Cures," lacking vertical partitions and some shelves to fitted interior, scattered areas of rust, pitting, and denting to embossed tin panels, refinished surface, 23 3/4" high x 17 1/4" wide x 8" deep. **$570**

The Blizzard Storm Front buggy apron company sign, tiny rust spots, very good-plus condition, framed under glass, 15 1/4" wide x 11 1/2" high. **$4,800**

Courtesy of Hake's Americana & Collectibles Auctions, www.hakes.com

Felix the Cat tin litho toffee container/pail with lid, mid-1920s, made in Liverpool, England by E.T. Gee & Sons, two bands of walking Felix figures at top and bottom, sides with two different scenes, one of beach with Felix family posing for photograph, other with Felix riding horse through fence as boy chases them, lid with full-body image of Felix, fine condition, exterior with scattered nicks/scratches, rim and edges of lid with moderate wear, interior with luster loss and some scattered oxidation, 8 1/4" high, 12" to top of wire handle. **$3,542**

Courtesy of Hake's Americana & Collectibles Auctions, www.hakes.com

Li'l Abner mechanical steel candy vending machine, 1949, narrow glass window in front, three sides with illustrations of Dogpatch characters, Li'l Abner, Daisy Mae, Mammy Yokum, Pappy Yokum, and Shmoo, four vending choices: "Daisy Mae Raisins (California Seedless Raisins), Li'l Abner Goobers (Selected Spanish Peanuts), Mammy Yokum Craws (Delicious Caramels), and Pappy Yokum Delight," very good/fine overall condition, works, no key, lower right corner with streak of oxidation, top with moderate paint wear and some bare metal, left side with heavy oxidation at rear bottom, back edge with dent at corner, 11 1/2" x 12 1/4" x 23" high. **$683**

Courtesy of Hake's Americana & Collectibles Auctions, www.hakes.com

◄ "TWENTY GRAND / Smoother SHAVES" razor blades tin sign, 1930s, single-sided, die-cut, painted heavy sign designed like razor blade, very fine overall condition, slight bends at holes at corners made for display, margins with scattered wear, small nicks and scattered trace oxidation, 15" x 29 3/4". **$536**

Chesterfield Cigarettes sign, "The Baseball Man's Cigarette," with Ted Williams, Stan Musial, Joe DiMaggio and others, 1947-1948, bright graphics, scattered wrinkles, sight 20 1/2" x 21 1/2", framed 27" x 28". $3,585

Havana Cigars round single-sided sign, "Reinken's Havana Plantation" across top with wavy-haired woman, Griselda, at center, very good condition, 14" diameter. $1,020

Imperial Cigar store wall-mounted oak display case with etched advertising on glass doors, case and brass trim cleaned and refinished, 26" wide x 24 1/2" high x 6 1/4" deep. $1,063

ART

American Art 64
Contemporary Art 82
Fine Art 94
Illustration Art 102

American Art

By Noah Fleisher

NOAH FLEISHER received his Bachelor of Fine Arts degree from New York University and brings more than a decade of newspaper, magazine, book, antiques and art experience to his position as Public Relations Director of Heritage Auctions, one of the country's foremost auction houses. He is the former editor of *Antique Trader, New England Antiques Journal* and *Northeast Antiques Journal,* is the author of *Warman's Modern Furniture* and co-author of *Collecting Children's Books,* and has been a longtime contributor to *Warman's Antiques & Collectibles.*

American art, described here as paintings, works on paper, and sculpture from roughly 1850 to 1950 – and on occasion even earlier than 1850 – is as fascinating, accessible, and varied a wrinkle in the art market as there is. The art and the artists now considered "American" have shifted significantly in the last decade.

"Everything from Colonial portraiture and Hudson River School paintings through to Modernism, Realism, and everything in between can be considered 'American,'" said Aviva Lehmann, Director of American Art at Heritage Auctions, New York. "Of all areas of fine art, I find American art to be the most diverse. Where else can you sell a Remington, an O'Keeffe, a Cassatt, and a Rockwell in one auction? As such, my catalogs often look like a syllabus of American art, even of American history in general."

What's even better news right now for both collectors and dealers in American art, especially if your bread and butter is in the middle market – say anything between $2,000 and $50,000 – and into the lower market, things are as good as they can be. It seems somewhat counter-intuitive to hear that, perhaps, given the obscene prices being paid for high profile Modern and contemporary works at top art auction houses, but it's the truth.

There is a plethora of quality work available in all corners, and with the malleable definition of "American art," this creates opportunities by the score, especially to a determined eye.

"The state of the American art market is as healthy as it's ever been," said Lehmann. "In 2007 and early 2008 we all thought that was the peak, yet in many areas the market is at a height never achieved before."

Several areas are driving the strength we see in American art right now, like Western art, regional art of various types, and early American Modernism, with very recent records being set at auction not just for Rockwell and O'Keeffe, but for secondary and tertiary artists in these areas, such as J.C. Leyendecker and Henry Lyman Sayan. This same pattern on down the hierarchical line of popular painters is repeating and resulting in ever better prices.

"Storm Sea," George Wesley Bellows (American, 1882-1925), 1913, oil on board, signed lower right: "Geo Bellows," 13 1/8" x 19 1/2". **$161,000**

"As they say, a rising tide lifts all boats," said Lehmann.

Nowhere has the shift been more pronounced, however, than in illustration art. It's rare when you have an opportunity to witness the exact moment when a paradigm shifts, but when Heritage Auctions began the 2009 auction of the estate of Charles Martignette, a legendary collector – and a series of auctions I was lucky enough to work on – it was obvious that things were changing. Suddenly art that was thought to be kitschy, dated, or transient had been given new life. Names like Elvgren, Moran, Armstrong, and many more were bringing real, undeniably good prices. The world of "fine art," which had thumbed its nose so long at illustration art, sat up and took notice.

"Illustration, in my opinion, has the most momentum right now," said Lehmann. "There are more buyers flocking to the category and more records being set by the season than anywhere else. I'm not just talking about Rockwell; it's Golden Age art, pulp art, pin-up art. Elvgren now regularly sells in the six-figure range, as do works by Patrick Nagel and even Leroy Neiman, an artist not even handled in fine art auctions until recently and now who regularly brings competitive bidding and six-figure results."

So, knowing now that the choice of "American" arenas is so broad – let your imagination go – the reality of price has to be considered. Most of us are not going to spend $50,000 or $100,000

Courtesy of Heritage Auctions, ha.com

"Manhattan Panorama," Leroy Neiman (American, 1921-2012), 1980-1984, oil on board, signed and dated lower right: "LeRoy Neiman / 80-84," 47" x 83". $137,000

on a painting. In fact, most of us will have to carefully consider spending more than $1,000-$2,000 on anything, let alone a painting. How do you decide?

"I always say to either choose a modest example by a very important artist – a Hopper drawing, for example – or a masterwork by a more obscure artist," said Lehmann. "At the end of the day, buy only what you love and cannot live without. Go from the heart."

This last bit of advice from Lehmann is perhaps the most important. It is also the most ubiquitous piece of advice a seeker in any category can get. At $100 million or so, it's probably okay to consider the investment aspect of it. At a few thousand? The market is going to hold its value at most levels right now. You're not going to get filthy rich on obscure Regionalism, but you're also not going to lose.

"I know that there is more 'investment buying' in the contemporary art arena and that there are portfolios being built by financial advisors based on art investment alone," said Lehmann. "I've never encouraged buying for investment purposes. American art is quite stable and not as erratic as contemporary art."

In the end, buy from those you trust, educate yourself – read books, go to museums, galleries, and auctions – and seek advice from seasoned collectors and curators.

"Never be afraid to ask too many questions," added Lehmann. "Above all, have fun."

Courtesy of Heritage Auctions, ha.com

"When He Was Fourteen, Michael Strogoff Had Killed His First Bear, Quite Alone," Newell Convers Wyeth (American, 1882-1945), 1927, oil on canvas, signed lower right: N.C. Wyeth, 40" x 30 1/4". **$269,000**

Courtesy of Heritage Auctions, ha.com

"Buckskins" (three works), Frederic Remington (American, 1861-1909), 1901, offset lithographs, all signed in plate, one dated in plate, 17 1/4" x 14 1/4". **$1,188**

Courtesy of Heritage Auctions, ha.com

"High and Shy," Gil Elvgren (American, 1914-1980), Brown & Bigelow calendar preliminary illustration, circa 1950, pencil on vellum, not signed, 24" x 17 3/4" (sheet). **$8,750**

Courtesy of Heritage Auctions, ha.com

"High and Shy," Gil Elvgren (American, 1914-1980), Brown & Bigelow calendar illustration, 1950, oil on canvas, signed lower right, 30" x 24". This painting was reproduced as figure 400 in *Gil Elvgren: All His Glamorous American Pin-Ups* by Charles G. Martignette and Louis K. Meisel, Taschen, 1999. **$161,000**

◀ "Harriet Tubman," Charles Wilbert White (American, 1918-1979), 1949, ink and pencil on board, signed and bears date lower left: "Charles White '49," 30" x 20". **$25,000**

▲ "The Risen Moon," Frederick Judd Waugh (American, 1861-1940), 1926, oil on canvas, signed lower right: Waugh, signed, titled, and dated on stretcher verso: '"The Risen Moon" Frederick Waugh 1926,' 25" x 30". **$11,875**

"The Summer House," Eric Sloane (American, 1905-1985), 1972, oil on Masonite, signed lower left: "Eric Sloane / The Summer / House," inscribed and dated verso: "To / Carl / 1972," 17 1/2" x 23 1/2". **$12,500**

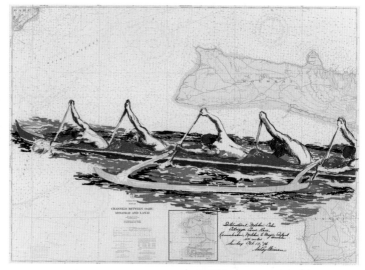

Courtesy of Heritage Auctions, ha.com

"International Molokai-Oahu Outrigger Canoe Race," Leroy Neiman (American, 1921-2012), Oct. 17, 1976, screenprint in colors on Hawaiian map, 24" x 32 1/2". **$500**

Courtesy of Heritage Auctions, ha.com

"Choosing Up (Four Sporting Boys: Baseball)," Norman Rockwell (American, 1894-1978), preliminary Brown & Bigelow Four Seasons calendar illustration, spring 1951, oil on glossy paper laid on board, 10 1/8" x 8" (sheet). **$125,000**

Courtesy of Heritage Auctions, ha.com

"Mirage," Patrick Nagel (American, 1945-1984), 1982, acrylic on canvas, signed and dated lower left, 36" x 23 7/8". **$131,000**

"Battery of the U.S. Field Artillery Going into Action," William Herbert Dunton (American, 1878-1936), oil on canvas, signed lower left: "W. Herbert Dunton," titled on label verso: "Battery of the U.S. Field Artillery Going into Action," 27 7/8" x 36 7/8". A founding member of the Taos Society of Artists, Dunton was a master draftsman. **$52,500**

"The Sergeant," Frederic Remington (American, 1861-1909), 1904, bronze with brown patina, authorized posthumous cast, inscribed along base: "copyright by / Frederic Remington / R.B.W.," stamped and numbered in red ink on underside: "N. 76," 10 1/4" high. **$11,000**

"The Texas Queen," David Michael Bates (American, b. 1952), 1982, oil on canvas, signed lower left: David Bates, signed, titled, dated, and inscribed on reverse: "David Bates - The Texas Queen - 90" x 67", 82," 90" x 67". **$221,000**

"Rocky Cliffs over Valley," Walter King Stone (American, 1875-1949), oil on canvas, signed lower right: Walter King Stone, 24 1/2" x 29 1/2". **$3,750**

"Waiting at the Doctor's Office," Norman Rockwell (American, 1894-1978), possible Smith Kline advertisement, circa 1952, pencil and ink on board, signed lower right: Norman Rockwell, 12" x 9" (sheet). **$87,500**

"Taking Off," Gil Elvgren (American, 1914-1980), Brown & Bigelow calendar illustration, 1955, oil on canvas, signed lower right, 30" x 24". This painting was reproduced as figure 333 in *Gil Elvgren: All His Glamorous American Pin-Ups* by Charles G. Martignette and Louis K. Meisel, Taschen, 1999. **$60,000**

"Racing," Leroy Neiman (American, 1921-2012), 1967, acrylic on Masonite, signed and dated lower right, 34" x 47 3/4" (sheet). **$50,000**

"Come Quitting Time," G. (Gerald Harvey Jones) Harvey (American, b. 1933), 1979, oil on canvas, signed and dated lower left: "G. Harvey 1979 ©," 18" x 24". **$37,500**

"Our Back Yard When I Was Young," Edward Emerson Simmons (American, 1852-1931), 1919, oil on canvasboard, signed and dated lower right: "Edward Simmons / 1919," signed, dated, and titled verso: "Our Back Yard When I Was Young / August 1919 / Edward Simmons," 12" x 16". Provenance: From the Jean and Graham Devoe Williford Charitable Trust. **$6,875**

Courtesy of Heritage Auctions, ha.com

"Lakeshore," Wolf Kahn (American, b. 1927), oil on canvas, signed lower right: "W. Kahn," 16" x 26". **$32,500**

Courtesy of Heritage Auctions, ha.com

"Sailor girl, preliminary," after Gil Elvgren (American, 1914-1980), pencil on board, figure done on separate cardstock cut-out and collaged together, not signed, 23" x 19 1/4". **$400**

Courtesy of Heritage Auctions, ha.com

"Study for Iris," David Michael Bates (American, b. 1952), 1998, lithograph in colors, ed. 11/20, signed and dated lower right: "BATES 98," 13 3/4" x 9 3/4". Provenance: From The Belo Collection. **$1,500**

Courtesy of Heritage Auctions, ha.com

"Margot Wearing a Bonnet (No. 3)," Mary Cassatt (American, 1844-1926), etching, 9" x 6" (plate). **$938**

Courtesy of Heritage Auctions, ha.com

"New England Summer, Late Afternoon," Mabel May Woodward (American, 1877-1945), oil on canvas, signed lower left: "M.M. Woodward," 16" x 20". **$2,000**

Courtesy of Heritage Auctions, ha.com

"A Glimpse of the Juniata from Sideling Hill," Russell Smith (American, 1812-1896), 1893, oil on panel with sculpted shadowbox relief, initialed lower right: RS, signed, dated and titled verso: "A Glimpse of the Juniata from Sideling Hill / Russell Smith 1893," 11 1/2" x 7 3/4" x 3". **$2,000**

Courtesy of Heritage Auctions, ha.com

"Russian Woman," Leon Gaspard (Russian/American, 1882-1964), 1914, oil on canvasboard, signed lower right: Leon Gaspard, dated, titled, and inscribed on label verso: "Leon Gaspard / Russian Woman / Painted in Russia in 1914," 8 1/2" x 10 1/2". **$20,000**

Courtesy of Heritage Auctions, ha.com

"Saratoga Trunk," Tom Lovell (American, 1909-1997), 1941, oil on canvas, signed upper right: "Tom / Lovell," 26 1/4" x 39". This painting was created for the film *Saratoga Trunk*, Warner Brothers Burbank Studios, 1945. **$8,125**

Courtesy of Heritage Auctions, ha.com

"Untitled ('Asgaard,' the farm of Sally and Rockwell Kent)," Rockwell Kent (American, 1882-1971), circa 1960-1965, oil on canvasboard, signed and inscribed lower right: "To my friends Vera and Yakov Tolchan / Rockwell Kent," inscribed verso: "Asgaard, the farm of Sally and Rockwell Kent / Au Sable Forks, New York, / USA," 14 7/8" x 18". **$50,000**

"Desert Waterhole at Nightfall,"
William Robinson Leigh
(American, 1866-1955), 1949,
oil on canvas laid on Masonite,
signed and dated lower left:
"W.R. Leigh 1949 ©," 16" x 20".
$40,000

"Mutiny," Dean Cornwell
(American, 1892-1960), oil
and pencil on board, signed
lower left: "Dean / Cornwell,"
29 1/2" x 23 1/4". **$15,000**

"Desert Sky at Evening, Tucson, Arizona," Maynard Dixon (American, 1875-1946), circa 1946, oil on board, signature added by artist's widow, lower left: "MD," inscription added by artist's widow, verso: "Desert Sky at Evening / 1945 - Tucson, Arizona. / by Maynard Dixon," 12" x 16". **$11,875**

"Backyard," Guy Pene Du Bois (American, 1884-1958), oil on canvas, 22 1/8" x 18". **$27,500**

"Path through a Rocky Landscape," Stephen Parrish (American, 1846-1938), 1915, oil on canvas, signed and dated lower right: "Stephen Parrish / 1915," 25" x 35". **$6,875**

"Cellist and Little Girl Dancing" preliminary study, Norman Rockwell (American, 1894-1978), 1923, pencil on paper, initialed lower right: "N / R," inscribed lower center: "My best wishes to / Mrs. Alden Barber / cordially / Norman Rockwell," 6" x 4 1/4" (sight). **$6,563**

"Going South," Joseph Christian Leyendecker (American, 1874-1951), *The Saturday Evening Post* cover, Oct. 19, 1935, oil on canvas, signed with monogram lower right: "JCLeyendecker," 29 1/4" x 24 1/4". **$137,000**

"Portrait Study of Young Girl,"
Mary Cassatt (American, 1844-
1926), watercolor and pencil on
paper, artist's estate stamp lower
right, 10 1/2" x 10 1/2" (sheet).
$15,000

"Alligator Pears," Georgia
O'Keeffe (American, 1887-1986),
circa 1923, oil on canvas, signed
on stretcher verso: O'Keeffe,
12" x 10". Provenance: From The
King Collection. **$461,000**

Contemporary Art

By Noah Fleisher

NOAH FLEISHER received his Bachelor of Fine Arts degree from New York University and brings more than a decade of newspaper, magazine, book, antiques and art experience to his position as Public Relations Director of Heritage Auctions, one of the country's foremost auction houses. He is the former editor of *Antique Trader, New England Antiques Journal* and *Northeast Antiques Journal,* is the author of *Warman's Modern Furniture* and co-author of *Collecting Children's Books,* and has been a longtime contributor to *Warman's Antiques & Collectibles.*

The proliferation of eight- and nine-figure artworks in the last five years has been hard to miss, unless you live in a cave, and no sector has seen a bigger uptick than contemporary art.

If you have a spare $10 million to $100 million, then the seasonal sales at high-end art auctions, where sums of money that equal or exceed some nations' GDP regularly change hands, are for you. One hundred million dollars for a couple of Warhols, anyone (Christie's, May 2014)? How about a Francis Bacon triptych for $142+ million (Christie's again, November 2013)? How about $1+ million for a Damien Hirst (Sotheby's, June 2104)? Look out your window now, toward the gilded art halls of New York, London and Paris, and tell me if you can see the bubble growing.

It sounds to me, sometimes, like the idle rich have too much monopoly money on their hands and are blowing it all in a battle royale aimed simply at keeping up with the Joneses, or buying art by the yard to decorate expansive chateaus and tony beach houses.

Forgive the cynicism, if you will, but it seems to me that the market is simply being ruined for the rest of us, meaning those of us who can't afford to spend eight figures on a canvas, who can often only spend a few thousand, if that, or the rarified air of those that can spend a few hundred thousand.

Really, though, where does the middle market – which has taken it in the shorts, by most accounts, across most categories, in the last decade – stand amidst all this conspicuous consumption? Is there a bubble forming? How can we even tell?

The truth is somewhere in-between, according to Brandon Kennedy, a Contemporary and Modern Art Specialist at Heritage Auctions, a specialty auction house that, while it hasn't seen $10 million or $100 million paintings, has seen an increase in prices and buyers for its modern auctions in the last few years.

"Now that we're almost six years beyond the economic downturn, things are definitely on the upswing," said Kennedy. "There's always a little bit of the 'good, bad, and the ugly' in the market and it largely depends on where you're standing. As of late, the talk is of a bubble and whether or not it exists. Only time will tell I suppose."

The best place to stand would be on your own two feet, I

"Standard Flower #2," Donald Baechler (b. 1956), oil, fabric, screen print, and mixed media collage on canvas; signed twice with artist's initials; signed, dated twice 95-96, dated 1995-96, and titled on reverse; 71 1/8" x 71 1/8". **$39,015**

have to guess, on a firm foundation. That foundation, first and foremost, has to be built on a solid understanding of exactly what you are looking at. Just what is the definition of contemporary art, and how is it separated from modern art?

According to Kennedy, the term 'modern art' is used to define a period starting in the late 19th century and extending to sometime in the 1960s-1970s, depending on who you ask, largely defined by styles and movements within a certain historical moment. 'Contemporary art,' therefore, is generally thought of taking shape post-1965 or so, when the lines between strict divisions and traditional mediums begin to dissolve and even wander outside the gallery or institutional framework."

Kennedy is quick to point out that, with the rapid evolution of mediums (including digital artwork, 3-D printers and new mediums for sculpture), even those definitions are becoming

**Untitled, Gerhard Richter
(b. 1932), watercolor on
paper, signed and dated
19.4.84, 8 7/8" x 13 1/8".
$251,257**

hazy. There is a definite post-modern movement, but is such a thing as post-contemporary even possible?

What can we make of recent sales at big auction houses and galleries of work by young artists done in those non-traditional mediums, specifically computer prints (or is it computer art?) that sell for seven and eight figures? How philosophically and financially sound or unsound is this?

"Artwork created by digital or other technological means is now always present and will continue to evolve with the available technology at hand," said Kennedy. "Whether sound or unsound, it largely boils down to the market and personal taste and where the two overlap."

Let's go a little further, then: Doesn't the very artificiality of such a medium change value for the lower in the long run?

"There are plenty of high rollers and lower-level speculators treating contemporary art like a futures market," Kennedy said, "and many others simply follow along and get burnt on the back-side of a transaction when they try to resell the work. A lot of the time, the contemporary art market can sound like it's somewhere in-between a horse race and interior decorating, and, unfortunately, it is sometimes as simple as that."

Can't an artist just print out another print, if it's a digital piece? Absolutely, and sometimes they do. In the topsy-turvy modern world, that can even enhance the value of a piece, at least in the short-term, even when an artist "creates" more digital work in a sort of protest against what could become a quickly bloated market.

Take the case of artist Wade Guyton, for example, a well-known, mid-career artist.

"Upon hearing that one of his Epson UltraChrome inkjet works on canvas would soon be offered at a major house with an estimate of $3.5 million to $4.5 million," Kennedy said, "he made dozens of duplicates and then posted photos to his Instagram account of them lingering about in his studio."

The original print that Kennedy is referring to, "If I Live I'll See You Tuesday," offered in Christie's late spring 2014 sale, still brought north of $3.5 million.

Most of us, again, don't play in those sandboxes. If you're serious about getting in, where do you even begin? What area of contemporary art is the hottest right now and who are the hottest artists who might not necessarily be household names?

"Names like Warhol, Bacon, and Gerhard Richter are still fetching premium prices, at all levels of work, and that's no surprise," Kennedy said. "Bruce Nauman and Ed Ruscha are still producing great work and fetching premium prices, as is the work of artists like David Hammons, John Baldessari, Jasper Johns, and Richard Serra. There are also a slew of hot, young artists who graduate from the gallery scene to the auction block in the blink of an eye and, by the time you realize that you could've capitalized on their ascendancy, they're already on the decline. I won't name names specifically because of the aforementioned problem."

Is contemporary art, then, a market that's even open to first-time buyers and those without massive bank accounts?

"Absolutely," said Kennedy. "Start small and look at editions and prints of an established artist that you have heard of before. Pop and abstract expressionism are good movements to consider when pondering this question. Otherwise, get out and visit local art galleries and the artists who show there. Spend a season or two surveying what's available and educating yourself, and eventually your heart and taste will lead you down the right road."

Kennedy is 100% right in this approach, which will work no matter what the category. Ask experts for their opinion. Get to know the people behind the industry, go to auctions and gallery openings and museum exhibitions. Continue to educate yourself in every aspect of art culture and the market.

"Educate yourself and continue to do so over the course of your life," he said, "but only buy what you love and can't stop thinking about."

Courtesy of Sotheby's, www.sothebys.com

"Maquette Diamond Wing," Lynn Chadwick (1914-2003), bronze with green patina, incised with artist's signature, dated 70 and numbered 1/6 on reverse, executed in 1970, number 1 from edition of six, 27 1/8" x 20" x 9 7/8". $107,291

Courtesy of Sotheby's, www.sothebys.com

"Cypress Hill," Hurvin Anderson
(b. 1965), acrylic on paper laid on
board, signed and dated March
2015 on reverse, 32 5/8" x 44 3/4".
$269,984

Courtesy of Sotheby's, www.sothebys.com

"Billiardzimmer 2," Mattias
Weischer (b. 1973), oil on
canvas, signed and dated 2002
on reverse, 55 7/8" x 67 1/2".
$152,159

Courtesy of Sotheby's, www.sothebys.com

"Rückenkratzen," Arnulf Rainer
(b. 1929), oil on cardboard,
signed, titled, and dated 1975,
28 3/4" x 40 1/8". **$48,769**

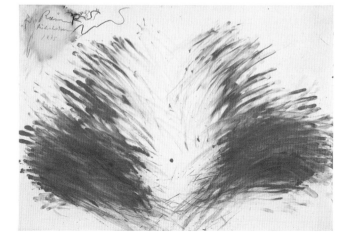

"Nestor," Joan Miró (Spanish, 1893-1983), lithograph in colors on Arches paper, 1975, edition 8/50, signed and numbered in pencil, 35" x 25". **$6,250**

"Pastoral Scene," Leonard Long (Australian, 1911-2013), oil on canvas, 1961, signed and dated lower left: Leonard Long '61, 29 3/4" x 35 3/4". **$600**

Courtesy of Heritage Auctions, ha.com

"Sandia #1 (Watermelon)," Rufino Tamayo (Mexican, 1899-1991), lithograph in colors, signed and inscribed in pencil in bottom margin, 20 1/2" x 27 1/4". **$3,250**

Courtesy of Heritage Auctions, ha.com

"Saint-Germain-des-Prés," Marc Chagall (French/Russian, 1887-1985), oil on canvas, 1953, signed lower right: Marc / Chagall, 13 3/4" x 10 5/8". **$275,000**

Courtesy of Heritage Auctions, ha.com

"Jonas' Boat," Marc Chagall (French/Russian, 1887-1985), lithograph in colors, 1977, AP IV/VII, signed and numbered in pencil in bottom margin, 16 3/8" x 12 3/8". **$3,750**

Courtesy of Heritage Auctions, ha.com

"Abstract Woman," Hugo Scheiber (Hungarian, 1873-1950), watercolor and gouache on paper laid on board, signed lower right: Scheiber / H., 23 1/8" x 16 7/8" (sheet). **$3,000**

Courtesy of Heritage Auctions, ha.com

Untitled, Toshimatsu Imai (Japanese, 1928-2002), oil on canvas, 1962, signed and dated lower right: Imai 1962, 28 3/4" x 23 1/2". **$161,000**

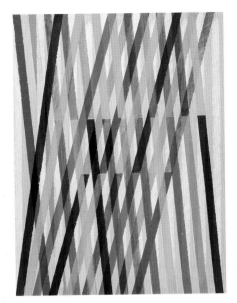

Courtesy of Heritage Auctions, ha.com

"Another Way," Piero Dorazio (Italian, 1927-2005), oil on canvas, 1965, signed and inscribed on stretcher verso: Dorazio to / M. Gerson Gallery; signed, titled, and dated on reverse: Piero Dorazio / "Another Way" / 1965, 72" x 53 3/4". **$149,000**

Courtesy of Heritage Auctions, ha.com

"Waterfall," M. C. Escher (Dutch, 1898-1972), lithograph on wove paper, 1961, edition 39/57 II, signed and numbered in pencil in bottom margin, initialed and dated in plate lower right, 15" x 11 3/4". **$25,000**

Courtesy of Heritage Auctions, ha.com

"The Hero," Sorel Etrog (Canadian, 1933-2014), oil on shaped panel, 1959, signed, titled, and dated verso: "The Hero" / etrog / 59, 25" x 20 1/2". **$16,250**

"Krakow (Cracow) 1," Wilhelm Sasnal (b. 1972), oil on canvas, 2007, 21 5/8" x 27 1/2". **$62,424**

"Three Fishermen," Julian Morales (Cuban, 1937-1990), oil on board, 1976, signed and dated lower right: Morales 76, 25 3/4" x 17 1/2". **$1,876**

"Red Composition with Blue Figure," Peter Max (American, b. 1937), acrylic on canvas, 1979, signed and dated upper right: Max / 1979, signed and dated verso: © Peter Max 1979, 34 3/4" x 23 1/2". **$7,500**

"Souvenir of Rio Grande City," Edward Muegge "Buck" Schiwetz (American, 1898-1984), gouache and pastel on paper, 1952, signed, titled, and dated: Souvenir of Rio Grand City / EM Schiwetz 52, 13 1/4" x 21 1/4" (sight). **$6,875**

"Floral," Clarice Smith (American, b. 1933), oil on canvas, 1987, signed lower left: C. Smith, 24" x 36". **$17,500**

"Formas," Miguel Angel Pareja (Uruguayan, 1908-1984), oil on cardboard, 1951, signed lower right: Pareja, 18 1/8" x 14 1/8". **$5,000**

"Meeting," Farhad Khalilov (b. 1946), acrylic on canvas, 2014-2015, 78 3/4" x 78 3/4". **$107,291**

Untitled, Kazuko Inoue (Japanese/American, b. 1946), acrylic on canvas, 1979, signed, titled, and dated verso: "Untitled" / © Kazuko Inoue 1979, 50" x 50". **$12,500**

"Bird House (Small)," Peter Doig (b. 1959), oil on canvas, signed, titled, and dated 95 on reverse, 16" x 12". **$1,655,797**

Fine Art

Fine art, created for aesthetic purposes and judged by its beauty rather than its utility, includes original painting and sculpture, drawing, watercolor, and graphics. It is appreciated primarily for its imaginative, aesthetic, or intellectual content.

The market is seeing more art in general sold and at faster rates, and is currently growing by six percent a year, according to Arts Economics' annual *Art Market Report*. Roughly $53.9 billion changed hands in 2014 in transactions involving fine and decorative art. The amount sold at art and antiques shows worldwide stands at $10.5 billion. In the middle market, post-war art is still strong and less speculative than contemporary art.

Courtesy of Heritage Auctions, ha.com

"Central Park Nocturne," Johann Berthelsen (1883-1972), oil on canvas, signed lower left: Johann Berthelsen, 16" x 20".
$4,750

"Girl on Bridge," Louisa Matthiasdottir (American, 1917-2000), oil on canvas, signed lower left: L. Matth, 9" x 12". **$6,250**

"Baby with Bottle," Ted Withers (American, 1896-1964), oil on canvas, signed lower right: Withers, 30" x 24". **$800**

"Vase of Flowers," Yolande Ardissone (French, b. 1927), oil on canvas, signed lower left: Ardissone, 10 3/4" x 6 5/8". **$1,000**

"Sir Mark Wood With His Dark Brown Filly Vespa, Winner of the Oaks in 1833, Her Trainer H Scott and a Groom With a Grey Hack," John Frederick Herring, Sr. (British, 1795-1865), oil on canvas, signed JF Herring and dated 1833 upper right, 28" x 36". **$706,000**

"Woman with Crimson Parasol," manner of William Merritt Chase (American, 1849-1916), oil on canvas, 34 1/2" x 24 1/4". **$7,500**

"Hooded Figure #2," Karl Zerbe (American, 1903-1972), 1952, polymer tempera on canvas laid on Masonite, signed lower right: Zerbe, titled, dated, and inscribed verso: Hooded Figure / #2 / June 52, 32" x 16". **$2,000**

Courtesy of Heritage Auctions, ha.com
"Oil Tanker," Edward Muegge
"Buck" Schiwetz (American, 1898-
1984), mixed media on board,
signed lower left: EM Schiwetz,
11 3/4" x 15 3/4" (sight). **$4,000**

Courtesy of Heritage Auctions, ha.com
"Looking Out," Robert Watson (American, 1923-
2004), 1951, oil on canvas, signed and dated lower
right: R Watson 51, 22" x 18". **$2,125**

Courtesy of Heritage Auctions, ha.com
"Coastal Landscape," Sidney Yates Johnson
(British, 1871-1940), 1907, oil on canvas, signed and
dated lower right: S. Y. Johnson / 1907, 30" x 20".
$600

Courtesy of Sotheby's, www.sothebys.com

"September Afternoon," Sir Alfred James Munnings, P.R.A., R.W.S. (English, 1878-1959), oil on canvas, signed lower left: A J. Munnings, 25" x 30". **$909,497**

Courtesy of Heritage Auctions, ha.com

"Sandwich and Soda" (from Ten Works by Ten Painters), Roy Lichtenstein (American, 1923-1997), 1964, screenprint in colors on clear plastic, from edition of 500 published by Wadsworth Atheneum, Hartford, 19" x 23". **$4,500**

Courtesy of Heritage Auctions, ha.com

"Cubist Composition," Henry Lyman Sayen (American, 1875-1918), 1917, casein tempera on paper, signed and dated lower right: H. Lyman Sayen / 1917, 20 5/8" x 17". **$100,000**

Courtesy of Sotheby's, www.sothebys.com

"Venetian Lovers," Eugen von Blaas (Austrian, 1843-1931), oil on canvas, signed Eug. de Blaas and dated 1906 lower right, 39 3/4" x 25". **$298,000**

▲ "Diagonal White Path," Charles B. Hinman (American, b. 1932), 1967, acrylic on shaped canvas, signed and dated on the reverse: Hinman / 67, 98" x 48" x 15". **$23,750**

◄ "Marchande De Fleurs À Londres," Jules Bastien-Lepage (French, 1848-1884), oil on canvas, signed J. BASTIEN-LEPAGE, dated 82 and inscribed Londres lower left, 68 1/4" x 35 1/2". **$1,507,000**

"Southwark Bridge From Blackfriars By Moonlight," John Atkinson Grimshaw (British, 1836-1893), oil on canvas, signed Atkinson Grimshaw and dated 1881+ lower left, 20" x 36". **$200,000**

ART

"Winter Landscape," American School, late 20th century, oil on canvas, initialed lower left: STI, 24 3/4" x 29 3/4". **$1,250**

"Hashknife of Stormy River," Nick Eggenhofer (American, 1897-1985), probable dust jacket illustration, gouache on board, signed lower right: N. Eggenhofer, inscribed verso: Hashknife of Stormy River – Jacket, 13 3/8" x 17 7/8" (sheet). **$1,500**

"La Marchande De Fleurs – Rue De Rivoli," Louis Marie de Schryver, (French, 1862-1942), oil on canvas, signed Louis de Schryver and dated 1892 lower right, 28 3/4" x 36 1/4". **$350,000**

Courtesy of Sotheby's, www.sothebys.com

"Prince's Dock, Hull," John Atkinson Grimshaw (English, 1836-1893), oil on board, signed and dated lower left: Atkinson Grimshaw 1882, 11 3/4" x 20". **$402,308**

Courtesy of Sotheby's, www.sothebys.com

"The Shadow," Edmund Blair Leighton, (English, 1853-1922), oil on canvas, signed with initials on the wall, lower left: E.B.L., signed and inscribed with artist's address on old label attached to reverse, 36" x 24". **$107,621**

Courtesy of Sotheby's, www.sothebys.com

"Ned Osborne on Grey Tick," Sir Alfred James Munnings, P.R.A., R.W.S. (English, 1878-1959), oil on canvas, signed lower left: A.J. MUNNINGS, 20" x 24". **$947,067**

Illustration Art

By Brent Frankenhoff and Maggie Thompson

MAGGIE THOMPSON was among the pioneering amateurs who formed the foundation in the 1960s of today's international anarchy of comic-book collecting. With her late husband, Don, she edited *Comics Buyer's Guide* and remains active as a collector and essayist.
BRENT FRANKENHOFF is a lifelong collector and former editor of *Comics Buyer's Guide*.

Collectors, whether looking for a distinctive decoration for a living room or seeking a rewarding long-term investment, will find something to fit their fancy – and their budget – when they turn to illustration art.

Pieces of representational art – often, art that tells some sort of story – are produced in a variety of forms, each appealing in a different way. They are created as the source material for political cartoons, magazine covers, posters, story illustrations, comic books and strips, animated cartoons, calendars, and book jackets. They may be in color or in black and white. Collectible forms include:

- Mass-market printed reproductions. These can range from art prints and movie posters to engravings, clipped advertising art, and bookplates. While this may be the least-expensive art to hang on your wall, a few rare items can bring record prices.

- Limited-run reproductions. These range from signed, numbered lithographs to numbered prints.

- Tangential items. These are hard-to-define, oddball pieces. One example is printing plates (some in actual lead; some in plastic fused to lightweight metal) used by newspapers and comic-book printers to reproduce the art.

- Unique original art. These pieces have the widest range of all, from amateur sketches to finished paintings. The term "original art" includes color roughs produced by a painter as a preliminary test for a work to be produced, finished oil paintings, animation cels for commercials as well as feature films, and black-and-white inked pages of comic books and strips. They may be signed and identifiable or unsigned and generic.

"Illustration art" is often differentiated from "fine art," but its pop culture nature may increase the pool of would-be purchasers. Alberto Vargas (1896-1982) and Gil Elvgren (1914-1980) bring high prices for pin-up art; Norman Rockwell (1894-1978), James Montgomery Flagg (1877-1960), and J.C. Leyendecker (1874-1951) were masters of mainstream illustration; and Margaret Brundage (1900-1976) and Virgil Finlay (1914-1971) are highly regarded pulp artists.

"When the living is easy," unknown artist, colored pencil and gouache on paper, advertisement for Coca-Cola, 20th century, light foxing, paper discoloration, some small tears, general age wear. **$2,750**

"A Swell-Looking Girl," James Avati, illustration for paperback cover, oil on board, signed lower left, published as cover for *A Swell-Looking Girl* (originally titled *American Earth*) by Erskin Caldwell, Signet Books 818, 1950, accompanied by copy of paperback, scattered surface scratches, minor surface dirt throughout, 14" x 12 3/4". **$23,750**

"Broken Gun," Richard Lillis, *Thrilling Western* pulp magazine cover, oil on canvas, November 1946, accompanied by copy of magazine, 30 1/2" x 21 1/8". **$1,750**

"Wonder Where Wally Went" illustrating story by R. Ross Annett, Amos Sewell, media on illustration board, signed lower right, published in June 10, 1994 issue of *The Saturday Evening Post*, *The Saturday Evening Post* label on verso, 28" x 35". **$5,250**

Courtesy Swann Auction Galleries,
www.swanngalleries.com

"Budgetary Control," Rico Tomaso, advertisement illustration for Remington Rand, oil on canvas, published in *Collier's*, April 5, 1930, accompanied by copy of magazine, restorer's small glued patch on verso, 34" x 26 1/4". **$3,380**

Courtesy Swann Auction Galleries,
www.swanngalleries.com

"Child Reading by Lamp Light," Norman Rockwell, graphite on paper mounted on card, likely rejected composition for advertisement for Armstrong Cork Co. in Lancaster, Pennsylvania, signed lower right in different color and weight pencil from that of drawing, thought to have been added at an earlier date for identification purposes, gifted from Rockwell to Hazel Dell-Brown, art director of Armstrong Cork Co., 1926, mild age toning, small chip on right corner, 11" x 9 3/4". **$16,875**

"As I Opened Fire," Roy Lichtenstein, set of three original offset lithographs, signed in pencil, lower right of third panel, text on reverse lower left: ROY LICHTENSTEIN 1923 / as i opened fire / 1964 – acryl on canvas /, 25 3/16" x 20 3/4". **$6,175**

Courtesy Heritage Auctions, ha.com

"Martian Emerges" from *The War of the Worlds*, Henrique Alvim Correa, Belgium edition, pencil and ink on paperboard, published as illustration in *Book I: The Coming of the Martians*, Chapter IV in "The Cylinder Opens," The War of the Worlds Archive, 1906, minor discoloration, light foxing, 20 1/8" x 16 3/4". **$32,500**

Courtesy Heritage Auctions, ha.com

▲ Ford holiday greeting card preliminary illustration, Norman Rockwell, pencil on board, signed on lower left, from family of original owner, Ralph H. Breding, artist and friend of Rockwell's, who was head of the art department at J. Walter Thompson Advertising, the company in charge of Ford's advertising; slight age discoloration and surface soiling, 9 3/4" x 17 3/4". **$26,250**

Courtesy Swann Auction Galleries, www.swanngalleries.com

"Ah! Sweet Mystery of Life," Jan B. Balet, illustration of famous Victor Herbert operetta "Naughty Marietta," gouache on board, signed in pencil lower left, published in Morrell Meat Dealer calendar Songs From Our Favorite Operettas, Ottumwa, Iowa: John & Co., 1952, 14 1/2" x 12 1/4". **$4,250**

Courtesy Swann Auction Galleries, www.swanngalleries.com

"The only remnant of her past magnificence being one of her little glass slippers" full-page illustration, Warwick Goble, pen and ink and watercolor, signed lower left, for *The Fairy Book*, Dinah Maria Mulock, London: Macmillan & Co., 1913, 13" x 9". **$2,340**

"The Beast Under the Wizard's Bridge," Edward Gorey, ink and watercolor on paper dust jacket, accompanied by Gorey's original pen and ink layout of cover and spine lettering, design for John Bellairs' *The Beast Under the Wizard Bridge*, Brad Strickland: Dial, 2000, 9 1/2" x 13". **$5,980**

"Printing Press," Edward McKnight Kauffer, advertisement for Charles Eneu Johnson Printing Inks, gouache on board, signed and dated lower right; artist's ink stamp verso: "Designed by E McK Kauffer, Mar 1926" and his original copyright label, signed and dated 3/15/26 in ink, 14 1/2" x 10 3/4". **$2,250**

"Fishing Contest," Arnold C. Holeywell, magazine cover image, gouache on board, signed lower left, cover for May 1952 issue of *Field & Stream*, 16 1/2" x 11 7/8". **$2,125**

Courtesy Swann Auction Galleries,
www.swanngalleries.com

"Dockside," Stevan Dohanos, unidentified image of New York City port by master artist for *The Saturday Evening Post*, watercolor with wash on board, slightly warped, strong colors, 14" x 11 1/4". **$1,750**

Courtesy Swann Auction Galleries,
www.swanngalleries.com

"Mother and Child with Swan," Maginel Wright Enright Barney, cover art, watercolor and pencil, signed in full in watercolor, lower right margin, published cover art for *Woman's World* magazine, June 1937, accompanied by copy of magazine, 14 1/2" x 13 1/2". **$1,875**

"Rip Van Winkle," Everett Shinn, published as vignette on foreword of 1939 publication of Washington Irving's *Rip Van Winkle*, pen and ink on paper, initialed lower right, Garden City Publishing Co., Garden City, New York, accompanied by copy of book, 9 1/2" x 13". **$6,250**

"Swimming," F. Earl Christy, illustration for American Art Works calendar, watercolor on board, signed lower right, minor surface soiling, light pigment fade, several pinholes, 39 1/4" x 31 1/4". **$3,125**

Asian

Art and antiques from Asia have fascinated collectors for centuries because they are linked to the rich culture and fascinating history of the Far East. Their beauty, artistry, and fine craftsmanship have lured collectors through the ages.

The category is vast and includes objects ranging from jade carvings to cloisonné to porcelain, the best known of these being porcelain.

Large quantities of porcelain have been made in China for export to America since the 1780s. A major source of this porcelain was Ching-te-Chen in the Kiangsi province, but the wares were also made elsewhere. The largest quantities were blue and white.

Prices for Asian antiques and art fluctuate considerably depending on age, condition, decoration, etc.

Courtesy of Heritage Auctions, ha.com

Pair of Chinese polychrome lacquered wood trunks with brass mounts, late 19th century, 20 1/4" x 42" x 20". $4,000

▲ Asian birds and floral watercolor on paper, bird surrounded by floral elements, wood frame, image 20" x 26". **$12,000**

◄ Chinese lapis lazuli mountain on rosewood stand, 10 1/4" x 8" x 5", including stand. **$3,000**

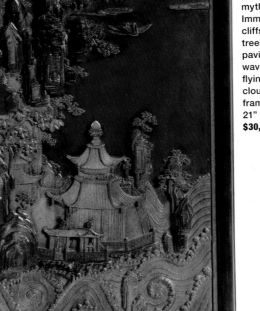

"Duan" stone "penglai" panel, Qing Dynasty, early 18th century, carved utilizing varied colors of layered stone, mythical islands of Immortals with rocky cliffs, evergreens, and trees, multi-tiered pavilions rising from waves, pair of cranes flying overhead amid clouds, hardwood frame, 21" high x 17 1/4" wide. **$30,000**

Courtesy of Heritage Auctions, ha.com

Monumental Chinese gourd-form cloisonné jardinière with gilt bronze and stand, Qing Dynasty, marks to stand: "18," lobed jardinière with cloisonné ground of blooming branches on blue ground, set in gilt bronze mounts with repeating ogee foliate rim on stand with four foo dog legs, on X-form base, 43 1/2" high x 28" diameter. **$32,500**

Repoussé gilt copper alloy figure depicting Makaramukha, Mongolia, Dolonor, 18th century, attendant to Palden Lhamo with arms raised to lead vehicle mount, with head of water monster, stag antlers and body of woman, with incised feathered jowls, skull affixed atop crown of head, mouth agape and fangs bared, wearing flayed human-skin cape, right arm extended and left hand raised to chest, with necklaces, armlets, bracelets and anklets inlaid with semi-precious stones, 17 1/4" high. **$20,000**

Chinese carved coral figural group on carved wood stand, central figure of Guanyin with two flanking figures, 10 1/4" high, 12" high with stand. **$18,500**

Rectangular inlaid zitan box and cover, Qing Dynasty, Kangxi period, slightly canted corners, cover inlaid depicting malachite-crested and hardstone bird perched on gnarled stained-bone branch with mother-of pearl, hardstone, and coral prunus blossoms and buds, with hibiscus blooms from rockwork of lapis lazuli and turquoise, stepped rim fitted to conforming lower section on slightly recessed base, 11" long. **$25,000**

Thangka panel, 35 1/4" high x 25" wide. **$2,500**

九死一生

Courtesy of Heritage Auctions, ha.com

Yoshitomo Nara (Japanese, b. 1959), unknown (Q), 1996, ink and colored pencil on paper, dated in pencil lower right: '96, 8" x 5 3/4". **$32,500**

Courtesy of International Auction Gallery, www.international-auction-gallery.com

▲ Important Chinese carved ivory standing Buddha, possibly Yongle, 17th century or earlier, 10" high. **$6,500**

Courtesy of Heritage Auctions, ha.com

◄ Japanese porcelain-covered koro, circa 1900, 12-character mark under lid, 7 1/2" x 8" x 6". **$1,000**

"Still Life with Asian Artifacts, Candlesticks, and Flowers," Anna S. Fisher (American, 1873-1942), oil on canvas, signed "Anna Fisher" left corner, framed, 40" x 36". **$6,500**

Large Chinese famille jaune porcelain fishbowl jardinière on giltwood stand, 17 3/4" high x 21 1/2" diameter. **$5,000**

▶ Gilt copper alloy figure of Garwa Nakpo, Tibeto-Chinese, 18th century, 10 3/4" high. **$137,000**

Courtesy of Heritage Auctions, ha.com

**Pair of monumental Chinese cloisonné
urns on stands, 65 1/4" high,
including stand. $7,500**

Courtesy of Heritage Auctions, ha.com

Japanese baluster-form palace vase with Imari floral and cloud decoration, gilt bronze C-scroll and S-curve mounts, double handle floral cornucopia joining large central cartouche to front and back, with gilt bronze cresting waves to base, 40" x 24" x 16". **$15,000**

Chinese glazed ceramic horse, Tang Dynasty (618-906 A.D.), tomb figure, depicted standing and saddled, with ground mane slot and hole to backside for horsehair mane and tail, on integral rectangular base, raised overall on wooden base, 24 1/2" high x 20" wide x 7" deep. **$25,000**

Carved Imperial green jade brush pot, Chinese, Kangxi Period (1662-1722), thick cylindrical sides carved in varying relief with large five-clawed dragon and four further dragons and chilong in pursuit of flaming pearl, bodies emerging through dense ground of ruyi-form clouds, 7" high x 5 1/2" diameter. **$16,000**

Rare and massive parcel-gilt bronze figure of Ananda China, Ming Dynasty, cast standing upright on lotus base with hands joined in anjalimudra, dressed in wide long-sleeved monk's robes, draped with kashaya fastened over left shoulder with loop and hook tied with chords, hems of garments chased and engraved with foliate sawtooth and wide scrolling lotus borders, full face with downcast eyes and reverent expression, on separately cast hexagonal waisted stand, each side centered with panel enclosing lotus, 84 5/8" high. **$845,000**

Autographs

By Zac Bissonnette

In *The Meaning and Beauty of Autographs,* first published in 1935 and translated from the German by David H. Lowenherz of Lion Heart Autographs, Inc. in 1995, Stefan Zweig explained that to love a manuscript, we must first love the human being "whose characteristics are immortalized in them." When we do, then "a single page with a few lines can contain the highest expression of human happiness, and ... the expression of deepest human sadness. To those who have eyes to look at such pages correctly, eyes not only in the head, but also in the soul, they will not receive less of an impression from these plain signs than from the obvious beauty of pictures and books."

John M. Reznikoff, founder and president of University Archives, has been a leading dealer and authority on historical letters and artifacts for 32 years. He described the current market for autographs as "very, very strong on many fronts. Possibly because of people being afraid to invest in the market and in real estate, we are seeing investment in autographs that seems to parallel gold and silver."

Reznikoff suspects that Civil War items peaked after Ken Burns' series but that Revolutionary War documents, included those by signers of the Declaration of Independence and the Constitution, are still undervalued and can be purchased for under $500.

Currently, space is in high demand, especially Apollo 11. Pop culture, previously looked at as secondary by people who dealt in Washingtons and Lincolns, has come into its own. Reznikoff anticipates continued growth in memorabilia that includes music, television, movies, and sports. Babe Ruth, Lou Gehrig, and Ty Cobb are still good investments, but Reznikoff warns that authentication is much more of a concern in sports than in any other field.

The Internet allows for a lot of disinformation and this is a significant issue with autographs. There are two widely accepted authentication services: Professional Sports Authenticator (PSA/DNA) and James Spence Authentication (JSA). A dealer's reliability can be evaluated by seeing whether he is a member of one or more of the major organizations in the field: the Antique

ZAC BISSONNETTE has been featured on The Today Show, The Suze Orman Show, CNN, and National Public Radio. In addition to his work in the antiques field, he has served as a financial journalist for *Glamour, The Daily Beast, The New York Times, The Huffington Post,* and *AOL Money & Finance.* He has a degree in art history from the University of Massachusetts.

Courtesy of Iconic Auctions, www.iconicauctions.com

Jimi Hendrix rare index card signature with "Best of Luck" inscription, PSA/DNA, 3" x 5". **$2,446**

to the Lending Agreement and the undersigned hereby acknowledges for this purpose that the rights granted to you and the undersigned's services thereunder are of a special, unique, unusual, extraordinary and intellectual character giving them peculiar value, the loss of which cannot be reasonably or adequately compensated in damages;

7.   That the undersigned will not amend or modify the Employment Agreement in any particular that would prevent or interfere with the performance of the undersigned's services for you or the use and ownership by you of the results and proceeds thereof, pursuant to the Lending Agreement; that any breach of the Employment Agreement by Lender shall not limit or affect any of the services, licenses, privileges and rights which are to be rendered and granted to you by the undersigned pursuant to the Lending Agreement, and in any such event, the undersigned hereby agrees to look solely to Lender for any remedies arising out of such breach or the failure by Lender to perform under the Employment Agreement, and the undersigned hereby expressly agrees that the undersigned shall continue to perform all services and obligations to be performed by the undersigned under the Lending Agreement and that you shall continue to have all rights, privileges and remedies specified therein;

8.   That the undersigned will indemnify and hold you, your successors and assigns harmless from and against any and all taxes and pension and welfare contributions which you may have to pay (except to the extent that you have agreed, if at all, to make any payment thereof pursuant to the Lending Agreement) and any and all liabilities including, without limitation, judgments, penalties, interest, damages, costs, expenses and reasonable attorneys' fees which may be obtained against, imposed upon or suffered by you or which you may incur by reason of Lender's failure to deduct and withhold from or pay on account of the compensation payable by Lender to the undersigned, by reason of or in connection with the services rendered by the undersigned pursuant to the Lending Agreement, any amounts required or permitted to be deducted and withheld from or paid on account of compensation paid to an employee under the provisions of applicable federal, state and local laws or regulations or any applicable collective bargaining agreement, as supplemented or amended. The undersigned further agrees to defend, at your request, all claims with respect to which indemnification may be required hereunder; and

9.   That if you shall serve Lender with any notices, demands, or instruments relating to the Lending Agreement, or to the rendition of the services of the undersigned thereunder, such service shall also constitute notice to the undersigned.

Very truly yours,

John Candy

LBM/50150.068
BHWP2608E/051587

Courtesy of Iconic Auctions, www.iconicauctions.com

Farrah Fawcett signed color photo, JSA, 8" x 10". **$184**

Courtesy of Iconic Auctions, www.iconicauctions.com

Betty Grable signed vintage sepia portrait photograph, inscribed "Sincere best wishes, Betty Grable," PSA/DNA, 8" x 10". **$198**

Courtesy of Iconic Auctions, www.iconicauctions.com

◀ John Candy signed contract for hit 1987 movie "Spaceballs," two-page document, signed on second page, PSA/DNA. **$472**

Booksellers Association of America, UACC Registered Dealers Program, and the National Professional Autograph Dealers Association (NPADA), which Reznikoff founded.

There is an additional caveat to remember and it is true for all collectibles: rarity. The value of an autograph is often determined less by the prominence of the signer than by the number of autographs he signed.

Courtesy of Nate D. Sanders, natedsanders.com

Document signed by Napoleon Bonaparte, boldly signed "Bonaparte" near upper left corner, the signature he used while gaining power in early 1800s; document in French concerns memorial service of a member of the French army, 7 3/4" x 12". **$2,188**

Courtesy of Collect Auctions, www.collectauctions.com

Adam West and Burt Ward signed Batman display, PSA/DNA, 16" x 20" framed. **$327**

Courtesy of Nate D. Sanders, natedsanders.com

Ray Bolger signed MGM publicity shot of himself in costume as the Scarecrow from "The Wizard of Oz," 1939 Loew's Inc. copyright mark on image and 1971 reprint copyright on border, 8" x 10". **$250**

Courtesy of Nate D. Sanders, natedsanders.com

Blaze Starr autographed letter regarding a tryst in the White House with President John F. Kennedy, "...I told J.F.K. about my fantasy with the Lincoln bedroom. He said lets go...," 8 1/2" x 11". **$1,031**

Courtesy of Collect Auctions, www.collectauctions.com

Signed index card by Robert Ripley, who added "Believe It or Not," PSA/DNA, 3" x 5". **$119**

Courtesy of Iconic Auctions,
www.iconicauctions.com

Charles M. Schulz "Snoopy"
sketch signed on album page,
PSA/DNA, 3-3/4" x 6-3/4".
$1,056

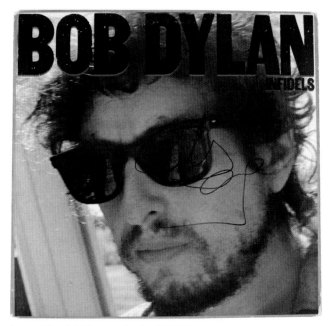

Courtesy of Iconic Auctions, www.iconicauctions.com

Bob Dylan signed "Infidels" album, rare signature among living
artists, PSA/DNA. **$1,595**

President Ulysses S. Grant
signed Presidential Pardon, May
8, 1876, when Grant authorized
the Secretary of State "to affix
the Seal of the United States to a
Warrant for the pardon of James
E. Marsh," PSA/DNA, 7 3/4" x
9 3/4". **$1,517**

Courtesy of Iconic Auctions,
www.iconicauctions.com

Courtesy of Nate D. Sanders, natedsanders.com

▲ Lucille Ball signature in pencil, inscribed, "For Lewis / Lucille Ball"
on album page, damp staining, 5 3/4" x 4 1/4". **$188**

Courtesy of Nate D. Sanders, natedsanders.com

◄ Lyndon B. Johnson signed print of his portrait by Norman
Rockwell, inscribed on left side of print to a family member of
his Assistant Secretary of the Interior Harry Anderson,
14" x 11". **$313**

Banks

By Eric Bradley & Karen Knapstein

ERIC BRADLEY is one of the young guns of the antiques and collectibles field. Bradley, who works for Heritage Auctions, is a former editor of *Antique Trader* magazine and an award-winning investigative journalist with a degree in economics. His work has received press from *The New York Times* and *The Wall Street Journal*. He also served as a featured guest speaker on investing with antiques. He has written several books, including the critically acclaimed *Mantiques: A Manly Guide to Cool Stuff*.

KAREN KNAPSTEIN is the print editor of *Antique Trader* magazine. A lifelong collector and student of antiques, she has written dozens of articles on antiques and collectibles. She lives in Wisconsin with her husband and daughter.

Banks that display some form of action while accepting a coin are considered mechanical banks. Mechanical banks date back to ancient Greece and Rome, but the majority of collectors are interested in those made between 1867 and 1928 in Germany, England, and the United States. More than 80 percent of all cast-iron mechanical banks produced between 1869 and 1928 were made by J. & E. Stevens Co. of Cromwell, Connecticut. Tin banks are usually of German origin.

The mechanical bank hobby continues to catch headlines as some of the best examples of rare banks head to the auction block. Morphy Auctions is a world leader in selling mechanical and still banks most desired by collectors; the firm has offered more than 6,000 mechanical banks in the last 12 years, and nearly 2,700 still banks.

According to Dan Morphy, owner and founder of Morphy Auctions, condition – like all other categories of collecting – is king. "Banks in top condition seem to be the trend these days," he said.

It's not uncommon for desirable banks to earn four and five figure results. But you don't need to be able to fill a bank to start collecting toy and mechanical banks. Auctions abound with more affordable character banks and premium banks from the mid-20th century. Designs are as varied as your imagination and cover a number of historical events, political figures, and landmarks. Unlike other collecting areas, many rare forms of mechanical and still banks (banks with no mechanical action) are highly valued, even if they are not in perfect condition. However, one should always buy the best condition afforded; when investing in a collection, quality should always outweigh quantity.

Those interested in mechanical banks are encouraged to learn more about the Mechanical Bank Collectors of America (www.mechanicalbanks.org), a non-profit organization consisting of around 400 members from the United States and several foreign countries. Organized in 1958, it is dedicated to expanding the knowledge and availability of antique mechanical banks. The

Courtesy of Bertoia Auctions,
www.bertoiaauctions.com

▲ Round Duck still bank,
blue version, Kenton,
circa 1925, cast iron,
desirable color variation,
trap appears at bottom,
4" high. **$247**

Courtesy of Morphy Auctions,
www.morphyauctions.com

▲ Roller Skating cast iron
mechanical bank, Kyser & Rex,
near mint condition, 9" long.
$88,800

Courtesy of Pook & Pook, Inc.,
www.pookandpook.com

◀ Mule Entering Barn cast
iron mechanical bank, J. & E.
Stevens Co., trap present,
overall good condition. **$425**

MBCA can be reached at info@mechanicalbanks.org or by writing to Mechanical Bank
Collectors of America, P.O. Box 13323, Pittsburgh, PA 15242.

Another valuable resource is the Still Bank Collectors Club of America (www.
stillbankclub.com), a non-profit organization founded in 1966 that now consists of nearly 500
collectors from the United States, Canada, Germany, Denmark, Australia and England. Learn
more about the SBCCA by writing to SBCCA Membership Chairman, 440 Homestead Ave.,
Metairie, LA 70005.

Ives Palace still bank, circa 1885, crisp casting details, 7 1/2" x 8". **$2,259**

State still bank, Kenton, circa 1900, japanned overall with gold and bronze highlights, 5 3/4" high. **$556**

▲ McKinley-Teddy elephant still bank, circa 1900, scarce example with busts embossed on sides, platform was "Prosperity," which appears on bank, 3 1/2" long. **$988**

▶ Mermaid still bank of woman in rowboat, United States, scarce example, cast iron, painted in gold overall, 4" long. **$216**

Baby in Cradle still bank of young baby sleeping under blanket, circa 1890s, rare still bank, made of nickeled cast iron and steel bed, 3 1/4" x 4". **$988**

Metropolitan Safe still bank, J. & E. Stevens Co., circa 1872, cast iron, painted in black with green panels, brass figure stands at key lock door, brass plaque lettered "Metropolitan Bank," ISB #303, 5 7/8" high. **$295**

The Cottage still bank, George Brown, circa 1870s, hand-painted tin, three-chimney version, red roof, yellow floor, tan sides and stenciling overall, marked "Bank" on façade, 6 1/8" high. **$370**

Whistling Boy in hat still bank, stoneware, appears German-made, hand-painted, fine molding design, slot on top of head, 3 1/2" high. **$463**

Lighthouse mechanical bank in working condition, 10" high. **$3,600**

▲ Uncle Remus cast iron mechanical bank, Kyser & Rex, fence at house repainted and club in cop's hand pinned, 6" long. **$33,000**

▶ Lion Hunter mechanical bank, J. & E. Stevens Co., circa 1911, cock device on gun's barrel and place coin in front, press lever and hunter takes aim and fires, causing coin to strike lion and fall into receptacle below, 7" high. **$2,000**

◀ Kicking Milk Cow painted cast iron mechanical bank, America, late 19th century, 5 1/4" high x 9 1/2" long. **$275**

*Courtesy of Morphy Auctions,
www.morphyauctions.com*

Penny Pineapple cast iron mechanical
bank, excellent condition, 9" high. **$330**

Courtesy of Heritage Auctions, ha.com

Hen and Chick mechanical bank in white, J. & E.
Stevens Co., circa 1901, slot in front of hen holds coin,
raise lever and hen moves her head as though calling
for chick, which emerges from beneath her and pecks
coin into bank; bellows simulates clucking sound,
4 1/2". **$896**

*Courtesy of Lloyd Ralston Gallery,
www.lloydralstontoys.com*

Bill E Grin mechanical bank, J. &
E. Stevens Co., painted cast iron,
working, missing trap. **$1,050**

Courtesy of Heritage Auctions, ha.com

Chief Big Moon mechanical bank, J. & E. Stevens Co.,
designed by Charles A. Bailey, circa 1899, press lever
and coin drops as frog springs from pond, tries to get
fish Native American woman is cooking, 5 3/4" high. **$900**

Books

By Noah Fleisher

NOAH FLEISHER received his Bachelor of Fine Arts degree from New York University and brings more than a decade of newspaper, magazine, book, antiques and art experience to his position as Public Relations Director of Heritage Auctions, one of the country's foremost auction houses. He is the former editor of *Antique Trader, New England Antiques Journal* and *Northeast Antiques Journal,* is the author of *Warman's Modern Furniture* and co-author of *Collecting Children's Books,* and has been a longtime contributor to *Warman's Antiques & Collectibles.*

Joe Fay is the manager of the Rare Books Department at Heritage Auctions. He's a young man, a devoted husband and father of two, an obsessive film buff and VHS tape aficionado. He also has an encyclopedic knowledge of the printed word.

He can wax poetic about the mysteries of incunabula, then turn around a breath later and extol the virtues of Stephen King or Sherlock Holmes, his personal favorite, finding the common thread between them – don't ask me, ask him. He's got an eye for early copies of *The Federalist Papers* and can spot a rare first edition of J.K. Rowling's *Harry Potter and the Philosopher's Stone,* reciting from memory exactly what makes it a true first edition.

We sat down for a conversation about the current market in rare books, which proved as entertaining as it did enlightening.

Warman's: Give me an overview of rare books.

Joe Fay: As always, the top of the market is very stable. The market seems to be holding steady against a fairly violent public assault on the printed word.

I hear the question all the time: "Will the Kindle kill the printed book?" Of course not. Folks bemoan the death of the printed word, but it's not going to happen anytime soon. It seems like every new technology that transmits information has called for the death of the book, but it hasn't happened yet and I don't think it will.

I think rare books will become increasingly more precious because of their physicality. People will come to interact with books in a different, more intimate way because of their relative scarcity.

Warman's: Is the market improving? Where are the best buying opportunities?

Joe Fay: The market is improving since the rather large hiccup of 2008. There is strength in special or unique books: examples with wonderful inscriptions, association copies, fine bindings, etc. Also, with the prevailing cultural obsession with superheroes and comic book-related material, there has never been a stronger market for science fiction and genre fiction.

You can also never go wrong with incunabula, books printed

Courtesy of Dreweatts &
Bloomsbury Auctions,
www.dreweatts.com

Sir Winston Churchill, *The Collected Works of Sir Winston Churchill*, London: Library of Imperial History in association with Hamlyn Publishing Group, Ltd., 1973-1976. Centenary Limited Edition, 34 volumes, original vellum, gilt, slip-cases; 8vo., along with proof copy of *My Early Life*. **$2,380**

before 1500, or great copies of great works in the major collecting categories.

Early printed books are always strong, the incunabula I just mentioned. Important first editions in the major categories, such as history, science and medicine, natural history, travel, religion, maps and atlases, literature, economics, early American imprints, children's books, and illustrated books.

Fine press printing and artists' books seem to be on the upward trend, too, as books become more of a specialty in the face of competing technologies.

Warman's: Is there room for new and younger collectors in rare books right now?

Joe Fay: I think it's a good market to get into at any time and any age. The rule I live by when talking about book collecting, as any expert in any category will tell you: Collect what you like. Find some focus within a subject area, author, printer or publisher, and collect everything you can.

Don't limit yourself to just the books, either. For a given author, seek out autograph material, posters, artifacts, original art if applicable, and so on. It can be very rewarding to walk into a person's personal library and not only see an incredible run of first editions by Ray Bradbury, but also find a *Fahrenheit 451* poster on the wall, next to a framed letter from the author. I guess this is a disguised version of diversification, in a way.

Warman's: It's a huge field. How do you go about starting or bolstering a collection if you've been out for a while?

Joe Fay: Vigilance. It's a great time to be a buyer of rare books because they are so readily available to be bought.

Build a relationship with a reputable dealer, save keyword searches at online sites like eBay and Heritage, places where you get email reminders when material matching your interests becomes available.

Warman's: What is it that draws people to rare books?

Joe Fay: That's a really big question. I think the desire to collect rare books started with a thirst to converse with the great minds of the past, which encompasses really anything. There

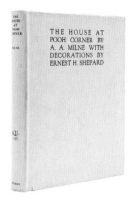

Courtesy of Dreweatts & Bloomsbury Auctions,
www.dreweatts.com

A.A. Milne, *The House At Pooh Corner*, London: Methuen Publishing Ltd., 1928. Number 41 of 350 large paper copies printed on handmade paper and signed by author and artist E.H. Shepard, folding map, dust jacket; endpapers browned, spine spotted and discolored. $2,090

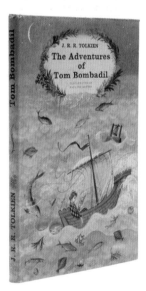

Courtesy of Dreweatts & Bloomsbury Auctions,
www.dreweatts.com

J.R.R. Tolkien, *The Adventures of Tom Bombadil*, a collection of 16 poems, England: George Allen & Unwin, 1962. Second impression, signed by author on half title, original pictorial boards, dust jacket; 8vo, light rubbing to top and bottom. $2,080

are practically limitless possibilities for a subject area to collect in rare books.

If you want to assemble the best collection of books bound in yellow cloth, you can do that. You want to collect signs made by homeless panhandlers? Let me introduce you to Michael Zinman, who already does that. You want to collect pamphlets and other imprints dealing with early 20th century American Communism? I hope you have a lifetime to devote to it and I would love to see your collection someday.

For me, personally, the allure of rare books comes down to both what they are, physically, and what they represent. Books are wonderful to handle. If a book is well put together, it fits nicely in the hand or lies well when opened on a table, it stimulates both the eye to flip through and the mind to read, and is a pleasure to look at on the shelf. Even the smell of a book is a unique phenomenon that evokes myriad emotions and memories.

A rare first printing of a given important novel is rare in itself, but it also represents a viewpoint and a cultural zeitgeist that is usually universal, that mattered both when the book was published and today. They are a window into the minds of people long gone, markers of our evolution as humans. This is not something you get with many other collecting categories.

Warman's: Looking back 10 years and looking ahead 10 years, how does/will the market look in comparison?

Joe Fay: A couple of generations ago everyone had books in their house. For 550 years books have been the primary method by which people learned. Now, there are so many competing delivery systems for information that print culture has obviously taken a hit.

I think the number of collectors 10 years from now will be smaller in number but more intense in terms of who is collecting. Rare books have become a bit of a niche market, but you can see the contraction markedly at regional book fairs. More people used to come to fairs than they do now. High-end fairs like the New York Antiquarian Book Fair are still going strong, and will likely continue to do so, because the top end of the market is not going anywhere. Truly valuable rarities always bring premium prices.

Warman's: You hear how technology has hurt books. Tell me how it has helped.

Joe Fay: The Internet and the eReader have certainly had an effect on the trade, no doubt – we have fewer

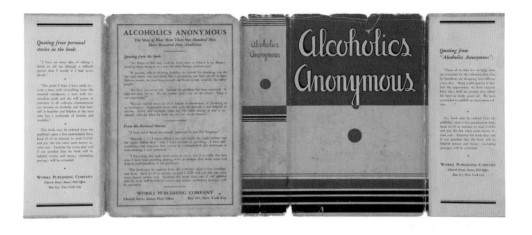

Courtesy of Heritage Auctions, ha.com

Alcoholics Anonymous' Big Red Book, New York City: Works Publishing, Inc., 1939. Rare first edition, first printing, octavo, original dust jacket, front cover lettered in gilt, spine lettered in gilt, in quarter brown morocco clamshell case; believed to be one of only 4,760 copies of ordered run of 5,000 printed, due to paper shortages. **$21,250**

and fewer bookstores these days – but the web has also opened up thousands upon millions of avenues for finding books, especially those that people once thought were very rare or even unique. The Internet has also had a positive effect on some titles by reinforcing their rarity.

The Internet helped to stratify the rare book world. With so much information, no one can pay – and no one will ask – unreasonable prices for common books. I talk to book dealers all the time who say something to the effect of, "I used to be able to get $500 for that book, now I can't give it away." Then they turn around and say, "You know that book I sold in your Internet weekly auction for $1,000? I've had that book on my table at book fairs for 10 years for $150 and barely anyone looked at it."

Obviously, the web can now help actually identify rarity instead of proving commonness.

Warman's: How much homework should a collector do before entering the category, or is it best to consult experts and let them fill in the gaps?

Joe Fay: Do a lot of homework. Many people have been burned by casually starting to collect books or by trusting the wrong dealer. Don't just do homework on the books; check out the dealer, the auction house, or whatever entity you might do business with.

Call other dealers and talk to them about a given dealer. Check with the Better Business Bureau. Call the auction house and talk to the book department.

Book dealers and rare books auctioneers, once trusted, can be a very important source of information for collectors, and can often "fill in gaps," as you say.

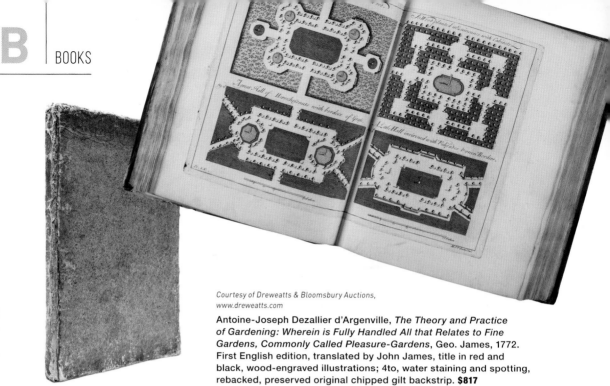

Antoine-Joseph Dezallier d'Argenville, *The Theory and Practice of Gardening: Wherein is Fully Handled All that Relates to Fine Gardens, Commonly Called Pleasure-Gardens*, Geo. James, 1772. First English edition, translated by John James, title in red and black, wood-engraved illustrations; 4to, water staining and spotting, rebacked, preserved original chipped gilt backstrip. **$817**

James Thomson, *The Seasons*, Parma: Bodoni, 1794. One of 50 large paper copies and one of few works printed by Bodoni in English, preserved in modern cloth drop-back box, slight marginal soiling, rubbed with few stains. **$1,490**

William Golding, *The Lord of the Flies*, London: Faber & Faber, 1954. First edition, dust jacket, light spotting, original cloth, slight shelf-lean, light fading to spine and margins, light creasing to head and foot; 8vo. **$1,630**

Edward Gibbon, *The History of the Decline and Fall of the Roman Empire*, London: W. Strahan & T. Cadell, 1776-1788. First edition, six-volume set, one of 500 copies; 4to, spines gilt with morocco labels, bumping and rubbing to corners with minor splitting near spine ends, pencil marginalia and highlighting found in volume one, foxing and hinges splitting superficially on vol. III. **$19,300**

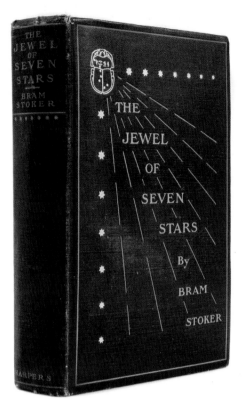

Courtesy of Dreweatts & Bloomsbury Auctions, www.dreweatts.com

Bram Stoker, *The Jewel of Seven Stars* (shown), New York & London: Harper & Brothers Publishers, 1904; and *Personal Reminiscences of Henry Irving*, New York: Macmillan, 1906. Both first American editions, 8vo; autographed signed letter from Stoker to Thomas P. Fowler of New York with *The Jewel of Seven Stars*: "My dear Fowler, I told Sir Henry about the letter & he is awfully sorry he never received it…," thanking Fowler for an invitation that Irving would have been unable to accept as "he has had such an overwhelming amount of work to do that he has had to refuse all pleasures of all kinds." **$475**

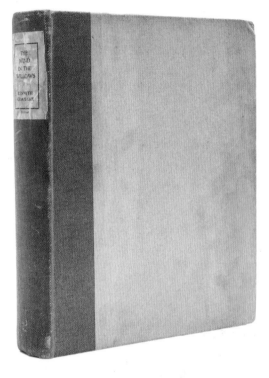

Courtesy of Dreweatts & Bloomsbury Auctions, www.dreweatts.com

William Grahame, *The Wind in the Willows*, London: Methuen Publishing Ltd, 1931. Number 155 of 200 large paper copies printed on handmade paper, signed by author and artist E.H. Shepard; 4to, original cloth-backed boards with paper label to spine, spare label tipped in at rear, light staining to endpapers, bumping to corners. **$1,340**

Courtesy of Dreweatts & Bloomsbury Auctions, www.dreweatts.com

Charles Dickens, *The Works*, 30-volume deluxe edition, 1881-1882. Number 996 of 1,000 copies, engraved portrait, some additional pictorial titles, hand-colored, tissue guards, slightly rubbed. **$3,270**

A.A. Milne, *Now We Are Six*, London: Methuen Publishing Ltd., 1927, and *The House at Pooh Corner*, 1928. First editions, first impressions, illustrations by E.H. Shepard, dust jackets on both, 8vo; ink inscription on *Now We Are Six*, surface soiling, tape repairs to verso head, browning to endpapers and fading of jacket spine. **$520**

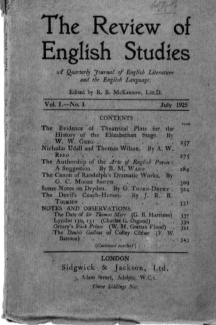

▲ J.R.R. Tolkien, "The Devil's Coach-Horses" in *The Review of English Studies*, Vol. 1, No. 3, 1925. First appearance, early seldom-seen work by Tolkien, original printed wrappers; 8vo, spine faded, spine ends chipped, creased at extremities. **$743**

▶ A.A. Milne, *When We Were Very Young*, London: Methuen Publishing Ltd., 1924. Number 46 of 100 large paper copies printed on handmade paper, signed by author and artist E.H. Shepard; 4to, original cloth-back boards, spine slightly faded, corners rubbed, uncut. **$3,270**

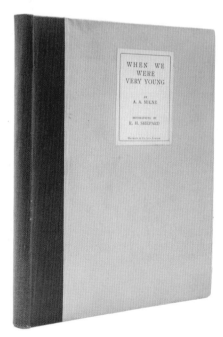

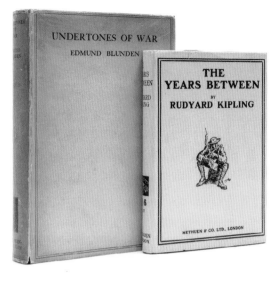

◀ Rudyard Kipling, *The Years Between*, New York: Doubleday, Page & Co., Garden City, 1919. Issue without 32 pp. advertisements, original buckram, blue-printed tan dust jacket, small closed tear and minor crease, with *Undertones of War* by Edmund Blunden, 1928, original cloth, uncut, dust jacket, some minor rubbing at corners, both first editions and 8vo. **$386**

▲ Jean de Brunhoff, *Histoire de Babar* (shown), *Le Voyage de Babar* and *Le Roi Babar*, France: 1931, 1932, 1933, respectively. First appearance of popular character Babar, and inspired English-language version *The Story of Babar* by A.A. Milne published in 1933; first editions, all signed and two inscribed by Brunhoff's son, Laurent; original pictorial cloth-backed boards, first and third rebacked, slight finger soiling and rubbing. **$446**

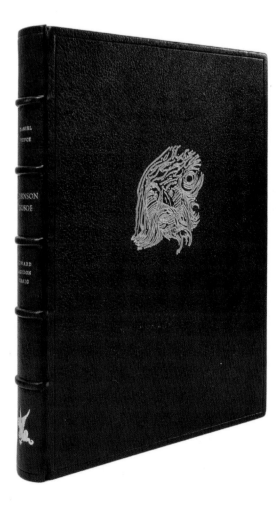

◀ Edward Gordon Craig and Daniel Defoe, *The Life & Strange Surprising Adventures of Robinson Crusoe of York*, London: Basilisk Press, 1979. Six of 25 specially bound copies with 10 original prints from an edition limited to 515; transparent dust jacket, six initialed and dated engravings in pencil, original pictorial dark blue morocco, gilt, 4to. **$2,380**

Bottles

By Michael Polak

MICHAEL POLAK has collected more than 3,000 bottles since entering the hobby in 1976. He is a regular contributor to a variety of antiques publications and is the author of *Antique Trader Bottles Identification & Price Guide*, 8th edition, and *Picker's Pocket Guide: Bottles*.

Glass bottles are not as new as some people believe. In fact, the glass bottle has been around for about 3,000 years. In the late first century B.C., the Romans, with the assistance of glassworker craftsmen from Syria and Egypt, began making glass vials that local doctors and pharmacists used to dispense pills, healing powders, and miscellaneous potions.

The first attempt to manufacture glass in America is thought to have taken place at the Jamestown settlement in Virginia around 1608 by the London Co. The first successful American glass house was opened in 1739 in New Jersey by Caspar Wistar, who immigrated from Germany to Philadelphia in 1717.

Throughout the 19th century, glasshouses opened and closed because of changes in demand and technological improvements. Between 1840 and 1890, an enormous demand for glass containers developed to satisfy the demands of the whiskey, beer, medical and food packing industries. Largely due to this steady demand, glass manufacturing in the United States evolved into a stable industry.

Unlike other businesses of the time that saw major changes in manufacturing processes, production of glass bottles remained unchanged. The process gave each bottle character, producing unique shapes, imperfections, irregularities, and various colors. That all changed at the turn of the 20th century when Michael J. Owens invented the first fully automated bottle making machine. Although many fine bottles were manufactured between 1900-1930, Owens' invention ended an era of unique bottle design that no machine process could ever duplicate.

The modern antique bottle collecting craze started in the 1960s with dump digging. Since then, interest in bottle collecting continues to grow, with new bottle clubs forming throughout the United States and Europe. More collectors are spending their free time digging through old dumps and foraging through ghost towns, digging out old outhouses where people often tossed empty bottles, exploring abandoned mine

Courtesy of Glass Works Auctions, www.glswrk-auction.com

Medicine bottle, "DR. TOWNSEND'S – SARSAPARILLA – ALBANY / N.Y.," New York, circa 1840-1860, teal blue with green tone, iron pontil, applied tapered collar mouth, 9 3/8" high. **$2,750**

Courtesy of Glass Works Auctions, www.glswrk-auction.com

▲ Medicine bottle, "DR. W.S. LOVE'S / VEGETABLE / ELIXIR / BALTIMORE," Maryland, circa 1840-1860, olive green cylinder, open pontil, applied tapered collar mouth, rare, last one sold at auction in 1994, 7 3/8" high. **$11,000**

Courtesy of Glass Works Auctions, www.glswrk-auction.com

◄ "POISON" – (one-wing owl sitting on mortar and pestle) – (TODCO monogram) / "THE OWL DRUG CO.," California, circa 1890-1910, cobalt blue, triangular form, smooth base, tooled lip, 9 3/4" high. **$700**

shafts, and searching favorite bottle or antique shows, swap meets, flea markets, and garage sales. In addition, the Internet offers collectors numerous opportunities and resources to buy and sell bottles with many new auction websites. Many bottle clubs now have websites providing even more information for the collector. These new technologies and resources have helped bottle collecting to continue to grow and gain interest.

Most collectors, however, still look beyond the type and value of a bottle to its origin and history. Researching the history of a bottle is almost as interesting as finding the bottle itself. Both pursuits have close ties to the rich history of the settling of the United States and the early methods of merchandising.

Civil War "U. S. A. / Hosp. Dept." glass bottle, very rare, clear with blue-green tint, logo embossed in relief inside 2 1/4" x 3 3/4" embossed panel on front, glob top with mold seam extending to base of spout, some fogging and air bubbles formed during fabrication, fine undamaged condition. **$813**

◄ French Wine Coca bottle with original paper labels, embossed at base of neck "Pemberton's Wine Coca," typical of medicinal bottles made during 1880s, with applied lip and some residue or "sickness" to inside, 11" high. **$13,750**

According to Heritage Auctions, Pemberton's French Wine Coca was designed to compete with Vin Mariani, a Bordeaux wine infused with cocaethylene (cocaine and alcohol). John Pemberton was an Atlanta druggist and Civil War veteran whose war injuries were assuaged with pain killers and other narcotics available at the time. His alcoholic "nerve tonic" was mixed with coca, kola nut, damiana, and cocaethylene. Pemberton marketed his version as a panacea to alleviate pain and improve sexual function. In 1885, Atlanta and Fulton County enacted temperance legislation. Fearing his new product might soon be banned from the market, Pemberton developed a new formula using the kola nut and the unrestricted coca. The result was the earliest formula for Coca-Cola. Financial difficulties and the need to finance his own drug habit prompted Pemberton to sell his formula to Asa Candler in 1886. For a period of years, Coca-Cola still contained small amounts of cocaine and was marketed as the "Ideal Brain Tonic" that would relieve headaches and fatigue.

Courtesy of Glass Works Auctions,
www.glswrk-auction.com

"R. C. & T. / NEW YORK – XX," soda
bottle, New York, circa 1840-1860,
dark reddish puce, iron pontil, applied
tapered collar mouth, possibly one of
only two known examples, 7 1/2" high.
$6,000

Courtesy of Glass Works Auctions,
www.glswrk-auction.com

Fire grenade, (motif of fireman's
helmet) / "HEATHMANS / SWIFT
/ FIRE / GRENADE," English,
circa 1880-1900, light pink,
smooth base, rough sheared
lip, original mouth plug with
embossed on red wax sealant,
"Parsons / Green / Heathman /
Fulham," 6 1/2" high. **$1,500**

Courtesy of Norman Heckler & Co.,
www.hecklerauction.com

"Hubbell" medicine bottle,
America, 1840-1860, medium
blue, oval with expanded
shoulder and base, applied
square collared mouth, pontil
scar, unusual form, 10" high,
only known example in this size.
$1,053

Courtesy of Norman Heckler & Co.,
www.hecklerauction.com

Medicine bottle, "Dr Townsend's
/ Sarsaparilla / Albany / N.Y.,"
America, 1845-1860, green,
square with beveled corners,
applied sloping collared mouth,
iron pontil mark, 9 1/2" high.
$995

Courtesy of Norman Heckler & Co.,
www.hecklerauction.com

Scroll flask, America, 1845-1860,
aquamarine, sheared mouth,
tubular pontil scar, slightly over
two quarts, 11 1/8" high, rare.
$3,510

Courtesy of Glass Works Auctions, www.glswrk-auction.com

"THE GLOBE / TONIC – BITTERS," Maine, circa 1865-1875, amber semi-cabin, smooth base, applied tapered collar mouth, 99% original labels on both side panels, 9 7/8" high. **$1,400**

Courtesy of Glass Works Auctions, www.glswrk-auction.com

Pattern molded chestnut flask, Midwestern Glass Works, Ohio, circa 1815-1835, pale greenish-aqua, 16 rib-pattern swirled to right, pontil scarred base, sheared and tooled mouth, 6 1/4" high. **$230**

Courtesy of Glass Works Auctions, www.glswrk-auction.com

Handled whiskey, "BUCKLEY, FISKE & CO. / BRANDY," American, circa 1855-1870, yellow green with aqua handle, chestnut form, iron pontil, applied ring mouth and handle, 8 1/2" high. **$9,500**

Courtesy of Glass Works Auctions, www.glswrk-auction.com

"G.H. / ARMSTRONG / 327 SH. ST.," (in oval panel), Pennsylvania, circa 1840-1860, emerald green, iron pontil, applied double collar mouth, rare Philadelphia bottle, 6 7/8" high. **$550**

Courtesy of Norman Heckler & Co., www.hecklerauction.com

"Poison / Pat. Appl'd. For" figural bottle, America, 1880-1900, cobalt blue, in form of skull, tooled flared mouth, smooth base with crossed bones, 4 1/8" high. **$1,112**

Courtesy of Heritage Auctions, ha.com

Chinese striped agate snuff bottle, compressed rectangular iridescent bottle with quartz stopper and applied paper label, monogrammed JS, 2 3/8" high. $1,750

Daisy pattern barber bottles, American, circa 1890-1925, opalescent cranberry red and white milk glass, melon rib sides, smooth bases, tooled lips, 7" high. **$80**

Barber bottles, American, circa 1885-1925, opaque milk glass, each with different hand-painted enamel scene of three cherubs playing, pontil scarred bases, sheared and tooled lips, 7 1/2" to 7 3/4" high. **$250**

▲ Pitkin flask, Midwestern, circa 1815-1825, bluish aqua, 32-broken rib pattern swirled to right, open pontil, sheared and tooled lip, blown in German half-post method, 7" high. **$600**

▶ Unger Brothers Love's Dream pattern silver and glass flask, Newark, New Jersey, circa 1900, cut glass bottle with silver hinged lid, silver base with putto kissing woman in cloud of waves, marks: UB (interlaced), STERLING, 925, FINE, 6 1/2" high. **$406**

CERAMICS

American 148
  Fiesta 148
  Fulper 155
  Grueby 162
  Rookwood 170
  Roseville 182
  Weller 192
European 200
  Select Makers 200
  KPM 219
  Limoges 232
  Majolica 237
  Meissen 246
  Sèvres 258
  Wedgwood 267

American Ceramics

Fiesta

The Homer Laughlin China Co. originated with a two-kiln pottery on the banks of the Ohio River in East Liverpool, Ohio. Built in 1873-1874 by Homer Laughlin and his brother, Shakespeare, the firm was first known as the Ohio Valley Pottery, and later Laughlin Bros. Pottery. It was one of the first white-ware plants in the country.

After a tentative beginning, the company was awarded a prize for having the best whiteware at the 1876 Centennial Exposition in Philadelphia.

Three years later, Shakespeare sold his interest in the business to Homer, who continued on until 1897. At that time, Homer Laughlin sold his interest in the newly incorporated firm to a group of investors, including Charles, Louis, and Marcus Aaron and the company bookkeeper, William E. Wells.

Under new ownership in 1907, the headquarters and a new 30-kiln plant were built across the Ohio River in Newell, West Virginia, the present manufacturing and headquarters location.

In the 1920s, two additions to the Homer Laughlin staff set the stage for the company's greatest success: the Fiesta line.

Dr. Albert V. Bleininger was hired in 1920. A scientist, author, and educator, he oversaw the conversion from bottle kilns to the more efficient tunnel kilns.

In 1927, the company hired designer Frederick

Courtesy of Strawser Auction Group,
www.strawserauctions.com

Onion soup bowl with cover, red. $787

Hurten Rhead, a member of a distinguished family of English ceramists. Having previously worked at Weller Pottery and Roseville Pottery, Rhead began to develop the artistic quality of the company's wares and to experiment with shapes and glazes. In 1935, this work culminated in his designs for the Fiesta line.

Fiesta was produced until 1973, when waning popularity and declining sales forced the company to discontinue the line. But renewed appreciation of Art Deco design, coupled with collectors scrambling to buy the discontinued Fiesta on the secondary market, prompted the company to reintroduce the line on Fiesta's 50th anniversary in 1986, spawning a whole new generation of collectors.

For more information on Fiesta, see *Warman's Fiesta Identification and Price Guide* by Glen Victorey.

Fiesta Colors

From 1936 to 1972, Fiesta was produced in 14 colors (other than special promotions). These colors are usually divided into the "original colors" of cobalt blue, light green, ivory, red, turquoise, and yellow (cobalt blue, light green, red, and yellow only on the Kitchen Kraft line, introduced in 1939); the "1950s colors" of chartreuse, forest green, gray, and rose (introduced in 1951); medium green (introduced in 1959); plus the later additions of Casuals, Amberstone, Fiesta Ironstone, and Casualstone ("Coventry") in antique gold, mango red, and turf green; and the striped, decal, and Lustre pieces. No Fiesta was produced from 1973 to 1985. The colors that make up the "original" and "1950s" groups are sometimes referred to as "the standard 11."

In many pieces, medium green is the hardest to find and the most expensive Fiesta color.

Seven-piece nested mixing bowl set, numbers 1-7, No. 1 in yellow, No. 2 in cobalt blue, No. 3 in red, No. 4 in ivory, No. 5 in light green, No. 6 in yellow, and No. 7 in cobalt blue, all marked Fiesta on bottom, No. 3 with area of glaze loss on bottom, largest 7 1/4" high. **$561**

Courtesy of Strawser Auction Group, www.strawserauctions.com

▶ Three individual salad bowls, two in medium green, one in yellow, various nicks. **$103**

Courtesy of Strawser Auction Group, www.strawserauctions.com

▼ Vase, turquoise, 12". **$908**

Fiesta Colors and Years of Production to 1972

Antique Gold – dark butterscotch............................1969-1972
Chartreuse – yellowish green....................................1951-1959
Cobalt Blue – dark or royal blue...............................1936-1951
Forest Green – dark hunter green 1951-1959
Gray – light or ash gray..1951-1959
Green – often called light green when comparing it to other
    green glazes; also called "original" green............1936-1951
Ivory – creamy, slightly yellow.................................1936-1951
Mango Red – same as original red 1970-1972
Medium Green – bright rich green...........................1959-1969
Red – reddish orange ....1936-1944 and 1959-1972
Rose – dusty, dark rose 1951-1959
Turf Green – olive...1969-1972
Turquoise – sky blue, like the stone 1937-1969
Yellow – golden yellow...1936-1969

In 1986, Laughlin offered five colors:

Rose – deep pink 1986-2005
Black...1986-2015
Cobalt – dark blue ....1986-still produced
White..1986-still produced
Apricot – pale peach 1986-1998

◀ Jubilee juice set, celadon disk juice pitcher and pink, beige, rose, and gray tumblers. **$484**

◀ Platter, medium green. **$67**

▲ Fiesta Kitchen Kraft stacking set, red lid with yellow, cobalt blue, and green units. **$169**

◀ Onion soup bowl with cover, ivory. **$605**

Courtesy of Strawser Auction Group, www.strawserauctions.com

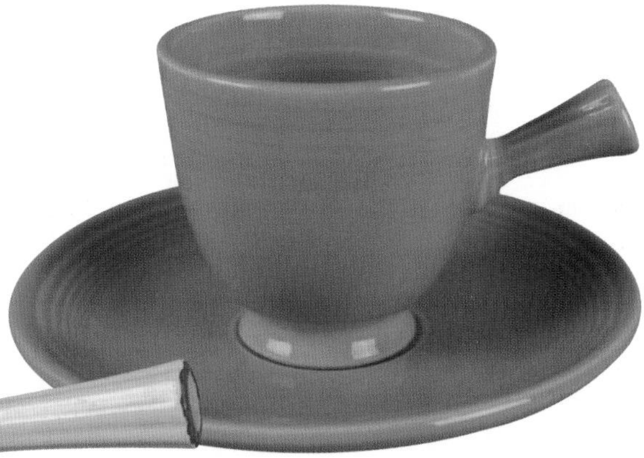

Demitasse cup and saucer, chartreuse. **$333**

Courtesy of Strawser Auction Group, www.strawserauctions.com

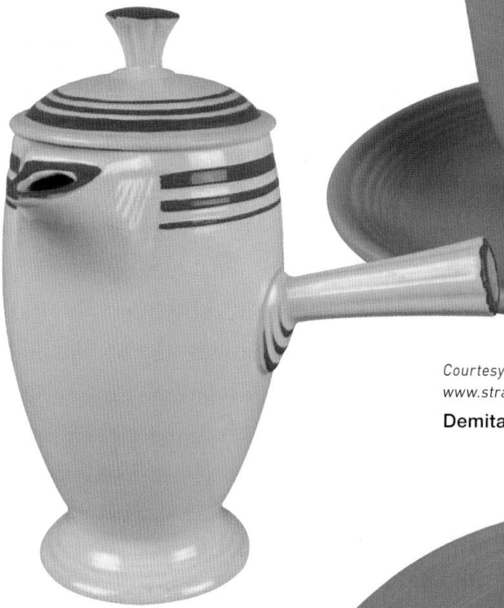

▲ Rare red stripe ivory demitasse pot, professional repair to lid. **$847**

Courtesy of Strawser Auction Group, www.strawserauctions.com

▶ Cake plate, yellow. **$514**

Courtesy of Strawser Auction Group, www.strawserauctions.com

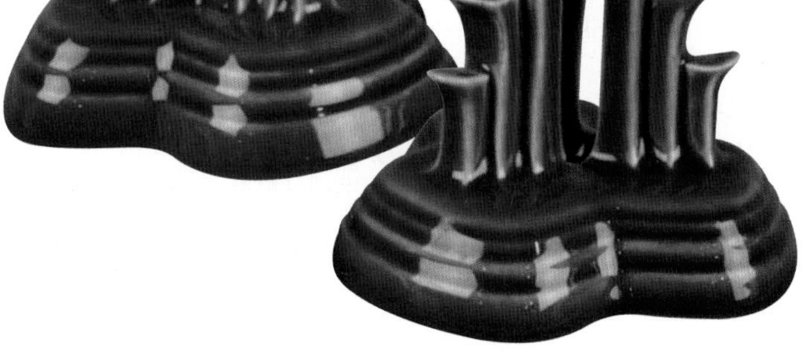

Rare Post-'86 sapphire pyramid candleholders, slight glaze rub to one pyramid, only pair known to exist. **$1,815**

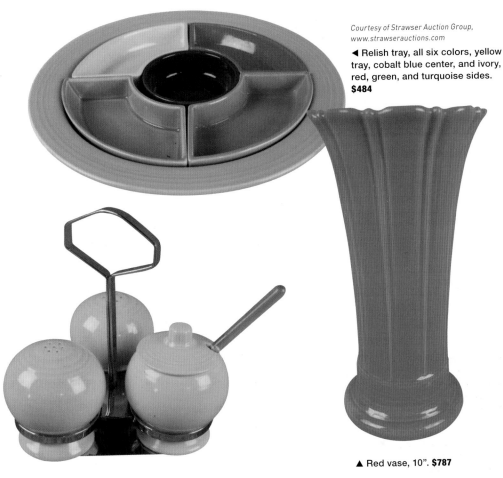

◄ Relish tray, all six colors, yellow tray, cobalt blue center, and ivory, red, green, and turquoise sides. **$484**

▲ Red vase, 10". **$787**

▲ Condiment set: ivory mustard and salt and pepper shakers with chrome holder. **$575**

▲ Footed salad bowl, ivory. **$272**

◄ Casserole, medium green, minor knick to finial. **$424**

Mustard, red. **$272**

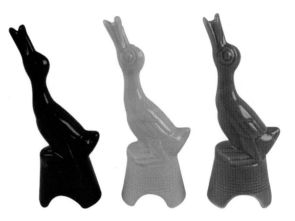

Three Post-'86 go-along piebirds in Fiesta colors, chip to yellow. **$79**

Utility tray group: red, green, cobalt blue, and turquoise. **$97**

Two eggcups, gray. **$121**

Fiesta creamer and sugar, medium green. **$182**

Fulper

The firm that became Fulper Pottery Co. of Flemington, New Jersey, originally made stoneware pottery and utilitarian wares beginning in the early 1800s. Fulper made art pottery from about 1909 to 1935.

The company's earliest artware was called the VaseKraft line (1910-1915). Its middle period (1915-1925) included some of the earlier shapes, but it also incorporated Oriental forms. Its glazing at this time was less consistent but more diverse. The last period (1925-1935) was characterized by Art Deco forms.

FULPER in a rectangle is known as the "ink mark" and dates from 1910-1915. The second mark, which dates from 1915-1925, was incised or in black ink. The final mark, FULPER, die-stamped, dates from about 1925 to 1935.

Courtesy of Mark Mussio, Humler & Nolan, www.humlernolan.com

▼ Chinese "Sleeping Cat" doorstop in flambé mirrored black with ivory glaze, larger rectangular ink stamp, restoration to right ear, 5" x 9 1/2". **$424**

Courtesy of Mark Mussio, Humler & Nolan, www.humlernolan.com

Uncommon "Sleeping Cat" figural in leopard skin crystalline glaze, Fulper oval ink stamp logo on bottom, excellent original condition, patches of crystals where glaze pooled, 3 1/8" high x 8 1/2" long. **$1,331**

Rare early reticulated VaseKraft vessel in leopard skin crystalline glaze, 1910s, rectangular ink stamp, 13 1/2" x 7 1/2". **$3,750**

◄ Twin-handled vase in blue snowflake crystalline glaze over tan flambé, marked with Fulper vertical racetrack ink stamp, excellent original condition, 9". **$182**

▼ Eight-sided vase, shape 511, in cucumber mat over ivory mat glazes, impressed on bottom with incised Fulper die stamp, excellent original condition, single minor stilt pull, 7 3/4" high. **$424**

Pair of early Ramses II bookends in cucumber mat glaze, 1910-1916, ink stamp mark to one, remnants of paper label to second, 8 1/2" x 4" x 4 1/2". **$563**

Courtesy of Rago Arts and Auctions, www.ragoarts.com

Early bulbous vase in rare Flemington green to ivory over famille rose glaze, 1910s, rectangular ink stamp, 11 1/2" x 7 1/2". $1,625

Courtesy of Rago Arts and Auctions, www.ragoarts.com

Large vase in Chinese blue flambé glaze, 1915-1920s, raised racetrack mark, 10" x 9 1/2". $1,750

Courtesy of Mark Mussio, Humler & Nolan, www.humlernolan.com

Pair of early "Liberty Bell" bookends in green mat finish, marked with early rectangular ink stamp logo, excellent original condition, 7 1/4" high. $514

Courtesy of Rago Arts and Auctions, www.ragoarts.com

Footed urn in pastel flambé and turquoise glaze, 1915-1920s, raised racetrack mark, 9 1/2" x 8 1/2". $625

Courtesy of Rago Arts and Auctions, www.ragoarts.com

Four-handled urn in blue flambé glaze, stamped racetrack mark, 13" x 12". $406

Courtesy of Rago Arts and Auctions, www.ragoarts.com
Large vessel in frothy crystalline over matte mustard glaze, 1910s, rectangular ink stamp, 8" x 10 1/4". $4,688

Courtesy of Rago Arts and Auctions, www.ragoarts.com
Rare vessel with cat's-eye flambé glaze, 1910s, rectangular ink stamp, 11" x 14". $10,625

▲ Baluster vase in frothy copperdust crystalline glaze, 1910s, rectangular ink stamp, 13 1/2" x 6 1/4". **$3,750**

◄ Rare early VaseKraft vessel in café au lait glaze, 1910s, VaseKraft paper label, rectangular ink stamp, 13" x 5 1/4". **$5,000**

Grueby

William Grueby was active in the ceramic industry for several years before he developed his own method of producing matte-glazed pottery and founded the Grueby Faience Co. of Boston in 1897.

The art pottery was hand-thrown in natural shapes, hand-molded, and hand-tooled. A variety of colored glazes, singly or in combinations, was produced, but green was the most popular. In 1908, the firm was divided into the Grueby Pottery Co. and the Grueby Faience and Tile Co. The Grueby Faience and Tile Co. made art tile until 1917, although its pottery production was phased out about 1910.

Courtesy of Treadway Toomey Auctions, www.treadwaygallery.com

Oak and matte green glazed tile table, Gustav Stickley and Grueby Faience Co., Eastwood, New York and Boston, early form with arched rails and 12 matched Grueby tiles, unsigned, some restoration to original finish, structurally sound, 24 1/2" wide x 20" deep x 26" high. $16,000

*Courtesy of Treadway Toomey Auctions,
www.treadwaygallery.com*

Viking ship tile, glazed ceramic
and oak, unsigned, initialed MK,
overall good condition without
chips, cracks or repairs, tile 8"
wide x 8" high, frame 13 1/2"
wide x 13 1/2" high. **$1,200**

Courtesy of Mark Mussio, Humler & Nolan, www.humlernolan.com

Two tiles with red clay body, neither marked, elephant with minor
nicks on rear edge, bird in excellent condition, elephant 4 1/8"
square x 3/4" thick, bird 4" square x 5/8" thick. **$363**

*Courtesy of Rago Arts and
Auctions, www.ragoarts.com*

**Vase with leaves,
curdled green glaze,
circa 1900, circular
Faience stamp/164,
incised AVL,
9 1/2" x 5". $2,000**

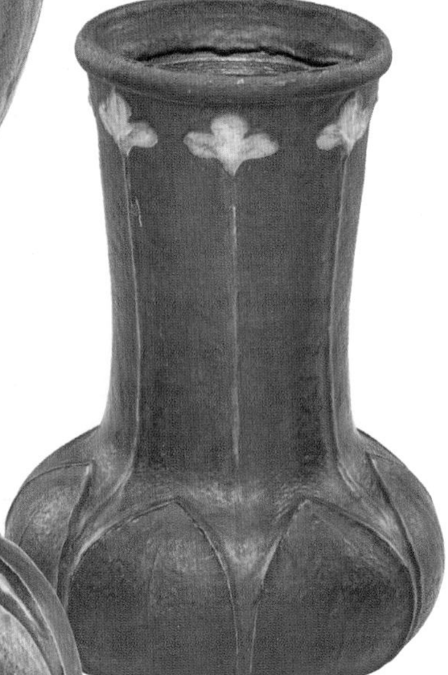

*Courtesy of Rago Arts and Auctions,
www.ragoarts.com*

▲ **Vase with yellow blossoms
by Wilhelmina Post, circa
1905, circular pottery stamp,
incised WP 32, 12 1/2" x
8 1/2". $8,125**

*Courtesy of Rago Arts and Auctions,
www.ragoarts.com*

◄ **Large vase with yellow buds
by artist Marie Seaman, circa
1905, circular pottery stamp,
13" x 8 1/2". $6,875**

Landscape tile, Grueby Faience Co./The C. Pardee Works, Boston, carved and polychrome glazed ceramic, painted "M.C." and raised logo on back, overall very good condition, tile 4" square, frame 10" square. **$1,300**

Rare rabbit tile, polychrome
glazed ceramic, signed, painted
MTC on back, overall good
condition, minor chips to corners,
6" square, unframed. **$6,500**

▲ Humidor in pale mat blue glaze
over round body with raised
shoulder design with veins reaching
base, pottery portion marked with
circular Grueby logo and possibly
artist's monogram, hinged metal
dome cover with impressed petal
design and green patina, impressed
factory mark obscured by patina and
impressed number, possibly Q303,
4" high x 4" wide. **$1,574**

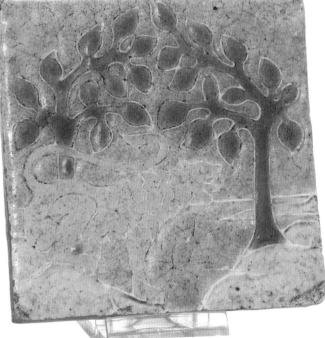

Tile with lion beneath pair of trees,
mat glazes on white clay body,
unmarked, small nicks at corners, 4"
square x 3/4" thick. **$605**

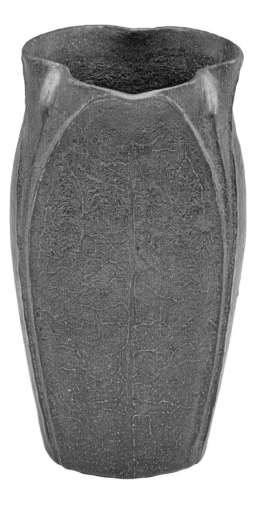

Courtesy of Rago Arts and Auctions,
www.ragoarts.com

**Tall vase with yellow buds, circa 1905,
circular pottery stamp, 9 1/2" x 4 1/2".
$5,313**

Courtesy of Rago Arts and Auctions,
www.ragoarts.com

**Lobed vase with yellow buds, circa
1905, glazed-over stamp, incised ERF
7-24, 8 1/4" x 5". $2,875**

Courtesy of Treadway Toomey Auctions, www.treadwaygallery.com

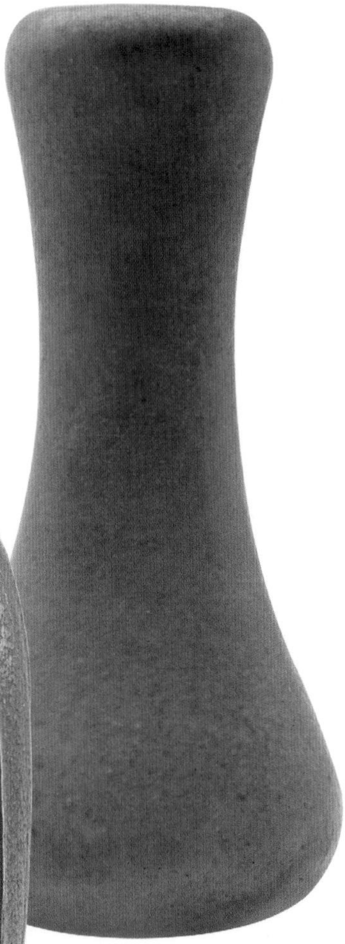

Bud vase in light blue glaze, unglazed bottom with impressed logo, overall very good condition with minor fine crazing, 6 1/2" high, 3 1/2" diameter. **$425**

Courtesy of Rago Arts and Auctions, www.ragoarts.com

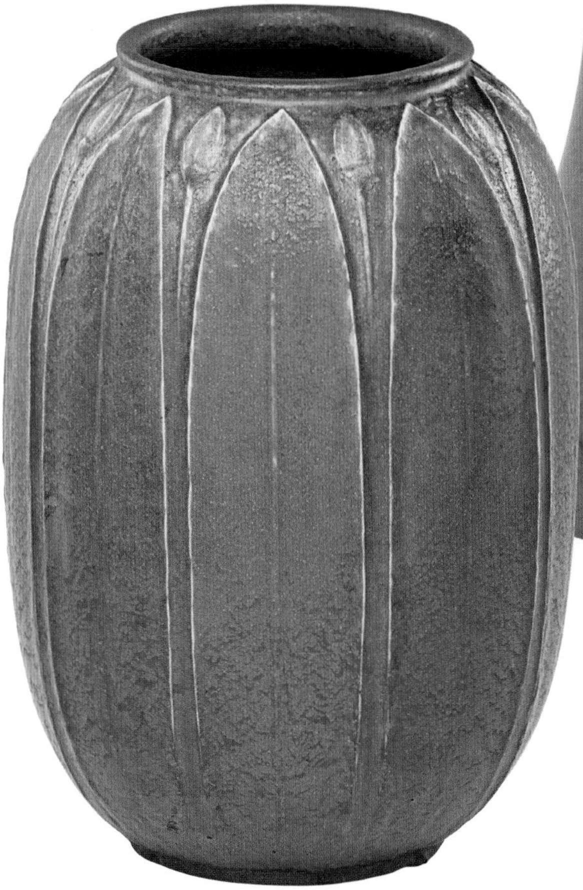

Melon-shaped vase with leaves and buds, circa 1905, circular pottery stamp, partial paper label and illegible numbers, 11 3/4" x 7 1/2". **$6,875**

Ship tile, circa 1905, framed, tile 8" square. **$2,000**

Rookwood

Maria Longworth Nichols founded Rookwood Pottery in Cincinnati in 1880. The name, she later reported, paid homage to the many crows (rooks) on her father's estate and was also designed to remind customers of Wedgwood. Production began on Thanksgiving Day 1880.

Rookwood's earliest productions demonstrated a continued reliance on European precedents and the Japanese aesthetic. Although the firm offered a variety of wares (Dull Glaze, Cameo, and Limoges for example), it lacked a clearly defined artistic identity. With the introduction of what became known as its "standard glaze" in 1884, Rookwood inaugurated a period in which the company won consistent recognition for its artistic merit and technical innovation.

Rookwood's first decade ended on a high note when the company was awarded two gold medals: one at the Exhibition of American Art Industry in Philadelphia and another later in the year at the Exposition Universelle in Paris. Significant, too, was Maria Longworth Nichols' decision to transfer her interest in the company to William W. Taylor, who had been the firm's manager since 1883. In May 1890, the board of a newly reorganized Rookwood Pottery Co. purchased "the real estate, personal property, goodwill, patents, trade-marks… now the sole property of William W. Taylor" for $40,000.

Under Taylor's leadership, Rookwood was transformed from a fledgling startup to successful business that expanded throughout the following decades to meet rising demand. Throughout the 1890s, Rookwood continued to attract critical notice as it kept the tradition of innovation alive. Taylor rolled out three new glaze lines – Iris, Sea Green and Aerial Blue – from late 1894 into early 1895. At the Paris Exposition in 1900, Rookwood cemented its reputation by winning the Grand Prix, a feat largely due to the favorable reception of the new Iris glaze and its variants. Over the next several years, Rookwood's record of achievement at domestic and international exhibitions remained unmatched.

Throughout the 1910s, Rookwood continued in a similar vein and began to more thoroughly embrace the simplified aesthetic promoted by many Arts and Crafts figures.

Production of the Iris line ceased around 1912. The company abandoned its older, fussier underglaze wares. The newer lines the pottery introduced trended toward simplicity.

The collapse of the stock market in October 1929 and ensuing economic depression dealt Rookwood a severe blow. The Great Depression eventually led to bankruptcy in April 1941. Rookwood's history might have ended were it not for the purchase of the firm by a group of investors led by automobile dealer Walter E. Schott and his wife, Margaret. Production started once again. In the years that followed, Rookwood changed hands a number of times before being moved to Starkville, Mississippi, in 1960. It finally closed its doors there in 1967.

In the 1980s, Dr. Arthur Townley, a Michigan art pottery collector, spent his life savings acquiring Rookwood's assets from a group of Florida investors. In 2006, The Rookwood Pottery Co. purchased the assets from Townley and eventually returned the company to Cincinnati, where it currently produces artisan wares.

For more information on Rookwood, see *Warman's Rookwood Pottery Identification and Price Guide* by Denise Rago and Jonathan Clancy.

Courtesy of Mark Mussio, Humler & Nolan, www.humlernolan.com

Rare Iris glaze plaque with four-masted ship near Kennebuck, Maine, by Sturgis Laurence in 1903, signed SL in lower left-hand corner and marked on back with large Rookwood logo, date, notation X1168X, and incised notation "Mouth of the Kennebuck Sturgis Laurence," uncrazed, 10 1/8" x 14 3/8". $12,100

Rare Vellum scenic tile, artist signed "L.A." for L. Asbury, label on back of frame indicates scene as "Autumn," no chips, cracks, or repairs, 6 1/4" x 9", 10" x 12 1/2" overall. **$4,425**

Carved and incised mat glaze vase with dandelion decoration by Kataro Shirayamadani in 1902, Arts & Crafts style, repeating dandelion leaves, stems, and flowers in green and yellow on rose-colored ground, concentric lines encircle shoulder with small dots of green between lines, marked with Rookwood logo, date, shape number 927 E, and incised cypher of artist, excellent condition, 6 5/8" high. **$6,655**

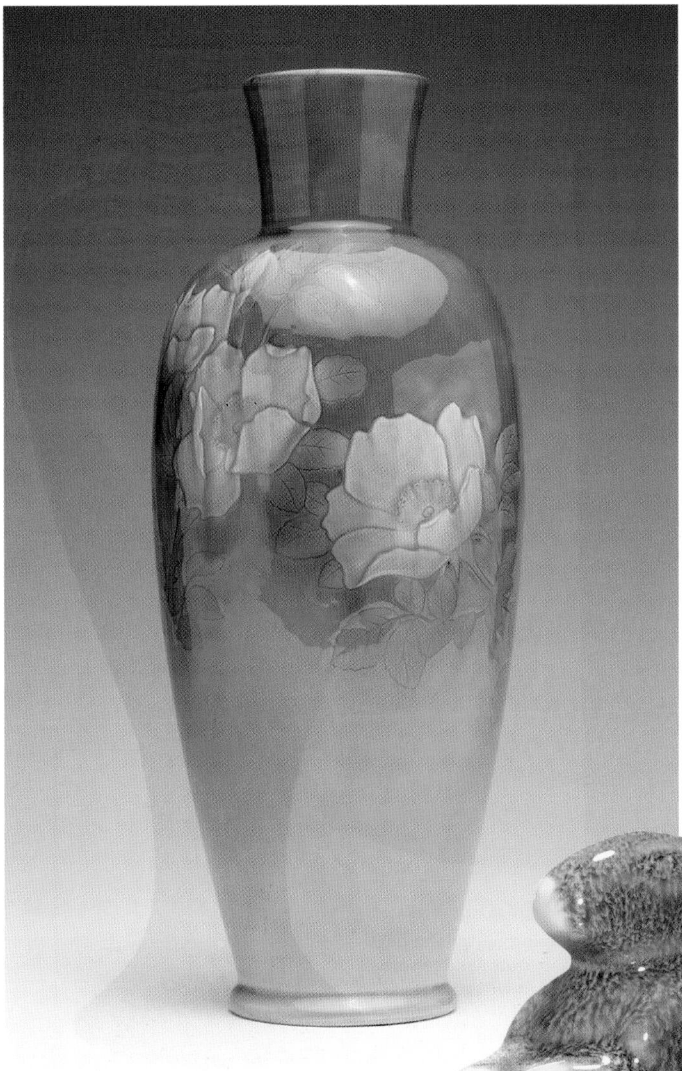

Vase by Albert Robert Valentien, circa 1900, flaring neck over baluster-form mustard-glazed body decorated with wild roses in green, fading to light yellowish-green at slightly spreading foot, impressed "RP" monogram with flame marks, "856C / G," and incised signature "A.R. Valentien," 13 1/4" high, 5 1/4" diameter. **$2,500**

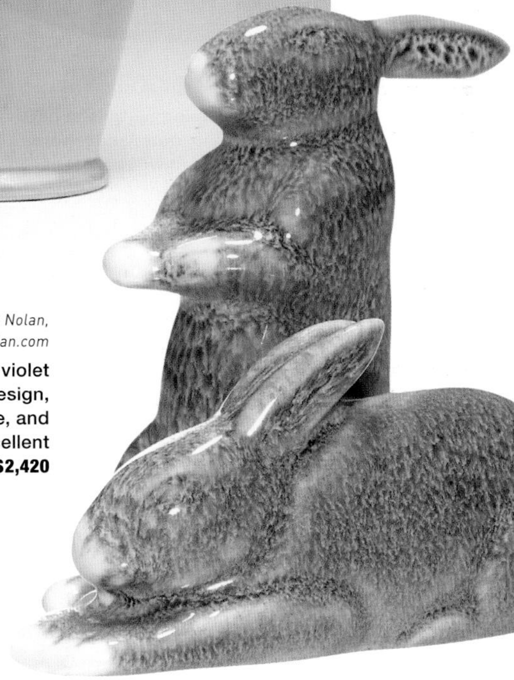

Rare Double Bunny paperweight in violet gray glaze, Kataro Shirayamadani design, 1953, marked with company logo, date, and shape number 6643, uncrazed excellent condition, 3" high. **$2,420**

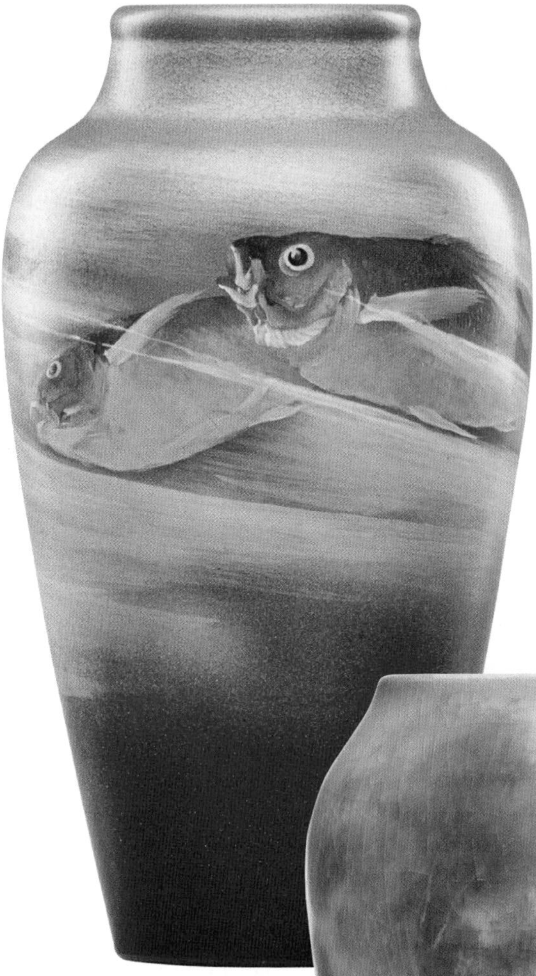

Courtesy of Rago Arts and Auctions, www.ragoarts.com
Vellum vase with carp by A.R. Valentien, 1905, flame mark / V / 948BV / A.R. VALENTIEN / V, 12" x 6". $6,875

Courtesy of Mark Mussio, Humler & Nolan, www.humlernolan.com
Scenic Vellum vase with trees in field by Ed Diers in 1920, impressed with Rookwood symbol, date, shape number 1343, and V for Vellum, and incised with artist's monogram, fine overall crazing, excellent condition, 4 3/4" high. $726

Courtesy of Rago Arts and Auctions, www.ragoarts.com

Rare banded Scenic Vellum vase with Native American scene by Ed Diers, 1908, flame mark / VIII / 999C / V / ED, 9" x 7". $4,063

Courtesy of John Moran Auctioneers, www.johnmoran.com

Curving conical vase painted with carp on yellow-green ground within pierced three-handled mount chased throughout with scrolling foliage and flowers and inscribed to lower reserve "Ut Pigmus Amicitia / Presented To / John R. Waters / By His Late Associates / At American Lloyds As A Token / Of Their Regard And Esteem / - From - / George C. Clarke / David S. Walton / Charles J. Follmer / Leo H. Wise / George A. Stanton / Jan 1st 1894," circa 1893, Providence, Rhode Island, in Art Nouveau style, with heavily rubbed maker's mark and standard mark and impressed partially rubbed Rookwood mark to underside of sterling silver-clad feet, marked to one foot "Alvin Mfg. Co." and "S?," 7 7/8" high, 8 3/4" diameter. **$1,599**

Jug, circa 1892, pointed spreading rim issuing silver-clad handle joining shoulder of bulbous body hand-painted with yellow irises and overlaid with chased foliate sterling silver overlay, marked to underside of overlay "Gorham Mfg. Co." and "R465," jug with maker's mark and impressed shape number 668 and iris glaze notation "W," signed with artist's monogram "E.D.F." for Emma D. Foertmeyer, 5 7/8" high x 5 3/4" wide, 5 1/2" diameter. **$1,722**

Jardiniere by Kataro Shirayamadani, circa 1890, standard glaze with polychrome foliate decoration, Rookwood logo on underside, incised Kataro Shirayamadani cipher, 10 1/4" high, 7 1/8" diameter rim. **$1,840**

Standard glaze vase of rook seated on pine bough by Sturgis Laurence in 1900, marked with Rookwood symbol indicating date, shape number 732 B, and incised mark of artist, fine crazing, drill hole to bottom professionally restored, 10 1/4" high. **$1,573**

Courtesy of Woody Auction, www.woodyauction.com

▲ Vase in brown tones with nasturtium décor, dated 1895, signed "A.V." (Albert Valentien) and shape number 787C, no chips, cracks, or repairs, 11 1/4" x 6 1/2". **$1,062**

Courtesy of Rago Arts and Auctions, www.ragoarts.com

◄ Large Later Mat/Mat Moderne urn, 1930, flame mark / XXX / 6010C / artist cipher, 11 1/2" x 10 1/2". **$1,000**

Courtesy of Mark Mussio, Humler & Nolan, www.humlernolan.com

Two-sided dealer advertising sign made for placement in commercial outlets that sold Rookwood Pottery, cast in 1946, tan high glaze, sign displays Rookwood name, pottery symbol, and Cincinnati, impressed on bottom with Rookwood symbol, date, and shape number 2788, excellent original condition without crazing, 4" x 13". **$968**

Rare Iris glaze scenic vase by John Dee Wareham in 1896, woman carrying large water vessel on her back, held on by rope, wooden fence in background, marked with company logo, date, shape number 80 B, incised W for white glaze and incised monogram of artist, fine overall crazing and small glaze nick off base, 6 7/8" high. **$1,452**

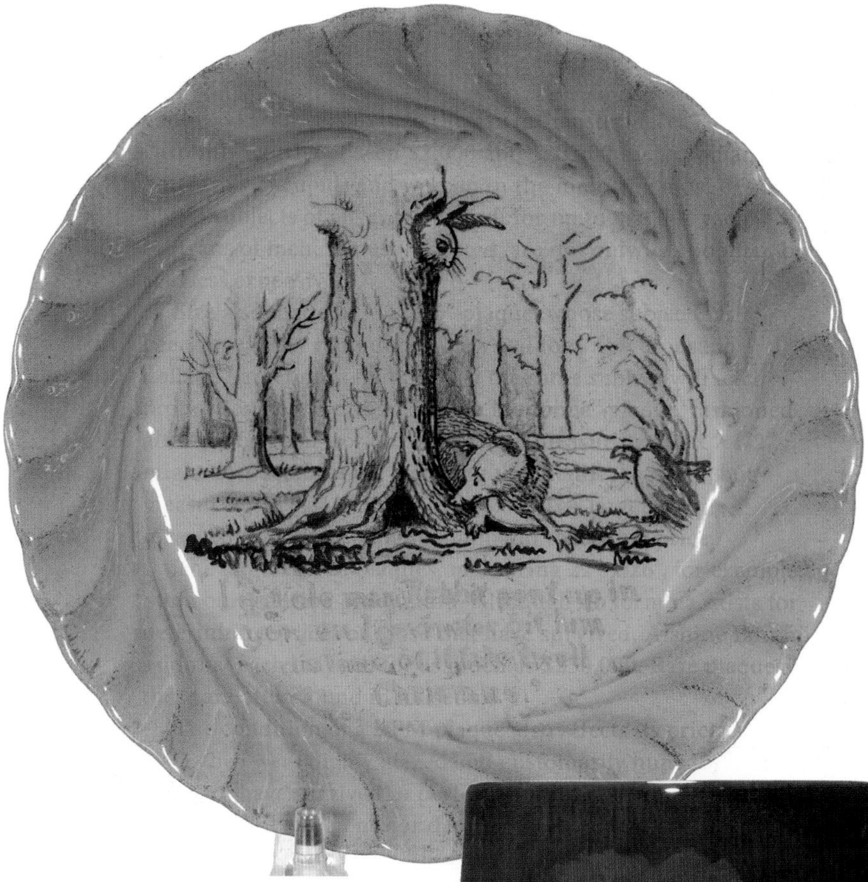

Rare child's dish with fox and rabbit, marked "Uncle Remus Tales," artist signed "EPC," dated 1887, no chips, cracks, or repairs, 6 1/2". **$472**

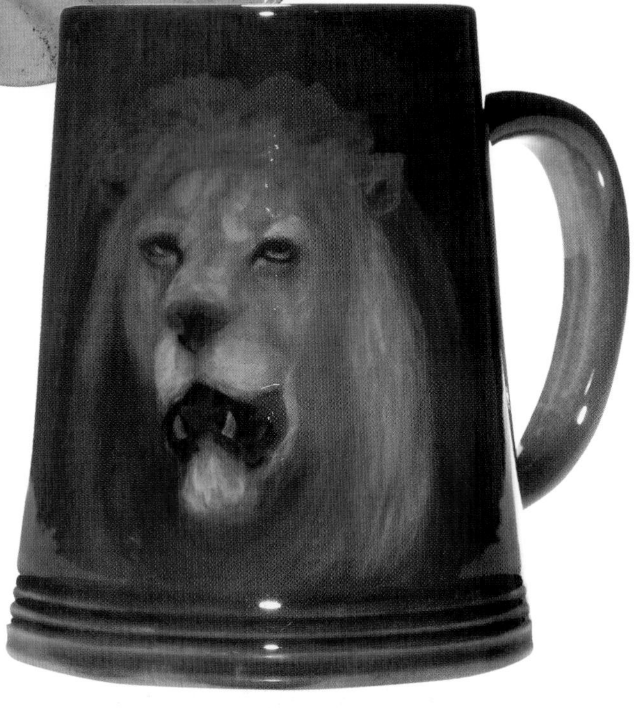

Standard Glaze mug of lion in midst of roar by E.T. Hurley in 1898, impressed Rookwood insignia indicating date and shape number 587 C, lightly incised with Hurley's cipher, excellent original condition with faint crazing, 4 5/8" high. **$726**

Courtesy of Mark Mussio, Humler & Nolan,
www.humlernolan.com

Rare Double Vellum trivet with pair of cows and windmill, 1940, marked with Rookwood logo, date, and shape number 6776, uncrazed excellent original condition, 5 7/8" square, 9 1/2" square framed. **$1,150**

Courtesy of Woody Auction,
www.woodyauction.com

Early marked vase in blue and cream tones with bird décor, dated 1886, artist signed "M.A.D." for Matthew A. Daly, shape number 283A, no chips, cracks, or repairs, 8 1/2" x 6". **$826**

Roseville Pottery

Roseville is one of the most widely recognizable of potteries across the United States. Having been sold in flower shops and drug stores around the country, its art and production wares became a staple in American homes through the time Roseville closed in the 1950s.

The Roseville Pottery Co., located in Roseville, Ohio, was incorporated on Jan. 4, 1892, with George F. Young as general manager. The company had been producing stoneware since 1890, when it purchased the J. B. Owens Pottery, also of Roseville.

The popularity of Roseville Pottery's original lines of stoneware continued to grow. The company acquired new plants in 1892 and 1898, and production started to shift to Zanesville, just a few miles away. By about 1910, all of the work was centered in Zanesville, but the company name was unchanged.

Young hired Ross C. Purdy as artistic designer in 1900, and Purdy created Rozane – a contraction of the words "Roseville" and "Zanesville." The first Roseville artwork pieces were marked either Rozane or RPCO, both impressed or ink-stamped on the bottom.

In 1902, a line was developed called Azurean. Some pieces were marked Azurean, but more often RPCO.

In 1904 at the St. Louis Exposition, Roseville's Rozane Mongol, a high-gloss oxblood red line, captured first prize, gaining recognition for the firm and its creator, John Herold.

Many Roseville lines were a response to the innovations of Weller Pottery, and in 1904 Frederick Rhead was hired away from Weller as artistic director. He created the Olympic and Della Robbia lines for Roseville. Frederick's brother, Harry, took over as artistic director in 1908, and in 1915 he introduced the popular Donatello line.

Courtesy of Mark Mussio, Humler & Nolan, www.humlernolan.com

Large Sunflower jardiniere on pedestal, marked with shape number and size 619-10 in red crayon beneath, pedestal with factory firing separation inside base rim, excellent condition, jardiniere 10 1/8" x 10 1/2" across rim, pedestal 18 1/2" high, 28 1/2" high combined. **$3,025**

Raymor vase in gold, shape number 63-7", marked on bottom Raymor Modern Artware by Roseville U.S.A. 63-7", fine overall crazing, 7 1/8" high. $545

Pine Cone window box/ planter, blue 469, with embossed decoration and raised Roseville mark to underside, 1939-1953, 4 3/4" high x 13 1/4" long x 5" wide. $219

By 1908, all handcrafting ended except for Rozane Royal. Roseville was the first pottery in Ohio to install a tunnel kiln, which increased its production capacity.

Frank Ferrell, who was a top decorator at the Weller Pottery by 1904, was Roseville's artistic director from 1917 until 1954. This Zanesville native created many of the most popular lines, including Pine Cone, which had scores of individual pieces.

Many collectors believe Roseville's circa 1925 glazes were the best of any Zanesville pottery. George Krause, who in 1915 became Roseville's technical supervisor responsible for glaze, remained with Roseville until the 1950s.

Company sales declined after World War II, especially in the early 1950s when cheap Japanese imports began to replace American wares, and a simpler, more modern style made many of Roseville's elaborate floral designs seem old-fashioned.

In the late 1940s, Roseville began to issue lines with glossy glazes. Roseville tried to offset its flagging artware sales by launching a dinnerware line – Raymor – in 1953. The line was a commercial failure.

Roseville issued its last new designs in 1953. On Nov. 29, 1954, the facilities of Roseville were sold to the Mosaic Tile Co.

For more information on Roseville, see *Warman's Roseville Pottery*, 2nd edition, by Denise Rago.

*Courtesy of Rago Arts
and Auctions,
www.ragoarts.com*

**Rozane Della
Robbia vase with
stylized trees, circa
1910, incised artist
initials to body,
10" x 5 1/2". $10,000**

*Courtesy of Rago Arts
and Auctions,
www.ragoarts.com*

**Futura spherical
vase with
diamond foot,
1924, unmarked,
8" high. $406**

Courtesy of Jeffrey S. Evans & Associates, www.jeffreysevans.com

Pine Cone jardinière and pedestal, blue 402 jardinière and blue 405 pedestal, each with embossed decoration and raised Roseville mark, second quarter 20th century, 25" high. **$805**

Courtesy of Mark Mussio, Humler & Nolan, www.humlernolan.com

Oversize Baneda vase, shape number 600, in mottled green glaze with flow of blue glaze extending from wide decorative band to dribbles of color on foot, marked with Roseville Pottery Rv foil sticker, excellent original condition, 15 1/4" high. **$1,573**

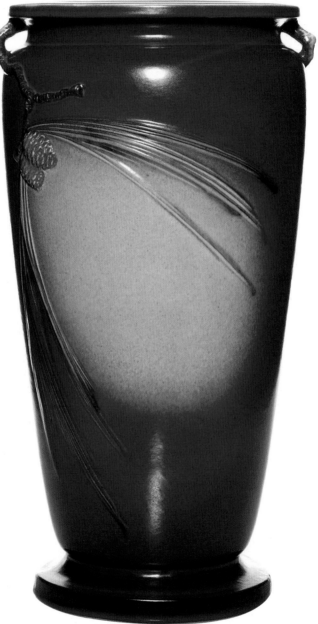

*Courtesy of Mark Mussio,
Humler & Nolan,
www.humlernolan.com*

Pine Cone umbrella stand in blue, shape number 777, impressed "Roseville 777-20" on bottom with old Cincinnati Art Galleries label from Rookwood VII, excellent original condition, uncrazed, 20 1/4" high. $1,150

Courtesy of Rago Arts and Auctions,
www.ragoarts.com

**Wisteria vase in blue, 1933,
unmarked, 8" high. $563**

Courtesy of Mark Mussio, Humler & Nolan,
www.humlernolan.com

**Crocus necked vase slip-
decorated with tulip-like flowers
with medium and dark green
petals, olive green serpentine
foliage against army green
backdrop, unmarked, excellent
condition, 8" high. $1,150**

Courtesy of Woody Auction, www.woodyauction.com

**Three-piece smoke set, "IT IS BETTER TO SMOKE IN THIS WORLD
THAN IN THE NEXT," no chips, cracks, or repairs, tray 10" diameter,
ashtray 4" diameter, match holder 2" high. $266**

Courtesy of Rago Arts and Auctions,
www.ragoarts.com

Futura vase in green with stepped neck and angular handles, 1924, foil label, 9" high. $438

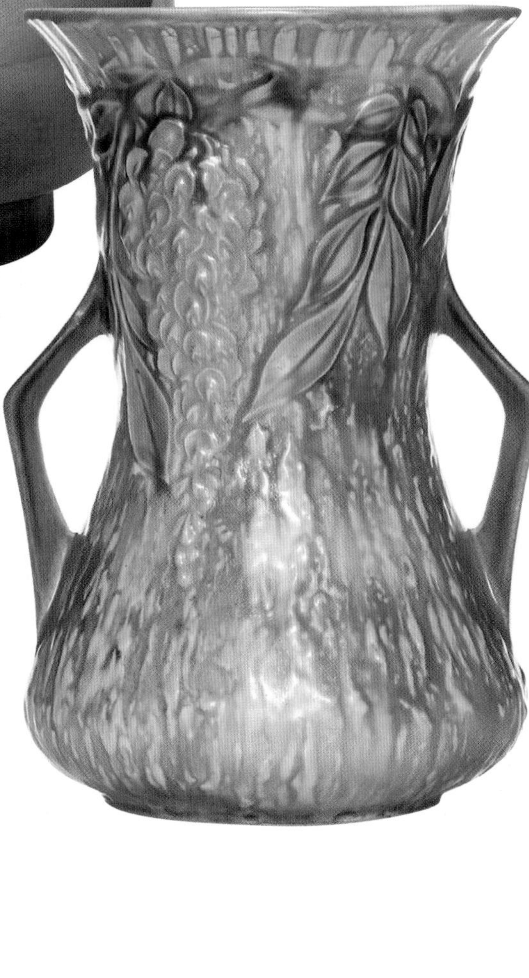

Courtesy of Mark Mussio, Humler & Nolan,
www.humlernolan.com

Wisteria vase in brown, shape number 682-10", marked 682 on bottom in orange crayon with original Roseville Pottery foil sticker, excellent original condition, 10 1/4" high. $484

Rare Earlam crocus pot in green and blue, shape number 90-8", unmarked, restoration to small chip at base, tight firing separation on bottom, 7 7/8" high. **$514**

Fudgi vase with angular and oval designs above seine pattern, earth tone slip decoration over biscuit clay body, raised Rozane Ware wafer and die-impressed 20 on bottom, conjoined artist monogram NE concealed within pattern, mild surface stains, excellent condition, 8 1/2" high. **$1,089**

Rozane Fudgi vase, shape number 971, marked with circular Rozane Ware wafer seal and impressed number 20, excellent color and condition, 8 3/4" high. **$2,057**

Courtesy of Mark Mussio, Humler & Nolan, www.humlernolan.com

Futura "Spaceship" vase, shape number 405-7.5", in pink and blue Carnelian II glaze, unmarked, excellent original condition, 7 3/4" high. **$4,235**

Panel footed vase with nudes posing with trees in mat green glaze, stamped Rv beneath, excellent condition, 11 3/8" high. **$968**

Panel vase with nudes on either side, marked with Rv ink stamp logo, excellent original condition with faint crazing, 8 1/8" high. **$424**

Silhouette fan vase with nudes in red, shape number 783-7", marked on bottom Roseville U.S.A. 783-7", 7 3/8" high. **$218**

Weller Pottery

Weller Pottery was made from 1872 to 1945 at a pottery established originally by Samuel A. Weller at Fultonham, Ohio and moved in 1882 to Zanesville, Ohio.

Weller's famous pottery slugged it out with several other important Zanesville potteries for decades. Cross-town rivals such as Roseville, Owens, La Moro, and McCoy were all serious fish in a fairly small and well-stocked lake. While Weller occasionally landed some solid body punches with many of his better art lines, the prevailing thought was that his later production ware just wasn't up to snuff.

Samuel Weller was a notorious copier and, it is said, a bit of a scallywag. He paid designers such as William Long to bring their famous discoveries to Zanesville. He then attempted to steal their secrets, and, when successful, renamed them and made them his own.

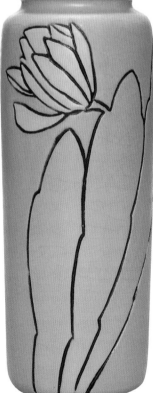

After World War I, when the cost of materials became less expensive than the cost of labor, many companies, including the famous Rookwood Pottery, increased their output of less expensive production ware. Weller Pottery followed along in the trend of production ware by introducing scores of interesting and unique lines, the likes of which have never been created anywhere else, before or since.

In addition to a number of noteworthy production lines, Weller continued in the creation of hand-painted ware long after Roseville abandoned them. Some of the more interesting Hudson pieces, for example, are post-World War I pieces. Even later lines, such as Bonito, were hand painted and often signed by important artists such as Hester Pillsbury. The closer you look at Weller's output after 1920, the more obvious the fact that it was the only Zanesville company still producing both quality art ware and quality production ware.

For more information on Weller pottery, see *Warman's Weller Pottery Identification and Price Guide* by Denise Rago and David Rago.

Courtesy of Mark Mussio, Humler & Nolan, www.humlernolan.com

Etched mat vase decorated by Frank Ferrell, incised yellow flower and green leaves against tan ground, signed Ferrell on side with incised Weller and White Pillars Museum label on bottom, overall crazing, 10 3/4" high. $1,331

"Dragon" Eocean bud vase in green, gray, white, and pink glazes, impressed "WELLER" in small block letters on bottom, fine overall crazing, 9 5/8" high. **$1,210**

▲ Hudson vase in blue and pink with blue and white floral décor, marked "England," no chips, cracks or repairs, 8 1/2" high. **$590**

◀ Green mat jardiniere with two handles and molded Mackintosh rose design, impressed WELLER in block letters on bottom, excellent original condition, 5 3/4" high, 7" diameter. **$575**

Courtesy of Mark Mussio, Humler & Nolan, www.humlernolan.com

▲ Woodcraft apple tree stump vase with black-faced owl perched at entrance of knothole with built-in floral arranger inside rim, impressed Weller and incised A, excellent condition, 15 1/2" high. **$1,331**

Courtesy of Mark Mussio, Humler & Nolan, www.humlernolan.com

▶ Tall Sicard vase with berry-filled branches, unsigned, shape number 472 on bottom, fine overall crazing and minor glaze rubs, 13 1/4" high. **$1,573**

Courtesy of Mark Mussio, Humler & Nolan, www.humlernolan.com

◀ Eocean vase with great horned owl perched on branch in front of full moon by Elizabeth Blake, who signed piece in black slip on side, incised Weller Eocean with impressed X 444 on bottom, fine overall crazing and glaze nick mid-body, 8 3/4" high. **$1,029**

Courtesy of Mark Mussio, Humler & Nolan, www.humlernolan.com

▼ Sicard vase with floral pattern, signed Weller Sicard on side, fine overall crazing, 7 3/8" high. **$1,694**

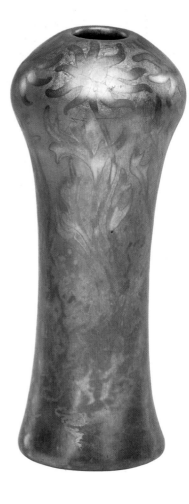

Courtesy of Mark Mussio, Humler & Nolan, www.humlernolan.com

Four-sided Sicard vase, deep maroon and blue with silver stars on each side, signed Weller Sicard on side, 5" high. $787

Courtesy of Rago Arts and Auctions, www.ragoarts.com

Sicard vase with tall flowers, 1902-1907, signed "Weller Sicard," 5 3/4" x 2 1/4". $469

Courtesy of Mark Mussio, Humler & Nolan,
www.humlernolan.com

Aurelian vase by former Rookwood decorator Ed Abel, large horned dragon with tail wrapped around vase, impressed Weller and incised "Aurelian K" on bottom, signed by artist on top of foot, glaze nick on foot, 12 7/8" high. Abel was one of the better figurative artists at Rookwood from 1890 to 1895. **$1,150**

Courtesy of Woody Auction,
www.woodyauction.com

Sicard cylindrical vase with large thistle design, no chips, cracks or repairs, 10" x 3 3/4". **$826**

Courtesy of Mark Mussio, Humler & Nolan,
www.humlernolan.com

Rare Majolica-style jardiniere
and pedestal with flora, fauna,
and scenes under high glaze,
design by Rudolph Lorber, rim
with great horned owl perched
in branch before full moon,
opposing side with landscape
and Dutch windmill; lug handles
on either side of jardiniere in
shape of owl's head, pedestal
with squirrel holding acorn,
opposing side with night scene
with castle and full moon; both
pieces with molded surround
of leaves, pinecones, and
acorns bordering each vignette,
conjoined initials of designer
molded into pedestal, both
pieces hand-incised; excellent
original condition, jardiniere 12"
x 14 1/2" wide, pedestal 22 1/2"
high, 34" high combined. **$3,630**

Courtesy of Mark Mussio,
Humler & Nolan,
www.humlernolan.com

◄ Hudson vase with white and red "Rose-O-Sharon" by Mae Timberlake, who signed piece in black slip near base, marked on bottom with Weller full-kiln ink stamp, faint crazing, 12" high. **$1,029**

Courtesy of Rago Arts and Auctions,
www.ragoarts.com

▲ Rare large mat green vase with snake and bird, circa 1905, stamped WELLER, 18" x 8 1/2". **$8,125**

Courtesy of Rago Arts and Auctions,
www.ragoarts.com

◄ Athens vase, 1915, unmarked, 10" x 4" x 4". **$313**

European Ceramics

Select English & European Makers

Amphora Porcelain Works

The Amphora Porcelain Works was one of several pottery companies located in the Teplitz-Turn region of Bohemia in the late 19th and early 20th centuries. It is best known for art pottery, especially Art Nouveau and Art Deco pieces. Several markings were used, including the name and location of the pottery and the Imperial mark, which included a crown. Prior to World War I, Bohemia was part of the Austro-Hungarian Empire, so the word "Austria" may appear as part of the mark. After World War I, the word "Czechoslovakia" may be part of the mark.

Belleek

Belleek is thin-bodied, ivory-colored, almost iridescent porcelain first made in 1857 in County Fermanagh, Ireland. Production continued until World War I, was discontinued for a period of time, and then resumed. The Shamrock pattern is most familiar, but many patterns were made, including Limpet, Tridacna, and Grasses.

Several American firms made a Belleek-type porcelain. The first was Ott and Brewer Co. of Trenton, New Jersey, in 1884. Other firms producing this ware included The Ceramic Art Co. (1889), American Art China Works (1892), Columbian Art Co. (1893) and Lenox Inc. (1904). Irish Belleek bore specific marks during given time periods, which makes it relatively easy to date. Variations in mark color are important, as well as the symbols and words.

Courtesy of Thomaston Place Auction Galleries, www.thomastonauction.com

▲ Large Belleek water pitcher with aftermarket decoration of primroses and blackberries on celery green upper portion, melon-colored base with gilt dividing line and large gilt dragon-form handle, initialed by decorator "L.O.M." on underside, very good condition, 15" high x 8" wide at handle. **$207**

Courtesy of Morphy Auctions, www.morphyauctions.com

◄ Amphora vase with embossed jewels, spiders, and webs, good condition, 13" high. **$30**

Capo-di-Monte

Capo-di-Monte serving platter, embossed classical scene border with family crest in center, gold stencil highlights, marked, good condition, 21" x 14 1/2". $295

Spode

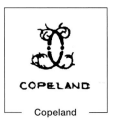

Copeland

Capo-di-Monte

In 1743, King Charles of Naples established a soft-paste porcelain factory. The firm made figurines and dinnerware. In 1760, many of the workmen and most of the molds were moved to Buen Retiro, near Madrid, Spain. A new factory, which also made hard-paste porcelains, opened in Naples in 1771. In 1834, the Doccia factory in Florence purchased the molds and continued production in Italy.

Capo-di-Monte was copied well into the 20th century by makers in Hungary, Germany, France, and Italy.

Copeland-Spode

In 1749, Josiah Spode was apprenticed to Thomas Whieldon and in 1754 worked for William Banks in Stoke-on-Trent, Staffordshire, England. In the early 1760s, Spode started his own pottery, making cream-colored earthenware and blueprinted whiteware. In 1770, he returned to Banks' factory as master, purchasing it in 1776.

Spode pioneered the use of steam-powered, pottery-making machinery and mastered the art of transfer printing from copper plates. Spode opened a London shop in 1778 and sent William Copeland there in about 1784. A number of larger London locations followed. At the turn of the 18th century, Spode introduced bone china. In 1805, Josiah Spode II and William Copeland entered into a partnership for the London business. A series of partnerships between Josiah Spode II, Josiah Spode III, and William Taylor Copeland resulted.

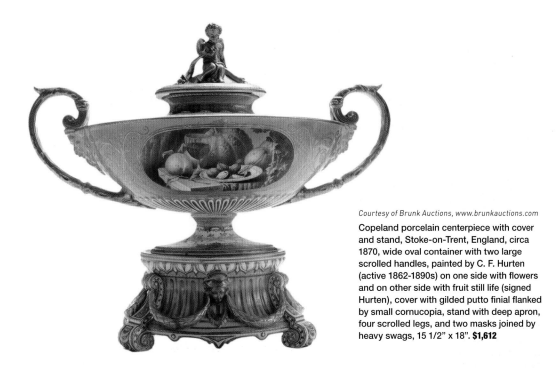

Copeland porcelain centerpiece with cover and stand, Stoke-on-Trent, England, circa 1870, wide oval container with two large scrolled handles, painted by C. F. Hurten (active 1862-1890s) on one side with flowers and on other side with fruit still life (signed Hurten), cover with gilded putto finial flanked by small cornucopia, stand with deep apron, four scrolled legs, and two masks joined by heavy swags, 15 1/2" x 18". **$1,612**

In 1833, Copeland acquired Spode's London operations and seven years later, the Stoke plants. William Taylor Copeland managed the business until his death in 1868. The firm remained in the hands of Copeland heirs. In 1923, the plant was electrified; other modernization followed.

In 1976, Spode merged with Worcester Royal Porcelain to become Royal Worcester Spode, Ltd.

Creamware

Creamware is cream-colored earthenware created about 1750 by the potters of Staffordshire, England, which proved ideal for domestic ware. It was also known as "tortoiseshell ware" or "Prattware" depending on the color of glaze used.

The most notable producer of creamware was Josiah Wedgwood. Around 1779, he was able to lighten the cream color to a bluish white and sold this product under the name "pearl ware." Wedgwood supplied his creamware to England's Queen Charlotte (1744-1818) and Russian Empress Catherine the Great (1729-1796), and used the trade name "Queen's ware."

Two early Delft platters in Chinese Canton style, 17th to 18th century, one floral, other figural with woman in garden, losses to edges, 1 1/2" x 11 3/4" and 2" x 14".
$649

Delftware

Delftware is pottery with a soft, red-clay body and tin-enamel glaze. The white, dense, opaque color came from adding tin ash to lead glaze. The first examples had blue designs on a white ground. Polychrome examples followed.

The name originally applied to pottery made in the region around Delft, Holland, beginning in the 16th century and ending in the late 18th century. The tin used came from the Cornish mines in England. By the 17th and 18th centuries, English potters in London, Bristol, and Liverpool were copying the glaze and designs. Some designs unique to English potters also developed.

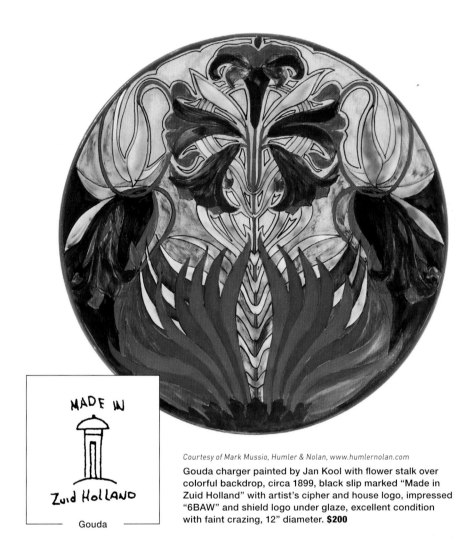

Courtesy of Mark Mussio, Humler & Nolan, www.humlernolan.com

Gouda charger painted by Jan Kool with flower stalk over colorful backdrop, circa 1899, black slip marked "Made in Zuid Holland" with artist's cipher and house logo, impressed "6BAW" and shield logo under glaze, excellent condition with faint crazing, 12" diameter. **$200**

Gouda

Gouda and the surrounding areas of Holland have been principal Dutch pottery centers for centuries. Originally, the potteries produced simple utilitarian, tin-glazed Delft-type earthenware and the famous clay smoker's pipes.

When pipe making declined in the early 1900s, Gouda turned to art pottery. Influenced by the Art Nouveau and Art Deco movements, artists expressed themselves with freeform and stylized designs in bold colors.

Haviland

In 1842, American china importer David Haviland moved to Limoges, France, where he began manufacturing and decorating china specifically for the U.S. market. Haviland is synonymous with fine, white, translucent porcelain, although early hand-painted patterns were generally larger and darker colored on heavier whiteware blanks than were later ones.

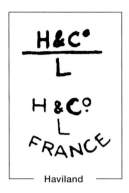
Haviland

Haviland revolutionized French china factories by both manufacturing the whiteware blank and decorating it at the same site. In addition, Haviland and Co. pioneered the use of decals in decorating china.

Haviland's sons, Charles Edward and Theodore, split the company in 1892. In 1936, Theodore opened an American division. In 1941, Theodore bought out Charles Edward's heirs and re-combined both companies under the original name of H. and Co. The Haviland family sold the firm in 1981.

Charles Field Haviland, cousin of Charles Edward and Theodore, worked for and then, after his marriage in 1857, ran the Casseaux Works until 1882. Items continued to carry his name as decorator until 1941.

Thousands of Haviland patterns were made, but not consistently named until after 1926. The similarities in many of the patterns make identification difficult. Numbers assigned by Arlene Schleiger and illustrated in her books have become the identification standard.

Leeds

The Leeds Pottery in Yorkshire, England, began production about 1758. Among its products was creamware that was competitive with that of Wedgwood. The original factory closed in 1820,

Leeds

but various subsequent owners continued until 1880. They made exceptional cream-colored ware – plain, salt glazed, or painted with colored enamels – and glazed and unglazed redware.

Pair of Leeds creamware basket-form bowls with flared and fluted pierce-work sides, late 18th century, twin intertwined handles ending in leaves, underside impressed Leeds Pottery, good condition, 3" x 10" x 9". **$708**

Early wares are unmarked. Later pieces are marked "Leeds Pottery," sometimes followed by "Hartley-Green and Co." or the letters "LP."

Liverpool

Liverpool is the name given to products made at several potteries in Liverpool, England, between 1750 and 1840. Seth and James Pennington and Richard Chaffers were among the early potters who made tin-enameled earthenware.

By the 1780s, tin-glazed earthenware gave way to cream-colored wares decorated with cobalt blue, enameled colors, and blue or black transfers.

Bubbles and frequent clouding under the foot rims characterize the Liverpool glaze. By 1800, about 80 potteries were working in the town producing not only creamware, but also soft paste, soapstone, and bone porcelain.

The reproduction pieces have a crackled glaze and often age cracks have been artificially produced. When compared to genuine pieces, reproductions are thicker and heavier and have weaker transfers, grayish color (not as crisp and black), ecru or gray body color instead of cream, and crazing that does not spiral upward.

Courtesy of Thomaston Place Auction Galleries,
www.thomastonauction.com

Minton cobalt blue glazed chinoiserie footed jardiniere, circa 1900, with two elephant head and ring handles, four dolphin head feet, stamped "England" and "1620" on underside, fine condition, 16" high, 15 1/2" diameter. $531

Minton

Minton

In 1793, Thomas Minton joined other entrepreneurs and formed a partnership to build a small pottery at Stoke-on-Trent, Staffordshire, England. Production began in 1798 with blueprinted earthenware, mostly in the Willow pattern. In 1798, cream-colored earthenware and bone china were introduced.

A wide range of styles and wares was produced. Minton introduced porcelain figures in 1826, Parian wares in 1846, encaustic tiles in the late 1840s, and majolica wares in 1850. In 1883, the modern company was formed and called Mintons Limited. The "s" was dropped in 1968.

Many early pieces are unmarked or have a Sevres-type marking. The "ermine" mark was used in the early 19th century. Date codes can be found on tableware and majolica. The mark used between 1873 and 1911 was a small globe with a crown on top and the word "Minton."

Mocha

Mocha decoration usually is found on utilitarian creamware and stoneware pieces and was produced through a simple chemical action. A color pigment of brown, blue, green or black was made acidic by an infusion of tobacco or hops. When the acidic colorant was applied in blobs to an alkaline ground, it reacted by spreading in feathery designs resembling sea plants. This type of decoration usually was supplemented with bands of light-colored slip.

Types of decoration vary greatly, from those done in a combination of motifs, such as Cat's Eye and Earthworm, to a plain pink mug decorated with green ribbed bands. Most forms of mocha are hollow, e.g., mugs, jugs, bowls and shakers.

English potters made the vast majority of the pieces. Collectors group the wares into three chronological periods: 1780-1820, 1820-1840, and 1840-1880.

Courtesy of Jeffrey S. Evans & Associates, www.jeffreysevans.com

Staffordshire Pottery mocha pitcher, circa 1820, incurvate neck over swollen shoulder, tapering cylindrical form to waisted foot, alternating black and gray bands, rouletted band at shoulder painted with green slip, gray bands with orange, black, and white Cat's Eye pattern, unmarked, 5 7/8" high. $1,560

Moorcroft

William Moorcroft was first employed as a potter by James Macintyre & Co., Ltd. of Burslem, Staffordshire, England, in 1897. He established the Moorcroft pottery in 1913.

The majority of the art pottery wares were hand thrown, resulting in a great variation among similarly styled pieces. Colors and marks are keys to determining age.

Walter Moorcroft, William's son, continued the business upon his father's death and made wares in the same style.

The company initially used an impressed mark, "Moorcroft, Burslem"; a signature mark, "W. Moorcroft," followed. Modern pieces are marked simply "Moorcroft," with export pieces also marked "Made in England."

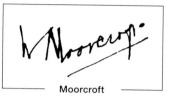

Moorcroft

Courtesy of Heritage Auctions, ha.com

◄ Moorcroft tiger lily vase, Burslem (Stoke-on-Trent), Staffordshire, England, circa 1930, marks: W. Moorcroft, POTTER TO THE QUEEN, MADE IN ENGLAND, WM, two minor fleabites to base edge, light scratch to body, 12 3/4" high. **$1,250**

Courtesy of Jeffrey S. Evans & Associates, www.jeffreysevans.com

▼ Moorcroft covered bowl, first half 20th century, cobalt blue and polychrome with polychrome grape and grape leaf decoration to cover and grape leaf decoration to body, impressed "MOORCROFT" to underside of cover and impressed "POTTER TO / H. M. THE QUEEN" and "MADE IN / ENGLAND" and incised "W. Moorcroft" signature to underside of bowl, 3 3/4" high overall, 5 3/8" diameter. **$271**

Courtesy of Jeffrey S. Evans & Associates, www.jeffreysevans.com

▲ Three Royal Bayreuth sunbonnet porcelain toothpick holders, fishing, sweeping, and washing examples, circa 1900-1920, one with printed blue mark to underside, 2 1/2" to 3 1/3" high overall. **$330**

Courtesy of Woody Auction, www.woodyauction.com

◄ Royal Bayreuth rose tapestry covered cracker jar, blue mark, good condition, 5" x 7". **$118**

Royal Bayreuth

In 1794, the Royal Bayreuth factory was founded in Tettau, Bavaria. Royal Bayreuth introduced its figural patterns in 1885. Designs of animals, people, fruits and vegetables decorated a wide array of tableware and inexpensive souvenir items.

Tapestry wares, in rose and other patterns, were made in the late 19th century. The surface of the pieces feel and look like woven cloth.

The Royal Bayreuth crest used to mark the wares varied in design and color.

Royal Bayreuth

Courtesy of Clars Auction Gallery, www.clars.com

Large Royal Crown Derby polychrome decorated ginger jar, retailed by Shreve Crump & Lowe, 19th century, rounded lid with raised gilt decoration above tapered body with floral sprays on crimson ground, circular base, 15" high. **$1,200-$1,600**

Courtesy of Brunk Auctions, www.brunkauctions.com

Royal Crown Derby perfume bottle, second half 19th century, pink bulbous form, applied rococo handles, foliate gilding to bottle, original stopper with retaining wires, signed on bottom of bottle and on side of plug "England/Royal Crown Derby," light wear to base, some losses to gilding, 7" high. **$248**

Royal Crown Derby

Derby Crown Porcelain Co., established in 1875 in Derby, England, had no connection with earlier Derby factories that operated in the late 18th and early 19th centuries. In 1890, the company was appointed "Manufacturers of Porcelain to Her Majesty" (Queen Victoria) and since that date has been known as Royal Crown Derby.

Most of these porcelains, both tableware and figural, were hand decorated. A variety of printing processes were used for additional adornment.

Derby porcelains from 1878 to 1890 carry only the standard crown printed mark. After 1891, the mark includes the "Royal Crown Derby" wording. In the 20th century, "Made in England" and "English Bone China" were added to the mark.

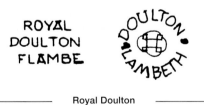

Royal Doulton

*Courtesy of Cottone Auctions,
www.cottoneauctions.com*

Two Royal Doulton flambé vases, early 20th century, excellent condition, taller vase 8 1/2" high. **$787**

Royal Doulton

Doulton pottery began in 1815 under the direction of John Doulton at the Doulton & Watts pottery in Lambeth, England. Early output was limited to salt-glazed industrial stoneware. After John Watts retired in 1854, the firm became Doulton and Co., and production was expanded to include hand-decorated stoneware such as figurines, vases, dinnerware and flasks.

In 1878, Doulton's son, Sir Henry Doulton, purchased Pinder Bourne & Co. in Burslem, Staffordshire. The companies became Doulton & Co., Ltd. in 1882. Decorated porcelain was added to Doulton's earthenware production in 1884.

Most Doulton figurines were produced at the Burslem plants, where they were made continuously from 1890 until 1978. After a short interruption, a new line of Doulton figurines was introduced in 1979.

Royal Doulton faience footed moon flask for Tiffany & Co., Lambeth, England, circa 1875, grotesque man and fowl to illustrated front, finches perched on budding branches to verso, brown and parcel gilt banded sides, neck, and feet with black and gilt striping, marked "TIFFANY & CO., NEW YORK," minor surface wear commensurate with age, 13 3/4" high. **$625**

Dickensware, in earthenware and porcelain, was introduced in 1908. The pieces were decorated with characters from Dickens' novels. Most of the line was withdrawn in the 1940s, except for plates, which continued to be made until 1974.

Character jugs, a 20th century revival of early Toby models, were designed by Charles J. Noke for Doulton in the 1930s. Character jugs are limited to bust portraits, while Royal Doulton Toby jugs are full figured. The character jugs come in four sizes and feature fictional characters from Dickens, Shakespeare, and other English and American novelists, as well as historical heroes. Marks on both character and Toby jugs must be carefully identified to determine dates and values.

Doulton's Rouge Flambé (Veined Sung) is a high-glazed, strong-colored ware.

Production of stoneware at Lambeth ceased in 1956.

Beginning in 1872, the "Royal Doulton" mark was used on all types of wares produced by the company.

Beginning in 1913, an "HN" number was assigned to each new Doulton figurine design. The "HN" numbers, which referred originally to Harry Nixon, a Doulton artist, were chronological until 1940, after which blocks of numbers were assigned to each modeler. From 1928 until 1954, a small number was placed to the right of the crown mark; this number, when added to 1927, gives the year of manufacture.

Royal Worcester

In 1751, the Worcester Porcelain Co., led by Dr. John Wall and William Davis, acquired the Bristol pottery of Benjamin Lund and moved it to Worcester. The first wares were painted blue under the glaze; soon thereafter decorating was accomplished by painting on the glaze in enamel colors. Among the most famous 18th century decorators were James Giles and Jeffery Hamet O'Neal. Transfer-

Courtesy of Jeffrey S. Evans & Associates, www.jeffreysevans.com

Royal Worcester hand-painted porcelain cabinet plates, set of 11, circa 1912, each depicting different orchid and artist signed "F. Roberts" for Frank Roberts (working 1872-1920), gilt outer and foot rims, appropriate back markings, "Rd. No. 571649, Ovington Brothers Co., New York Retailers," and name of orchid in script, undamaged condition, 10 5/8" diameter. **$7,200**

Royal Worcester pate-sur-pate vase, circa 1900, marked "ROYAL CHINA WORKS WORCESTER ENGLAND, B, 191/G 4056," good condition, wear commensurate with age, 8 3/4" high. **$406**

print decoration was developed by the 1760s.

A series of partnerships took place after Davis' death in 1783: Flight (1783-1793); Flight & Barr (1793-1807); Barr, Flight & Barr (1807-1813); and Flight, Barr & Barr (1813-1840). In 1840, the factory was moved to Chamberlain & Co. in Diglis, Worcester. Decorative wares were discontinued. In 1852, W.H. Kerr and R.W. Binns formed a new company and revived the production of ornamental wares.

In 1862, the firm became the Royal Worcester Porcelain Co. Among the key modelers of the late 19th century were James Hadley, his three sons, and George Owen, an expert with pierced clay pieces. Royal Worcester absorbed the Grainger factory in 1889 and the James Hadley factory in 1905. Modern designers include Dorothy Doughty and Doris Lindner.

Spatterware

Spatterware generally was made of common earthenware, although occasionally creamware was used. The earliest English examples were made about 1780. The peak period of production was from 1810 to 1840. Firms known to have made spatterware are Adams, Barlow, and Harvey and Cotton.

The amount of spatter decoration varies from piece to piece. Some objects simply have decorated borders. These often were decorated with a brush, requiring several hundred touches per square inch to achieve the spatter effect. Other pieces have the entire surface covered with spatter. Marked pieces are rare.

Collectors today focus on the patterns – Cannon, Castle, Fort, Peafowl, Rainbow, Rose, Thistle, Schoolhouse, etc. The decoration on flat ware is in the center of the piece; on hollow ware, it occurs on both sides.

Aesthetics and the colors of the spatter are keys to determining value. Blue and red are the most common colors; green, purple, and brown are in a middle group; black and yellow are scarce.

Courtesy of Quinn's Auction Gallery, www.quinnsauction.com

Eight pieces of English spatterware in Castle/Fort and Peafowl patterns, mid-19th century, two plates, two handless cups, two shallow bowls, small plate, and creamer. $514

Zsolnay

Vilmos Zsolnay (1828-1900) assumed control of his brother's factory in Pécs, Hungary, in the mid-19th century. In 1899, Vilmos' son, Miklos, became manager. The firm still produces ceramic ware.

The early wares are highly ornamental, glazed, and have a cream-colored ground. Eosin glaze, a deep, rich play of colors reminiscent of Tiffany's iridescent wares, received a gold medal at the 1900 Paris exhibition.

Originally no trademark was used, but in 1878 the company began to use a blue mark depicting the five towers of the cathedral at Pécs. The initials "TJM" represent the names of Miklos' three children.

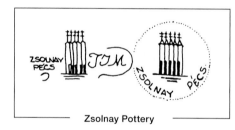

Zsolnay Pottery

Courtesy of Heritage Auctions, ha.com

Zsolnay Pécs two-handled luster vase with daisies and maple leaves, circa 1900, marked "ZOLNAY PECS (impressed five-tower mark), 6816, 86," very good condition, 12" high. $11,950

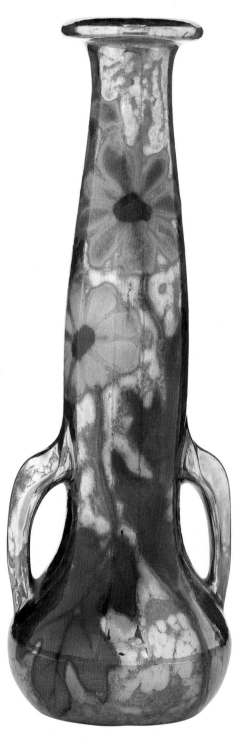

KPM

By Melody Amsel-Arieli

KPM plaques are highly glazed, enamel paintings on porcelain bases that were produced by Konigliche Porzellan Manufaktur (KPM), the King's Porcelain Factory, in Berlin, Germany, between 1880 and 1901.

Their secret, according to Afshine Emrani, dealer and appraiser at www.some-of-my-favorite-things.com, is KPM's highly superior, smooth, hard paste porcelain, which could be fired at very high temperatures.

"The magic of a KPM plaque is that it will look as crisp and beautiful 100 years from now as it does today," he said. Even when they were introduced, these plaques proved highly collectible, with art lovers, collectors, tourists, and the wealthy acquiring them for extravagant sums.

KPM rarely marketed painted porcelain plaques itself, however. Instead, it usually supplied white, undecorated ones to independent artists who specialized in this genre. Not all artists signed their KPM paintings, however.

While most KPM plaques were copies of famous paintings, some, commissioned by wealthy Americans and Europeans in the 1920s, bear images of actual people in contemporary clothing. These least collectible of KPM plaques command between $500 and $1,500 each, depending on the attractiveness of their subjects.

Gilded, hand-painted plaques featuring Middle Eastern or female Gypsy subjects and bearing round red "Made in Germany" stamps were produced just before and after World War I for export. They command between $500 and $2,000 each. Plaques portraying religious subjects, such as the Virgin Mary or the Flight into Egypt, command higher prices but are less popular.

Popular scenes of hunters, merrymakers, musicians, etc., generally fetch less than $10,000 apiece because they have been reproduced time and again. Rarer, more elaborate scenes, however, like "The Dance Lesson" and "Turkish Card Players" may be worth many times more.

Highly stylized portraits copied from famous paintings – especially those of attractive children or décolleté women

MELODY AMSEI-ARIELI is a freelance writer and frequent contributor to *Antique Trader* magazine. She is the author of *Between Galicia and Hungary: The Jews of Stropkov* as well as *Jewish Lives: Britain 1750-1950* (Pen & Sword, 2013). She lives in Israel.

– allowed art lovers to own their own "masterpieces." These are currently worth between $2,000 and $20,000 each. Romanticized portrayals of cupids and women in the nude, the most desirable KPMs subjects of all, currently sell for up to $40,000 each. Portraits of men, it must be noted, are not only less popular, but also less expensive.

Size also matters. A 4" x 6" plaque, whose subject has been repeatedly reproduced, may sell for a few thousand dollars. Larger ones that portray the same subject will fetch proportionately more. A "Sistine Madonna" plaque, fashioned after the original work by Rafael and measuring 10" x 7 1/2", might cost $4,200. One featuring the identical subject, but measuring 15" x 11", might cost $7,800. A larger plaque, measuring 22" x 16", might command twice that price.

The largest KPM plaques, measuring 22" x 26", for example, often burst during production. Although no formula exists for determining prices of those that have survived, Afshine Emrani said that each may sell for as much as $250,000. Rare plaques like these are often found in museums.

The condition of a KPM plaque also affects its price. Most, since they were highly glazed and customarily hung instead of handled, have survived in perfect condition. Thus those that have sustained even minor damage, like scratches, cracks, or chips, fetch considerably lower prices. Those suffering major damage are worthless.

KPM's painted plaques arouse so much interest and command such high prices that, over the last couple of years, unscrupulous dealers have entered the market. According to dealer Balazs Benedek, KPM plaques are "the mother of all fakes. About 90 percent of KPM plaques are mid- to late-20th century reproductions. And about 70 percent are not hand painted."

Collectors should be aware that genuine KPM paintings always boast rich, shiny, glazes that preserve their colors, and though subject matter may vary, they typically feature nude scenes, indoor portraits of women, or group gatherings in lush settings. Anything wildly different should raise suspicion.

Genuine KPMs, on their backs or edges, feature small icons of scepters deeply set in the porcelain, over the letters KPM. These marks are sometimes accompanied by an "H" or some other letter, which may indicate their production date or size. Some are imprinted with the size of the plaque as well, which facilitated sorting or shipping. Shallow or crooked imprints may reveal a fake.

▲ Porcelain plaque of Roman ruins, women and children in Roman market scene, late 19th/early 20th century, carved and gilded frame, mark on verso, very good condition throughout with no cracks, chips, or restorations, 8 1/4" x 10 3/8" (sight). **$6,150**

◄ Oval plaque with hand-painted portrait of black-haired gypsy woman, late 19th/early 20th century, pierced and carved giltwood frame, impressed KPM and scepter marks, impressed "F / 5," unsigned, plaque 10 1/2" high x 8 1/2" wide. **$6,000**

Courtesy of Fontaine's Auction Gallery, fontainesauction.com

Painted porcelain plaque, "Murder of Edward IV's Sons," after Ferdinand Theodor Hildebrandt (1835), two men in shadows leaning over two sleeping princes, sons of Edward IV of England, signed on back with KPM and scepter mark, excellent condition, in gilt carved frame with repainted surface, 8 3/4" high x 10 3/4" wide, 12" high x 14" wide (framed). **$3,025**

Courtesy of Fontaine's Auction Gallery, fontainesauction.com

Large hand-painted porcelain plaque titled "In Deinem Auge Liegt Mein Himmel" ("In Your Eyes My Heaven Lies") in gilt carved frame, interior scene with woman standing by open window holding baby, artist signed R. Dittrich, signed on back with KPM and scepter marks, size marks 407-263, titled "In Deinem Auge Liegt Mein Himmel" and signed with blue Royal Vienna beehive mark, excellent condition, 15 3/4" high x 10 1/4" wide, 17" high x 23 3/4" wide (framed). **$7,563**

Courtesy of Fontaine's Auction Gallery, fontainesauction.com

Hand-painted portrait plaque of young girl with pearl necklace carrying basket on her left arm with book inside and portfolio under her right arm, gilt carved inset frame with tan felt-lined border, signed on back with KPM and scepter mark, 12 3/4" high x 7 3/4" wide (sight), 19 3/4" high x 13 1/2" wide (framed). **$5,143**

Courtesy of John Moran Auctioneers, Inc., www.johnmoran.com

Oval plaque of maiden after Italian artist Angelo Asti (1847-1903), "Meditation," late 19th century, impressed KPM scepter mark and monogram, incised with two ciphers and "5," signed to right edge "Wagner," in giltwood frame with burgundy liner, plaque 10 1/2" high x 8 1/2" wide. **$3,750**

Courtesy of Fontaine's Auction Gallery, fontainesauction.com

Hand-painted portrait plaque of standing figure of woman wearing long garments with carved stone structure behind her and foliage to her right, artist signed "B. Barry, 99," signed on back with KPM and scepter mark and size marks 330-200, in gilt pierced and carved filigree frame, overall good condition with minor losses, 13" high x 7 3/4" wide, 20" high x 14 1/2" wide (framed). **$3,025**

Porcelain portrait plaque
of painter Titian's daughter,
Lavinia, carrying tray of fruit
over her head, her back to
painter and looking over her
right shoulder, signed with
KPM and scepter mark on
back, in gilt carved frame,
excellent condition, plaque 8"
high x 7" wide, 10 3/4" high x
9 1/2" wide (framed). **$2,420**

Hand-painted oval porcelain
plaque of long-haired woman,
late 19th/early 20th century, in
carved gilt rectangular frame
housed in glazed rectangular
shadowbox, impressed
"K.P.M" and scepter marks
and "4 / G," signed to face
"Wagner," with partially
obscured label verso "No. 4 /
Gio??? / Lef??re," plaque
8 7/8" high x 6 1/2" wide.
$1,680

Five-piece porcelain tea service, all white with matching floral décor and floral finials, 12" x 8 3/4" oval tray, 5 1/4" teapot, 4" creamer, 3 1/2" covered sugar and underplate, no chips, cracks or repairs. **$295**

Porcelain cabinet ewer, third quarter 19th century, ornate scrollwork, molded body and handle, C-scroll foot, hand-painted polychrome floral decoration and gilt highlights, marked with red orb above "KPM" and underglaze blue scepter, 5 1/2" high. **$345**

Courtesy of Woody Auction,
www.woodyauction.com

Scenic plate with reticulated white with pink floral border, scene titled "Sternberg Liebenstein," marked "KPM," no chips, cracks or repairs, 9 1/2". **$148**

Courtesy of Rago Arts and Auctions,
www.ragoarts.com

Porcelain jardinière with slip-decorated Aesthetic Movement design in teal and deep pantone glaze with gilt highlights and trim, circa 1880, scepter mark with "Srg. P," 13" high. **$375**

Rectangular plaque of young maiden, late 19th century, impressed KPM scepter mark and monogram, further impressed "v" and "A(?)," inscribed "275.223," titled lower left "m. Sabr. Mase," signed lower right with artist's monogram device "THK," in giltwood and gesso frame, plaque 11" high x 9" wide. **$3,750**

Two plates of temple ruins and passing figures, late 19th/early 20th century, each with underglaze blue scepter and overglaze gold orb marks, each with original "Konigl Porzellan Manufactur / Berlin" and title paper labels, smaller titled "Temple of Peace" and impressed "G / 3," larger titled "Temple of Venus" and impressed "G / 4," on short circular foot, larger 2" high, 15 3/4" diameter, smaller 1 3/4" high, 14" diameter. **$750**

Courtesy of Skinner, Inc., www.skinnerinc.com

Porcelain plaque of child with lamb, last quarter 19th century, in gilded frame with cartouche ornaments at corners, plaque in good condition, loss of gilding to frame, to lower right corner, and evidence of cracking to applied ornaments at corners, 6 5/8" high (sight), 12" high (frame). **$738**

Pair of jeweled porcelain lidded urns, each with tapered form in green with gilt scrolls and raised enameling, circular base, each signed with underglaze scepter mark, 7 1/4" high. **$3,050**

Painted and gilt porcelain vase, circa 1880, marked KPM, (orb and cross), (scepter), 29" high. **$7,500**

Porcelain plaque of boy and girl, late 19th/early 20th century, boy whispering to girl as she carries lit chamberstick, in carved frame, impressed mark, signed "R. Dittrich," very good condition throughout, 10 5/8" x 8 3/8" (sight). **$3,690**

Courtesy of Skinner, Inc., www.skinnerinc.com

Porcelain plaque of guardian angel in green, gray, blue, and gold, 19th/early 20th century, factory mark on reverse, with "Sz" and "315-235" and name, surface grime, wear to gilding and scattered small losses on edges and corners of frame, wear appropriate with age, 12 3/8" high x 10 1/4" wide (sight). **$4,920**

Limoges

"Limoges" has become the generic identifier for porcelain produced in Limoges, France, and the surrounding vicinity. Over 40 manufacturers in the area have, at some point, used the term as a descriptor of their work, and there are at least 400 different Limoges identification marks. The common denominator is the product itself – fine hard paste porcelain created from the necessary components found in abundance in the Limoges region: kaolin and feldspar.

Until the 1700s, porcelain was exclusively a product of China, introduced to the Western world by Marco Polo and imported at great expense. In 1765, the discovery of kaolin in St. Yrieixin, a small town near Limoges, made French production of porcelain possible. (The chemist's wife credited with the kaolin discovery thought at first that it would prove useful in making soap.)

Limoges entrepreneurs quickly capitalized on the find. Adding to the area's allure were expansive forests providing fuel for wood-burning kilns; the nearby Vienne River, with water for working clay; and a workforce eager to trade farming for a (hopefully) more lucrative pursuit. Additionally, as

Courtesy of Clars Auction Gallery, www.clars.com

Fish service with scalloped gilt border centering trout in river, 12 luncheon plates, 9 1/2" diameter; large serving tray, 24" wide; and sauce boat with undertray, signed de Solis. **$671**

the companies would be operating outside metropolitan Paris, labor and production costs would be significantly less.

By the early 1770s, numerous porcelain manufacturers were at work in Limoges and its environs. Demand for the porcelain was high because it was both useful and decorative. To meet that demand, firms employed trained, as well as untrained, artisans for the detailed hand painting required. (Although nearly every type of Limoges has its fans, the most sought-after – and valuable – are those pieces decorated by a company's professional artists.) At its industrial peak in 1900, Limoges factories employed over 8,000 workers in some aspect of porcelain production.

A myriad of products classified as Limoges flooded the marketplace from the late 1700s onward. Among them were tableware pieces, such as tea and punch sets, trays, pitchers, compotes, bowls, and plates. Also popular were vases and flower baskets, dresser sets, trinket boxes, ash receivers, figural busts, and decorative plaques.

Although produced in France, Limoges porcelain was soon destined for export overseas; eventually over 80 percent of Limoges porcelain was exported. The United States proved a particularly reliable customer. Notable among the importers was the Haviland China Co.; until the 1940s, its superior, exquisitely decorated china was produced in Limoges and then distributed in the United States.

By the early 20th century, many exporters in the United States were purchasing porcelain blanks from the Limoges factories for decoration stateside. The base product was authentically made in France, but production costs were significantly lower: Thousands of untrained porcelain painters put their skills to work for a minimal wage. Domestic decoration of the blanks also meant that importers could select designs suited to the specific tastes of target audiences.

Because Limoges was a regional designation rather than the identifier of a specific manufacturer, imported pieces were often marked with the name of the exporting firm, followed by the word "Limoges." Beginning in 1891, "France" was added. Some confusion has arisen from products marked "Limoges China Co." (aka "American Limoges"). This Ohio-based firm, in business from 1902-1955, has no connection to the porcelain produced in France.

The heyday of quality French Limoges lasted roughly into the 1930s. Production continues today, but after World War II, designs and painting techniques became much more standardized.

Vintage Limoges is highly sought-after by today's collectors. They're drawn to the delicacy of the porcelain as well as the colors and skill of decoration. Viewing a well-conceived Limoges piece is like seeing a painting in a new form. Valuation is based on age, decorative execution and, as with any collectible, individual visual appeal.

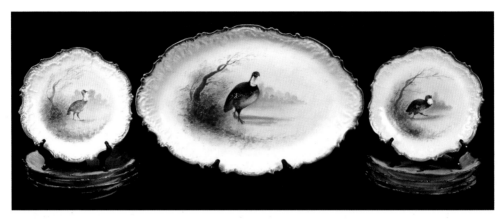

Game service with scrolled gilt border centering scenic reserve of pheasants in naturalistic setting, large serving platter, 18" long, and 10 dinner plates, 9" diameter. $275

Thirteen-piece game set by Delinieres & Co., late 19th century, platter and 12 plates with game bird in foliate setting and all-over gilt tracery decoration, red and green "D & Co." back markings, 10 3/4" x 18 1/2", 8 7/8" diameter. $288

Vase with hand-painted polychrome decoration, slight baluster form, rose bouquet and gold-painted rim, Tressermann & Vogt, late 19th/first quarter 20th century, printed "T &V / LIMOGES / FRANCE" mark to underside, 12 1/2" high, 4 3/4" diameter rim. $403

▲ Twelve place settings of Hermès black and white Estampe de Toucans: 11 teacups, 2 1/2" wide x 2 1/2" high; 12 saucers, 5 1/2" diameter; 12 bread plates, 6" diameter; 12 salad plates, 8 1/2" diameter; 12 dinner plates, 11" diameter; and 12 bowls, 12" diameter; excellent condition, one missing teacup, each bowl with dustbag. **$5,750**

◄ Unusual Haviland & Co. barbotine vase painted by Emile-Justin Merlot, circa 1875, scenic decoration of houses on bank of river with chickens in foreground, signed by Merlot on front of form and impressed "Haviland & Co. Limoges" on bottom, fine overall crazing and professional restoration to small chip on back of foot, 8 7/8" high x 13 1/4" wide. **$1,694**

▲ Hand-painted porcelain plaque with two women, one lying and one seated on garden bench, with scenic background, gilded edge, artist signed "Dubois," signed on back "Coronet, Limoges, France," excellent condition with no scratches, chips, or repairs, 15 1/2". **$726**

Courtesy of Woody Auction,
www.woodyauction.com

Teapot in green tones
with white floral
décor, artist signed
"M.K.," no chips,
cracks, or repairs,
6 1/2" x 7". **$106**

Courtesy of Woody Auction,
www.woodyauction.com

Two-handled footed porcelain
bowl and matching 11" tray,
green tones with berry and vine
décor, artist marked "LHS,"
no chips, cracks, or repairs,
4 3/4" x 12 1/2". **$266**

Courtesy of Heritage Auctions,
ha.com

Hermès gray and white
Fil d'Argent porcelain
serving bowl and
platter set, very good
to excellent condition,
serving bowl with light
wear to base edges
and small spot on base,
serving platter with light
wear and small marks
to base edges, serving
bowl, 8" diameter x
4" high; serving platter,
23" wide x 11 1/2" long.
$475

Majolica

In 1851, an English potter was hoping that his new interpretation of a centuries-old style of ceramics would be well received at the Great Exhibition of the Industries of All Nations set to open May 1 in London's Hyde Park.

Potter Herbert Minton had high hopes for his display. His father, Thomas Minton, founded a pottery works in the mid-1790s in Stoke-on-Trent, Staffordshire. Herbert Minton had designed a "new" line of pottery, and his chemist, Leon Arnoux, had developed a process that resulted in vibrant, colorful glazes that came to be called "majolica."

Trained as an engineer, Arnoux also studied the making of encaustic tiles, and had been appointed art director at Minton's works in 1848. His job was to introduce and promote new products. Victorian fascination with the natural world prompted Arnoux to reintroduce the work of Bernard Palissy, whose naturalistic, bright-colored "maiolica" wares had been created in the 16th century. But Arnoux used a thicker body to make pieces sturdier. This body was given a coating of opaque white glaze,

Courtesy of Heritage Auctions, ha.com

French neoclassical jardinière, 19th century, 14" high x 24" wide x 13 1/2" deep. $6,875

which provided a surface for decoration.

Pieces were modeled in high relief, featuring butterflies and other insects, flowers and leaves, fruit, shells, animals, and fish. Queen Victoria's endorsement of the new pottery prompted its acceptance by the general public.

When Minton introduced his wares at Philadelphia's 1876 Centennial Exhibition, American potters also began to produce majolica.

For more information on majolica, see *Warman's Majolica Identification and Price Guide* by Mark F. Moran.

Other Majolica Makers

John Adams & Co., Hanley, Stoke-on-Trent, Staffordshire, England, operated the Victoria Works, producing earthenware, jasperware, Parian, and majolica, 1864-1873.

Another Staffordshire pottery, **Samuel Alcock & Co.,** Cobridge, 1828-1853; Burslem, 1830-1859, produced earthenware, china, and Parian.

The **W. & J.A. Bailey Alloa Pottery** was founded in Alloa, the principal town in Clackmannanshire, located near Edinburgh, Scotland.

The **Bevington** family of potters worked in Hanley, Staffordshire, England in the late 19th century.

W. Brownfield & Son operated in Burslem and Cobridge, Staffordshire, England, from 1850-1891.

T.C. Brown-Westhead, Moore & Co. produced earthenware and porcelain at Hanley, Stoke-on-Trent, Staffordshire, from about 1862 to 1904.

The **Choisy-le-Roi** faience factory of Choisy-le-Roi, France, produced majolica from 1860 until 1910. The firm's wares are not always marked. The common mark is usually a black ink stamp "Choisy-le-Roi" pictured to the right with a large "HBm," which stands for Hippolyte Boulenger, a director at the pottery.

William T. Copeland & Sons pottery of Stoke-on-Trent, Staffordshire, England, began producing porcelain and earthenware in 1847. (Josiah Spode established a pottery at Stoke-on-Trent in 1770. In 1833, the firm was purchased by William Copeland and Thomas Garrett. In 1847, Copeland became the sole owner. W.T. Copeland & Sons continued until a 1976 merger when it became Royal Worcester Spode. Copeland majolica pieces are sometimes marked with an impressed "COPELAND," but many are unmarked.)

Jose A. Cunha, Caldas da Rainha, southern Portugal, also worked in the style of Bernard Palissy, the great French Renaissance potter.

Julius Dressler, Bela, Czech Republic, was founded 1888, producing faience, majolica and porcelain. In 1920, the name was changed to EPIAG. The firm closed about 1945.

Eureka Pottery was located in Trenton, New Jersey, circa 1883-1887.

Railway Pottery was established by S. Fielding & Co., Stoke-on-Trent, Staffordshire, England, 1879.

There were two **Thomas Forester** potteries active in the late 19th century in Staffordshire, England. Some sources list the more famous of the two as Thomas Forester & Sons, Ltd. at the Phoenix Works, Longton.

Established in the early 19th century, the **Gien** pottery works is located on the banks of France's Loire River near Orleans.

Joseph Holdcroft majolica ware was produced at Daisy Bank in Longton, Staffordshire, England, from 1870 to 1885. Items can be found marked with "J HOLDCROFT," but many pieces can only be attributed by the patterns and colors that are documented to have come from the Holdcroft potteries.

George Jones & Sons, Ltd., Stoke, Staffordshire, started operation in about 1864 as George Jones and in 1873 became George Jones & Sons, Ltd. The firm operated the Trent Potteries in Stoke-on-Trent (renamed "Crescent Potteries" in about 1907).

In about 1877, **Samuel Lear** erected a small china works in Hanley, Staffordshire. Lear produced domestic china and, in addition, decorated all kinds of earthenware made by other manufacturers, including "spirit kegs." In 1882, the firm expanded to include production of majolica, ivory-body earthenware, and Wedgwood-type jasperware. The business closed in 1886.

Robert Charbonnier founded the **Longchamp** tile works in 1847 to make red clay tiles, but the factory soon started to produce majolica. Longchamp is known for its "barbotine" pieces (a paste of clay used in decorating coarse pottery in relief) made with vivid colors, especially oyster plates.

Hugo Lonitz operated in Haldensleben, Germany, from 1868-1886, and later Hugo Lonitz & Co., 1886-1904, producing household and decorative porcelain, earthenware, and metalwares. Look for a mark of two entwined fish.

The **Lunéville** pottery was founded about 1728 by Jacques Chambrette in the city that bears its name, in the Alsace-Lorraine region of northeastern France. The firm became famous for its blue monochromatic and floral patterns. Around 1750, ceramist Paul-Louis Cyfflé introduced a pattern with animals and historical figures. Lunéville products range from hand-painted faience and majolica to pieces influenced by the Art Deco movement.

The **Massier** family began producing ceramics in Vallauris, France, in the mid-18th century.

François Maurice, School of Paris, was active from 1875-1885 and also worked in the style of Bernard Palissy.

Courtesy Leslie Hindman Auctioneers,
www.lesliehindman.com

◀ Cylindrical umbrella stand in three-color glaze with griffins and foliate scrolls, 21 3/4" high, 12" diameter. **$250**

George Morley & Co. was located in East Liverpool, Ohio, 1884-1891.

Morley & Co. Pottery was founded in 1879, Wellsville, Ohio, making graniteware and majolica.

Orchies, a majolica manufacturer in northern France near Lille, is also known under the mark "Moulin des Loups & Hamage," 1920s.

Faïencerie de Pornic is located near Quimper, France.

Quimper pottery has a long history. Tin-glazed, hand-painted pottery has been made in Quimper, France, since the late 17th century. The earliest firm, founded in 1685 by Jean Baptiste Bousquet, was known as HB Quimper. Another firm, founded in 1772 by Francois Eloury, was known as Porquier. A third firm, founded by Guillaume Dumaine in 1778, was known as HR or Henriot Quimper. All three companies made similar pottery decorated with designs of Breton peasants and sea and flower motifs.

The **Rörstrand** factory made the first faience (tin-glazed earthenware) produced in Sweden. It was established in 1725 by Johann Wolff, near Stockholm.

The earthenware factory of **Salins** was established in 1857 in Salins-les-Bains, near the French border with Switzerland. Salins was awarded the gold medal at the International Exhibition of Decorative Arts in Paris in 1912.

Sarreguemines wares are named for the city in the Lorraine region of northeastern France. The pottery was founded in 1790 by Nicholas-Henri Jacobi. For more than 100 years, it flourished under the direction of the Utzschneider family.

Wilhelm Schiller and Sons, Bodenbach, Bohemia, was established 1885.

Thomas-Victor Sergent was one of the School of Paris ceramists of the late 19th century who was influenced by the works of Bernard Palissy.

St. Clement was founded by Jacques Chambrette in Saint-Clément, France, in 1758. Chambrette also established works in Lunéville.

The **St. Jean de Bretagne** pottery works are located near Quimper, France.

Vallauris is a pottery center in southeastern France, near Cannes. Companies in production there include Massier and Foucard-Jourdan.

Victoria Pottery Co. was located in Hanley, Staffordshire, England, from 1895-1927.

Wardle & Co. was established 1871 at Hanley, Staffordshire, England.

Josiah Wedgwood was born in Burslem, Staffordshire, England, on July 12, 1730, into a family with a long pottery tradition. At the age of nine, after the death of his father, he joined the family business. In 1759, he set up his own pottery works in Burslem. There he produced cream-colored earthenware that found favor with Queen Charlotte. In 1762, she appointed him royal supplier of dinnerware. From the public sale of "Queen's Ware," as it came to be known, Wedgwood was able to build a production community in 1768, which he named Etruria, near Stoke-on-Trent, and a second factory equipped with tools and ovens of his own design. (Etruria is the ancient land of the Etruscans, in what is now northern Italy.)

Courtesy of Clars Auction Gallery,
www.clars.com

▲ French Palissy-style centerpiece, late 19th century, front and back with applied Bacchic masks, each with gaping mouth, flanked by grapevine handles, 12 1/2" high, together with pair of wall brackets, late 19th century, each with putto grasping bulrushes, painted "TS," probably for Thomas Sergent, 10" high. **$1,220**

Courtesy Leslie Hindman Auctioneers,
www.lesliehindman.com

▶ Pair of large figures, gentleman musician and lady, taller one 38 1/2" high. **$750**

Courtesy Leslie Hindman Auctioneers,
www.lesliehindman.com

◀ Jardiniere with leaf motif on white ground, 8 1/4 high, 9 1/4" diameter. **$438**

Pair of Schweidnitz compotes, late 19th/early 20th century, each in form of leafy tree, one depicting leopard attacking flamingo, other depicting heron grasping fish, underside with impressed crowned MK monogram, shield marks, model numbers 381 and 371, each 14" high. **$915**

Pair of Minton urns with ram's head handles, Stoke-on-Trent, Staffordshire, England, 19th century, cobalt blue with Greek key border to spouts, garlands supporting blue cartouches to each side, pedestal bases, marked "M, 30," repair to ram handle, chips to glaze on bases, hairline crack to spout, light crazing, wear commensurate with age, 21 1/2" high. **$3,250**

◄ French figural centerpiece with seaweed texture, 19th century, lozenge-form bowl flanked by swimming maidens with diaphanous covering forming standard above four shell-form dishes, stepped diamond foot, 14 1/2" x 19" x 10". **$625**

Minton vintagers figural sweetmeat dish, Stoke-on-Trent, Staffordshire, England, 1867, male vintager carrying round basket with basket on his back, circular base, marked "MINTON, 375, (date mark), F," fine condition, 16 1/2" high. **$1,625**

Continental rectangular umbrella stand, pierced draped sides with stylized flowers and foliage, 22" high. **$519**

Courtesy of Woody Auction,
www.woodyauction.com

▲ Figural double dolphin head pitcher with strong colors, circa 1870s, marked Brownfield & Son, no chips, cracks or repairs, 11 1/2". **$826**

Courtesy of Heritage Auctions, ha.com

▶ Monumental Italian ewer with bifurcated serpent-form handle, circa 1890, painted continuous battle scene to body, raised on circular foot with putti and shell decoration, missing flakes to lip rim and handle, some craquelure throughout, surface wear commensurate with age, 51" high. **$750**

Courtesy of Woody Auction,
www.woodyauction.com

Etruscan cider pitcher, shell
and seaweed mold, marked,
no chips, cracks or repairs,
5 1/2" x 8 1/2". **$177**

Courtesy of Heritage Auctions, ha.com

French figural jardinière in form of cart pulled
by lion and tiger and driven by pair of putti, 19th
century, raised on naturalistically textured ground
on scroll and shell base, marked with four leaf
clover and "1115," 13" high x 19 1/2" wide x 7 1/2"
deep. **$475**

Courtesy of Heritage Auctions, ha.com

German Wilhelm Schiller & Sons pitcher, circa
1860, bulbous seashells and coral with crawfish
handle, marked "5403, WS&S," surface wear
commensurate with age, repairs to foot and all
lower seashells, 11" high. **$656**

Meissen

Augustus II, Elector of Saxony and King of Poland, founded the Royal Saxon Porcelain Manufactory in Albrechtsburg, Meissen, in 1710. Johann Friedrich Bottger, an alchemist, and Tschirnhaus, a nobleman, experimented with kaolin from the Dresden area to produce porcelain. By 1720, the factory produced a whiter hard-paste porcelain than that from the Far East.

The Meissen factory experienced its golden age from the 1730s to the 1750s. By the 1730s, Meissen employed nearly 100 workers. It became known for its porcelain sculptures; Meissen dinnerware also won acclaim.

The Meissen factory was destroyed and looted by the forces of Frederick the Great during the Seven Years' War (1756-1763). It was reopened later but never achieved its former greatness. By the early 1800s, Meissen's popularity began to wane. In the 19th century, the factory reissued some of its earlier forms.

Many marks were used by the Meissen factory. The famous crossed swords mark was adopted in 1724. The swords mark with a small dot between the hilts was used from 1763 to 1774, and the mark with a star between the hilts from 1774 to 1814.

Courtesy of Skinner, Inc., www.skinnerinc.com

Box with gilt-metal mounts and high-relief polychrome allegorical scenes, second half 19th century, minor chips on edge of base, high-relief scenes in good condition, 7 1/2" high x 12" wide. $7,380

Courtesy of Skinner, Inc., www.skinnerinc.com

Four porcelain figures of garden children, late 19th to 20th century, each polychrome enamel-decorated and gilt-accented, with first quality crossed swords mark, boy with rake, incised "10," boy with hoe and basket of flowers, incised "11," and two girls collecting apples in their aprons, incised "12," height to 5 5/8". **$1,046**

Courtesy of John Moran Auctioneers, www.johnmoran.com

Figural group depicting drunken Silenus atop donkey, with Bacchus and cherub and bacchante feeding donkey grapes, late 19th/early 20th century, on integral base with gilt-highlighted rocaille surround, likely modeled in 1760 by Friedrich Elias Meyer, underglaze blue crossed swords mark, incised model number "2724" and impressed "21," marked with overglaze painter's mark "4.," 8 1/4" high x 8 1/2" wide x 4 1/2" deep. **$1,320**

Courtesy Leslie Hindman Auctioneers,
www.lesliehindman.com

Figural centerpiece with pierced oval floral- and shell-decorated bowl on standard in form of woman and man gathering flowers, gilt-decorated rocaille base with blue crossed swords mark in underglaze, 18 3/4" high. **$813**

Courtesy of Clars Auction Gallery, www.clars.com

Pair of "Snowball" fruit-decorated urns, 19th century, each with floral-encrusted finial surmounting bulbous body with fruit and bird-form reserves, underside with blue crossed swords mark, 17 1/2" high x 9" wide. **$1,830**

Courtesy of Clars Auction Gallery, www.clars.com

Figural Bolognese dog, after model by Kändler, dog seated with scrolled curls and hand-painted features, marked with blue crossed swords, 9" high. **$1,342**

Courtesy of Woody Auction, www.woodyauction.com

Figure of woman seated on two baskets with floral highlights, blue crossed swords mark, no chips, cracks, or repairs, 4 1/2" x 5 1/2". **$354**

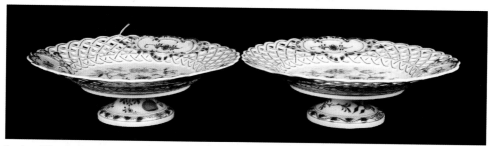

Courtesy of Clars Auction Gallery, www.clars.com

Pair of blue and white footed compotes, each with latticework bowl, 3" high, 9 1/2" diameter. **$275**

Courtesy of Clars Auction Gallery, www.clars.com

Pate-sur-pate lidded potpourri urn, 19th century, with gilded wreath and ribbon finial surmounting pierced lid, floral reticulated band above gilt acanthus and ribbon rim, classical urn-form blue body with applied gilt twisted snake handles, centering oval medallion with pate-sur-pate cherub en grisaille, with gilt frame, on flared standard with gilt laurel leaf edge and square plinth with gilt accents, blue underglaze crossed swords mark and impressed numbers "20 19 26," 11" high x 5 1/2" wide. **$4,575**

Courtesy of Skinner, Inc., www.skinnerinc.com

Fourteen assembled porcelain monkey band figures, 19th and 20th century, each polychrome enamel- and gilt-decorated, with crossed swords and other various marks, three choral singers, keyboardist, harpist, cellist, hurdy-gurdy player, bagpiper, flutist, drummer, mandolinist, violinist, clarinetist, and bassoonist, 4 3/4" to 5 3/4" high, together with Meissen-type conductor, flutist, clarinetist, choral singer, and five music stands. **$7,995**

Courtesy of Jeffrey S. Evans & Associates, www.jeffreysevans.com

Two figures, blue and white example of seated winged putti in domestic setting holding coffee grinder, other of two cherubs, one holding grapes, on circular plinth base, 19th/20th century, underglaze blue crossed swords mark and incised/impressed numbers to each base, blue and white example undamaged, 5 1/2" high, other with professional restoration to figures. **$518**

Courtesy of Clars Auction Gallery, www.clars.com

Pair of urns in Neoclassical style with gadrooned gilt rims above cobalt bodies with entwined snake handles, each on circular fluted and gilded base, marked with underglaze blue crossed swords, 11" high x 6" wide. **$854**

Courtesy of Skinner, Inc., www.skinnerinc.com

Figural mantel clock, late 19th century, enameled and gilded with cherub seated to one side of rectangular case with lovebird finial and floral and foliate festoons, enameled clock face inscribed "Exam.d by / Lund & Blockley / 42 Pall Mall / London," big toe missing from extended foot, end of bow missing, chipping to petals of flowers on floral festoon, one foot reglued, 12" high. **$1,476**

Polychrome parrot in yellow, green, blue, and red holding cherries in his talons, on stump with flowers, late 19th century/first quarter 20th century, factory marks, restorations surrounding base along foot rim, 17" high. **$3,075**

Large elements ewer, "Air," circa 1880, after 18th century models by Johann Kändler (1706-1776), decorated in high relief, lip and foot encircled with polychrome feathers, drapery handle surmounted by putti, body of painted and high-relief clouds with figure of Juno with peacock and Zephyr, factory marks, inscribed "327," old and discolored repairs, 26 1/2" high. **$8,610**

Courtesy of Clars Auction Gallery, www.clars.com

Urn with stylized gilt-accented snake-form handles above Classical-form body centered with hand-painted pansies, on circular base, 19" high. **$976**

Set of 23 pieces of Meissen, circa mid-20th century, coffeepot (10 1/2" high x 10" wide x 5 1/2" deep), teapot (7" high x 8 3/4" wide x 6" deep), rectangular two-handled platter (11 3/4" wide x 6" deep), sugar bowl (4 3/4" high, 4" diameter), milk jug (5" high x 4 3/4" wide x 3 1/4" deep), six teacups (3 1/8" high x 4 1/2" wide x 3 3/4" deep), six saucers (6 1/2" diameter), and six dessert plates (7 3/4" diameter), each hand-painted with floral sprays within white ground reserves, bordered by raised gilt decoration over cobalt, coffeepot and teapot each with dragon's-head spout, each piece with blue underglaze crossed swords mark. **$5,000**

Porcelain figural group, circa 1940, marked with crossed swords in blue underglaze and "47, F. 93," 5 7/8" high. **$475**

Courtesy of Skinner, Inc., www.skinnerinc.com

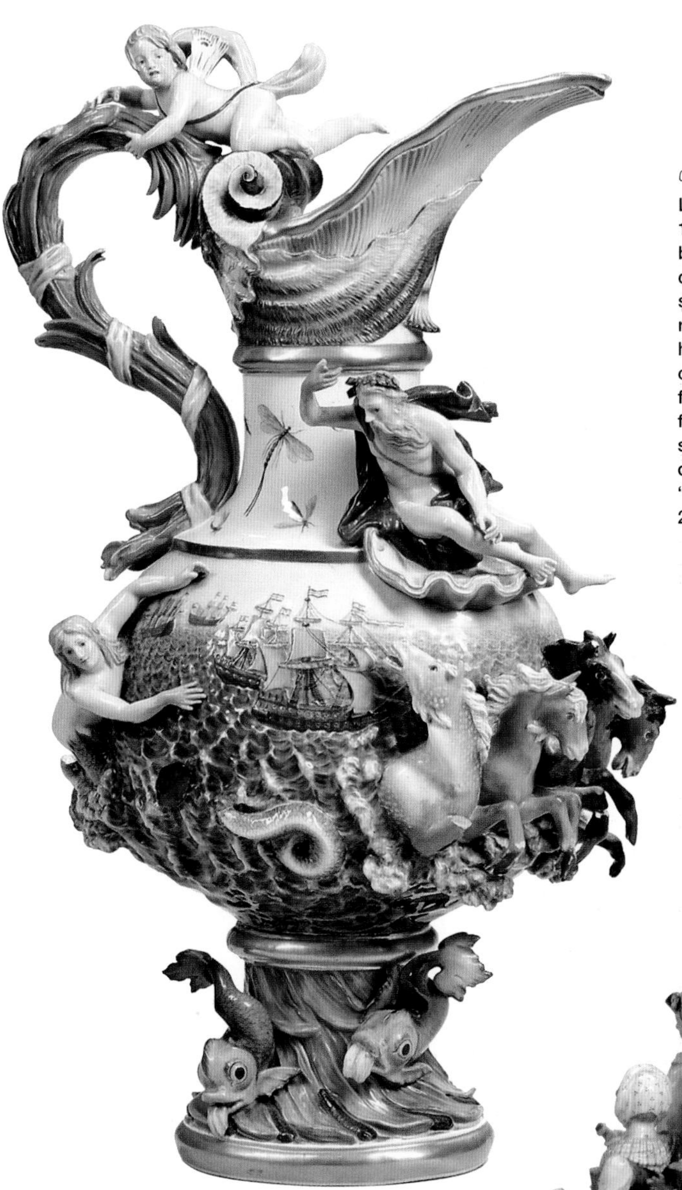

Large elements ewer, "Water," circa 1880, after 18th century models by Johann Kändler (1706-1776), decorated in high relief, mouth with shell decoration and winged putto resting on ribbon-tied seaweed handle, fleet of ships and sea creatures encircling waist, with flanking Nereid and Neptune in shell-form chariot drawn by Hippocampi, spreading foot with dolphin decoration, factory marks, inscribed "320," old and discolored repairs, 26 1/2" high. **$7,995**

Courtesy of Skinner, Inc., www.skinnerinc.com

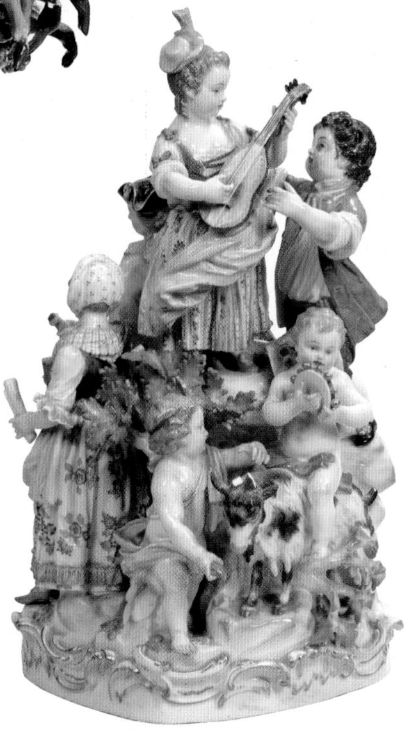

Figural group of musicians, circa 1924-1934, pyramidal-form polychrome figures with woman playing mandolin, man with violin, cherub with tambourine, and goat with missing horns at base, scattered losses on foliage throughout, 14 1/2" high. **$1,476**

Sèvres

Some of the most desirable porcelain ever produced was made at the Sèvres factory, originally established at Vincennes, France, and transferred, through permission of Madame de Pompadour, to Sèvres as the Royal Manufactory about the middle of the 18th century. King Louis XV took sole responsibility for the works in 1759, when production of hard paste wares began. Between 1850 and 1900, many biscuit and soft-paste pieces were made again. Fine early pieces are scarce and high-priced. Many of those available today are late productions. The various Sèvres marks have been copied, and pieces in the "Sèvres style" are similar to actual Sèvres wares but not necessarily from that factory.

Courtesy of Fontaine's Auction Gallery, fontainesauction.com

Pair of monumental covered urns with cobalt and gilt borders, mythical male heads with ram horns on sides, four oval porcelain-relief decorated panels with putti, domical lids with pinecone finials and bronze bases, signed with Sèvres mark under base, one lid repaired, repair to bowl-form body of one urn below one figural head, other urn body with hairlines and one horn repaired, 30" high. **$8,168**

Six hand-painted porcelain cabinet plates, each with gilt bands flanking mauve border surrounding central floral medallion, underside with conjoined L mark with Sèvres in center, 9 1/4" wide. **$23,180**

Covered low bowl with cylindrical handle above circular lid with reserve of putti, base with gilt floral swags and polychrome floral sprays on red, white, and green ground, marked on underside, 6" high. **$915**

Courtesy of Clars Auction Gallery, www.clars.com

Monumental porcelain urn with dore bronze mounts, 19th century, lid with artichoke finial above floral reserves on turquoise ground, body with scene of courting couple in bucolic setting on one side and landscape on other, flanked by high-relief acanthus mounts, circular foot with floral reserves on turquoise ground, gilt plinth, signed Maxant, 38" high, 11" diameter.
$6,100

Courtesy of Mark Mussio, Humler & Nolan, www.humlernolan.com

◀ Pair of porcelain vases from 1894 in teal and blue, marked with circular "Decore A Sèvres 94" ink stamp logo and number S 94, excellent condition with minor wear to gold trim at rim and base, each 9 1/2" high. **$545**

Courtesy of Fontaine's Auction Gallery, fontainesauction.com

▼ Pair of porcelain urns with pierced handles and domical lids with finials, early 19th century, painted panels on front with scenes of Cupid and woman, floral painted panels on back with green-decorated body with gilt highlights and borders, excellent condition with no chips or hairlines, 12 1/2" high. **$3,025**

Pair of porcelain dessert plates painted with border of florettes between gilt bands above view of Maleherbes or Villebon, within etched gilt banderole, blue printed factory marks with name of view in puce, various initials to underside near foot, signed Julienne in red, dated 1828, 9 1/4" diameter. **$173**

Pair of compotes with allover gilt and floral decoration, each with pierced rim above flared stem on square base, 6" high. **$188**

Courtesy of Clars Auction Gallery, www.clars.com

Pair of signed Sèvres covered urns, 19th century, with gilt brass lids with acorn finials surmounting long necks with raised gilt decoration above urn-form bodies painted in round with scenes of 18th century courtiers relaxing in bucolic landscapes on rose pink grounds, flared standards with raised gilt decoration and shaped gilt brass plinths, signed F. Garnier, 16" high, 6 1/2" diameter. **$1,220**

Courtesy of Clars Auction Gallery,
www.clars.com

Monumental signed
porcelain urn with
dore bronze mounts,
body with scenic river
landscape, reverse
decorated with classical
partially nude woman
surrounded by putti,
circular foot, 36" high.
$4,880

Courtesy Neal Auction, www.nealauction.com

Polychrome porcelain plateau painted with Louis XVI in center surrounded by eight portrait busts of court beauties, 19th/20th century, interlaced Ls mark, ringed base with sitter's names, 19 7/8" diameter. **$960**

Courtesy of Rago Arts and Auctions, www.ragoarts.com

Porcelain gourd-shaped pitcher by artist Leon Kann, 1900, triangular Sèvres mark, 1900, incised letters and numbers, 8" x 6" x 5". **$1,125**

Courtesy Leslie Hindman Auctioneers, www.lesliehindman.com
Gilt bronze-mounted porcelain urn (front and back shown), 36" high. **$8,125**

Wedgwood

In 1754, Josiah Wedgwood and Thomas Whieldon of Fenton Vivian, Staffordshire, England, became partners in a pottery enterprise. Their products included marbled, agate, tortoiseshell, green glaze, and Egyptian black wares.

In 1759, Wedgwood opened his own pottery at the Ivy House works, Burslem. In 1764, he moved to the Brick House (Bell Works) at Burslem. The pottery concentrated on utilitarian pieces.

Between 1766 and 1769, Wedgwood built the famous works at Etruria. Among the most-renowned products of this plant were the Empress Catherina of Russia dinner service (1774) and the Portland Vase (1790s). The firm also made caneware, unglazed earthenwares (drabwares), piecrust wares, variegated and marbled wares, black basalt (developed in 1768), Queen's or creamware, and Jasperware (perfected in 1774).

Bone china was produced under the direction of Josiah Wedgwood II between 1812 and 1822, and was revived in 1878. Moonlight Lustre was made from 1805 to 1815. Fairyland Lustre began in 1920. All Lustre production ended in 1932.

A museum was established at the Etruria pottery in 1906. When Wedgwood moved to its modern plant at Barlaston, North Staffordshire, the museum was expanded.

Courtesy of Skinner, Inc.,
www.skinnerinc.com

Black basalt encaustic-decorated sauceboat, early 19th century, oval, with loop handles, cream and red-decorated anthemion band, impressed mark, 8 1/2" long. **$1,169**

▲ Pearlware peafowl plate with press-molded scallop-shell rim, circa 1800-1820, painted with cobalt blue band above long-tailed peafowl painted in blue, ocher, orange, and brown on curling brown branch, surrounded by green-sponged foliage, impressed WEDGWOOD, 7 3/4" diameter. **$690**

▶ Two-handled cabinet vase and cover, circa 1900, vase of campana shape on square stepped base, domed cover with inverted onion knop, painted turquoise blue with raised paste gold rouletted floral swags and garlands, molded with neoclassical leaves and anthemia to cover and waist, gilt knop, handles, bands, etc., brown urn mark to underside, excellent undamaged condition, 8 1/2" high. **$460**

Courtesy of Woody Auction, www.woodyauction.com

Four majolica plates, cobalt blue, green, and yellow tones with reticulated edges, circa 1870s, marked, no chips, cracks, or repairs, 9". **$413**

Courtesy of Skinner, Inc., www.skinnerinc.com

Majolica bee-form matchbox and cover, 1878, back and wings formed as cover with striker underneath, impressed mark, very good condition throughout with no cracks, chips, or restorations, 5" long. **$5,228**

Courtesy of Skinner, Inc., www.skinnerinc.com

▲ Black basalt bacchanalian sacrifice plaque, late 18th/early 19th century, rectangular, with figures in relief, impressed mark, set in giltwood frame, sight 8 1/4" x 19 3/4". **$3,444**

Courtesy of Skinner, Inc.,
www.skinnerinc.com

▶ Gilded and bronzed black basalt teapot and cover, late 19th century, oval shape with ball finial and various foliate relief, impressed mark, 6 1/2" high. **$5,228**

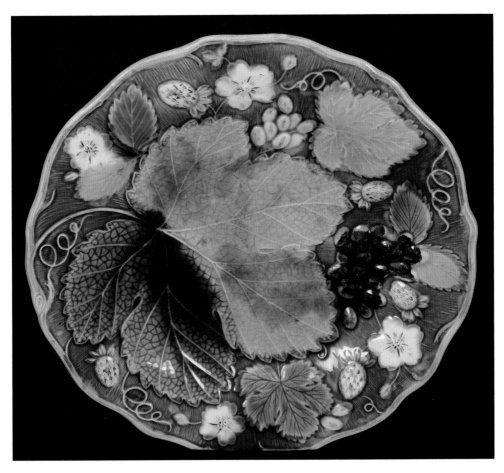

Pedestal majolica cake plate with embossed fruit and leaf décor, marked, no chips, cracks, or repairs, 2" x 8 3/4". **$236**

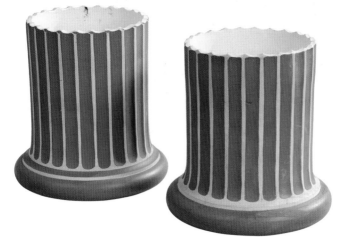

Pair of Wedgwood & Bentley white terracotta biscuit pillar vases, circa 1775, cylindrical fluted bodies with rosso antico slip, glazed interiors, impressed marks, one with black stain spots, 4 7/8" high. **$4,920**

Courtesy of Skinner, Inc.; www.skinnerinc.com

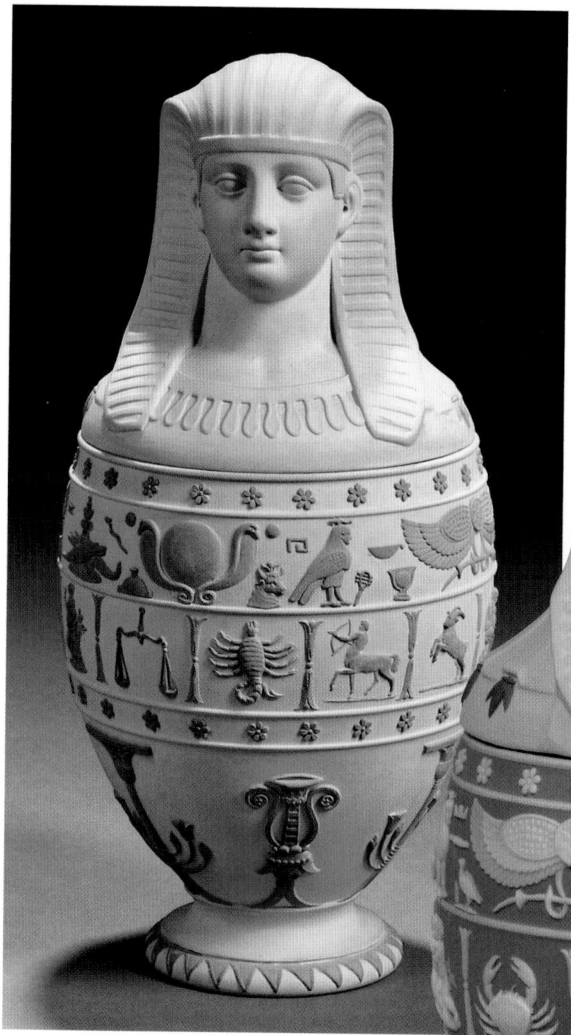

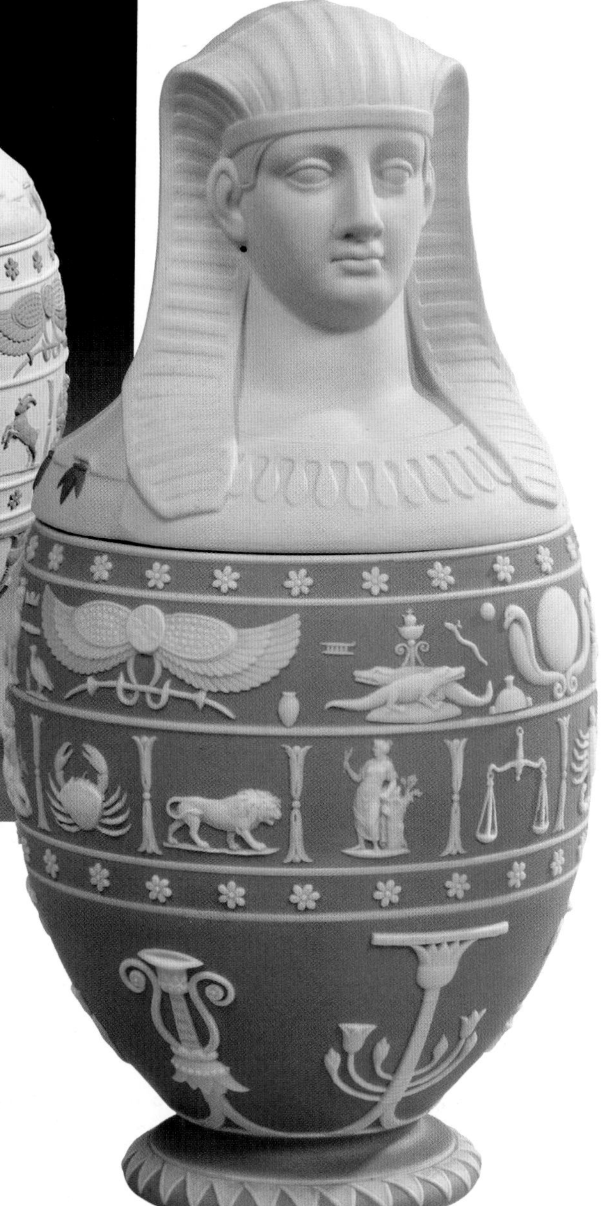

▲ Caneware canopic jar and cover, England, 19th century, applied blue-gray bands of hieroglyphs and zodiac symbols above Egyptian motifs, impressed mark, 10 1/4" high. **$6,765**

Courtesy of Skinner, Inc., www.skinnerinc.com

▶ Green Jasper dip canopic jar and cover, 19th century, applied white bands of hieroglyphs and zodiac symbols in white relief, impressed mark, 9 1/2" high. **$7,995**

Courtesy of James D. Julia Auctioneers, Fairfield, Maine, www.jamesdjulia.com

Fairyland Lustre commemorative plaque in Enchanted Palace pattern of white palace with long torchlit stairway leading to palace with large tree to side with snake climbing tree toward bird nest with chicks, imps, and gnomes looking on, marked on back "The Enchanted Palace Based upon original Wedgwood Design in Fairyland Lustre Produced in 1922, No. 167 in Limited Edition of 250, Wedgwood Bone China Made in England," in gold and silver frame, very good to excellent condition, 9 3/8" wide x 13" high including frame. **$5,333**

Fairyland Lustre Melba center bowl decorated on exterior in Garden of Paradise pattern against pink sky, interior of bowl decorated in Jumping Fawn pattern, signed on underside with Portland vase mark "MADE IN ENGLAND Z-4968," very good to excellent condition, 8" diameter. **$7,110**

Fairyland Lustre punch bowl, England, circa 1920, pattern Z5481 with flame sky to Woodland Elves III exterior, interior with Jumping Faun, printed mark, patches of interior wear and glaze abrasions, 9 3/8" diameter. **$5,400**

Courtesy of Skinner, Inc., www.skinnerinc.com

Majolica game pie dish and cover, circa 1871, oval shape with molded rabbit finial and dead game, fruiting grapevine festoons, insert liner, impressed mark, liner with glaze loss to rim, dish with glaze loss to areas of highest relief, 9 1/2" long. **$984**

Courtesy of James D. Julia Auctioneers, Fairfield, Maine, www.jamesdjulia.com

Fairyland Lustre Imperial bowl with Flight of Birds pattern encircling bottom with mottled green medallion with gilded flowers, inside rim decorated with band of multicolored bubbles, exterior with band of white Flight of Birds pattern with gilded detail, birds flying against shaded background of green, red, and yellow against mottled blue glaze, signed on underside with gold Portland vase mark "Wedgwood England Z5088," very good to excellent condition, 8 3/4" diameter. **$4,740**

Children's Books

By Noah Fleisher

NOAH FLEISHER received his Bachelor of Fine Arts degree from New York University and brings more than a decade of newspaper, magazine, book, antiques and art experience to his position as Public Relations Director of Heritage Auctions, one of the country's foremost auction houses. He is the former editor of *Antique Trader*, *New England Antiques Journal* and *Northeast Antiques Journal*, is the author of *Warman's Modern Furniture* and co-author of *Collecting Children's Books*, and has been a longtime contributor to *Warman's Antiques & Collectibles*.

To accurately encompass the entire scope of children's books is impossible, let's just get that out of the way. To fully illustrate the form you would need an encyclopedia. While this is not that, it should give you a good snapshot the children's book market for 2017. Armed with the knowledge I hope you can glean here and your own natural curiosity, the journey before you should unfold with the inherent delight of the subject matter itself.

Collecting children's books as an adult is a trip back through time and childhood. Hopefully more than a few people who read this – and have no experience in the collecting marketplace – will see something that piques their interest and decide to pursue it further. To me, that is the very essence of collecting: pursuing something because it *speaks* to you.

Values and value ranges have been assigned to the images you'll see here, and they have been culled from auction results in the years leading up to the publication of this volume. They are not meant to be a strict price guide that stridently quantifies every dog-ear and split spine. There are variations on first editions, first printings, signed volumes and author inscriptions – all things that can affect the value of a given book. Above all, however, it has to be about the chase, it has to be because it *speaks* to you.

Collecting is an emotional pursuit. Ask the experts and they will tell you: If you don't love it, don't go after it. This holds true with children's books. If this section is your entrée into the marketplace, have fun, but make sure to do your due diligence when it comes to buying.

It always a good idea to get to know dealers and collectors, to find shows and auctions and attend them. Ask questions. Any good auctioneer or dealer will be happy to spend as much time with you as you are willing to spend. Their level of accessibility will rise with your interest and enthusiasm.

Courtesy of Justin Benttinen/PBA Galleries,
www.pbagalleries.com

How The Grinch Stole Christmas by Dr.
Seuss, 1957, Random House, New York,
illustrated throughout by author, first
edition, first printing. **$390**

The best examples of first edition children's literature, where the biggest names are concerned, is still a competitive market and one that requires a solid foundation to make the right choices. Meanwhile, however, at the lower and mid-levels of the market, there are simply a ton of great books waiting to be discovered, and at bargain prices. If you are focused, willing to invest the time to learn what's out there and what to pay for it, there's a broad world of charming books awaiting.

What do you look for in first edition kids' lit, besides the titles you love?

"Three words: Condition, condition, condition," said James Gannon, Director of Rare Books at Heritage Auctions. "Does it have its original dust jacket? Is it signed or inscribed? Is it in good shape or is it torn? Is the hardback cover in good condition? Are the corners bent or shredded? Are the pages dog-eared? Does it have all the pages in it and, most importantly, does it say 'first printing' on that title page?"

The Auction Archives at PBA Galleries in San Francisco (pbagalleries.com), Bloomsbury in London (bloomsbury.com), and liveauctioneers.com or Heritage Auctions (ha.com) are good places to start any search and to get a good sense of price and condition. Mainstream booksellers like Barnes & Noble, Half-Price Books, and Powell's Books (Portland, Oregon) all feature good first edition kids' lit and can give you a good idea of what the retail value is on a given title. Smart collectors or would-be collectors are all also well-served to check out online booksellers like alibris.com, biblio.com, and abebooks.com.

Any and all of the above are enough to give you a sense of what's out there and, hopefully, a good bead on that signed first-edition *Harry Potter* you've been coveting since your kids starting reading the books.

A last word of advice from Gannon to the neophyte: This is a true buyer's market right now.

"In the end, I would urge any new collector to find a dealer or an auctioneer that you trust and have a good rapport with," said Gannon. "There has been and will continue to be a proliferation of small auction houses selling collections of good books. This is a side effect of the closing of so many brick and mortar stores due to current market conditions."

This means patience, it means not rushing out immediately and buying from the top auctioneers and dealers in the field as they tend to be on the expensive side. A good relationship with a reputable dealer is desirable, but there are many tools available to speed along an education.

"Find offerings that others are missing," said Gannon. "With a computer you can do this from home mostly by looking at auctions and specialty sites and using want lists and keywords to get what you want. The fun comes in getting a great kid's book before anyone else and paying much less for the effort."

For more information on children's books, see *Collecting Children's Books* by Noah Fleisher and Lauren Zittle (Krause Publications, 2015).

Courtesy of Justin Benttinen/PBA Galleries, www.pbagalleries.com

Where the Wild Things Are by Maurice Sendak, New York: Harper & Row, 1963: first edition, first issue jacket with $3.50 price intact and no mention of Caldecott Medal on jacket flaps and no metallic medal sticker on front of jacket. **$8,400**

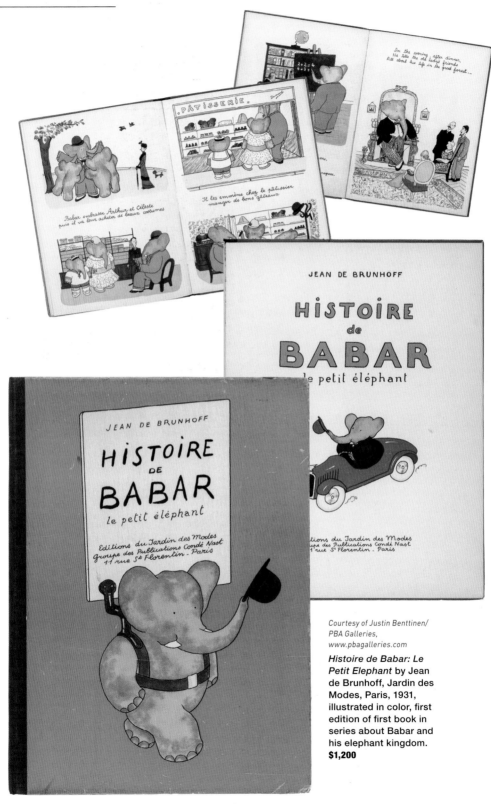

*Courtesy of Justin Benttinen/
PBA Galleries,
www.pbagalleries.com*

**Histoire de Babar: Le
Petit Elephant** by Jean
de Brunhoff, Jardin des
Modes, Paris, 1931,
illustrated in color, first
edition of first book in
series about Babar and
his elephant kingdom.
$1,200

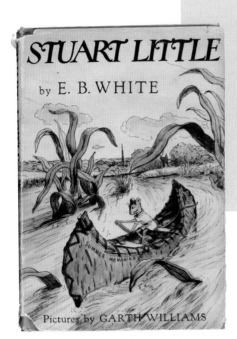

Courtesy of Heritage Auctions, ha.com

Stuart Little by E.B. White, New York: Harper & Brothers, 1945: first edition, first printing, inscribed by White on half-title page, "For Max / from E B White," illustrated by Garth Williams and signed by him in pencil on lower margin of frontispiece. **$3,500**

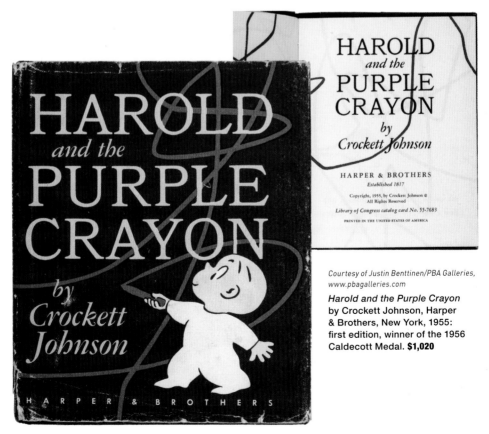

Courtesy of Justin Benttinen/PBA Galleries, www.pbagalleries.com

Harold and the Purple Crayon by Crockett Johnson, Harper & Brothers, New York, 1955: first edition, winner of the 1956 Caldecott Medal. **$1,020**

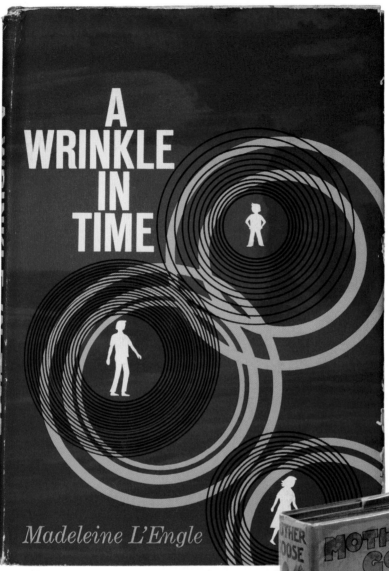

Courtesy of Heritage Auctions, ha.com

A Wrinkle in Time by Madeline L'Engle, New York: Ariel Books/Farrar, Straus and Cudahy, 1962: first edition, first printing with bookplate signed by author laid in, Newberry winner. **$3,500**

Courtesy of Justin Benttinen/PBA Galleries, www.pbagalleries.com

Mother Goose's Nursery Rhymes by Walter Jerrold, Blackie & Sons Limited, London, 1909: illustrations include frontispiece by John Hassall, English artist known for poster designs and advertisements. **$540**

Courtesy of Justin Benttinen/
PBA Galleries, www.pbagalleries.com

▲ *The Story of Ferdinand* by Leaf Munro, The Viking Press, New York, 1936: first edition. **$5,700**

Courtesy of Heritage Auctions, ha.com

◄ *Flotsam* by David Wiesner, New York: Clarion Books, 2006: no edition stated, signed by author on title page, Caldecott Medal winner, signed. **$15**

Courtesy of Justin Benttinen/PBA Galleries

Green Eggs and Ham by Dr. Seuss, 1960: first London edition. **$938**

Courtesy of Justin Benttinen/PBA Galleries, www.pbagalleries.com

The Cat in the Hat by Dr. Seuss, Random House, New York, 1957: first edition, first Dr. Seuss book specifically targeted for beginning readers that kicked off Beginner Books series. **$2,400**

◄ *And to Think That I Saw it on Mulberry Street* by Dr. Seuss, Vanguard Press, New York, 1937: first edition, first issue with boy in white shorts on front cover of volume and on dust jacket (versus blue shorts of later issues), Seuss's first book. **$1,920**

▲ *The Story About Ping* by Marjorie Flack, 1933, Viking Press, New York, illustrations by Kurt Wiese, first edition. **$780**

The Brownies Around the World by Palmer Cox, Century Co., New York, late 1800s/early 1900s: first edition, fourth book in Brownies series, inscribed by Cox on front free endpaper with small sketch of brownie, inscription dated 1908. **$330**

Courtesy of Heritage Auctions, ha.com

Curious George by H.A. Rey, Boston: Houghton Mifflin, 1941: first edition, original dust jacket with $1.75 price, near fine condition, scarce. **$26,290**

Princess Badoura: A Tale from the Arabian Nights by Laurence Housman, illustrated by Edmund Dulac, Hodder and Stoughton, London, 1913. **$510**

The Fairy Tales of the Brothers Grimm, illustrated by Arthur Rackham, Constable and Co., London, 1909: translated by Mrs. Edgar Lucas, illustrated by Arthur Rackham, 40 tipped-in color plates, first trade edition. **$480**

Courtesy of Justin Benttinen/PBA Galleries, www.pbagalleries.com

Millions of Cats by Wanda Ga'g, Coward McCann, New York, 1928: No. 184 of 250 copies, first edition with original signed woodcut by Ga'g laid in, as issued, signed by author/illustrator at limitation statement, winner of Newberry Honor award in 1929. *Millions of Cats* has remained in print since its initial publication, the oldest American picture book to claim this. **$7,200**

Courtesy of Justin Benttinen/ PBA Galleries, www.pbagalleries.com

Outside Over There by Maurice Sendak, Harper & Row, New York, 1981: first edition, signed by author on front free endpaper. **$150**

Courtesy of Heritage Auctions, ha.com

Officer Buckle and Gloria by Peggy Rathman, Putnam, 1995: later printing, signed and inscribed by author, Caldecott Medal winner. **$15**

Courtesy of Heritage Auctions, ha.com

The Cricket in Times Square by George Selden, New York: Ariel Books/Farrar, Straus and Cudahy, 1960: first edition, first printing, illustrations by Garth Williams. **$388**

Civil War Collectibles

By Noah Fleisher

NOAH FLEISHER received his Bachelor of Fine Arts degree from New York University and brings more than a decade of newspaper, magazine, book, antiques and art experience to his position as Public Relations Director of Heritage Auctions, one of the country's foremost auction houses. He is the former editor of *Antique Trader, New England Antiques Journal* and *Northeast Antiques Journal,* is the author of *Warman's Modern Furniture* and co-author of *Collecting Children's Books,* and has been a longtime contributor to *Warman's Antiques & Collectibles.*

The Civil War, in its way, was the single most important event in American history. The nation's tortured relationship with slavery and abolition was kicked down the road by every founding father and every president until Lincoln had the courage to stand up to and stop it.

The ramifications of the conflict still play out today, though an increasingly large segment of the population has less and less familiarity with the particulars. Films like Spielberg's 2012 epic *Lincoln* help keep the conflict current in the broadest sense, but the true scope of the war, its players and battles, its massive reach and devastating effects, requires a healthy intellectual curiosity and the time to nurture it.

The War Between the States also left behind a rich material history to bolster any study of the era. From uniforms to guns to photographs, writings and various printed ephemera, the field of Civil War collecting is vast and intricate, with pieces from most every corner of the war available to serious collecting.

The market of Civil War collecting is a market, however, that is somewhat in flux.

Prices are down from a decade or two ago, when common and mid-range pieces were bringing high prices, respective to their previous comparables, and the very best material – those things tied to big names in the war, or important regiments, with impeccable provenance – were simply exorbitant.

Things seemed to reach a bottom of sorts a few years ago and now, as we mark the sesquicentennial of the war's end, the best material is experiencing a balancing out, perhaps even a comeback. No matter how you come at it, there are good opportunities if you know where to look.

"The Civil War market is evolving to meet the demands of a changing collector base," said Eric Smylie, noted historian and an expert in Civil War and Arms & Militaria at Heritage

Courtesy of Case Antiques - Auctions & Appraisers, caseantiques.com

Confederate CSS Shenandoah ship diary archive of Lieutenant Dabney Scales: 1865 diary journal (85 pages, 104 pages total), ambrotype and CDV of Scales in uniform, CDV of Shenandoah, and author-signed book/pamplet titled, "Cruises of the Confederate States Steamers Shenandoah" and "Nashville" by Captain William C. Whittle, 1910. The CSS Shenandoah fired the last shot of the Civil War and marked the final surrender of Confederate forces on Nov. 6, 1865. $16,500

Auctions. "Most dealers and collectors have finally realized that if the market is going to grow and thrive, they need to cultivate a new generation of collectors to follow the current generation. The prospects for that happening are very good, even if it will be a smaller number of collectors. I've seen movement in the last few years of collectors from other areas moving into the Civil War market. They're generally buying high-quality, identified, and unique pieces."

The exuberance of a decade ago has worn off and with it, for several years, the exuberance of collectors, which – as Smylie points out – has led to a contracted market and a generation of collectors that was almost passed over altogether. As current trends at auction seem to indicate, however, there is a younger generation of collectors (men and women in their 30s and 40s) beginning to show interest in the history. The prices also support Smylie's observation that the pool is smaller and that they are interested in paying good money for top-level material and let the bottom fall away.

"The market shows sustained strength of late led by high quality, well-provenanced weapons, uniforms, and more showy equipment," Smylie said. "The more common material, bullets, run-of-the mill cartridge boxes, U.S. belt plates, and ephemera have suffered in recent years."

The prices realized on the images that follow certainly seem to bear this out.

While the overall market, at the top end, follows the truism that quality will always sell, smart collectors would indeed do well to look at the more generic parts of the market because there are sure to be good deals on the areas that have "suffered," plenty of which are more than sufficient to start a collection, bolster an existing grouping, or hook a beginner who doesn't have the discretionary income yet to go after the big stuff.

Items of Civil War Capt. Watson W. Bush: Union frock coat and pants; period photograph of him in uniform, 4 3/4" x 2 3/4"; Remington & Sons pistol, Ilion, New York, New Model, Pat. Sept. 14, 1858; original holster, belt, and eagle buckle; Spencer Repeating Rifle Co. carbine, Boston; eagle, brass hilted sword, etched; rifle, marked Potsdam, Co. B 20, #19580, 2B, 12, 1R; cartridge belt and strap with eagle brass plate; cartridge box and brass eagle buckle; gloves, horse's bit and spurs; leather and brass sword straps; platoon map and books, *Cavalry Tactics*, Vol. 1-3, *Manual of Arms for 10th NY Cavalry*; field desk and contents; diaries, Bible; revised "Regulations and for the Army," 1861; instructions to mustering officers; and other items. **$29,000**

"Indeed there are always opportunities," said Smylie. "There are many older collections coming on the market right now. You'll often see the large collections accompanied by fanfare, but there are smaller collections, with good material, coming out of rural attics and suburban cellars and quietly slipping onto the market. Finding that hidden or overlooked treasure is often a matter of knowledge and lots of luck."

Most any Civil War dealer or auctioneer worth his salt is going to be happy to spend some time with you if you are new to the market, or thinking of getting back in after staying away for a while, and neophyte collectors should find someone they like and trust. That, coupled with some time spent in self-erudition on what you like – North? South? Uniforms? Correspondence? Battlefield artifacts? – should lead you into a very rewarding and infinitely fascinating area.

"Study the items that interest you before you buy," said Smylie. "Go to shows, touch the material, ask questions, carefully read auction catalogs, and follow the prices realized prices. Buy from well-established and reputable dealers and auction houses, as they will stand by the material they sell. In time, you will recognize a genuine piece from a reproduction in a booth bulging with items."

"To all collectors, perhaps the best advice is to buy the best you can afford," added Smylie. "Don't try to save a few dollars by purchasing a faded or repaired item if a better one is available. Buying quality is always better than settling for something less."

More than 650,000 soldiers died in the brutal bloodshed of the Civil War, in fighting that was obviously horrifying to endure and still shocking to learn about. The war nearly destroyed America and helped forge the Union as it is today – infinitely diverse and prone to disagreement, as ever, but decidedly united when push comes to shove.

The artifacts of the conflict carry that heavy history; the rifle a soldier carried into battle, or the coarse wool tunic that provided scant protection from cold and was suffocating in the heat, they tie us to our past and thrill us with their immediacy to such a charged and important moment in time.

The important material is out there, waiting to be appreciated, 250 years after its intended purpose expired. Now it is waiting for a new generation to make it new again.

Courtesy of Sotheby's, www.sothebys.com

Monument by sculptor David Richards (American, 1828-1897), dedicated in 1885 to honor Enfield, Connecticut's Civil War heroes, bronze with natural green oxidation, signed "D. RICHARDS / SCULPT / 1879" and "M.J. POWER / BRONZE FOUNDRY, N.Y.," 6' 9". $68,750

Abraham Lincoln presidential
document dated Feb. 23, 1863,
Civil War appointment, partially
printed on vellum, from office
of The President of the United
States of America: "... reposing
special trust and confidence
in the patriotism, valor, fidelity,
and abilities of Orrin E. Davis,
I ... appoint him Second
Lieutenant in the Eighteenth
Regiment of Infantry," signed by
Lincoln and Edwin M. Stanton,
his Secretary of War, very
good condition with evidence
of folds, darkening in spots,
label on back states it was
professionally conserved and
framed in conservation clear UV
protected glass, 18" x 13 1/2",
25 1/2" x 21" in frame. **$5,000**

Brass gunnery caliper, engraved "Franklin
Buchanan," stamped "LIEUT M. THOMAS
U.S. ORDNANCE. FRANKFORT PA. 1819," 7".
Buchanan was an admiral in the Confederate
Navy during the Civil War. He was captain of
the ironclad CSS Virginia (formerly the USS
Merrimack) during the Battle of Merrimack,
March 1862. **$11,000**

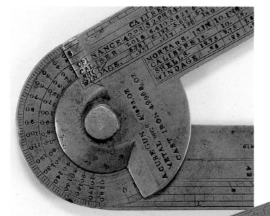

▲ Officer's pork pie slouch hat belonging to Col.
George W. Roberts, killed in action at Stone's River,
Tennessee, in December 1862; polished silk lining,
manufactured for Gadfley, Porter & Co., Nashville,
embroidered infantry insignia on front, general's
star inset with embroidered Jeff Davis insignia on
left side pinning up hat, right side retains officer's
plumes with infantry officer's cockade attaching it to
hat with officer's netted hat cords underneath, wide
sweat band; near mint condition, silk lining partially
detached. **$7,000**

Double-breasted colonel's frock coat
belonging to George W. Roberts of
42nd Regiment of Illinois Volunteers,
identified on inside collar "Col. Roberts
February 11th, 1862," missing two
Infantry officer buttons, polished cotton
lining and velvet collar with reinforced
eyelets with tie-on shoulder straps,
near mint condition. Roberts was
killed in action on Dec. 31, 1862, while
in command of the third brigade of
Sheridan's division at Stone's River in
Tennessee. **$9,000**

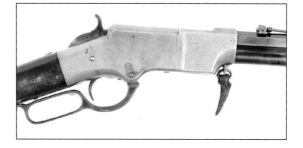

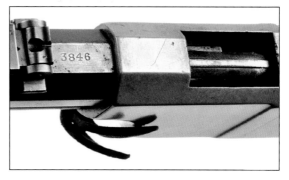

Courtesy of Morphy Auctions, www.morphyauctions.com

Rifle with serial No. 3846, fine condition, standard 24" octagon barrel (blued), full magazine (blued), brass frame, walnut stock, barrel and tube with smooth brown patina and no pitting, factory stamps perfect, brass frame with no signs of having been cleaned or polished, right side of brass frame etched "P.M.C.," stocks excellent with original finish, military cartouche in right side of stock, brass ring in loading tube, 3846 stamped on lower tang on left side, same number stamped on buttplate and buttplate screws. According to Wylies book on serial numbers, serial No. 3846 was issued to Company B of the First D.C. Cavalry, which participated in many major battles, including the capture of John Mosby, the Battle of Gettysburg in 1863, Spotsylvania in 1864, and Cold Harbor in 1865, and was present at Appomattox at Gen. Robert E. Lee's surrender. **$27,000**

Courtesy of Artemis Gallery Live Online Auctioneers, www.artemisgallerylive.com

Iron cannonball from Fort Sumter, Charleston, South Carolina, circa 1861, 12 pounds, 4 1/2" diameter. **$2,200**

Courtesy of Centurion Auctions – Militaria | Firearms, www.centurionauctions.com

▶ Union drum found at Battle of Gettysburg, with eagle painted on front and brass rivet design, 14". **$8,000**

Courtesy of Morphy Auctions,
www.morphyauctions.com

French fitted, cased multi-barrel set, Maynard First Model sporting rifle, given in appreciation for service to then-secretary William G. Freeman, serial #3822: 20" barrel in .35 Maynard, 20" barrel in .50 Maynard, 26" barrel with .54 smooth bore, Maynard-marked bullet mould, loading tools for each barrel, cleaning brushes for each barrel, patch cutter, rosewood-handled turnscrew, two cartridge inserts with leather lanyards, powder flask with original lacquer, four tin canisters with embossed brass caps, one with nine rolls of Maynard tape primers, tin of Eley percussion caps, and cleaning kit, each partitioned in fitted and specially made walnut casing; rifle with early style stock of fiery grain walnut with oval presentation plaque of either silver or white gold on right side engraved "Maynard Arms Co. to / Wm. G. Freeman," no signs of ever having been fired. **$20,000**

Courtesy of Rago Arts and Auctions,
www.ragoarts.com

Wood-carved gilded figure of eagle on ball, circa 1860, 43 1/2" x 32" x 11". **$4,500**

Courtesy of Louis J. Dianni, LLC Antiques Auctions, louisjdianni.com

Painting of famed Civil War photographer Matthew B. Brady by Chas. Loring Elliott, oil on canvas. **$5,500**

Clocks

The clock is one of the oldest human inventions. The word "clock" (from the Latin word *clocca*, "bell") suggests that it was the sound of bells that also characterized early timepieces.

The first mechanical clocks to be driven by weights and gears were invented by medieval Muslim engineers. The first geared mechanical clock was invented by an 11th century Arab engineer in Islamic Spain. The knowledge of weight-driven mechanical clocks produced by Muslim engineers was transmitted to other parts of Europe through Latin translations of Arabic and Spanish texts.

In the early 14th century, existing clock mechanisms that used water-power were being adapted to take their driving power from falling weights. This power was controlled by some form of oscillating mechanism. This controlled release of power – the escapement – marks the beginning of the true mechanical clock.

Courtesy of Clars Auction Gallery, www.clars.com

Chinese export automaton bracket clock with shell-carved crest above mother-of-pearl marquetry-decorated case with foliate banding centering automaton and Roman numeral enamel dial, quarter striking movement with two attendants striking bell, central elder strikes hands on hour, with inlaid rectangular rotating stand, 32" high x 17" wide x 9" deep. **$28,060**

Courtesy of Guernsey's, www.guernseys.com

◄ Union Depot train station clock, originally in Troy, New York, as part of renovation to third version of terminal completed in early 1900s, white terracotta glazed in green with Grecian-style relief, locomotive breaking through tunnel of steam, same design concepts were used by Reed & Stern in their development of Grand Central Station, 88" high x 122" wide x 18" deep. **$43,750**

Courtesy of Clars Auction Gallery, www.clars.com

▲ French champleve-decorated mantle clock with bronze case and domed top above multi-color champleve inlay surrounding Arabic numeral dial, interspersed with floral garland, flanked with Corinthian columnar supports, pendulum decorated with miniature putto with bow and arrow, stepped plinth, 18" high. **$17,080**

Courtesy of Clars Auction Gallery, www.clars.com

◄ Chinese triple fusee and gilt bronze bracket clock with automation, top with animated acrobats rotating around glazed portion, lifting and flipping as automaton turns, dial surmounted with flowing water and moving ducks, gilt bronze case, advanced eight-bell musical movement with engraved rear panel, footed base, 30" high x 17" wide. **$282,500**

◄ Imperial Immortal Mountain musical and automation clock, Qianlong period (1736-1795), made in Guangzhou Workshop, gilt bronze, brass, copper, enamel, ivory, carved wood, silver, and paste stones with brass plate movement with fusees and chord, hour striking on bell, in shape of mountain with waterfall, with small figures depicting Eight Immortals and attendants along with Three Star Deities mounted throughout, in good condition and fully functional, 29" high. **$3.8 million**

Colonial mahogany "Maiden" figural nine-tube tall case clock with carved partial gilt crest above brass and silvered Arabic numeral dial, flanked by figural supports, above single door with beveled glass panel, opening to tubes, weights, and pendulum, on conforming base flanked with winged griffins, paw feet, 99" high x 26" wide x 19" deep. **$21,960**

Courtesy of Heritage Auctions, ha.com

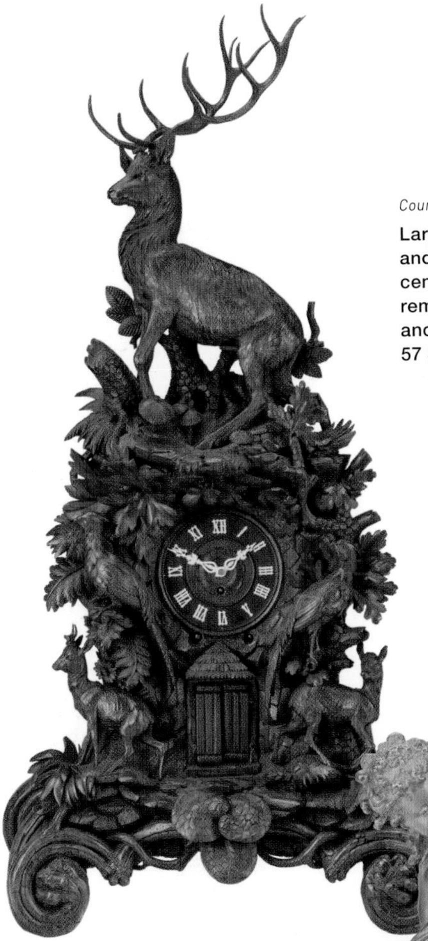

Large Black Forest carved wood and ivory mantle clock, 19th century, minor restoration to elk's removable antlers, scuffing at anchor for clock key, 57 3/4" x 27" x 15". $23,750

Courtesy of Heritage Auctions, ha.com

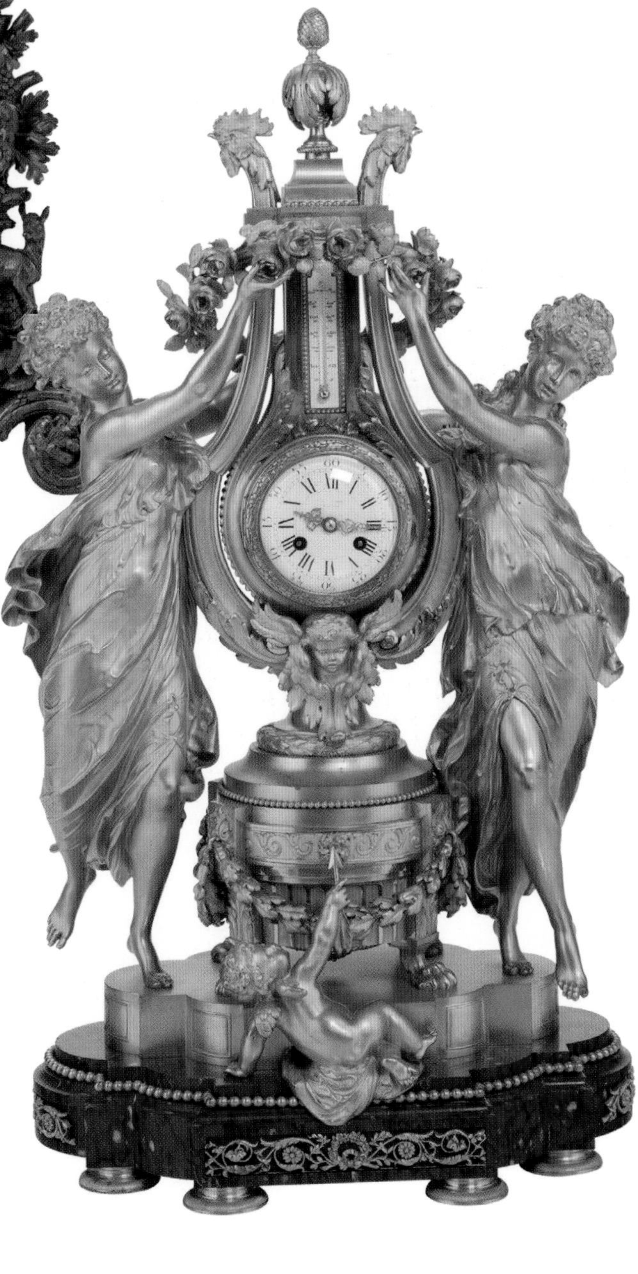

Lemerle Charpentier & Cie French gilt bronze figural mantle clock and thermometer, 19th century, pomegranate finial flanked by rooster heads, floral garland held aloft by two allegorical robed women, central harp-style standard with thermometer and porcelain clock face, decorated on sides with foliate swag, gilt pedestal on red marble pedestal, wear to gilt, with original key and pendulum, 33" x 18 1/2" x 11". $25,000

▶ Symphonion Eroica No. 38B disc music box and clock, circa 1895, with 300 teeth in total of six combs, two-train Lenzkirch movement striking hours on gong and releasing musical movement, carved walnut hall clock case with domed top flanked by turned pillars about putto, with 14" disks in sets of three. **$57,440**

Mahogany regulator clock with stamped movement, E. Howard & Co., Boston, reproduction, 91" high. **$5,658**

Double fusee skeleton clock under dome (shown without dome), 21 3/4" high. **$3,013**

Uncommon George Nelson & Associates wall clock, model 2241, by Howard Miller Clock Co., circa 1957, brass, lacquered wood, and enameled aluminum, signed with manufacturer's mark to reverse, "Howard Miller Clock Company Zeeland, Michigan 2241," 27 1/4" deep x 40 1/2" high. **$11,520**

▲ Silver Cymric mantel clock by Liberty & Co., with slight tapering form embossed with foliate motif and stylized numerals with replacement hands and going barrel drum movement, marked "Liberty & Co Ltd, Birmingham, 1902," abrasively cleaned with scratched appearance, some loss of definition, hallmarks clear and legible, 7 1/4" high. **$22,800**

◄ Japanese double-foliot lantern clock, double weight-driven with striking, in brass case with engraved flowers, Japanese character time ring with hand center rotating to indicate time, both doors on side open to reveal movement, clock strikes on large domed bell, all parts original with replaced weight cables, 14 1/2" high x 6" wide. **$6,710**

Courtesy of Pook & Pook, Inc., www.pookandpook.com

▲ Mahogany carved column and mirror shelf clock, Asa Munger & Co., 39" high. **$1,132**

Courtesy of Pook & Pook, Inc., www.pookandpook.com

▶ Pennsylvania Chippendale walnut tall case clock with eight-day movement and painted dial, inscribed "Seneca Lukens – Samuel Maulsby 1792," 98" high. **$1,537**

Courtesy of Fellows, www.fellows.co.uk

Brass dial chiming clock by Thomas Clay, London, circa early 18th century, with 13" break-arched dial with silvered chapter ring, Arabic minutes, fleur-de-lis half-hour divisions and inner quarter-hour track framing matted center with silvered subsidiary seconds dial framing terrestrial calendar aperture, molded detail to front of case is damaged, figures regilded, 105" high. **$18,786**

Courtesy of Pook & Pook, Inc., www.pookandpook.com

Oak calendar wall clock, Prentiss Clock Improvement Co., 36 1/2" high. **$1,230**

Courtesy of Applebrook Auctions & Estate Sales, www.applebrookauctions.com

◄ Train with clock, barometer, and compass, likely with stone base originally, good condition overall, clock dial with light age lines and paint loss, 19" long x 15 1/4" wide x 8" deep. **$22,800**

Coca-Cola Collectibles

By Allan Petretti

ALLAN PETRETTI is one of the world's top authorities on Coca-Cola memorabilia. He conducts seminars for Coca-Cola collector groups and has been interviewed by the *Wall Street Journal*, *USA Today*, *London Times*, and *New York Times*, and has appeared on many television shows, including "History Detectives."

Organized Coca-Cola collecting began in the early 1970s. The advertising art of the Coca-Cola Co., which used to be thought of as a simple area of collecting, has reached a whole new level of appreciation. Because of their artistic quality, these images deserve to be considered true Americana.

Coca-Cola art is more than bottles and trays, more than calendars and signage, more than trinkets, giveaways, and displays. It incorporates all the best that America has to offer. The Coca-Cola Co., since its conception in 1886, has taken advertising to a whole new level. So much so that it has been studied and dissected by scholars as to why it has proved to be so successful for nearly 130 years.

Can soda pop advertising be considered true art? Without a doubt! The very best artists in America were an integral part of that honorary place in art history. Renowned artists like Rockwell, Sundbloom, Elvgren, and Wyeth helped take a quality product and advance it to the status of an American icon and all that exemplifies the very best about America.

This beautiful advertising directly reflects the history of our country: its styles and fashion, patriotism, family life, the best of times, and the worst of times. Everything this country has gone through since 1886 can be seen in these wonderful images.

For more information on Coca-Cola collectibles, see *Petretti's Coca-Cola Collectibles Price Guide*, 12th edition, by Allan Petretti.

Courtesy of Morphy Auctions, www.morphyauctions.com

Lighted lamp sign, circa 1968, lampshade with pictures of glasses of Coca-Cola, reads, "Delicious with Food / Drink Coca-Cola / Coke brightens every bite," 14" high. **$1,440**

Courtesy of Richard Opfer Auctioneering, www.opferauction.com

Festoon with "Girl on Hammock," 1913. $94,400

Courtesy of LeMar Auctions and Estate Services, www.lemarauctions.com

Coca-Cola syrup bottle, one-gallon, 1950s, original label and contents, unopened. $75

Courtesy of Bright Star Antiques Co., www.brightstarantiques.com

"Drink Coca-Cola" cooler with opener, 34 1/4" high x 42" long x 25 1/2" wide. $590

Early leaded glass globe, all original
hardware, 13" long. **$165,200**

1900 calendar, one of two known to exist, near mint condition,
framed, 16" x 20". **$211,200**

Smith-Miller pressed steel truck with original box marked 1-420
Coca-Cola and all four original Coke cases with bottles. **$976**

"Drink Coca-Cola" wooden menu
board, 24 1/2" high x 13 3/4"
long. **$660**

Courtesy of Morphy Auctions, www.morphyauctions.com

Vintage Coca-Cola soda fountain dispenser with oak base, three silver spigots with white marble handles, and contemporary embossed metal "Fountain Service" sign, 23" x 16" x 19 1/2". **$210**

Courtesy of Morphy Auctions, www.morphyauctions.com

"Drink Coca-Cola" countertop dispenser, 16" high. **$600**

Courtesy of Bright Star Antiques Co., www.brightstarantiques.com

"Fountain Service" porcelain sign. **$500**

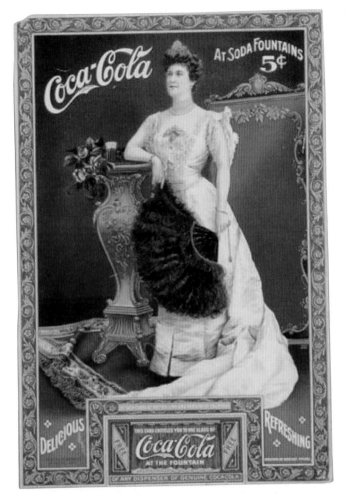

Courtesy of Morphy Auctions, www.morphyauctions.com
"Coca-Cola AT SODA FOUNTAINS" ad, 1904, coupon still attached, 6 1/2" x 10". **$180**

Courtesy of Morphy Auctions, www.morphyauctions.com
Coca-Cola button calendar sign with partial 1960 calendar pad, 19" long. **$420**

Courtesy of Morphy Auctions, www.morphyauctions.com
"ICE COLD / Coca-Cola / ENJOY THAT Refreshing NEW Feeling" tin advertising sign, 1950s, 27 1/2" x 19 1/2". **$420**

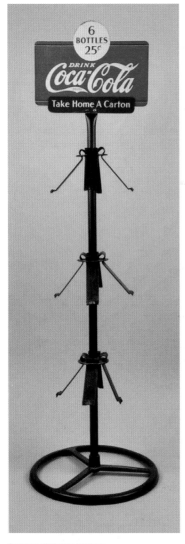

"Drink Coca-Cola / Take Home A
Carton" store display rack,
53" high. **$420**

**Tiffany Foundry embossed belt buckle, "Coca-Cola /
REFRESHING / AND / DELICIOUS." $89**

"Drink Coca-Cola"
vending machine, Vendo
Co., No. 5352, 53" high
x 27" wide x 22" deep.
$185

"Drink Coca-Cola" glass sign, 11 3/4" x 22". **$480**

Buddy Lee doll, circa 1930, in striped
Coca-Cola uniform, 13" high. **$215**

"Drink Coca-Cola" tin serving
tray, 1927, with soda jerk artwork,
made by American Art Works Inc.,
10" x 13". **$390**

Early Coca-Cola paper and rattan
hand fan, 16" long. **$120**

Coin-Operated Devices

Coin-operated devices fall into three main categories: amusement or arcade games, trade stimulators, and vending machines.

Vending machines have been around longer than any other kind of coin-op, and the 1880s witnessed the invention of many varieties. Gambling devices and amusement machines soon followed suit. The industry swelled during the 1890s and early 1900s but slowed during World War I. It rebounded in the 1920s and 1930s, which is considered the Golden Age of coin-ops.

Coin-ops reflect the prevailing art form of the era in which they were produced. Early machines exhibit designs ranging from Victorian to Art Nouveau and Art Deco, while later devices manufactured from 1940 on feature modernism.

For more information on coin-operated devices, visit the website of the Coin Operated Collectors Association at http://coinopclub.org.

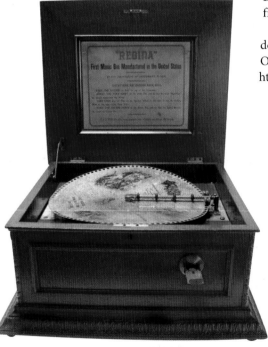

Courtesy of Wickliff Auctioneers, www.wickliffauctioneers.com

Regina music box in mahogany case, serial No. 26007, single comb, sold with 12 16" discs, 22 1/2" x 20 1/2" x 12". $1,495

Courtesy of Fontaines Auction Gallery, fontainesauction.com

Football match soccer half-cent game, glass top and sides with oak framing, signed C.J. Griffiths Bar Fitter, Liverpool, 48" high with base x 48" wide x 21 1/2" deep. $2,057

Courtesy of Clars Auction Gallery, www.clars.com

▲ **Ohio Blue Tip Matches vending machine, red-painted metal with blue decal, 12 1/2" high x 6" wide. $366**

Courtesy of Morphy Auctions, www.morphyauctions.com

◄ **Roll Out the Barrel countertop reel trade stimulator vendor, 18" x 9" x 24". $1,680**

Courtesy of Bright Star Antiques Co.,
www.brightstarantiques.com

**Ride the Champion 10¢ horse
ride, 57" high x 71" long x 25 1/2"
wide. $1,180**

Courtesy of Morphy Auctions,
www.morphyauctions.com

**Caille Ben Hur counter
wheel slot machine, 1908,
16" x 10" x 25". $1,020**

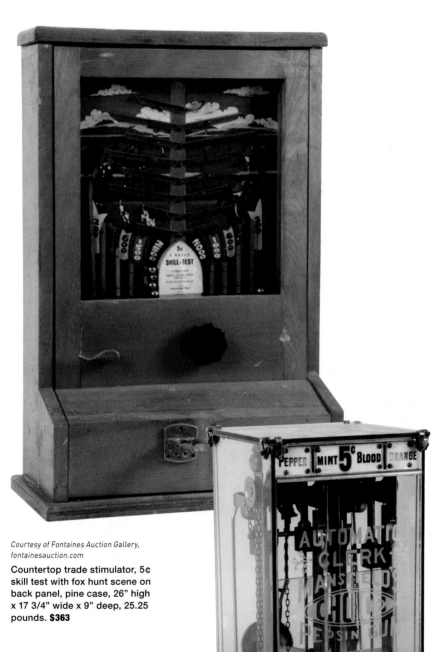

Courtesy of Fontaines Auction Gallery,
fontainesauction.com

**Countertop trade stimulator, 5¢
skill test with fox hunt scene on
back panel, pine case, 26" high
x 17 3/4" wide x 9" deep, 25.25
pounds. $363**

Courtesy of Morphy Auctions,
www.morphyauctions.com

**Mansfield's Choice 5¢
Pepsin Gum Automatic
Clerk, 12" high. $1,200**

Pink elephant kiddie ride. **$1,440**

French crane digger machine,
mahogany case with beveled
front door glass, 66" high x 22"
wide x 21" deep. **$605**

Marvel's Pop-Up baseball flipball countertop skill game,
1947. **$570**

The Hotel Radio, "Tradio," on stand, decal radio face, 36" high with stand x 6 3/4" wide x 12 1/2" deep. **$270**

▲ Robot figural popcorn machine, 25¢, circa 1980s, 29" x 22" x 57". **$660**

◄ Smilin' Sam from Alabam' / The Salted Peanut Man vending machine manufactured by General Merchandising Co. of Chicago, 13" high. **$720**

Courtesy of Morphy Auctions,
www.morphyauctions.com

Saloon mutoscope viewer, International Mutoscope Reel Co. of New York, restored, 52" high. $2,400

Courtesy of Manifest Auctions,
manifestauctions.com

Mills Novelty Co. Art Deco scale, porcelain, Chicago, 13" x 52" x 24". $293

Courtesy of Fontaines Auction Gallery,
fontainesauction.com

All American Drop Kick 5¢ arcade game, Mutoscope International Corp., circa 1949, testing kick strength, 76" high x 18" wide x 36" deep. $3,933

Courtesy of Morphy Auctions,
www.morphyauctions.com

Penny-Lag Legal Skill Game manufactured by Gillespie Games Co. of Long Beach, California, 13 1/2" x 25 1/2". $510

Courtesy of Milestone Auctions, Inc.,
www.milestoneauctions.com

▲ U.S. Postage Stamps machine, all original, with keys. $108

Courtesy of Milestone Auctions, Inc.,
www.milestoneauctions.com

◄ Challenger Rocket Patrol game, 5¢, 23" x 15" x 9". $192

Comics

By Barry Sandoval

BARRY SANDOVAL is Director of Operations for Comics and Comic Art, Heritage Auctions. In addition to managing Heritage's Comics division, which sells some $20 million worth of comics and original comic art each year, Sandoval is a noted comic book evaluator and serves as an advisor to the *Overstreet Comic Book Price Guide*.

Back in 1993, Sotheby's auctioned a copy of *Fantastic Four #1* (1961) that was said to be the finest copy known to exist. It sold for $27,600, which at the time was considered an unheard-of price for a 1960s comic. A couple of years ago, Heritage Auctions sold that same copy for $203,000 … and it's not even the finest known copy anymore.

It used to be that only comics from the 1930s or 1940s could be worth thousands of dollars. Now, truly high-grade copies of comics from the Silver Age (1956-1969 by most people's reckoning) can sell for four, five, or even six figures. Note I said truly high-grade. Long gone are the days when a near mint condition copy was only worth triple the price of a good condition copy. Now near mint is more like 10-20 times good, and sometimes it's as much as a factor of 1,000.

A trend of the last couple of years has been that the "key" issues have separated even further from the pack, value-wise. Note that not every key is a "#1" issue – if you have *Amazing Fantasy #15, Tales of Suspense #39,* and *Journey into Mystery #83,* you've got the first appearances of Spider-Man, Iron Man, and Thor. (Beware of reprints and replica editions, however.)

The most expensive comics of all remain the Golden Age (1938-1949) first appearances, like Superman's 1938 debut in *Action Comics #1,* several copies of which have sold for $1 million or more. However, not every single comic from the old days is going up in value. Take western-themed comics. Values are actually going down in this genre as the generation that grew up watching westerns is at the age where they're looking to sell, and there are more sellers than potential buyers.

Comics from the 1970s and later, while increasing in value, rarely garner anywhere near the same value as 1960s issues, primarily because in the 1970s comics were increasingly seen as a potentially valuable collectible. People took better care of them, and in many cases hoarded multiple copies.

What about 1980s favorites like *The Dark Knight Returns* and *Watchmen*? Here the demand is high, but the supply is really high. These series were heavily hyped at the time and were done

Courtesy of Heritage Auctions, ha.com

Whiz Comics #4 (#3), Fawcett Publications, 1940, first appearance of Beautia Sivana, graded CGC VF- 7.5. **$4,780**

by well-known creators, so copies were socked away in great quantities. We've come across more than one dealer who has 20-30 mint copies of every single 1980s comic socked away in a warehouse, waiting for the day when they're worth selling.

I should mention one surprise hit of the last couple of years. When Image Comics published *The Walking Dead #1* in 2003, it had a low print run and made no particular splash in the comics world. Once AMC made it into a television series, however, it was a whole different story. High-grade copies of #1 have been fetching $1,000 and up lately.

If you've bought comics at an auction house or on eBay, you might have seen some in CGC holders. Certified Guaranty Co., or CGC, is a third-party grading service that grades a comic book on a scale from 0.5 to 10. These numbers correspond with traditional descriptive grades of good, very fine, near mint, and mint, with the higher numbers indicating a better grade. Once graded, CGC encapsulates the comic book in plastic. The grade remains valid as long as the plastic holder is not broken open. CGC has been a boon to the hobby, allowing people to buy comics with more confidence and with the subjectivity of grading taken out of the equation. Unless extremely rare, it's usually only high-grade comics that are worth certifying.

One aspect of collecting that has absolutely exploded in the last 20 years has been original

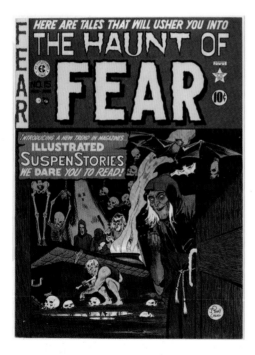

Courtesy of Hake's Americana, www.hakes.com

The Haunt of Fear #15 (#1), EC Comics, May-June 1950, first issue as "Haunt of Fear" – formerly "Gunfighter, graded CGC 9.0 VF/NM. **$3,431**

Courtesy of Hake's Americana, www.hakes.com

Captain Marvel Adventures, #NN, Fawcett Publications, 1946, Wheaties Giveaway, graded CGC 8.5 VF+. **$3,795**

comic art, and not just art for the vintage stuff. In fact, the most expensive piece Heritage Auctions has ever sold was from 1990: Todd McFarlane's cover art for *Amazing Spider-Man #328*, which sold for more than $650,000. It's not unusual for a page that was bought for $20 in the 1980s to be worth $5,000 now.

If you want to get into collecting original comic art, McFarlane would not be the place to start unless you've got a really fat wallet. I suggest picking a current comic artist you like who isn't yet a major "name." Chances are his originals will be a lot more affordable. Another idea is to collect the original art for comic strips. You can find originals for as little as $20, as long as you're not expecting a Peanuts or a Prince Valiant. Heritage Auctions (HA.com) maintains a free online archive of every piece of art they've sold and it is an excellent research tool.

As expensive as both comic books and comic art can be at the high-end of the spectrum, in many ways this is a buyer's market. In the old days you might search for years to find a given issue of a comic; now you can often search eBay and see 10 different copies for sale. Also, comics conventions seem to be thriving in almost every major city – and while the people in crazy costumes get all the publicity, you can also find plenty of vintage comics dealers at these shows. From that point of view, it's a great time to be a comics collector.

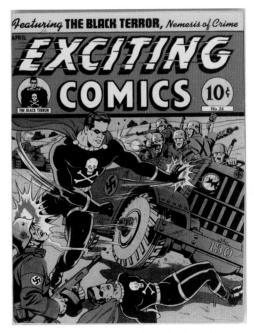

Courtesy of Heritage Auctions, ha.com

Exciting Comics #26, Nedor/Better/Standard, 1943, first Schomburg cover, graded CGC NM- 9.2. **$3,346**

Courtesy of Heritage Auctions, ha.com

Planet Comics #43, Fiction House, 1946, Futura stories begin, cover by Joe Dooli, graded CGC NM- 9.4. **$1,434**

Courtesy of Hake's Americana, www.hakes.com

Superman Sunday Page McClure Newspaper Syndicate promotional folder, New York City, 1959, 10 7/8" x 17" stiff paper folder titled "The Man of Tomorrow." **$9,867**

Courtesy of Heritage Auctions, ha.com

More Fun Comics #54, DC, 1940, graded CGC NM- 9.2. **$38,240**

Courtesy of Heritage Auctions, ha.com

Detective Comics #60, DC, 1942, first appearance of Air Wave, graded CGC VF- 8.0. **$1,315**

Courtesy of Heritage Auctions, ha.com

Century of Comics #nn, Eastern Color, 1933, recognized as third comic book ever produced, given away as a premium, graded CGC FN- 5.5. **$5,019**

Courtesy of Heritage Auctions, ha.com

Superman #1, DC, 1939, origin of Superman, restored, graded CGC Apparent GD+ 2.5 Moderate (C-3). **$33,460**

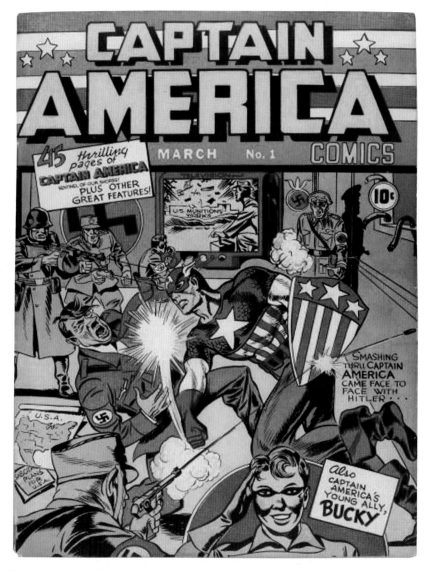

Courtesy of Heritage Auctions, ha.com

Captain America Comics #1, Timely, 1941, origin and first appearance of Captain America and Bucky, first appearance of Red Skull, graded CGC FN- 5.5. **$77,675**

Courtesy of Hake's Americana, www.hakes.com

Amazing Fantasy #15, Marvel Comics, August 1962, first appearance of Spider-Man, Aunt May, and Uncle Ben, graded CGC 5.0 VG/Fine. **$19,482**

Courtesy of Hake's Americana, www.hakes.com

Tales of Suspense #1, Atlas Comics, January 1959, first issue in series that spawned Iron Man (#39), graded CGC 5.5 Fine. **$1,553**

Courtesy of Hake's Americana, www.hakes.com

X-Men #4, Marvel Comics, March 1964, first appearances of Quicksilver and Scarlet Witch. **$380**

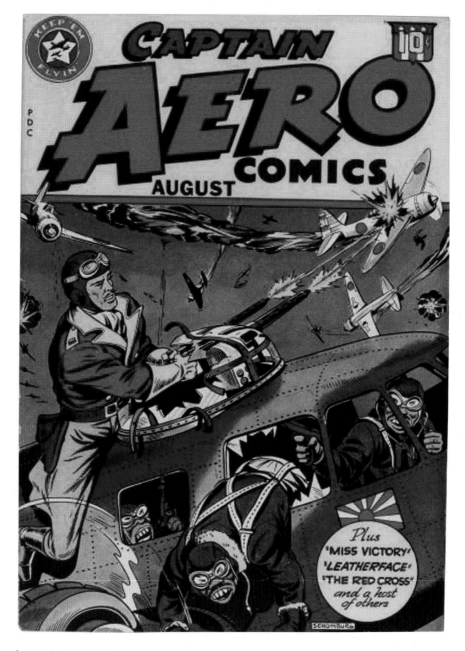

Courtesy of Heritage Auctions, ha.com

Captain Aero Comics #16, Holyoke Publications, 1944, graded CGC NM- 9.2. **$3,585**

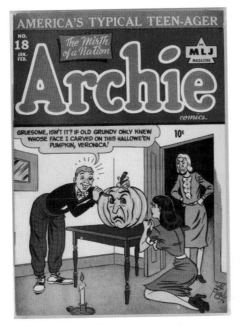

Courtesy of Heritage Auctions, ha.com

Archie Comics #18, MLJ, 1946, graded CGC NM- 9.2. **$3,107**

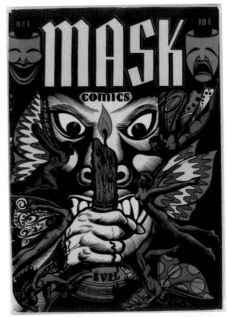

Courtesy of Heritage Auctions, ha.com

Mask Comics #1, Rural Home, 1945, graded CGC FN- 5.5. **$2,271**

Courtesy of Hake's Americana, www.hakes.com

The Incredible Hulk #1, Marvel Comics, May 1962, first appearance of The Incredible Hulk, graded CGC 4.0 VG. **$11,243**

Courtesy of Heritage Auctions, ha.com

Walt Disney's Comics and Stories #35, Dell, 1943, graded CGC NM- 9.2. **$2,868**

Courtesy of Heritage Auctions, ha.com

Captain America Comics #74, one of just two issues that experimented with venue-blending, combining the Captain America title with "Weird Tales," Timely, 1949, graded CGC FN 6.0. **$8,066**

Courtesy of Hake's Americana, www.hakes.com

Weird Fantasy #21, EC Comics, September-October 1953, graded CGC 9.8 NM.MT. **$9,108**

Cookie Jars

Cookie jars, colorful and often whimsical, are popular with collectors. They were made by almost every manufacturer in all types of materials. Figural character cookie jars are the most popular with collectors.

Cookie jars often were redesigned to reflect newer tastes. Hence, the same jar may be found in several different variations, and these variations can affect the price.

Many cookie-jar shapes were manufactured by more than one company and, as a result, can be found with different marks. This often happened because of mergers. Molds also were traded and sold among companies.

Some cookie jars by American Bisque were enhanced with flashers – a plastic piece, technically known as a lenticular image, that changes when the item is moved back and forth.

For more information on cookie jars, see *Warman's Cookie Jars Identification and Price Guide* by Mark F. Moran.

Courtesy of Morphy Auctions, www.morphyauctions.com

Buick convertible cookie jar, Glenn Appleman, Appleman Autoworks, Inc., signed by artist, near mint condition, 15" long. $540

Courtesy of Strawser Auctions, www.strawserauctions.com

Little Red Riding Hood cookie jar, Hull. $104

Courtesy of Morphy Auctions, www.morphyauctions.com

Flintstones cookie jar with Barney and Betty Rubble, American Bisque, circa 1960s, bird head on top repaired, near mint-plus condition, 10" x 7" x 6". $83

Courtesy of Strawser Auctions, www.strawserauctions.com

Blue Magnolia pattern cookie jar, Roseville Pottery Co. 2-8". $64

Courtesy of Morphy Auctions, www.morphyauctions.com

Bear cookie jar, American Bisque, excellent condition, 10" high. $150

Two large glass cookie jars with metal lids, one with decal reading "Calirox / King of Cook-E-Dom / Mothers Only Rival" and metal lid stamped "Calirox Co.," and one with etched lettering reading "Property of Dad's Cookie Co." and metal lid stamped "Calirox Co.," excellent condition, 15" high. **$180**

Green painted and glazed ceramic tyrannosaurus rex cookie jar with "Sinclair Oil" etched on front, marked "1942 USA" on bottom, excellent condition, 13" high. **$1,200**

Sunnybrook pressed cookie jar, black, original cover and wrapped bail handle, H. C. Fry Glass Co., first half 20th century, 7 1/4" high overall. **$48**

Wishing well brown-glazed cookie jar, McCoy, reads, "Wish I Had a Cookie," maker's mark on bottom: McCoy, USA, very good condition, 9" high. **$12**

Freesia pattern cookie jar,
Roseville Pottery Co., #4-8",
brown tones. $207

Freesia pattern cookie jar,
Roseville Pottery Co., #4-8",
green tones, good condition, no
chips, cracks or repairs. $148

Zephyr Lily pattern cookie jar,
Roseville Pottery Co., maker's
mark on bottom: Roseville, USA
5-8", very good condition,
10 1/2" high. $210

Courtesy of Jeffrey S. Evans & Associates, www.jeffreysevans.com

Blue and white salt-glazed ceramic cookie jar in Flying Birds pattern, with likely original cover and in strong coloration, together with handled measuring cup in Spear Point and Flower Panels pattern, first quarter 20th century, excellent condition, chip on interior rim of cover, firing imperfections as made, 5 1/8" and 9" high overall. **$240**

Courtesy of Morphy Auctions, www.morphyauctions.com

Dad's cookie jar, circa 1940s-1950s, with original decal and heavy large embossing on jar, small lid nicks, near mint condition, 13 1/2" high. **$150**

Courtesy of Jeffrey S. Evans & Associates, www.jeffreysevans.com

Blue and white salt-glazed ceramic cookie jar with cover, Brickers, first quarter 20th century, excellent condition, firing imperfections as made, 7 3/8" high overall. **$168**

Courtesy of Humler & Nolan, www.humlernolan.com

◄ Earthenware cookie jar made in 1942 by Carlton Ball while teaching at Mills College, gingerbread men, cats, dog, boy and girl seated at table with cookies, lid with finial of gingerbread man holding cookie, exterior in bluish glaze, interior in white, bottom incised "Kathryn + Carlton Mills College April 22, 1942 Made by Carlton Ball Decoration put on by Kathryn Uhl Ball," two small open separations beneath boy occurring during firing, 10 1/4" h. **$847**

Courtesy of Humler & Nolan, www.humlernolan.com

Mammy cookie jar, Weller, with incised "Weller Pottery Since 1872" on bottom, professional repair to chip on rim of lid, fine overall crazing, 11 1/4" high to top of lid. **$303**

Courtesy of Slotin Folk Art, www.slotinfolkart.com

Pair of cookie face jars by Jerry Brown, 1992, signed and dated, mixed glazes, mint condition, 12 1/2" high with lids. **$123**

CLOSE-UP!

Courtesy of Elite Decorative Arts, www.eliteauction.com

Rare Old King Cole cookie jar, Red Wing Pottery, stamped Red Wing Pottery to base, circa early 20th century, 9 1/2" high. Provenance: From estate of Count Adrian Toati de Suiza de Bourbon, great-grandson of Queen Isabella II of Spain. **$545**

Disneyana

By Noah Fleisher

NOAH FLEISHER received his Bachelor of Fine Arts degree from New York University and brings more than a decade of newspaper, magazine, book, antiques and art experience to his position as Public Relations Director of Heritage Auctions, one of the country's foremost auction houses. He is the former editor of *Antique Trader, New England Antiques Journal* and *Northeast Antiques Journal,* is the author of *Warman's Modern Furniture* and co-author of *Collecting Children's Books,* and has been a longtime contributor to *Warman's Antiques & Collectibles.*

There is no single cultural force of the 20th century stronger than Walt Disney. To fully understand the American experience, I believe you have to understand Walt Disney, his work and – perhaps most importantly – his greatest masterpiece: Disneyland.

Disneyland was the full realization of Walt's dream, to create and control a world that gave concrete realization to his vision of America itself; a land steeped in nostalgia and sunshine, soaking in the goodness of days past, irretrievable except in our collective memory. In fact, America's very sense of itself, the wistfulness that defines our view of our history, did not exist before Walt Disney and exists now only because of him and, in particular, his amazing accomplishment in creating Disneyland.

While Disneyana has been written about extensively, it still continues to fascinate us. It's hard to find a wrinkle that has not been covered. For the sake of this section, at least as far as the images go, with a nod to the staples of Disneyana (for other collectors Disneyana can mean toys, movie posters, pins, bean plush, and dolls, just to name a few of the endless categories of merchandise that has been produced by the Disney Co. or its licensees), I'd like to focus on what is an important and emergent sector of the market: "collectibles" that come from the theme park itself, that are actually part of the original park (though you will find plenty that deals with other forms here, too).

There are few people in the collectibles business who can claim a better grasp on Disneyana than Phil Sears of Phil Sears Collectibles, LLC in Laguna Nigel, California. Sears, who grew up in Southern California, steeped in the influence of Disney, is the foremost expert on Disney's autograph and all things Disneyana.

"My admiration for Walt Disney is connected strongly to Disneyland," Sears said. "In addition to collecting Disneyland memorabilia and Disney Studio artwork, 25 years ago I set out to own my first 'something' signed by the man who

Courtesy of Heritage Auctions, ha.com

Snow White and the Seven Dwarfs (RKO, 1937) half sheet, Style A movie poster, with artwork by children's book/animator Gustaf Tenggren. **$4,481**

started Disney entertainment. I soon discovered that Disney's autograph was tricky because he had employees [who were] allowed to sign on his behalf, and because of outright forgeries. Disney Studios archivist David R. Smith graciously invited me down to the Disney Studio and let me make photocopies of Walt's signature from their files for comparison in my collecting. I was the proverbial 'kid in a candy store' and didn't realize I had taken the first steps to becoming the world's expert on Disney's autograph."

Since then, Sears has added Disney theme park props, signage, ride vehicles, and Disney Studio art to the categories of Disneyana that interest him most.

In Sears' own words, "Disneyana is the quintessential American 20th century collectible. Since the day in 1929 when Walt Disney accepted $300 to license Mickey Mouse's image for school paper tablets, Disneyana collectibles were destined to become among the most ubiquitous and popular of all American collectibles," Sears said. "Every Disney collectible – and especially those created in Walt Disney's lifetime – tells a deeper story than just that of the plucky Mickey Mouse or vulnerable Snow White. They also speak to the American

WALT DISNEY'S Snow White and the Seven Dwarfs

April 27, 1938.

Miss Rose Marie Daughenbaugh,
Happyland,
2041 Hillhurst Ave.,
Los Angeles, Calif.

Dear Rose Marie:

I am very glad to have your note, telling me
how much you liked SNOW WHITE AND THE SEVEN
DWARFS. This makes us all very happy, as we
always enjoy hearing from our little friends.

And just because you liked SNOW WHITE so much,
I am going to send you a colored sketch of
her -- and another of one of the dwarfs -- I
hope he's the one you like best!

There's something else in your letter that
pleases me very much, too -- and that is you
haven't forgotten THE THREE LITTLE PIGS. I'm
so glad to know that -- it's sort of like not
forgetting your old friends! And here's a
secret I'll tell you -- we're going to have
another Pig Picture soon -- it's about the
Practical Pig - you know, the one who wears
the blue overalls - and his two little
brothers who are always having narrow escapes
with the Big, Bad Wolf! It's called the
"PRACTICAL PIG" and we hope when you see it
you shall like it as much as you did THE THREE
LITTLE PIGS.

Many more thanks for writing to me and please
tell all my little friends "hello" at Happyland.

Sincerely,

Walt Disney

WALT DISNEY PRODUCTIONS, Ltd.
2719 HYPERION · HOLLYWOOD, CAL.

Courtesy of Phil Sears, LLC, www.philsears.com

1938 letter on *Snow White and the Seven Dwarfs* **letterhead signed by Walt Disney. $5,000-$7,000**

Courtesy of Phil Sears, LLC, www.philsears.com

Tinker Bell 25-year Disney employee award statuette. **$450-$650**

dream, of a Missouri farm boy named Walt Disney, who, with only one year of high school but plenty of ambition and the talent to back it up, persevered to become one of the most influential figures of the 20th century."

Well said. The philosophical implications of Disney are clearly not lost on Sears. When it comes to nuts and bolts collecting, however, what does he recommend?

"When I'm asked what type of things someone should collect, I always recommend that a collector follow their heart," he said. "On a more specific note, if buying artwork, buy original artwork instead of limited edition reproductions. For example, a collector can often find an original 1937 drawing from *Snow White and the Seven Dwarfs* for less than the cost of a limited edition reproduction of a cel from the film."

Sears points out that the market for Disneyana has gone in two different directions in the Internet Age.

"Very common items, which were produced by the thousands, can be had for bargain prices," he said. "Sites like eBay make it easy for people to flood the market with items that, 20 years ago, were considered scarce because they were sitting in the back of a drawer or closet in Iowa – or Indonesia – with no easy way of getting to market. Now, with a few keystrokes, that item is on eBay.

"On the other hand," he said, "the Internet also allows for truly rare items to be exposed to more hungry buyers and bidders than ever before, and competition can drive the price of truly precious items into the stratosphere. However, whether the collectible is a common $20 beanie or a rare $20,000 Disney movie poster, we like these things because they trigger an emotion. When it comes to Disney, that emotion is always fun."

Finally, because Sears is not only an authority but also a collector, what does the expert himself consider his most beloved personal Disney collectible?

"Because my interest in Disney collecting traces right back to the original source – Walt Disney himself – the favorite piece in my collection is a typed manuscript for a 1966 *Fortune Magazine* article about the history of the Disney Co., which was given to Walt Disney for his review

Disneyana expert Phil Sears.

and notes," Sears said. "Walt doesn't like the tone of the article and has passionately made his notes and corrections in the margins of the 30-page manuscript. I love it because it's the real Walt Disney forcefully making his points about building his company, creating his movies, and inventing his amusement park. Walt Disney's passion about his career is so clearly evident, and all of it is written in his own hand. Now *that's* a Disney collectible."

Phil Sears Collectibles, LLC can be reached online at www.PhilSears.com, or via mail at P.O. Box 6359, Laguna Niguel, CA 92607.

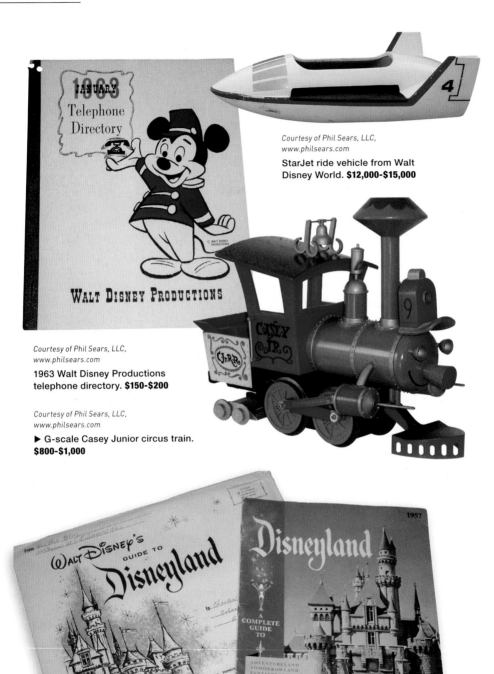

Courtesy of Phil Sears, LLC, www.philsears.com

StarJet ride vehicle from Walt Disney World. $12,000-$15,000

Courtesy of Phil Sears, LLC, www.philsears.com

1963 Walt Disney Productions telephone directory. $150-$200

Courtesy of Phil Sears, LLC, www.philsears.com

▶ **G-scale Casey Junior circus train. $800-$1,000**

Courtesy of Phil Sears, LLC, www.philsears.com

1957 Disneyland souvenir book with original mailing envelope. $150-$175

Courtesy of Heritage Auctions, ha.com

Peter Pan (RKO, 1953) one-sheet movie poster, 1953, rendered by Disney's famed "Nine Old Men," the animators who were responsible for the distinctive Disney animation style. **$2,868**

Courtesy of Phil Sears, LLC,
www.philsears.com

▲ 1983 Disneyland The New Fantasyland grand opening press gifts and publications. **$200-$300**

Courtesy of Phil Sears, LLC,
www.philsears.com

▲ Disneyland Space Mountain roller coaster vehicle. **$15,000-$20,000**

Courtesy of Phil Sears, LLC,
www.philsears.com

◄ Production rough drawing of Stromboli from *Pinocchio*. **$275-$350**

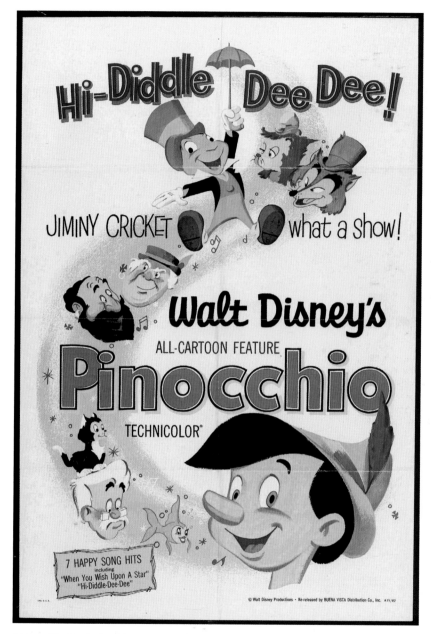

Courtesy of Heritage Auctions, ha.com

Pinocchio (Buena Vista, R-1971) one-sheet movie poster, starring voices of Dick Jones, Cliff Edwards, Walter Catlett, Evelyn Venable, and Christian Rub, from 1972 re-release of film. **$62**

Courtesy of Phil Sears, LLC, www.philsears.com

▲ Disneyland opening day press ticket, July 17, 1955. **$1,500-$2,000**

Courtesy of Phil Sears, LLC, www.philsears.com

▲ Disneyland Pirates of the Caribbean plaque with voice chip. **$300-$500**

Courtesy of Phil Sears, LLC, www.philsears.com

▲ Walt Disney autographed Mickey Mouse note sheet. **$4,000-$5,000**

Courtesy of Phil Sears, LLC, www.philsears.com

1980s Sears department store Disney World Town Square play set and accessories. **$200-$300**

Courtesy of Heritage Auctions, ha.com

Walt Disney Studios,
The "Pop-Up" *Silly
Symphonies Babes in the
Woods King Neptune*,
New York: Blue Ribbon
Books, Inc., 1933:
first edition, with 34
illustrations including
four double-page pop-
ups illustrated by the
staff of Walt Disney
Studios. **$938**

Courtesy of Heritage Auctions, ha.com

Al White (American, 20th century), *Walt Disney's Mary Poppins*, Little Golden Book cover illustration, 1964, gouache on board with acetate and acrylic paint overlay, not signed, 16" x 13". **$567**

Courtesy of Heritage Auctions, ha.com

Mary Poppins (Buena Vista, 1964), British quad movie poster, starring Julie Andrews and Dick Van Dyke, directed by Robert Stevenson. **$191**

Courtesy of Heritage Auctions, ha.com

Gustaf Tenggren (American, 1896-1970), *Snow White and the Seven Dwarfs* original promotional art, 1937, mixed media on paper. The coming of Walt Disney's first feature-length animated film shook the world of animation with its innovation and resulted in this detailed movie poster illustration by children's book artist Gustaf Tenggren. In 1936 Tenggren was hired by The Walt Disney Co. to work as the stylist on *Snow White and the Seven Dwarfs*, the first American feature-length animated film. He created the distinctive Old World look that Walt Disney sought for his breakthrough animated feature. This was the original art used as the centerpiece of the *Snow White* movie poster. **$59,750**

Courtesy of Heritage Auctions, ha.com

Mary Poppins (Buena Vista, 1964), set of nine lobby cards, starring Julie Andrews, Dick Van Dyke, David Tomlinson, Glynis Johns, Hermione Baddeley, Elsa Lanchester, Arthur Treacher, Reginald Owen, Ed Wynn, and Jane Darwell; lightly used, unrestored near-mint condition. **$388**

Peter Pan, Peter and the Darling family production cel and master background (Walt Disney, 1953), with hand-painted Key Master background of Darling residence. **$8,963**

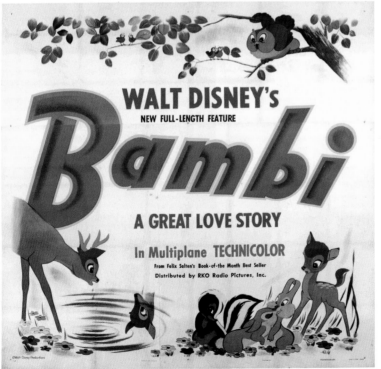

Bambi (RKO, 1942) six-sheet movie poster, best paper on Disney's revolutionary Multiplane Technicolor feature based on the Felix Salter book, originally written in French, rare. **$3,107**

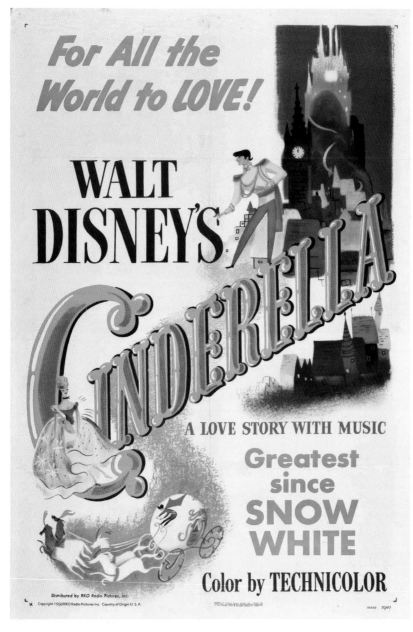

Courtesy of Heritage Auctions, ha.com

Cinderella (RKO, 1950) one-sheet movie poster. **$777**

Disney Theme Park *Mr. Toad's Wild Ride* vehicle. **$25,000-$35,000**

Pirates of the Caribbean – Dead Man's Chest authentic movie skull prop. **$400-$500**

Walt Disney World The Haunted Mansion secret panel chest. **$150-$250**

Walt Disney signed bank check. **$1,900-$2,500**

Folk Art & Americana

Folk art generally refers to items that originated among the common people of a region, usually reflecting the traditional culture, especially regarding everyday or festive items. Unlike fine art, folk art is primarily utilitarian and decorative rather than purely aesthetic.

Exactly what constitutes the genre is a question that continues to be vigorously debated among collectors, dealers, museum curators, and scholars. Some want to confine folk art to non-academic, handmade objects. Others are willing to include manufactured material. Folk art can range from crude drawings by children to academically trained artists' paintings of "common" people and scenery. It encompasses items made from a variety of materials, from wood and metal to cloth and paper. The accepted timetable for folk art runs from its earliest origins up to the mid-20th century.

Americana applies to items representing key figures and times in American history.

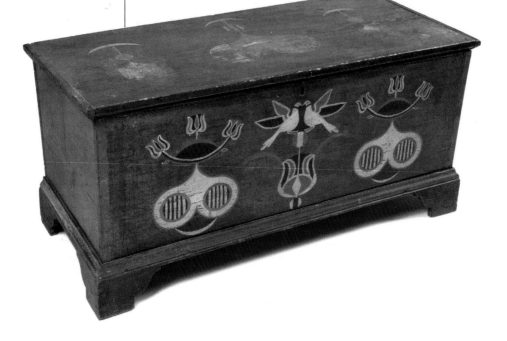

Courtesy of Pook & Pook, Inc., www.pookandpook.com
Carved and painted hanging shelf, circa 1870, found in Oneonta, New York, scrolled crest with three high-relief carvings of eagle with tin wings and busts of two stags with tin ears above shelf with scrolled supports and swag and tassel apron, 39" high x 45 1/2" wide. **$9,225**

Courtesy of Pook & Pook, Inc., www.pookandpook.com
▲ "Ham and Eggs" hooked rug, American, mid-20th century, 30" x 49". **$4,428**

Courtesy of Jeffrey S. Evans & Assoc., www.jeffreysevans.com
◀ Uncommon paint-decorated yellow pine blanket chest, Johannes Spitler, Shenandoah Valley, Virginia, circa 1800; hinged rectangular lid with applied edge molding of square profile with angled lower edge over dovetailed case with applied ogee base molding and cut-out bracket feet; original wrought iron strap hinges with triangular terminals; moldings, feet, and bottom board attached with wooden pins, top corners of dovetailed case secured with wooden pins, two wrought iron nails used to attach rear foot supports; painted decoration to lid incorporates inverted hearts balancing inverted crescents suspended on thin knopped stems; front panel central zone with lovebirds perched atop abstract tulip form flanked by parallel outer zones, each with triple-bloom tulip-like form issuing from tip of inverted heart with dual barred orbs, 23" high x 47 1/2" wide x 21 1/4" deep. **$372,000**

Courtesy of Pook & Pook, Inc., www.pookandpook.com
Carved fish-form walnut wall shelf with inset mirror plate, 19th century, 16 1/4" x 6 1/2". **$1,599**

Courtesy of Slotin Folk Art, www.slotinfolkart.com

▲ "GOD IS OUR REFUGE" carved wood relief plaque with paint and glitter by Elijah Pierce (Columbus, Ohio, 1892-1984), circa 1960, signed and dated, titled "Mr. and Mrs. James Morgan, presented by Mr. & Mrs. Pierce 'It's a part of me,'" excellent condition, 18" wide x 14 1/2" high. **$24,600**

Courtesy of Conestoga Auction Co., www.conestogaauction.com

◄ Sheet iron rooster silhouette weathervane, dated 1909, red and gold painted highlights on black ground, good condition with some rust and pitting, silhouette 23 1/2" high x 20 1/2" wide, 53" mounted on iron bar. **$5,445**

Courtesy of Slotin Folk Art, www.slotinfolkart.com

"Wind Storm in the Valley" carved wood relief plaque with varnish by Daniel Pressley, signed and titled, excellent condition, three natural wood splits, all minor, 32" wide x 24" high. **$7,995**

Battle of Vicksburg painted vellum drum head after lithograph published by Kurz and Allison, hand-painted in oil, depicting Union soldiers in trenches during siege of Vicksburg, captioned by hand at bottom of scene "Battle of Vicksburg," framed and matted under glass, 36" x 36". **$2,500**

▲ Fraktur sampler by Barbara Ebersol, Lancaster County, Pennsylvania, circa 1864, with geometric hex sign, birds with potted tulips, floral devices, and soldier on horseback motifs, very fine condition with tears, creases, edge loss and stains, 11" x 14 1/2". Sampler was gifted to a friend at age 18 and is considered the best-known example of Ebersol's work and only known human figure she created. **$6,050**

◀ Early 19th century carved and polychromed wood figure with articulated joints at shoulders, elbows, and wrists, arms extended forward, wear commensurate with age and use, 12 3/4" wide x 19" deep x 18 1/4" high. **$3,690**

Courtesy of Heritage Auctions, ha.com

Hand-painted banner from 1844 presidential campaign of Henry Clay and James K. Polk, muslin mounted on linen, depicts Clay giving Polk a sound drubbing before election that Polk would win; above candidates eagle flies bearing streamer reading "PROTECTIVE TARIFF," one of signal issues addressed by Clay's Whig candidacy; annexation of Texas was major plank in Polk's platform and small ball labeled "Texas" may have implied diminished importance of issue; verse underneath: "Thus Polk the scoundrel tries / Our tariff low to lay / While to its rescue flies / Our gallant Henry Clay," excellent condition, light signs of aging, 35" x 42 1/2". **$31,250**

Painting of ship Russell in port with applied laminated half hull, oil on canvas, signed and dated lower right "I Hudson, Nov. 1881," vertical tear in sky, upper right, 22" high x 40" wide in frame. **$6,150**

Seldom-seen Taufschein fraktur attributed to Jacob Strickler, Shenandoah Valley of Virginia, circa 1806, watercolor and ink on paper, two federal eagles with heart-shaped breast medallions, tulips and other floral scenes, polychrome diamond border, very good condition overall, treatment of small edge losses, 7 5/8" x 12 1/4". This is the only recorded composition by Strickler to include American eagles and was commissioned by members of the Rothgeb/Roadcap family. **$31,000**

Uncommon four-gallon stoneware jar with large cobalt elephant decoration, circa 1880, applied lug handles and flared rim with narrow opening, stamped "WEST TROY / N.Y. / POTTERY," excellent condition overall with two surface flakes to bottom edge of jar, 14 1/2" high. **$166,750**

Courtesy of Heritage Auctions, ha.com

George Sosnak baseball depicting 1971 World Series and Pittsburgh Pirates with impressions of Roberto Clemente, Bruce Kilson, and Steve Blass and text describing story of series. $6,572

FURNITURE

Styles 366
Antique 382
Modern 390

Furniture Styles
AMERICAN

PILGRIM CENTURY 1620–1700

MAJOR WOOD(S): Oak

GENERAL CHARACTERISTICS:

- **Case pieces:** Rectilinear low-relief carved panels; blocky and bulbous turnings; splint-spindle trim

- **Seating pieces:** Shallow carved panels; spindle turnings

WILLIAM AND MARY 1685–1720

MAJOR WOOD(S): Maple and walnut

GENERAL CHARACTERISTICS:

- **Case pieces:** Paint-decorated chests on ball feet; chests on frames; chests with two-part construction; trumpet-turned legs; slant-front desks

- **Seating pieces:** Molded, carved crest rails; banister backs; cane, rush (leather) seats; baluster, ball and block turnings; ball and Spanish feet

QUEEN ANNE · 1720–1750

MAJOR WOOD(S): Walnut

GENERAL CHARACTERISTICS:

- **Case pieces:** Mathematical proportions of elements; use of the cyma or S-curve broken-arch pediments; arched panels, shell carving, star inlay; blocked fronts; cabriole legs and pad feet

- **Seating pieces:** Molded yoke-shaped crest rails; solid vase-shaped splats; rush or upholstered seats; cabriole legs; baluster, ring, ball and block-turned stretchers; pad and slipper feet

CHIPPENDALE 1750–1785

MAJOR WOOD(S): Mahogany and walnut

GENERAL CHARACTERISTICS:

- **Case pieces:** Relief-carved broken-arch pediments; foliate, scroll, shell, fretwork carving; straight, bow or serpentine fronts; carved cabriole legs; claw and ball, bracket or ogee feet
- **Seating pieces:** Carved, shaped crest rails with out-turned ears; pierced, shaped splats; ladder (ribbon) backs; upholstered seats; scrolled arms; carved cabriole legs or straight (Marlboro) legs; claw and ball feet

FEDERAL (HEPPLEWHITE) 1785-1800

MAJOR WOOD(S): Mahogany and light inlays

GENERAL CHARACTERISTICS:

- **Case pieces:** More delicate rectilinear forms; inlay with eagle and classical motifs; bow, serpentine or tambour fronts; reeded quarter columns at sides; flared bracket feet

- **Seating pieces:** Shield backs; upholstered seats; tapered square legs

FEDERAL (SHERATON) 1800-1820

MAJOR WOOD(S): Mahogany, mahogany veneer, and maple

GENERAL CHARACTERISTICS:

- **Case pieces:** Architectural pediments; acanthus carving; outset (cookie or ovolu) corners and reeded columns; paneled sides; tapered, turned, reeded or spiral-turned legs; bow or tambour fronts; mirrors on dressing tables

- **Seating pieces:** Rectangular or square backs; slender carved banisters; tapered, turned or reeded legs

CLASSICAL (AMERICAN EMPIRE) 1815–1850

MAJOR WOOD(S): Mahogany, mahogany veneer, and rosewood

GENERAL CHARACTERISTICS:

- **Case pieces:** Increasingly heavy proportions; pillar and scroll construction; lyre, eagle, Greco-Roman and Egyptian motifs; marble tops; projecting top drawer; large ball feet, tapered fluted feet or hairy paw feet; brass, ormolu decoration

- **Seating pieces:** High-relief carving; curved backs; out-scrolled arms; ring turnings; sabre legs, curule (scrolled-S) legs; brass-capped feet, casters

VICTORIAN – EARLY VICTORIAN 1840–1850

MAJOR WOOD(S): Mahogany veneer, black walnut, and rosewood

GENERAL CHARACTERISTICS:

- **Case pieces:** Pieces tend to carry over the Classical style with the beginnings of the Rococo substyle, especially in seating pieces.

VICTORIAN – GOTHIC REVIVAL 1840–1890

MAJOR WOOD(S): Black walnut, mahogany, and rosewood

GENERAL CHARACTERISTICS:

- **Case pieces:** Architectural motifs; triangular arched pediments; arched panels; marble tops; paneled or molded drawer fronts; cluster columns; bracket feet, block feet or plinth bases

- **Seating pieces:** Tall backs; pierced arabesque backs with trefoils or quatrefoils; spool turning; drop pendants

VICTORIAN – ROCOCO (LOUIS XV) 1845–1870

MAJOR WOOD(S): Black walnut, mahogany, and rosewood

GENERAL CHARACTERISTICS:

- **Case pieces:** Arched carved pediments; high-relief carving, S- and C-scrolls, floral, fruit motifs, busts and cartouches; mirror panels; carved slender cabriole legs; scroll feet; bedroom suites (bed, dresser, commode)

- **Seating pieces:** High-relief carved crest rails; balloon-shaped backs; urn-shaped splats; upholstery (tufting); demi-cabriole legs; laminated, pierced and carved construction (Belter and Meeks); parlor suites (sets of chairs, love seats, sofas)

VICTORIAN – RENAISSANCE REVIVAL 1860–1885

MAJOR WOOD(S): Black walnut, burl veneer, painted and grained pine

GENERAL CHARACTERISTICS:

- **Case pieces:** Rectilinear arched pediments; arched panels; burl veneer; applied moldings; bracket feet, block feet, plinth bases; medium and high-relief carving, floral and fruit, cartouches, masks and animal heads; cyma-curve brackets; Wooton patent desks

- **Seating pieces:** Oval or rectangular backs with floral or figural cresting; upholstery outlined with brass tacks; padded armrests; tapered turned front legs, flared square rear legs

VICTORIAN – LOUIS XVI 1865–1875

MAJOR WOOD(S): Black walnut and ebonized maple

GENERAL CHARACTERISTICS:

- **Case pieces:** Gilt decoration, marquetry, inlay; egg and dart carving; tapered turned legs, fluted

- **Seating pieces:** Molded, slightly arched crest rails; keystone-shaped backs; circular seats; fluted tapered legs

VICTORIAN – EASTLAKE 1870–1895

MAJOR WOOD(S): Black walnut, burl veneer, cherry, and oak

GENERAL CHARACTERISTICS:

- **Case pieces:** Flat cornices; stile and rail construction; burl veneer panels; low-relief geometric and floral machine carving; incised horizontal lines

- **Seating pieces:** Rectilinear; spindles; tapered, turned legs, trumpet-shaped legs

VICTORIAN JACOBEAN AND TURKISH REVIVAL 1870–1890

MAJOR WOOD(S): Black walnut and maple

GENERAL CHARACTERISTICS:

- **Case pieces:** A revival of some heavy 17th century forms, most commonly in dining room pieces

- **Seating pieces:** Turkish Revival style features: oversized, low forms; overstuffed upholstery; padded arms; short baluster, vase-turned legs; ottomans, circular sofas

- **Jacobean Revival style features:** heavy bold carving; spool and spiral turnings

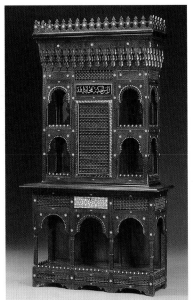

VICTORIAN – AESTHETIC MOVEMENT 1880–1900

MAJOR WOOD(S): Painted hardwoods, black walnut, ebonized finishes

GENERAL CHARACTERISTICS:

- **Case pieces:** Rectilinear forms; bamboo turnings, spaced ball turnings; incised stylized geometric and floral designs, sometimes highlighted with gilt

- **Seating pieces:** Bamboo turning; rectangular backs; patented folding chairs

ART NOUVEAU 1895–1918

MAJOR WOOD(S): Ebonized hardwoods, fruitwoods

GENERAL CHARACTERISTICS:

- **Case pieces:** Curvilinear shapes; floral marquetry; whiplash curves

- **Seating pieces:** Elongated forms; relief-carved floral decoration; spindle backs, pierced floral backs; cabriole legs

TURN-OF-THE-CENTURY (EARLY 20TH CENTURY) 1895-1910

MAJOR WOOD(S): Golden (quarter-sawn) oak, mahogany, hardwood stained to resemble mahogany

GENERAL CHARACTERISTICS:

- **Case pieces:** Rectilinear and bulky forms; applied scroll carving or machine-pressed designs; some Colonial and Classical Revival detailing

- **Seating pieces:** Heavy framing or high spindle-trimmed backs; applied carved or machine-pressed back designs; heavy scrolled or slender turned legs; Colonial Revival or Classical Revival detailing such as claw and ball feet

MISSION (ARTS & CRAFTS MOVEMENT) 1900-1915

MAJOR WOOD(S): Oak

GENERAL CHARACTERISTICS:

- **Case pieces:** Rectilinear through-tenon construction; copper decoration, hand-hammered hardware; square legs

- **Seating pieces:** Rectangular splats; medial and side stretchers; exposed pegs; corbel supports

COLONIAL REVIVAL 1890–1930

MAJOR WOOD(S): Oak, walnut and walnut veneer, mahogany veneer

GENERAL CHARACTERISTICS:

- **Case pieces:** Forms generally following designs of the 17th, 18th, and early 19th centuries; details for the styles such as William and Mary, Federal, Queen Anne, Chippendale, or early Classical were used but often in a simplified or stylized form; mass-production in the early 20th century flooded the market with pieces that often mixed and matched design details and used a great deal of thin veneering to dress up designs; dining room and bedroom suites were especially popular.

- **Seating pieces:** Designs again generally followed early period designs with some mixing of design elements.

ART DECO 1925–1940

MAJOR WOOD(S): Bleached woods, exotic woods, steel, and chrome

GENERAL CHARACTERISTICS:

- **Case pieces:** Heavy geometric forms
- **Seating pieces:** Streamlined, attenuated geometric forms; overstuffed upholstery

MODERNIST OR MID-CENTURY 1945–1970

MAJOR WOOD(S): Plywood, hardwood, or metal frames

GENERAL CHARACTERISTICS: Modernistic designers such as the Eames, Vladimir Kagan, George Nelson, and Isamu Noguchi led the way in post-war design. Carrying on the tradition of Modernist designers of the 1920s and 1930s, they focused on designs for the machine age that could be mass-produced for the popular market. By the late 1950s many of their pieces were used in commercial office spaces and schools as well as in private homes.

- **Case pieces:** Streamlined or curvilinear abstract designs with simple detailing; plain round or flattened legs and arms; mixed materials including wood, plywood, metal, glass, and molded plastics

- **Seating pieces:** Streamlined or abstract curvilinear designs generally using newer materials such as plywood or simple hardwood framing; fabric and synthetics such as vinyl used for upholstery with finer fabrics and real leather featured on more expensive pieces; seating made of molded plastic shells on metal frames and legs used on many mass-produced designs

DANISH MODERN 1950–1970

MAJOR WOOD(S): Teak

GENERAL CHARACTERISTICS:

- **Case and seating pieces:** This variation of Modernistic post-war design originated in Scandinavia, hence the name; designs were simple and restrained with case pieces often having simple boxy forms with short rounded tapering legs; seating pieces have a simple teak framework with lines coordinating with case pieces; vinyl or natural fabric were most often used for upholstery; in the United States dining room suites were the most popular use for this style although some bedroom suites and general seating pieces were available.

ENGLISH

JACOBEAN MID-17TH CENTURY

MAJOR WOOD(S): Oak, walnut

GENERAL CHARACTERISTICS:

- **Case pieces:** Low-relief carving; geometrics and florals; panel, rail and stile construction; applied split balusters

- **Seating pieces:** Rectangular backs; carved and pierced crests; spiral turnings ball feet

WILLIAM AND MARY 1689–1702

MAJOR WOOD(S): Walnut, burl walnut veneer

GENERAL CHARACTERISTICS:

- **Case pieces:** Marquetry, veneering; shaped aprons; 6-8 trumpet-form legs; curved flat stretchers

- **Seating pieces:** Carved, pierced crests; tall caned backs and seats; trumpet-form legs; Spanish feet

QUEEN ANNE 1702–1714

MAJOR WOOD(S): Walnut, mahogany, veneer

GENERAL CHARACTERISTICS:

- **Case pieces:** Cyma curves; broken arch pediments and finials; bracket feet
- **Seating pieces:** Carved crest rails; high, rounded backs; solid vase-shaped splats; cabriole legs; pad feet

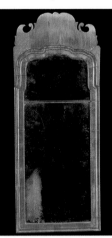

GEORGE I 1714–1727

MAJOR WOOD(S): Walnut, mahogany, veneer, and yew wood

GENERAL CHARACTERISTICS:

- **Case pieces:** Broken arch pediments; gilt decoration, japanning; bracket feet
- **Seating pieces:** Curvilinear forms; yoke-shaped crests; shaped solid splats; shell carving; upholstered seats; carved cabriole legs; claw and ball feet, pad feet

GEORGE II 1727–1760

MAJOR WOOD(S): Mahogany

GENERAL CHARACTERISTICS:

- **Case pieces:** Broken arch pediments; relief-carved foliate, scroll and shell carving; carved cabriole legs; claw and ball feet, bracket feet, ogee bracket feet

- **Seating pieces:** Carved, shaped crest rails, out-turned ears; pierced shaped splats; ladder (ribbon) backs; upholstered seats; scrolled arms; carved cabriole legs or straight (Marlboro) legs; claw and ball feet

GEORGE III 1760–1820

MAJOR WOOD(S): Mahogany, veneer, satinwood

GENERAL CHARACTERISTICS:

- **Case pieces:** Rectilinear forms; parcel gilt decoration; inlaid ovals, circles, banding or marquetry; carved columns, urns; tambour fronts or bow fronts; plinth bases

- **Seating pieces:** Shield backs; upholstered seats; tapered square legs, square legs

REGENCY 1811–1820

MAJOR WOOD(S): Mahogany, mahogany veneer, satinwood, and rosewood

GENERAL CHARACTERISTICS:

- **Case pieces:** Greco-Roman and Egyptian motifs; inlay, ormolu mounts; marble tops; round columns, pilasters; mirrored backs; scroll feet

- **Seating pieces:** Straight backs; latticework; caned seats; sabre legs, tapered turned legs, flared turned legs; parcel gilt, ebonizing

GEORGE IV 1820–1830

MAJOR WOOD(S): Mahogany, mahogany veneer, and rosewood

GENERAL CHARACTERISTICS: Continuation of Regency designs

WILLIAM IV 1830–1837

MAJOR WOOD(S): Mahogany, mahogany veneer

GENERAL CHARACTERISTICS:

- **Case pieces:** Rectilinear; brass mounts, grillwork; carved moldings; plinth bases
- **Seating pieces:** Rectangular backs; carved straight crest rails; acanthus, animal carving; carved cabriole legs; paw feet

VICTORIAN 1837–1901

MAJOR WOOD(S): Black walnut, mahogany, veneers, and rosewood

GENERAL CHARACTERISTICS:

- **Case pieces:** Applied floral carving; surmounting mirrors, drawers, candle shelves; marble tops
- **Seating pieces:** High-relief carved crest rails; floral and fruit carving; balloon backs, oval backs; upholstered seats, backs; spool, spiral turnings; cabriole legs, fluted tapered legs; scrolled feet

EDWARDIAN 1901–1910

MAJOR WOOD(S): Mahogany, mahogany veneer, and satinwood

GENERAL CHARACTERISTICS: Neo-Classical motifs and revivals of earlier 18th century and early 19th century styles

Antique Furniture

L. & J.G. Stickley Arts & Crafts oak sideboard, circa 1912, Fayetteville, New York, Model 7351/2, mirrored back over rectangular top, two central half drawers over two drawers flanked by cabinet doors, long drawer at base, marked "Work of L.J.G. Stickley" in white decal, 50" high x 56" wide x 22" deep. **$1,107**

Pair of Empire-style upholstered mahogany fauteuils with gilt bronze mounts, second half 20th century, rubbing of lacquered finish to edges of armrests and nicking to crest rail and legs, kick marks to legs, rubbing of gilt bronze mounts, minor wear to upholstery, 40 1/2" x 27" x 25". **$3,000**

Courtesy of Heritage Auctions, ha.com

Dutch walnut and oak bonnet secretary bookcase, circa 1800, original lock, new screws to handles, light wear to leather writing surface, cracks to veneer of drop-front and sides, surface wear commensurate with age, 91" x 40" x 25". **$12,500**

Courtesy of Brunk Auctions, www.brunkauctions.com

Southern Federal tassel inlaid walnut corner cupboard, probably Washington County, Tennessee, 19th century, rope and tassel inlaid frieze over two eight-pane glazed doors, shelved interior with silk lining, inlaid dovetailed drawer flanked by two false drawer facings, above two fan and quarter-fan inlaid panel doors, refinished, foot facings replaced, original back boards reset, some glass panes probably original, upper case interior now lighted, 90" x 48 1/2" x 22". **$9,000**

Courtesy of Skinner, Inc., www.skinnerinc.com

Gerson & Wolf Arts & Crafts display cabinet in oak, glass, and brass, Stuttgart, Germany, early 20th century, rectangular form centered by beveled glass door with stylized flowers over long drawer, sides with four open cabinets for display and two cabinets with doors, brass hardware, Gerson & Wolf interior label, 76" high x 43 3/4" wide x 14" deep. **$984**

Miniature carved and paint-decorated pine six-board chest, possibly New England, late 18th century, hinged lid with applied molded edge above nail-constructed box, facade carved with fans, pinwheels, and notches centering heart above carved initials "ME," many carved areas paint-decorated in yellow, green, black, white, and red, molded base, 8 3/4" high x 20" wide x 11" deep. **$10,455**

Painted Windsor settee, probably Pennsylvania, circa 1800-1810, bowed crest rail above bamboo-turned spindles, scrolled arms on shaped supports, seat with shaped ends on splayed bamboo-turned legs joined by stretchers, old green paint over earlier red, 34 1/2" high x 78 1/2" long x 17" deep. **$8,610**

Arts & Crafts even-arm settle, oak, United States, circa 1912, back and side rails with through tenons over seven back slats and three side slats, brown upholstered seat, unmarked, 34 1/2" high x 55 3/4" wide x 26 1/4" deep. **$1,476**

Chippendale carved mahogany side chair, Boston, with carving possibly by John Welch (1711-1789), serpentine crest centering carved shell with flanking acanthus leaves, on vasiform splat and shaped stiles above upholstered compass seat and shaped rails, frontal cabriole legs with shell-and-pendant carved knees and webbed claw-and-ball feet joined to raking chamfered rear legs by block, vase, and ring-turned stretchers, old refinish, 39 1/2" high, seat 18" high. **$28,290**

Louis Majorelle mahogany and marquetry writing desk, Nancy, France, circa 1900, includes key, sliding writing surface with light surface wear commensurate with age and indicative of use, 44" x 38" x 27 1/2". **$8,125**

Courtesy of Skinner, Inc., www.skinnerinc.com

Black-painted cherry dressing table, Connecticut, 18th century, overhanging molded top on case of thumb-molded long drawer and three short drawers, centering fan on concave carved valanced skirt joining cabriole legs with arris knees ending in pad feet on platforms, replaced brasses, 29 1/2" high, case 30 3/4" wide x 17 1/4" deep. **$17,220**

Courtesy of Heritage Auctions, ha.com

Empire-style mahogany and gilt bronze table with specimen marble games table top, 20th century, scratches to apron, surface wear commensurate with age and indicative of use, 28 1/2" x 35 1/2". **$4,500**

Courtesy of Heritage Auctions, ha.com

Pair of neoclassical gilt bronze and malachite side tables, 20th century, surface wear commensurate with age and indicative of light use, 28 1/2" high, 23 1/2" diameter. **$5,000**

Courtesy of Heritage Auctions, ha.com

George III mahogany and gilt bronze demilune sideboard with satinwood stringing, late 18th century, surface scratches to top, minor kick marks to spade-form feet, surface wear commensurate with age and indicative of use, 35 1/4" x 72" x 28". **$3,125**

Virginia carved mahogany ceremonial desk attributed to Robert Walker (1710-1777) of King George County, slant lid opening to fitted interior centering profile bust-carved prospect door flanked by two inlaid document drawers, one document drawer inscribed on side in red pencil "RL" and verso "James M..." over five dovetailed drawers set with large original batwing brasses, base with gadrooned molding and legs carved with lion-mask knees and hairy paw feet, early surface, formerly fitted with upper case now capped with 19th century top, original feet with some later blocking, top drawer lacking lock and set with probably 19th century dividers, minor repairs to secondary surfaces including three interior drawers with replaced bottoms, interior desk valances restored, minor distress at escutcheon hole in prospect door, other cracks and flaws consistent with age and use, 44" x 43" x 23". **$185,000**

Louis XV amaranth, tulipwood, mahogany, and gilt bronze commode with marble top, Paris, circa 1775, with molded rectangular gris marble top, over frieze with mounted ovolu border continuing to sides, rosette mounts to corners, zigzag tulipwood parquetry to drawers, canted corners and sides, gilt bronze acanthus wreath-form handles to corners of both drawers, acorn and foliate mount to skirt, four cabriole legs terminating in gilt bronze scrolling foliate feet, stamped to top "M. CARLIN," restoration to joints, original hardware, lacking key, chipping of marble to far edge, wear commensurate with age, 34 1/2" x 38 1/2" x 21". **$71,875**

Mid-Century Modern Furniture

Paper knife chair, Kai Kristiansen (Danish, b. 1929), 1955, teak with upholstered cushions, light surface wear commensurate with age, 29 3/4" x 25" x 29". **$813**

Corona chair, Poul Volther (1923-2001), design date 1958, licensed manufacturer Erik Jorgensen, Denmark, brown upholstered seat on metal framework, 38" high x 32" deep x 34 1/2" wide. **$1,476**

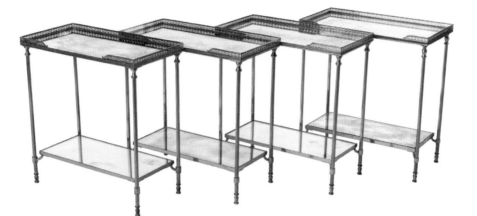

Courtesy of Heritage Auctions, ha.com

Four Directoire-style brass and mirrored side tables, circa 1940, surface scratches to mirrored surfaces, all with surface wear commensurate with age, 21" x 20" x 10". **$1,125**

Courtesy of Heritage Auctions, ha.com

Large round dining table with tulip base, Eero Saarinen (American, 1910-1961), marble, wood, enameled aluminum, later Knoll International edition, 26" x 49 1/2" x 49 1/2". **$2,750**

Courtesy of Skinner, Inc., www.skinnerinc.com

Elizabeth chair and ottoman, Ib Kofod Larson, Denmark, circa 1956, rosewood and leather, stamped manufacturer's mark to underside of chair, chair 28" high x 31" wide x 30" deep, ottoman 14 1/2" high x 22 1/2" wide x 17 1/2" deep. $20,910

Courtesy of Skinner, Inc., www.skinnerinc.com

Butterfly or BKF chair, Jorge Ferrari Hardoy, circa 1957, painted wrought iron and leather, thick brown leather cover, unmarked, 32 3/4" high x 34 3/8" wide. $1,046

Courtesy of Skinner, Inc., www.skinnerinc.com

Bird chair and ottoman, Harry Bertoia, design date 1952, Knoll International, Park Avenue, New York, circa 1974, welded steel rods, blue upholstery on steel rod frame, paper label, chair 40 1/4" high x 33" deep x 38 1/4" wide, ottoman 14 1/2" high x 17 1/4" deep x 23 1/2" wide. $984

▲ Pair of Italian Art Deco mahogany veneered upholstered armchairs, circa 1930, club-style with upholstered seats and backs with continuous veneered arms, missing veneer to front skirts, one chair with lifting veneer to left facing arm front, each arm with slight buckle and lift to arm veneers, 29" x 27" x 30". **$3,500**

◄ RAR rocker, Charles Eames (American, 1907-1978) and Ray Kaiser Eames (American, 1912-1988), circa 1950, Herman Miller, fiberglass shell, zinc wire, and walnut, overall good condition, 27" x 25" x 27". **$550**

Four Model 3107 chairs,
Arne Jacobsen (Danish,
1902-1971), 1955, cherry
and chromed steel,
good condition, 29 1/2" x
17 3/4" x 18 1/2". **$1,500**

"PL Uddebo" (desk),
Svante Skogh (Swedish,
20th century), circa
1950, Mobelfabrikken
Balder, oak, without
key, light surface wear
commensurate with age,
28 7/8" x 53 1/4" x 27 1/2".
$2,250

Long sofa, William "Billy"
Haines, designer, custom
designed, commissioned
1960, 30" x 132" x 36".
$12,500

▲ Sofa, Florence Knoll
(American, b. 1917), 1954, felt
upholstery, steel, wood frame,
polished chrome finish, later
Knoll International edition,
32" x 90" x 33". **$4,375**

▲ Credenza, Tommi Parzinger (1903-
1981), Charak Modern, United States,
circa 1955, leather and wood, green
leather finish tooled and gilded in
lozenge pattern, cabinet with two double
doors with circular brass hardware,
interior of each cabinet fitted with single
drawer over shelf and painted coral pink,
Charak Modern mark on drawer, black
finish on base, indentations in leather
surface, wear, 33" high x 64 1/2" wide x
16" deep. **$6,765**

◀ Sheaf of wheat table, Edward
Wormley for Dunbar, Berne, Indiana,
1958, mahogany, Carrera marble, and
brass, circular top over steam-bent
mahogany base joined by brass ring,
metal Dunbar label, 25 1/2" high,
27" diameter. **$1,353**

Console table, Ico and Luisa Parisi, designed circa 1955, M. Singer & Sons, with label reading "M. Singer & Sons/New York Chicago," 30" x 71" x 19 3/4". **$22,500**

Art Deco oval faux marble dining table, Paul T. Frankl, Los Angeles, circa 1948, extending oval table with faux marble top and brass trim to apron, two matching leaf inserts each 14" wide, gilt wood, reeded standard with faux marble base, brass X-form foot, restored, minor surface scratches to table top, 29 1/2" x 71" x 48". **$3,500**

Mid-century Danish table, inlaid teak with graduating tiers, 22" x 25" x 20" deep. **$338**

GLASS

Art Glass 398
Carnival 402
Daum Nancy 409
Depression 420
Fenton 438
Lalique 444
Quezal 454

Art Glass

Art glass is artistic novelty glassware created for decorative purposes. Types of art glass include leaded glass, molded glass, blown glass, and sandblasted glass. Tiffany, Lalique, and Steuben are some of the best-known types of art glass. Daum Nancy, Baccarat, Gallé, Moser, Mt. Washington, Fenton, and Quezal are a few others.

Courtesy of James D. Julia Auctioneers, Fairfield, Maine, www.jamesdjulia.com

Loetz Titania vase, free-form pulled design in brown and platinum extending upward from foot against green background, unsigned, very good to excellent condition, 5 1/4" high. **$5,629**

Courtesy of Mark Mussio, Humler & Nolan, www.humlernolan.com

Loetz cobalt Papillon bottle vase with cobalt reeded fleur-de-lis scroll handles, oval acid stamp logo reads "Czecho-Slovakia" beneath, excellent original condition, 7 7/8" high. **$325**

Pair of Bohemian gilded and enameled cranberry glass vases, late 19th century, each with crenulated rim over central oval medallion polychrome painted with floral bouquet, on three pulled feet, unmarked, 11 3/8" high. **$800**

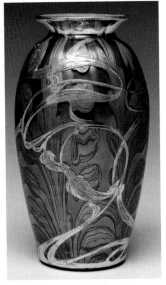

Loetz Cytus vase, copper-colored iridescent ground with platinum iridescent oil spots, light green glass background, pinched shoulder and tricorn lip, unsigned, very good to excellent condition, 7" high. **$5,333**

Large Moser blue glass vase with enameled bird perched on limb with yellow, blue, and red flowers, edge of vase trimmed with floral band, foot trimmed with dental band in blue and gray with gilded outline, backside with floral design and butterfly and bumblebee, unsigned, flake to side of foot and wear to gilding on foot and lip, 16" high. **$652**

Loetz Phanomen 2/450 genre vase with blue iridescent decoration and violet highlights against green iridescent background, sterling silver overlay of stems and leaves with curving, unengraved cartouche, unsigned, very good to excellent condition, 6 7/8" high. **$13,035**

G | GLASS

Courtesy of James D. Julia Auctioneers, Fairfield, Maine, www.jamesdjulia.com

Moser vase with dark red cameo glass decoration of grapevines, leaves, and clusters against swirling yellow and white background with acid-textured surface, center of one grape with etched signature "Moser," original Moser paper label on underside, very good to excellent condition, 10 1/4" high. **$474**

Courtesy of James D. Julia Auctioneers, Fairfield, Maine, www.jamesdjulia.com

Moser vase with cranberry shading to clear body with applied amber glass foot, allover decoration of oak leaves in red, yellow, green, and blue with yellow branches, single enameled bumblebee at shoulder, applied and gilded glass acorns, signed on underside in gold "622/ D180 Moser," very good to excellent condition, 5 1/4" high. **$948**

Courtesy of James D. Julia Auctioneers, Fairfield, Maine, www.jamesdjulia.com

Loetz Titania vase with silvery blue pulled design against brown and orange background, Art Nouveau silver overlay design of twining stems and leaves, silver overlay plain with no engraved detail, unsigned, very good to excellent condition, 12 1/4" high. **$7,110**

Courtesy of Skinner, Inc.; www.skinnerinc.com

Pair of Bohemian gilded and enameled cranberry glass vases, late 19th century, each balustroid with central medallion polychrome hand-painted with putti in clouds, unmarked, 14 1/4" high. **$861**

Monumental marquetry Moser vase with wheel-carved dark red marquetry flower on front with two dark green marquetry buds on sides, applied green thread forming stem of flower, remainder intaglio carved with flowers, leaves and stems in all-around design, top rim with irregular border, shading from clear to transparent olive green at base, unsigned, very good to excellent condition, 15 1/2" high. **$4,444**

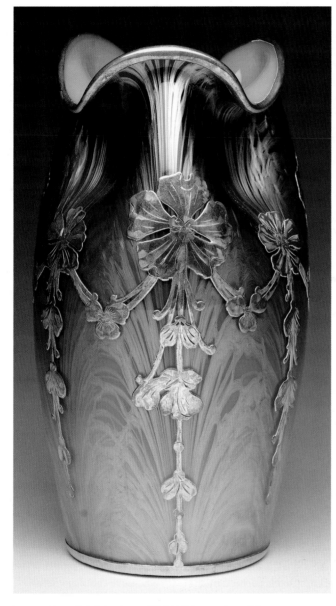

Loetz silver overlay vase in Titania pattern with silvery blue dragged loop design against yellow background, pinched shoulder and ruffled lip, sterling silver overlay of garland of flowers surrounding shoulder with leaves and buds dangling below, unsigned, very good to excellent condition, 9 1/2" high. **$8,295**

Carnival Glass

By Ellen T. Schroy

Carnival glass is what is fondly called mass-produced iridescent glassware. The term "carnival glass" has evolved through the years as glass collectors have responded to the idea that much of this beautiful glassware was made as giveaway glass at local carnivals and fairs. However, more of it was made and sold through the same channels as pattern glass and Depression glass. Some patterns were indeed giveaways, and others were used as advertising premiums, souvenirs, etc. Whatever the origin, the term "carnival glass" today encompasses glassware that is usually pattern molded and treated with metallic salts, creating that unique coloration that is so desirable to collectors.

Early names for iridescent glassware, which early 20th century consumers believed to have all come from foreign manufacturers, include Pompeiian Iridescent, Venetian Art, and Mexican Aurora. Another popular early name was "Nancy Glass," as some patterns were believed to have come from the Daum, Nancy, glassmaking area in France. This was at a time when the artistic cameo glass was enjoying great success. While the iridescent glassware being made by such European glassmakers as Loetz influenced the American marketplace, it was Louis Tiffany's Favrile glass that really caught the eye of glass consumers of the early 1900s. It seems an easy leap to transform Tiffany's shimmering glassware to something that could be mass-produced, allowing what we call carnival glass today to become "poor man's Tiffany."

Carnival glass is iridized glassware that is created by pressing hot molten glass into molds, just as pattern glass had evolved. Some forms are hand finished, while others are completely formed by molds. To achieve the marvelous iridescent colors that carnival glass collectors seek, a process was developed where a liquid solution of metallic salts was put onto the still-hot glass form after it was unmolded. As the liquid evaporated, a fine metallic surface was left which refracts light into wonderful colors. The name given to the iridescent spray by early glassmakers was "dope."

Many of the forms created by carnival glass manufacturers

ELLEN T. SCHROY, one of the leading experts in her field, is the author of *Warman's Carnival Glass Identification and Price Guide* and other books on collectible glass. Her books are the definitive references for glass collectors.

Courtesy of Jeffrey S. Evans & Associates, www.jeffreysevans.com

◄ Daisy and Drape pattern vase in aqua opalescent with three feet, H. Northwood Co., first quarter 20th century, undamaged, 6 1/4" high. **$219**

Courtesy of Jeffrey S. Evans & Associates, www.jeffreysevans.com

▲ Peacocks on the Fence pattern bowl in amethyst iridescent, ruffled and serrated rim, ribbed back, and strong iridescence, H. Northwood Co., first quarter 20th century, undamaged, 2 1/2" high, 9" diameter. **$230**

were accessories to the china American housewives so loved. By the early 1900s, consumers could find carnival glassware at such popular stores as F. W. Woolworth and McCrory's. To capitalize on the popular fancy for these colored wares, some other industries bought large quantities of carnival glass and turned them into "packers." This term reflects the practice where baking powder, mustard, or other household products were packed into a special piece of glass that could take on another life after the original product was used. Lee Manufacturing Co. used iridized carnival glass as premiums for its baking powder and other products, causing some early carnival glass to be known by the generic term "Baking Powder Glass."

Classic carnival glass production began in the early 1900s and continued

Grape Arbor pattern four-piece water set in amethyst iridescent, water pitcher and three tumblers, Northwood Glass Co., late 19th/first quarter 20th century, undamaged, pitcher 11 5/8" high, tumblers 4 1/4" high. $161

for about 20 years. Fenton Art Glass became the top producer with more than 150 patterns. No one really documented or researched production until the first collecting wave struck in 1960.

It is important to remember that carnival glasswares were sold in department stores as well as mass merchants rather than through the general store often associated with a young America. Glassware by this time was mass-produced and sold in large quantities by such enterprising companies as Butler Brothers. When the economics of the country soured in the 1920s, those interested in purchasing iridized glassware were not spared. Many of the leftover inventories of glasshouses that hoped to sell this mass-produced glassware found their way to wholesalers who, in turn, sold the wares to those who offered the glittering glass as prizes at carnivals, fairs, circuses, etc. Possibly because this was the last venue people associated with the iridized glassware, it became known as "carnival glass."

For more information on carnival glass, see *Warman's Carnival Glass Identification and Price Guide,* 2nd edition, by Ellen T. Schroy.

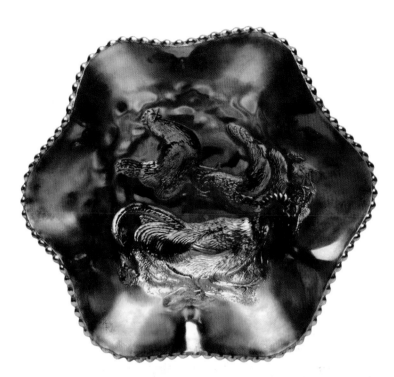

Farmyard pattern bowl with six ruffles and beaded rim in amethyst iridescent, Jeweled Heart exterior pattern, Dugan Glass Co., near mint condition with three minute rim nicks, 3 1/4" high, 10 7/8" diameter.
$2,204

Grape and Cable pattern punch bowl in amethyst iridescent, relief decorated on exterior with grape cluster and leaves hanging from cable, on matching trumpeted base, H. Northwood Co., signed with Northwood "N" in circle mark, excellent condition with no chips or cracks, 10 1/2" high overall, bowl 6" high, 11"diameter.
$393

Grape and Cable pattern footed bowl in amethyst iridescent, relief decorated on exterior with grape cluster and leaves hanging from cable, three scrolled feet, H. Northwood Co., signed on bottom with Northwood "N" in circle mark, excellent condition with no chips or cracks, 6 1/2" high, 11" diameter. **$182**

Rare Orange Tree pattern cobalt blue iridescent candy ribbon-edge bowl with unusual variant tree trunk center and Bearded Berry exterior, Fenton Art Glass Co., only known example with candy ribbon edge, very good condition, bottom with faint scratches and "straw mark," minute rim nick, 2 5/8" high overall, 7 3/4" diameter top, 3 1/4" diameter base. **$464**

*Courtesy of Green Valley
Auctions & Moving, Inc.,
www.greenvalleyauctions.com*

Rare Christmas pattern compote in amethyst iridescent, Dugan/Diamond Glass Co., light wear to base, several "straw marks" on exterior made during firing process, 5 7/8" high, 9 3/4" diameter. **$1,972**

Courtesy of Jeffrey S. Evans & Associates, www.jeffreysevans.com

Nippon pattern bowl in ice blue, ribbed exterior, ruffled and serrated/piecrust rim, signed, H. Northwood Co., first quarter 20th century, undamaged, 2" high, 8 3/4" diameter. **$184**

Courtesy of Jeffrey S. Evans & Associates, www.jeffreysevans.com

▲ Poinsettia and Lattice pattern bowl in amethyst, ruffled rim, three feet, H. Northwood Co., first quarter 20th century, undamaged, 2 3/4" high, 9" diameter. **$230**

Courtesy of Green Valley Auctions & Moving, Inc., www.greenvalleyauctions.com

◄ Wishbone pattern water pitcher with applied handle in green iridescent, Northwood Glass Co., undamaged, "straw mark" in spout, 10 1/8" high. **$522**

Daum Nancy

Daum Nancy fine glass, much of it cameo, was made by Auguste and Antonin Daum, who founded a factory in 1875 in Nancy, France. Most of their cameo and enameled glass was made from the 1890s into the early 20th century.

Cameo glass is made by carving into multiple layers of colored glass to create a design in relief. It is at least as old as the Romans.

Courtesy of Woody Auction, www.woodyauction.com
Ashtray in green shading to clear glass, heavy blank with cameo-carved floral and banner design, signed "AVGVI L'ANNEVF," gold stencil highlights with slight wear, no chips, cracks, or repairs, 6" high. **$295**

Lamp with cameo and enameled winter scene of barren trees on snow-covered ground, trees enameled in brown, shade in triangular shape with flared apron, with original hammered iron collar and spider, signed on underside of base with enamel signature "Daum Nancy" with Cross of Lorraine, very good to excellent condition, some wear to finish on iron spider and replacement socket, rewired, 18" high. **$16,590**

Table lamp with cameo decoration of large green leaves encircling shade and base with orange cameo oranges or peaches against mottled pink shading to orange background, lamp base with hammered metal collar and four-arm spider, shade signed on side in cameo "Daum Nancy" with Cross of Lorraine, base signed near bottom "DN," very good to excellent condition, rewired, 10 1/2" wide x 19 3/4" high. **$9,480**

Courtesy of James D. Julia Auctioneers, Fairfield, Maine, www.jamesdjulia.com
Vase with red cameo leaves, stems, and flowers extending from foot against frosted amber background, flowers and some leaves detailed with wheel carving, background near foot with wheel-carved texture, signed on side of foot with engraved signature "Daum Nancy France" with Cross of Lorraine, very good to excellent condition, 9 1/2" high. **$8,295**

Courtesy of James D. Julia Auctioneers, Fairfield, Maine, www.jamesdjulia.com
Cylindrical vase with mottled green cameo Impressionistic trees against acid-textured brown shading to orange shading to mottled light blue background, cameo birds in flight above trees, signed on underside with etched signature "Daum Nancy" with Cross of Lorraine, very good to excellent condition, 8 5/8" high. **$4,631**

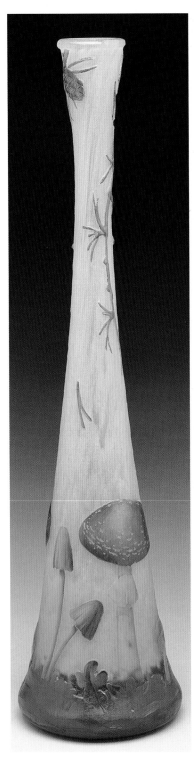

Courtesy of James D. Julia Auctioneers, Fairfield, Maine, www.jamesdjulia.com

▲ Vase with brownish-red cameo floral decoration surrounding body against clear glass background with cased yellow interior, patches of wheel-carved martele around body and on foot, signed on underside with etched signature "Daum Nancy" with Cross of Lorraine, very good to excellent condition, 5 3/4" high. **$1,422**

Courtesy of James D. Julia Auctioneers, Fairfield, Maine, www.jamesdjulia.com

◄ Vase with cameo decoration of various colored mushrooms with pine tree limbs, needles and pinecones near top of vase against mottled yellow and cream background, wheel-carved detailing to grasses at bottom of vase and underside of mushrooms, mushrooms enameled in orange, green, brown, and tan, signed on underside with etched signature "Daum Nancy" with Cross of Lorraine, very good to excellent condition, small grind mark to outside lip and small acid burn on lip from manufacture, 15 3/4" high. **$11,850**

Vase with mottled green and orange cameo leaves and stems leading to large cameo flowers in red, purple, lavender, and yellow against frosted background of mottled purple shading to yellow shading to cream, signed on underside with lightly etched signature "Daum Nancy" with Cross of Lorraine, very good to excellent condition, 10" high. **$5,558**

Vase with bulbous body and long slender neck, green cameo leaves and stems ascending from foot with pink cameo flowers hanging from stems, green cameo flowers on neck, purple shading to cream-colored full martele background, signed on underside with engraved and gilded signature "Daum Nancy" with Cross of Lorraine, very good to excellent condition, 9 7/8" high. **$7,110**

Vase with dark reddish-amber cameo tobacco leaves ascending from foot with stems leading to wheel-carved tobacco flowers and buds against yellow mottled background, textured surface near top of vase, signed on side with engraved signature "Daum Nancy" with Cross of Lorraine, very good to excellent condition with minor roughness on top of foot from manufacture, 19" high. **$3,556**

Bowl with cameo morning glories, stems, and leaves surrounding side, leaves enameled in green, morning glories enameled in white, yellow, and gray against frosted background, signed on side in cameo "Daum Nancy" with Cross of Lorraine, very good to excellent condition, 6" diameter. **$2,015**

Miniature vase with cameo and enameled red orchids on front and back with stems and leaves enameled in green along with cameo spiderwebs around flowers, mottled brown shading to yellow shading to cream background, signed on side in cameo "Daum Nancy" with Cross of Lorraine, very good to excellent condition, 2 1/2" high. **$2,548**

Large vase with dark brown cameo trees in foreground framing lake with two sailboats and mountains in distance against mottled yellow and orange background, signed on side in cameo "Daum Nancy" with Cross of Lorraine, very good to excellent condition, 12 1/2" high. **$2,074**

Courtesy of James D. Julia Auctioneers, Fairfield, Maine, www.jamesdjulia.com

Blown-out vase with internally decorated glass body in mottled purple and pink glass within Majorelle iron frame with stylized leaves, wires, and tooled bands encircling vase, signed on underside with engraved signature "Daum Nancy" with Cross of Lorraine and "Majorelle," very good to excellent condition, 9 3/4" high. **$2,161**

Courtesy of Woody Auction, www.woodyauction.com

Cameo cabinet vase, yellow and purple mottled background with carved floral, wasp, and spiderweb design, signed, no chips, cracks or repairs, 4" high x 4 1/2" wide. **$3,835**

Large mold-blown vase with mottled green and brown trees, branches and leaves surrounding vase against sky of mottled orange and yellow, foliage at bottom between wheel-carved trees, signed in polished pontil with engraved "Daum Nancy" with Cross of Lorraine, very good to excellent condition with tiny open bubbles around foot from manufacture, 17 1/4" high. **$9,480**

Vase with brown cameo stems and leaves ascending from foot, terminating in red tobacco flowers against mottled orange and pink background, each flower with wheel-carved details, signed on top of foot with engraved signature "Daum Nancy" with Cross of Lorraine, very good to excellent condition, small burst bubble on bottom edge of foot from manufacture, 13 1/2" high. **$2,161**

Courtesy of James D. Julia Auctioneers, Fairfield, Maine, www.jamesdjulia.com

Vase with cranberry acid-etched wild roses and green stems and leaves on frosted and textured background with green foot and rim, top and bottom of vase with wheel-carved martele background, engraved signature on underside "Daum Nancy," very good to excellent condition with small open bubbles from manufacture, 7" high. **$2,074**

ELLEN T. SCHROY, one of the leading experts in her field, is the author of *Warman's Depression Glass Identification and Price Guide* and *Warman's Depression Glass Field Guide.* Her books are the definitive references for Depression glass collectors.

Depression Glass

By Ellen T. Schroy

Depression glass is the name of the colorful glassware manufactured during the years surrounding the Great Depression in America. Homemakers of the era enjoyed this new, inexpensive dinnerware because they received pieces of their favorite patterns and colors packed in boxes of soap or as premiums on "dish night" at the local movie theater. Merchandisers, such as Sears & Roebuck and F.W. Woolworth, enticed young brides with the colorful wares that they could afford even when economic times were harsh.

Because of advancements in glassware technology, Depression-era patterns were mass-produced and could be purchased for a fraction of what cut glass or lead crystal cost. As one manufacturer found a pattern that was pleasing to the buying public, other companies soon followed with their adaptations of a similar design. Hundreds of patterns exist and include several design motifs, such as florals, geometrics, and even patterns that looked back to Early American patterns like Sandwich glass.

As America emerged from the Great Depression and life became more leisure-oriented again, new glassware patterns were created to reflect the new tastes of this generation. More elegant shapes and forms were designed, leading to what is sometimes called "Elegant Glass." Today's collectors often include these more elegant patterns when they talk about Depression glass.

Depression glass researchers have many accurate sources, including company records, catalogs, magazine advertisements, and oral and written histories from sales staff, factory workers, etc. It is one of the best-researched collecting areas available to the American marketplace. This is due in large part to the careful research of several people, including Hazel Marie Weatherman, Gene Florence, Barbara Mauzy, Carl F. Luckey, and Kent Washburn, whose books are held in high regard by researchers and collectors today.

Courtesy of Specialists of the South, www.specialistsofthesouth.com
Adam pattern pink butter dish, Jeannette Glass Co., 1932-1934. $40

Avocado pattern green creamer and sugar, Indiana Glass Co., 1923-1933. **$65/set**

Aurora pattern cobalt blue tumbler, Hazel Atlas Glass Co., late 1930s. **$22**

Bubble pattern royal ruby two-tier tidbit tray, Hocking Glass Co./Anchor Hocking Glass Co., 1937-1965. **$35**

Capri pattern azure blue boxed seashell snack set, Hazel Ware, a division of Continental Can, 1960s. **$75**

Regarding values for Depression glass, rarity does not always equate to a high dollar amount. Some more readily found items command lofty prices because of high demand or other factors, not because they are necessarily rare. As collectors' tastes range from the simple patterns to the more elaborate patterns, so does the ability of their budget to invest in inexpensive patterns to multi-hundreds of dollars per form patterns.

For more information on Depression glass, see *Warman's Depression Glass Identification and Price Guide, 6th Edition*, or *Warman's Depression Glass Field Guide, 5th Edition*, both by Ellen T. Schroy.

PATTERN SILHOUETTE Identification Guide

Depression-era glassware can be confusing. Many times a manufacturer came up with a neat new design, and as soon as it was successful, other companies started to make patterns that were similar. To help you figure out what pattern you might be trying to research, here's a quick identification guide. The patterns are broken down into several different classifications by design elements.

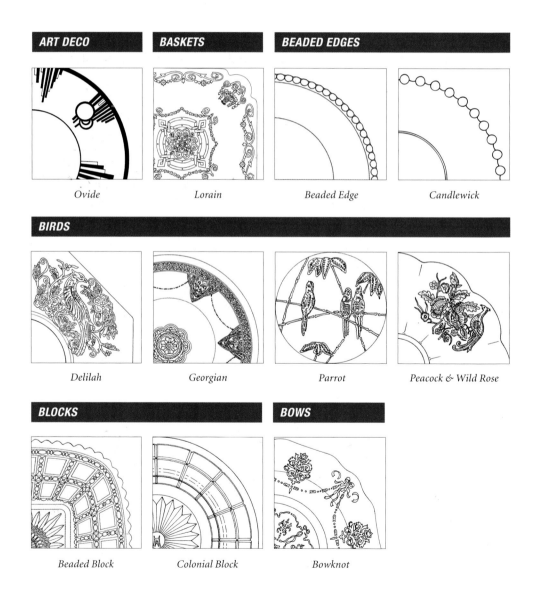

ART DECO

Ovide

BASKETS

Lorain

BEADED EDGES

Beaded Edge

Candlewick

BIRDS

Delilah

Georgian

Parrot

Peacock & Wild Rose

BLOCKS

Beaded Block

Colonial Block

BOWS

Bowknot

COINS

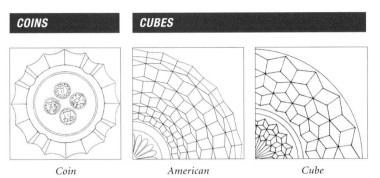

Coin

CUBES

American

Cube

DIAMONDS

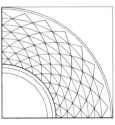

Cape Cod

Diamond Quilted

English Hobnail

Holiday

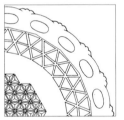

Laced Edge

Miss America

Peanut Butter

Waterford

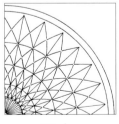

Windsor

ELLIPSES (FANS)

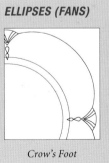

Crow's Foot

Newport

Romanesque

FIGURES

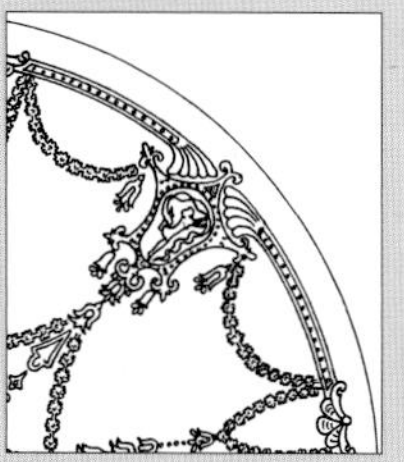

Cameo

Cupid

FLORALS

Alice

Cherry Blossom

Cloverleaf

Daisy

Dogwood

Doric

Doric & Pansy

Floragold

Floral

Floral and Diamond Band

Flower Garden with
Butterflies

Indiana Custard

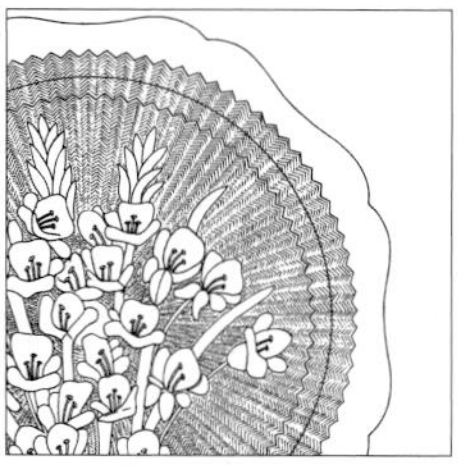

Iris

Jubilee

FLORALS *continued*

Mayfair (Federal)

Mayfair (Open Rose)

Normandie

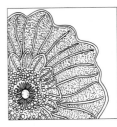

Orange Blossom

Pineapple & Floral

Primrose

Rosemary

Rose Cameo

Royal Lace

Seville

Sharon

Sunflower

Thistle

Tulip

Vitrock

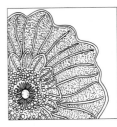

Wild Rose

FRUITS

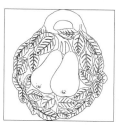

Avocado

Cherryberry

Della Robbia

Fruits

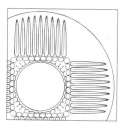

Paneled Grape

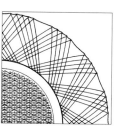

Strawberry

GEOMETIC & LINE DESIGNS

Cracked Ice

Cape Cod

Cremax

Early American Prescut

Park Avenue

Pioneer

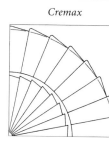

Sierra

Star

Starlight

Tea Room

HONEYCOMB

Aunt Polly

Hex Optic

HORSESHOE

Horseshoe

LEAVES

Laurel Leaf

Sunburst

LACY DESIGNS

Harp

Heritage

S-Pattern

Sandwich (Duncan Miller)

Sandwich (Hocking)

Sandwich (Indiana)

LOOPS

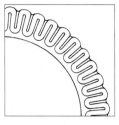

Christmas Candy

Crocheted Crystal

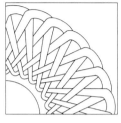

Pretzel

PETALS

Aurora

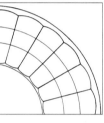

Block Optic

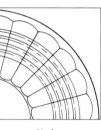

Circle

Colonial

National

New Century

Old Café

Ribbon

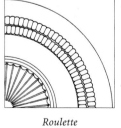

Roulette

Round Robin

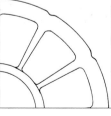

Victory

PETALS/RIDGES WITH DIAMOND ACCENTS

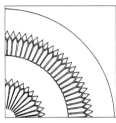
Anniversary

Coronation

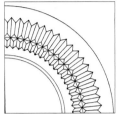
Fortune

Lincoln Inn

Petalware

Queen Mary

PLAIN

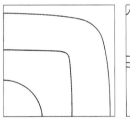
Charm

Mt. Pleasant

PYRAMIDS

Pyramid

RAISED BAND

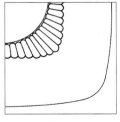
Charm

Forest Green

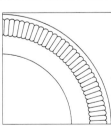
Jane Ray

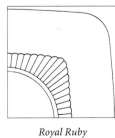
Royal Ruby

RAISED CIRCLES

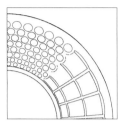
American Pioneer

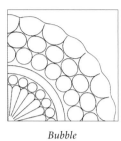
Bubble

Columbia

Dewdrop

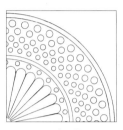
Hobnail

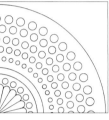
Moonstone

Oyster & Pearl

Raindrops

Radiance

Ships

Teardrop

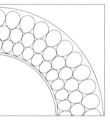
Thumbprint

RIBS

Homespun

RINGS (CIRCLES)

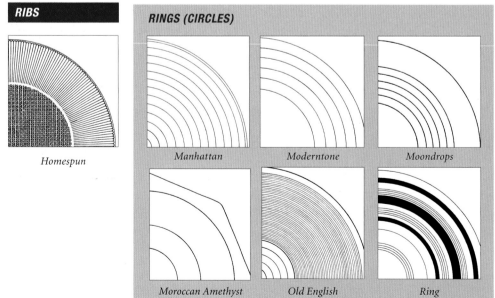

Manhattan *Moderntone* *Moondrops*

Moroccan Amethyst *Old English* *Ring*

SCENES

Chinex Classic

Lake Como

SCROLLING DESIGNS

Adam

American Sweetheart

Florentine No. 1

Florentine No. 2

Madrid

Patrick

Philbe

Primo

Princess

Rock Crystal

Roxana

Vernon

SWIRLS

Colony   *Diana*   *Fairfax*   *Jamestown*

Spiral   *Swirl*   *Swirl (Fire King)*   *Twisted Optic*

TEXTURED

U.S. Swirl   *By Cracky*   *Twiggy*

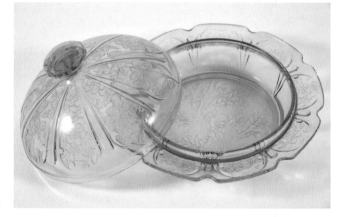

Cherry Blossom pattern green covered butter dish, Jeannette Glass Co., 1930-1939. $34

Circle pattern green saltshaker, Hocking Glass Co., 1930s. **$95**

Colonial Block green covered candy jar, Hazel Atlas Glass Co., early 1930s. **$40**

Courtesy of Milestone Auctions, www.milestoneauctions.com

Colony pattern pink candlesticks, Fostoria Glass Co., 1930s-1983, excellent condition, 8" high. **$48**

Delilah pattern amber candlesticks, Paden City Glass Co., 1930s. **$90**

Constellation pattern amber water goblet, Indiana Glass Co., circa 1940. **$15**

English Hobnail pattern pink covered puff box, Westmoreland Glass Co., 1920s-1983, 6" diameter. **$80**

Courtesy of Specialists of the South, www.specialistsofthesouth.com

▼ Holiday/Buttons and Bows pink covered butter dish, Jeannette Glass Co., 1947-1950s, 6" diameter. **$40**

Courtesy of East Coast Auctions, www.eastcoastauctions.org

Floragold pattern iridescent pitcher with six footed tumblers, Jeannette Glass Co., 1950s. Pitcher **$30**, Tumblers **$15 ea.**

▲ Iris/Iris and Herringbone pattern crystal candlesticks, two lights each, Jeannette Glass Co., 1928-1932, 1950s, 1970s, 6 1/4" x 5 3/4". **$24**

◄ Eight Jamestown pattern green ice tea tumblers, Fostoria Glass Co., 1958-1982, 6" high. **$96**

Jubilee pattern yellow centerpiece, three legs, Lancaster Glass Co., early 1930s, 14" diameter. **$210**

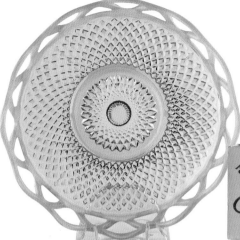

▲ Laced Edge pattern blue bowl, Imperial Glass Co., early 1930s, also known as Katy Blue, Sugar Cane, and Line 7455, 5 1/2" diameter. **$30**

▶ Moroccan Amethyst pattern four-piece cocktail set in box, Hazel Ware, a division of Continental Can, 1960s. **$75**

Courtesy of Specialists of the South, www.specialistsofthesouth.com

Newport pattern cobalt blue pitcher with ice lip, creamer, sugar, five cups, four saucers, four plates, and sherbet, plates 8 1/4" diameter. **$34**

◀ Paneled Grape white soap dish, Westmoreland Glass Co., 1950s-1970s. **$75**

Courtesy of Specialists of the South, www.specialistsofthesouth.com

Poinsettia/Floral pattern green covered butter dish, Jeannette Glass Co., 1931-1935, 6 1/2" diameter. **$51**

Courtesy of Specialists of the South, www.specialistsofthesouth.com

Sierra pattern green bowl, Jeannette Glass Co., 1931-1933, 8 1/2" diameter, 3 1/2" high. **$29**

Courtesy of Specialists of the South, www.specialistsofthesouth.com

▲ Sunflower pattern pink cake plate, Jeannette Glass Co., 1930s, 10" diameter. **$40**

Courtesy of Specialists of the South, www.specialistsofthesouth.com

◀ Thumbprint & Cherries pattern pink butter dish, plate 7 3/4" diameter. **$23**

Fenton Art Glass

The Fenton Art Glass Co. was founded in 1905 by Frank L. Fenton and his brother, John W., in Martins Ferry, Ohio. They initially sold hand-painted glass made by other manufacturers, but it wasn't long before they decided to produce their own glass.

The new Fenton factory in Williamstown, West Virginia, opened on Jan. 2, 1907. From that point on, the company expanded by developing unusual colors and continued to decorate glassware in innovative ways. Two more brothers, James and Robert, joined the firm.

But despite the company's initial success, John W. left to establish the Millersburg Glass Co. of Millersburg, Ohio, in 1909. The first months of the new operation were devoted to the production of crystal glass only. Later iridized glass was called "Radium Glass." After only two years, Millersburg filed for bankruptcy.

Fenton's iridescent glass had a metallic luster over a colored, pressed pattern and was sold in dime stores. It was only after the sales of this glass decreased and it was sold in bulk as carnival prizes that it came to be known as carnival glass.

Fenton became the top producer of carnival glass, with more than 150 patterns. The quality of the glass, and its popularity with the public, enabled the new company to be profitable through the late 1920s. As interest in carnival glass subsided, Fenton moved on to stretch glass and opalescent patterns. A line of colorful blown glass (called "off-hand" by Fenton) was also produced in the mid-1920s.

During the Great Depression, Fenton survived by producing functional colored glass tableware and other household items, including water sets, table sets, bowls, mugs, plates, perfume bottles, and vases.

Restrictions on European imports during World War II ushered in the arrival of Fenton's opaque colored glass, and the lines of "Crest" pieces soon followed.

In the 1950s, production continued to diversify with a focus on milk glass, particularly in Hobnail patterns.

In the third quarter of Fenton's history, the company returned to themes that had proved popular to preceding generations, and began adding special lines, such as the Bicentennial series.

Innovations included the line of Colonial colors that debuted

**Lattice and Grape
pattern seven-piece
water set, circa 1912,
colorless, blown-
molded tankard
pitcher with applied
handle and six
pressed tumblers,
pitcher 11 5/8" high,
tumblers 4" high. $69**

in 1963, including amber, blue, green, orange and ruby. Based on a special order for an Ohio museum, Fenton in 1969 revisited its early success with "Original Formula Carnival Glass." Fenton also started marking its glass in molds for the first time.

The star of the 1970s was the yellow and blushing pink creation known as Burmese, which remains popular today. This was followed closely by a menagerie of animals, birds, and children.

In 1975, Robert Barber was hired by Fenton to begin an artist-in-residence program, producing a limited line of art glass vases in a return to the off-hand, blown-glass creations of the mid-1920s.

Shopping at home via television was a phenomenon in the late 1980s when the "Birthstone Bears" became the first Fenton product to appear on QVC (established in 1986 by Joseph Segel, founder of The Franklin Mint).

In August 2007, Fenton discontinued all but a few of its more popular lines, and in 2011 ceased production entirely.

For more information on Fenton Art Glass, see *Warman's Fenton Glass Identification and Price Guide*, 2nd edition, by Mark F. Moran.

Two **Empress vases**, one in deep orange and one in jadite, marked Fenton on underside, each decorated with Buddha in garden with bridge and water fowl, 7 3/4" high. **$72**

▲ Large **art glass vase** with "Hanging Hearts" design by Robert Barber, custard base, flared ribbed rim, marked and dated 1976, 15 1/4" high. **$354**

▶ **Mosiac off-hand art glass vase** with colorful inclusions bound by spider-webbing in shadow balancing above deep cobalt blue foot, iridescent black interior, excellent original condition, 10 1/8" high. **$2,541**

Cactus pattern cracker jar in topaz/vaseline (uranium) opalescent, circa 1959, undamaged, 8" high. $300

Optic-Ribbed pattern glass lemonade set, No. 222, circa 1926, lidded pitcher with applied cobalt handle and six conforming tumblers in green opal, cobalt, and clear glass, pitcher 10" high x 7" wide. $366

Cherry and Scale pattern seven-piece water set, circa 1908, water pitcher and six tumblers in custard (uranium) with nutmeg stain, pitcher 9 1/4" high, tumblers 4" high. **$92**

Grape and Cable Fernery pattern bowl in chocolate glass, No. 920, first quarter 20th century, beaded rim, with three feet, 3 1/4" high, 6 1/8" diameter. **$58**

Paperweights in egg form, each signed "Fenton/1976," one retaining original sales sticker, undamaged, 4 1/8" and 4 1/2" high. **$204**

▲ Orange Tree pattern carnival glass bowl in blue, No. 921, first quarter 20th century, upright scalloped rim, collared foot, undamaged, 2 1/2" high, 8 1/8" diameter rim. **$69**

◄ Colonial pattern candlesticks in jade green, No. 349, circa 1920-1930, hexagonal form with open base, 10 1/4" high. **$115**

Lalique

René Jules Lalique was born on April 6, 1860, in the village of Ay, in the Champagne region of France. In 1862, his family moved to the suburbs of Paris.

In 1872, Lalique attended College Turgot where he studied drawing with Justin-Marie Lequien. After the death of his father in 1876, Lalique began working as an apprentice to Louis Aucoc, who was a prominent jeweler and goldsmith in Paris.

Lalique moved to London in 1878 to continue his studies. He spent two years attending Sydenham College, developing his graphic design skills. He returned to Paris in 1880 and worked as an illustrator of jewelry, creating designs for Cartier, among others. In 1884, Lalique's drawings were displayed at the National Exhibition of Industrial Arts, organized at the Louvre.

At the end of 1885, Lalique took over Jules Destapes' jewelry workshop. Lalique's design incorporated translucent enamels, semiprecious stones, ivory, and hard stones. In 1889, at the Universal Exhibition in Paris, the jewelry firms of Vever and Boucheron included collaborative works by Lalique in their displays.

In the early 1890s, Lalique began to incorporate glass into his jewelry, and in 1893 he took part in a competition organized by the Union Centrale des Arts Decoratifs to design a drinking vessel. He won second prize.

Courtesy of Rago Arts and Auctions, www.ragoarts.com

"Tulipes" vase, opalescent glass with blue patina, designed in 1927, (M p. 438, No. 995), etched "R. Lalique France," 8" x 8". **$2,500**

Lalique opened his first Paris retail shop in 1905, near the perfume business of François Coty, who commissioned Lalique to design his perfume labels in 1907. Lalique also created his first perfume bottles for Coty.

In the first decade of the 20th century, Lalique continued to experiment with glass manufacturing techniques and mounted his first show devoted entirely to glass in 1911.

During World War I, Lalique's first factory was forced to close, but the construction of a new factory was soon begun in Wingen-sur-Moder, in the Alsace region. It was completed in 1921 and still produces Lalique crystal today.

In 1925, Lalique designed the first car mascot (hood ornament) for Citroën, the French automobile company. For the next six years, Lalique designed 29 models for

Courtesy of James D. Julia Auctioneers, Fairfield, Maine, www.jamesdjulia.com

Mascot with circular medallion with frosted intaglio carved image of Saint Christophe carrying a child on his shoulders with radiant lines emanating from child, signed on medallion in impressed block letters "R. Lalique France," (Marcilhac 1142), very good to excellent condition, 4 3/4" high.
$2,074

Vase with bulbous clear glass body molded in relief with overlapping rows of leaves, tapering neck surmounted by flared circular mouth, circa 1927, etched in script "R. Lalique France" with model number "1014," 9" high, 6 1/2" diameter. $780

automotive companies such as Bentley, Bugatti, Delage, Hispano-Suiza, Rolls Royce, and Voisin.

Lalique's second boutique opened in 1931, and this location continues to serve as the main Lalique showroom today.

René Lalique died on May 5, 1945, at the age of 85. His son, Marc, took over the business at that time, and when Marc died in 1977, his daughter, Marie-Claude Lalique Dedouvre, assumed control of the company. She sold her interest in the firm and retired in 1994.

For more information on Lalique, see *Warman's Lalique Identification and Price Guide* by Mark F. Moran.

(**Editor's Note:** In some of the descriptions of Lalique pieces that follow, you will find notations like "M p. 478, No. 1100" or "Marcilhac 952, pg. 428." This refers to the page and serial numbers found in *René Lalique, maître-verrier, 1860-1945: Analyse de L'oeuvre et Catalogue Raisonné* by Félix Marcilhac, published in 1989 and revised in 1994. Printed entirely in French, this book of more than 1,000 pages is the definitive guide to Lalique's work, and listings from auction catalogs typically cite the Marcilhac guide as a reference.)

Courtesy of John Moran Auctioneers, www.johnmoran.com
Clear and frosted tapering rectangular crystal bottle relief-decorated with fruits and foliage with black enameled highlights, flanked by outset green tassels and surmounted by oval-shaped foliate-decorated stopper, circa 1919, with molded signature "R. Lalique" to one face and "Volnay Paris" to other, etched to underside "50," 5 3/8" high x 1 5/8" wide x 1 1/8" deep. **$7,995**

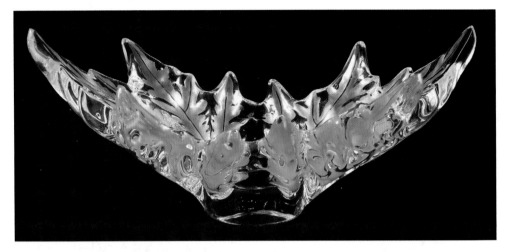

Courtesy of Clars Auction Gallery, www.clars.com

"Champs Elysees" centerpiece with frosted leaf decoration on clear glass, signed in etched script "Lalique, France," 7 1/2" high x 17 1/2" wide. **$915**

Courtesy of Rago Arts and Auctions, www.ragoarts.com

▲ Rare "Mûres" inkwell, frosted and polished glass, designed in 1920, (M p. 316, No. 431), base etched "Lalique," 2 1/4" x 6 1/4". **$1,000**

Courtesy of Rago Arts and Auctions, www.ragoarts.com

◄ "L'Elegance" perfume bottle, frosted and clear glass with amber patina, after 1914, (M p. 934, No. 10), etched "R. Lalique France 850," stopper etched "850," 3 3/4" x 2 3/4" x 3/4". **$4,375**

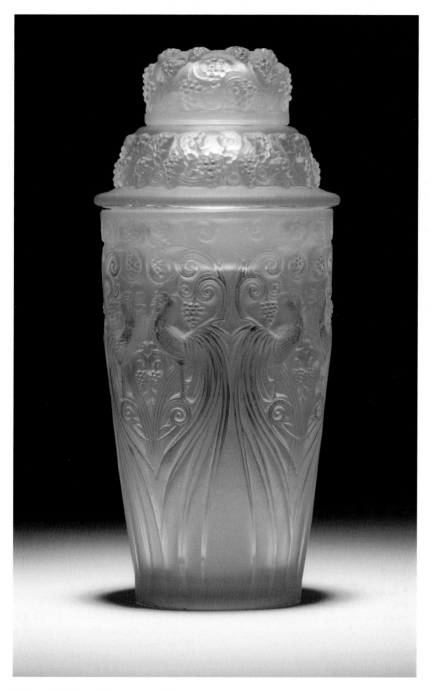

Courtesy of John Moran Auctioneers, www.johnmoran.com

Covered tumbler of slightly tapering cylindrical clear and frosted art glass molded with scrolling grapevines and roosters with trailing tails, inset with removable strainer with fruiting grapevines, surmounted by similarly molded domed cover, designed in 1928, tumbler signed "R. Lalique France," model no. 3879, 8 3/4" high, 3 3/4" diameter. **$4,200**

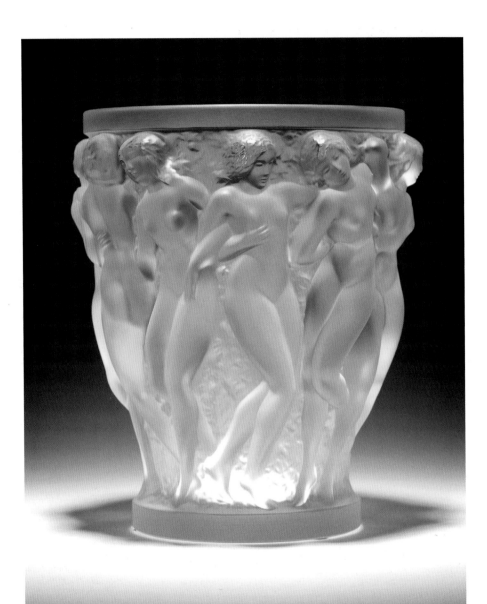

Vessel of clear and frosted glass with tapering cylindrical body decorated in high relief with continuous scene of dancing bacchantes, third quarter 20th century, numbered "F016" and etched in script "Lalique France" with copyright symbol to foot, "Lalique / Paris" sticker to underside, with original box, 9 3/4" high, 8 3/4"diameter. **$2,160**

Courtesy of Clars Auction Gallery, www.clars.com

Frosted glass "Mask De Femme" plaque with maiden surrounded by fish-form relief-decorated reserves on silvered stand, with original double box and original stand, signed with script "Lalique France" mark, purchased at Shreve & Co., San Francisco, 12 1/2" square. **$4,880**

Courtesy of Rago Arts and Auctions, www.ragoarts.com

▲ "Lepage" perfume bottle, frosted and clear glass with amber patina, designed in 1920, (M p. 333, No. 506), molded "R. LALIQUE," 4 5/8" x 1 1/2" x 3/4". **$7,500**

Courtesy of John Moran Auctioneers, www.johnmoran.com

◄ Vase with clear and frosted relief-molded seed pod base beneath cylindrical body decorated with eucalyptus leaves in high relief, wide flaring mouth, circa 1920s, molded signature "R. Lalique," etched "France" and "No. 936," 6 1/2" high, 5 5/8" diameter. **$1,320**

Courtesy of John Moran Auctioneers, www.johnmoran.com

"Le Jade" perfume bottle for Roger et Gallet, molded flask-form green glass body relief-decorated with bird-of-paradise among scrolling vines, surmounted by vine-molded domed stopper, circa 1926, molded signature to underside "R.L. France," impressed verso "Roger et Gallet / Paris," 3 1/4" high x 2 3/8" wide x 1 1/8" deep. **$2,337**

Courtesy of John Moran Auctioneers, www.johnmoran.com

▲ Light source of barrel-shaped reeded frosted glass surmounted by clear and frosted glass fan-shaped "veil" cut in relief with swans in flight, designed in 1990 by Marie-Claude Lalique, etched in script "Lalique France," base etched "Lalique," with original Lalique, Paris fitted box, description card, and European-to-American outlet adapter, 16 1/2" high x 21 3/4" wide x 5 1/2" deep. **$4,200**

Courtesy of Rago Arts and Auctions, www.ragoarts.com

◄ Etched glass crucifix, 1930s, acid-etched "R LALIQUE," 6 3/4" x 5" x 2". **$500**

Quezal

The Quezal Art Glass Decorating Co., named for the quetzal – a bird with brilliantly colored feathers found in tropical regions of the Americas – was organized in 1901 in Brooklyn, New York, by Martin Bach and Thomas Johnson, two disgruntled Tiffany workers. They soon hired Percy Britton and William Wiedebine, two more former Tiffany employees. The first products, unmarked, were exact Tiffany imitations.

Quezal pieces differ from Tiffany pieces in that they are more defined and the decorations are more visible and brighter. No new techniques were developed by Quezal.

Johnson left in 1905. T. Conrad Vahlsing, Bach's son-in-law, joined the firm in 1918, but left with Paul Frank in 1920 to form Lustre Art Glass Co., which in turn copied Quezal pieces. Martin Bach died in 1924, and by 1925, Quezal had ceased operations.

The "Quezal" trademark was first used in 1902 and was placed on the base of vases and bowls and the rims of shades. The acid-etched or engraved letters vary in size and may be found in amber, black, or gold. A printed label that includes an illustration of a quetzal was used briefly in 1907.

Courtesy of Heritage Auctions, ha.com

Iridescent glass footed vase, circa 1900, marked Quezal, rubbing to lip rim, light scuffing and label residue to underside, 7 3/8" high. $475

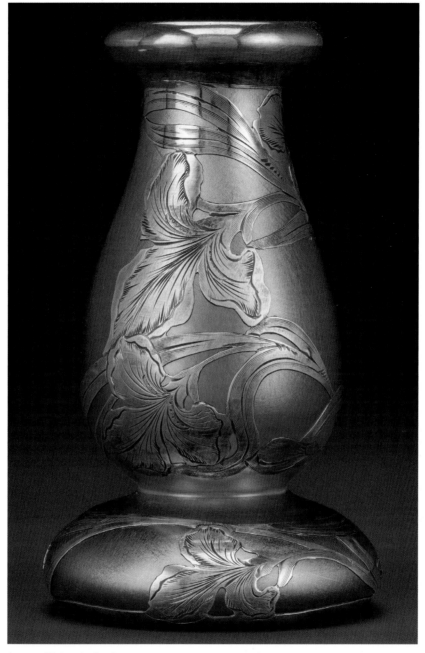

Courtesy of Heritage Auctions, ha.com

Vase with Alvin Silver overlay, circa 1900, iridescent blue and violet glass with silver overlay in chased floral motif, marked to glass "Quezal, 13," marked to silver "A, 999-1000 FINE, PATENTED, 15," 5 1/2" high. **$1,125**

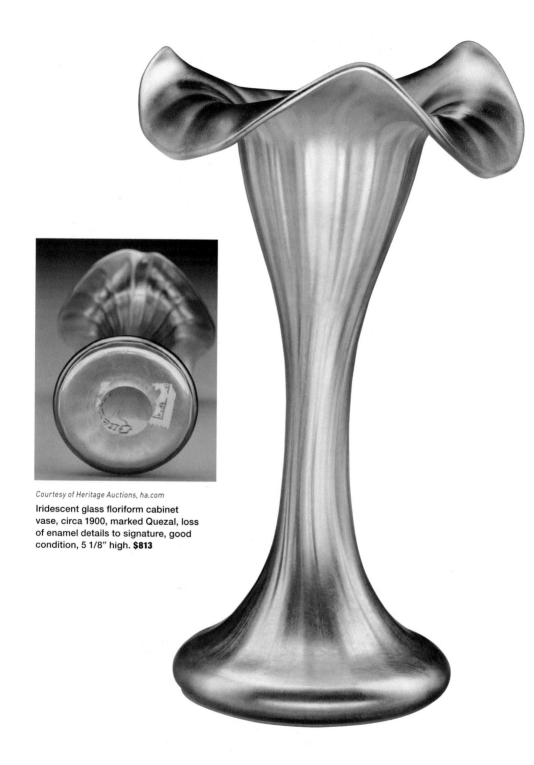

Courtesy of Heritage Auctions, ha.com

Iridescent glass floriform cabinet vase, circa 1900, marked Quezal, loss of enamel details to signature, good condition, 5 1/8" high. **$813**

Courtesy of Heritage Auctions, ha.com

Iridescent glass cabinet vase, circa 1910, marked Quezal, minor scuffing to underside, good condition, 3 7/8" high. **$213**

Courtesy of Brunk Auctions;
www.brunkauctions.com

Perfume bottle made for Melba Perfume Co., Chicago, early 20th century, bottom marked "Quezal/ Melba," matching stopper, light wear to base, good condition, 5 3/4" high. $1,240

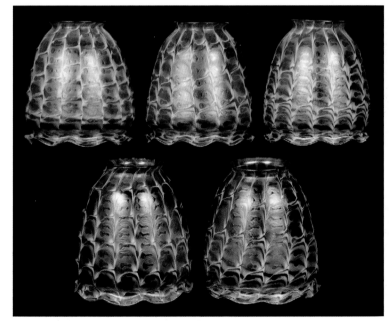

Courtesy of Woody Auction,
www.woodyauction.com

Five signed lampshades, gold iridescent with white spiderweb design, no chips, cracks, or repairs, 4 1/2". $1,121

Courtesy of Heritage Auctions, ha.com

Blue iridescent glass vase, circa 1915, enameled Quezal, fleabite and minor rubbing of iridescence to base, good condition, 7" high. **$906**

Courtesy of Woody Auction, www.woodyauction.com

▲ Vase with green/blue iridescence, signed, no chips, cracks, or repairs, 6 1/2" high. **$295**

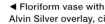

Courtesy of Heritage Auctions, ha.com

◀ Floriform vase with Alvin Silver overlay, circa 1900, iridescent green and gold glass with everted and ruffled rim with silver overlay in etched floral motif, marked to silver "A, 925-1000, FINE, 3413, PATENTED," light surface scratches to silver, glass in good condition, 4 7/8" high. **$1,125**

Halloween Collectibles

By Mark B. Ledenbach

MARK B. LEDENBACH, longtime collector and expert on all things Halloween, is the author of *Vintage Halloween Collectibles,* 3rd edition, published in 2014. His website is HalloweenCollector.com.

As a collector of vintage Halloween memorabilia for nearly 25 years, I find the evolution of the imagery for this fun hobby endlessly fascinating.

Halloween became quite the event in the first decade of the last century, mainly through the exchange of festive postcards. Those cards, with the art drawn by such luminaries as Winsch and Clapsaddle, typically accented the agricultural roots of Halloween, then branched out into the more whimsical realm of witches, black cats, blazing jack-o-lanterns, bats, cavorting devils, and the like.

As Halloween became an event to be celebrated with parties – primarily given by and for adults through the 1920s – the imagery began to change. From about 1909 through 1913, manufacturers of party supplies like Dennison of Framingham, Massachusetts, simply offered an array of seasonally decorated crepe papers from which the host would fashion decorations and party favors. The imagery from this period tends to be more subdued and somewhat pedestrian. However, as the manufacturers became more entranced by the business possibilities of offering finished goods for sale, the lines of available products exploded into a dazzling array of seals, silhouettes, tally cards, placecards, invitations, die-cuts, aprons, and costumes. To keep up with the seemingly endless kinds of products to be sold to adults, the imagery became more complex, scary, and perhaps sometimes chilling.

The most innovative purveyor of such complex Halloween imagery was the Beistle Co. of Shippensburg, Pennsylvania. They provided nut cups, die-cuts, lanterns, games, table decorations, and other small paper decorations that are especially coveted by collectors today. The firm's design sensibilities are easily recognized today for their ingenuity in extending Halloween imagery beyond what was offered previously by other manufacturers. Examples of this would be Beistle's 1930-1931 identical dual-sided lantern and 1923 fairy clock.

Imagery through about 1940 tends to be more adult-focused. However, as trick-or-treating become more of an entrenched feature of Halloween celebrations, the target market segment for parties ceased to be adults and moved inexorably toward juveniles. The impact on Halloween imagery was profound. Out were the more complex and scary images of devils, witches, and black cats, to be replaced by less threatening, less interesting, and less memorable imagery of apple-cheeked witches, grinning plump devils, and friendly black cats. The air of implied menace, so evocative of early Halloween imagery, had been replaced by a sugar-high-inducing cuteness that any retailer could carry without censure.

Through the present day, cuteness has been dethroned by goriness. One can shop at any mass retailer and find die-cuts of skulls with worms wriggling through eye sockets, costumes complete with wretch-inducing masks trumpeting various deformities or tortures, and other horrors meant to shock and perhaps dismay. The sense of subtlety and artistry so apparent in the majority of decorations made prior to 1940 is nowhere in evidence today.

As with many hobbies, certain sub-categories have done better than others. Hotter categories are embossed German die-cuts; U.S. die-cuts, especially those made by Dennison and

Courtesy of Morphy Auctions, www.morphyauctions.com

Cast iron hunchback cat doorstop, signed, "Copyright 1927, A.M. Greenblatt Studio, 19," excellent condition, 9" high. $519

Courtesy of Bertoia Auctions,
www.bertoiaauctions.com

Victorian-era table centerpiece, stuffed velvet vegetable man with pumpkin head, in black and orange suit with two brass buttons, 20" long. $3,088

Gibson; Beistle paper products; boxed seals, silhouettes, and cut-outs from Dennison; tin tambourines; and German candy containers and figurals as well as Halloween-themed games. Colder categories include tin noisemakers, U.S. pulp, and hard plastic.

Collecting vintage Halloween memorabilia became a red-hot hobby complete with skyrocketing prices and scarce supply in the early 1990s. Even with all of the economic cycles since and the rise of more efficient supply channels like eBay, prices continue to climb for nearly all genres of near-mint condition or better items. For example, embossed German die-cuts sold then for between $30-$75. Today many examples bring $100-$400, with the rarest items like a winged bat devil and a large fireplace screen topping $2,250. Even ephemera like a 1932 Beistle grandfather clock mechanical invitation bring astronomical prices. One recently sold for over $1,700.

Not all categories have benefited. The garish hard plastic made in such huge quantities during the 1950s used to command head-scratching prices of $40-$1,000. Today prices have decreased to about half of the market's height given more collector awareness of the ubiquity of these items.

Unlike Christmas items, Halloween decorations were purchased with the intention of using them once, then tossing them out after the event with no sentiment. This is the primary supply driver behind the rapid escalation of prices today. The primary demand driver is the large number of new collectors entering this fun field as each Halloween season comes around.

As with all hobbies wherein the values have risen tremendously, reproductions and fantasy pieces are a problem. Consult other collectors and buy the right references before plunking down cash. Get in the habit of asking a lot of questions. Don't be shy!

SUGGESTED READING: Vintage Halloween Collectibles, 3rd edition, contains nearly 550 new photographs showing over 600 new Halloween items, all in full color. Most of the new items shown have never appeared in other books on vintage Halloween. **http://HalloweenCollector.com.**

Courtesy of Morphy Auctions, www.morphyauctions.com
Witch wind-up toy, original clothes and broom, very good-plus condition, when wound, toy rocks from side to side, 10 1/4" high. **$1,159**

Courtesy of Morphy Auctions, www.morphyauctions.com
Veggie man on pumpkin candy container with carrot arms, original near mint condition, 8 1/2" high. **$2,745**

▲ Mechanical postcards by Ellen Clapsaddle, very good condition, minor corner bumping on card with white child, heavier corner bumping on card with black child, 6" x 4 3/8". **$240**

◄ Wooden double noisemaker with witch and cat figures, papier maché heads, excellent condition, 9" high. **$458**

Courtesy of Morphy Auctions, www.morphyauctions.com
Large Veggie Man candy container with jack-o-lantern in each hand, paper insert eyes and mouth, head is candle lantern, very good-plus condition, all original, no damage or repaint, 9 1/2" high. $10,980

Courtesy of Morphy Auctions, www.morphyauctions.com
Rare jack-o-lantern figure with wood frame body and pumpkin head with paper insert, unmarked, probably German, place for candle in head, excellent condition, squeaks when pushed in middle, 15" high. $4,800

**Two early tin parade
jack-o-lanterns,
good original surface
with even wear and
corrosion, possibly
missing paper inserts,
8 1/2" high. $1,700**

**Pumpkin head wind-up toy
dressed in Mexican attire with
poncho and sombrero, all original
clothes, very good-plus condition,
when wound, toy rocks from side
to side, 7" high. $549**

Courtesy of Heritage Auctions, ha.com

"Halloween Scare," Frederic Stanley (American, 1892-1967), oil on canvas, *The Saturday Evening Post* cover, Nov. 2, 1935, signed and inscribed lower right: Frederic Stanley – / To / George and Helene / with best wishes – / "Ted" –, 32" x 22". **$56,250**

Egg carton jack-o-lantern with paper insert; litho cardboard jack-o-lantern with paper insert; and plastic black cat candleholder; good to very good condition, some melting, tallest 7" high. **$73**

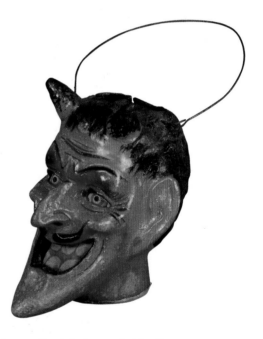

American folk art paint-decorated tin Halloween parade jack-o-lantern, probably by Ohio Art Co., late 19th/early 20th century, with original interior paper face elements, candleholder, and remnants of original stenciled mark to reverse, mounted on custom black-painted wood and metal stand, scattered areas of wear to painted surface, losses to paper face insert, 13 1/8" high including stand. **$2,280**

Early composition devil lantern with long pointy chin, Germany, original paper insert and bale handle, detailed throughout, very good condition, 4 1/2" long. **$1,853**

Four blown-glass ornaments, two jack-o-lanterns, devil head with molded horns, and grinning clown, very good to excellent condition, 3" long. $401

Two paper decorations, witch with long arms and legs, 31", and Beistle Co. pumpkin with long arms and legs, 27", wear, some tape on witch, pumpkin in good condition. $61

Rare German papier maché monkey lantern with original paper inserts. Provenance: Tom Pritchard's Halloween collection. $1,853

JEWELRY

Styles 470

Jewelry Listings 474
  Bracelets 474
  Brooches, Pins, & Clips 477
  Earrings 481
  Necklaces & Pendants 485
  Art Nouveau 472
  Rings 480

Jewelry
Styles

Jewelry has been a part of every culture throughout time, reflecting the times as well as social and aesthetic movements. Jewelry is usually divided into periods and styles. Each period may have several styles, with some of the same styles and types of jewelry being made in both precious and non-precious materials. Elements of one period may also overlap into others.

Georgian, 1760-1837. Fine jewelry from this period is quite desirable, but few good-quality pieces have found their way to auction in recent years. Sadly, much jewelry from this period has been lost.

Victorian, 1837-1901. Queen Victoria of England ascended the throne in 1837 and remained queen until her death in 1901. The Victorian period is a long and prolific one, abundant with many styles of jewelry. It warrants being divided into three sub-periods: Early or Romantic period dating from 1837-1860; Mid or Grand period dating from 1860-1880; and Late or Aesthetic period dating from 1880-1901.

Sentiment and romance were significant factors in Victorian jewelry. Often, jewelry and clothing represented love and affection, with symbolic motifs such as hearts, crosses, hands, flowers, anchors, doves, crowns, knots, stars, thistles, wheat, garlands, horseshoes and moons. The materials of the time were also abundant and varied. They included silver, gold, diamonds, onyx, glass, cameo, paste, carnelian, agate, coral, amber, garnet, emeralds, opals, pearls, peridot, rubies, sapphires, marcasites, cut steel, enameling, tortoise shell, topaz, turquoise, bog oak, ivory, jet, hair, gutta percha and vulcanite.

Courtesy of Heritage Auctions, ha.com

Diamond and silver-topped gold pendant-brooch, European-, mine- and rose-cut diamonds weighing approximately 7.35 carats, set in silver-topped 14k gold, pendant wire, removable pinstem and catch on reverse, 1 1/8" x 1 3/8". **$4,780**

Courtesy of Heritage Auctions, ha.com

Edwardian diamond, platinum and gold brooch, European-cut diamond measuring 6.92 x 6.85 x 4.71 mm and weighing approximately 1.35 carats, European-cut diamonds weighing approximately 1.30 carats, set in platinum, 14k gold pinstem and catch, total diamond weight 2.65 carats, gross weight 8.50 grams, 2 5/8" x 1/2". **$4,062**

Sentiments of love were often expressed in miniatures. Sometimes they were representative of deceased loved ones, but often the miniatures were of the living. Occasionally, the miniatures depicted landscapes, cherubs or religious themes.

Hair jewelry was a popular expression of love and sentiment. The hair of a loved one was placed in a special compartment in a brooch or a locket, or used to form a picture under a glass compartment. Later in the mid-19th century, pieces of jewelry were made completely of woven hair. Individual strands of hair would be woven together to create necklaces, watch chains, brooches, earrings and rings.

In 1861, Queen Victoria's husband, Prince Albert, died. The queen went into mourning for the rest of her life, and Victoria required that the royal court wear black. This atmosphere spread to the populace and created a demand for mourning jewelry, which is typically black. When it first came into fashion, it was made from jet, fossilized wood. By 1850, there were dozens of English workshops making jet brooches, lockets, bracelets and necklaces. As the supply of jet dwindled, other materials were used such as vulcanite, gutta percha, bog oak and French jet.

By the 1880s, somber mourning jewelry was losing popularity. Fashions had changed and the clothing was simpler and had an air of delicacy. The Industrial Revolution, which had begun in the early part of the century, was now in full swing and machine-manufactured jewelry was affordable to the working class.

Edwardian, 1890-1920. The Edwardian period takes its name from England's King Edward VII. Though he ascended the throne in 1901, he and his wife, Alexandria of Denmark, exerted influence over the period before and after his ascension. The 1890s were known as La Belle Epoque. This was a time known for ostentation and extravagance. As the years passed, jewelry became simpler and smaller. Instead of wearing

Courtesy of Heritage Auctions, ha.com

Early Victorian Vacheron & Constantin diamond, enamel and gold hunting case pocket watch with accompanying brooch, fob and key, circa 1850. Victorian gold mourning brooch with applied black and white enamel accents supports watch, key and fob. Case: 38 mm, hinged, circular 18k yellow gold with smooth edge and decorated case front and back, black champleve enamel, rose-cut diamonds; No. 83139 dial: white enamel with black Roman numerals, gilt "moon" hour and minute hands. Movement: 31 mm, gilt, 13 jewels, detached lever, keywind and set, No. 83139, signed Vacheron & Constantin on center bridge, lateral bridge escapement; signed and numbered Vacheron & Constantin in Geneve. E. E. Rodgers on cuvette, triple signed Vacheron & Constantin on dial, movement and dustcover. **$3,107**

▲ ABOVE **Art Nouveau leaves brooch**, demantoid garnet, diamond, plique à jour enamel, and silver-topped gold, round-shaped demantoid garnets weighing approximately 2.30 carats, European- and single-cut diamonds weighing approximately 0.90 carat, green plique à jour enamel, set in silver-topped gold, pinstem and catch, gross weight 13.55 grams, 3" x 2 1/8". **$4,687**

TOP OF PAGE **Arts & Crafts moonstone, sapphire and diamond necklace**, Louis Comfort Tiffany, circa 1915, designed as cabochon moonstone within twisted ropework frame with circular-cut sapphires and diamonds, three row fancy link chain and clasp similarly set, signed Tiffany & Co., approximately 18 1/2" long. **$25,103**

one large brooch, women were often found wearing several small lapel pins.

In the early 1900s, platinum, diamonds and pearls were prevalent in the jewelry of the wealthy, while paste was being used by the masses to imitate the real thing. The styles were reminiscent of the neo-classical and rococo motifs. The jewelry was lacy and ornate, feminine and delicate.

Arts & Crafts, 1890-1920. The Arts & Crafts movement was focused on artisans and craftsmanship. There was a simplification of form where the material was secondary to the design. Guilds of artisans banded together. Some jewelry was mass-produced, but the most highly prized examples of this period are handmade and signed by their makers. The pieces were simple and at times abstract. They could be hammered, patinated and acid etched. Common materials were brass, bronze, copper, silver, blister pearls, freshwater pearls, turquoise, agate, opals, moonstones, coral, horn, ivory, base metals, amber, cabochon-cut garnets and amethysts.

Art Nouveau, 1895-1910. In 1895, Samuel Bing opened a shop called "Maison de l'Art Nouveau" at 22 Rue de Provence in Paris. Art Nouveau designs in the jewelry were characterized by a sensuality that took on the forms of the female figure, butterflies, dragonflies, peacocks, snakes, wasps, swans, bats, orchids, irises and other exotic flowers. The lines used whiplash curves to create a feeling of lushness and opulence.

1920s-1930s. Costume jewelry began its steady ascent to popularity in the 1920s. Since it was relatively inexpensive to produce, it was mass-produced. The sizes and designs of the jewelry varied. Often, it was worn a few times, disposed of and then replaced with a new piece. It was thought of as expendable, a cheap throwaway to dress up an outfit. Costume jewelry became so popular that it was sold in both upscale and "five and dime" stores.

During the 1920s, fashions were often accompanied by

jewelry that drew on the Art Deco movement, which got its beginning in Paris at the "Exposition Internationale des Arts Décoratifs et Industriels Modernes" held in 1925. The idea behind this movement was that form follows function. The style was characterized by simple, straight, clean lines, stylized motifs and geometric shapes. Favored materials included chrome, rhodium, pot metal, glass, rhinestones, Bakelite and celluloid.

One designer who played an important role was Coco Chanel. Though previously reserved for evening wear, the jewelry was worn by Chanel during the day, making it fashionable for millions of other women to do so, too.

With the 1930s came the Depression and the advent of World War II. Perhaps in response to the gloom, designers began using enameling and brightly colored rhinestones to create whimsical birds, flowers, circus animals, bows, dogs and just about every other figural form imaginable.

Retro Modern, 1939-1950. Other jewelry designs of the 1940s were big and bold. Retro Modern had a more substantial feel to it and designers began using larger stones to enhance the dramatic pieces. The jewelry was stylized and exaggerated. Common motifs included flowing scrolls, bows, ribbons, birds, animals, snakes, flowers and knots.

Sterling silver now became the metal of choice, often dipped in a gold wash known as vermeil.

Designers often incorporated patriotic themes of American flags, the V-sign, Uncle Sam's hat, airplanes, anchors and eagles.

Post-War Modern, 1945-1965. This was a movement that emphasized the artistic approach to jewelry making. It is also referred to as Mid-Century Modern. This approach was occurring at a time when the Beat Generation was prevalent. These avant-garde designers created jewelry that was handcrafted to illustrate the artist's own concepts and ideas. The materials often used were sterling, gold, copper, brass, enamel, cabochons, wood, quartz and amber.

1950s-1960s. The 1950s saw the rise of jewelry that was made purely of rhinestones: necklaces, bracelets, earrings and pins. The focus of the early 1960s was on clean lines: Pillbox hats and A-line dresses with short jackets were a mainstay for the conservative woman. The large, bold rhinestone pieces were no longer the must-have accessory. They were now replaced with smaller, more delicate gold-tone metal and faux pearls with only a hint of rhinestones.

At the other end of the spectrum were psychedelic-colored clothing, Nehru jackets, thigh-high miniskirts and go-go boots. These clothes were accessorized with beads, large metal pendants and occasionally big, bold rhinestones. By the late 1960s, there was a movement back to Mother Nature and the "hippie" look was born. Ethnic clothing, tie-dye, long skirts, fringe and jeans were the prevalent style, and the rhinestone had, for the most part, been left behind.

Courtesy of Heritage Auctions, ha.com

Diamond and gold bracelet with full-cut diamonds weighing approximately 6.00 carats, set in 10k gold, very good condition, gross weight 29.30 grams. **$1,250**

Courtesy of Heritage Auctions, ha.com

Art Deco amethyst, diamond, and platinum-topped gold bracelet with sugarloaf-shaped amethyst cabochon measuring 8.06 mm x 8.12 mm x 6.28 mm and weighing approximately 2.90 carats, with rose-cut diamonds, set in platinum-topped 14k gold, good condition, 7" long, gross weight 7.60 grams. **$375**

Courtesy of Heritage Auctions, ha.com

Garnet and gold bracelet with oval-shaped garnet cabochons weighing approximately 43.10 carats, set in 18k gold, very good condition, 6 3/4" x 15/16", gross weight 33.40 grams. **$3,125**

BRACELETS

Courtesy of Heritage Auctions, ha.com

Sapphire, diamond, and gold hinged bangle bracelet with cushion-shaped sapphires from 12.02 mm x 9.89 mm x 7.24 mm to 7.37 mm x 6.31 mm x 2.94 mm and weighing approximately 25.35 carats, with European- and mine-cut diamonds weighing approximately 1.00 carat, set in 14k gold, 6 5/8" x 1/2", gross weight 30.90 grams. **$5,938**

Courtesy of Heritage Auctions

▲ Multi-stone 18k gold bracelet with eight charms: silver gilt heart set with rose- and European-cut garnets; silver gilt crescent charm set with rose-cut garnets; 18k gold claw set with oval-shaped turquoise cabochon measuring 5.91 mm x 4.91 mm; 14k gold charm set with cultured pearl measuring 4.21 mm x 4.03 mm and European-cut diamonds weighing approximately 0.05 carat; 14k gold charm set with seed pearls and round rubies weighing approximately 0.10 carat; 18k gold enamel bird set with European and native-cut diamonds; 14k crescent moon and star charm set with European-cut diamond weighing approximately 0.03 carat; and 14k gold face engraved charm; 7" long, gross weight 19.60 grams. **$625**

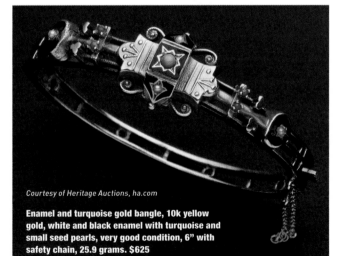

Courtesy of Heritage Auctions, ha.com

Enamel and turquoise gold bangle, 10k yellow gold, white and black enamel with turquoise and small seed pearls, very good condition, 6" with safety chain, 25.9 grams. $625

Art Deco-era platinum, diamond, and emerald bracelet, bead-set with approximately 990 single-cut diamonds, 111 late European-cut diamonds and two emerald-cut diamonds, estimated total combined diamond weight 8.53 carats, bezel set with one emerald-cut emerald, estimated weight 1.71 carats, four triangle-shaped faceted emeralds, two straight baguette emeralds, estimated combined emerald weight 2.37 carats, platinum mount, good condition, 6 1/2" x 8 mm to 13 mm, gross weight 30.7 grams. **$24,800**

Turquoise bracelet with oval-shaped clasp with center oval cabochon with 16 3.5 mm round cabochon turquoises, set in 18k yellow gold mount, four stands of 5 mm round beads, three separator bars set with nine 2.5 mm round turquoise beads, light grime and tarnish, 6 1/2", gross weight 36 grams. **$1,054**

Gold cannetille and amethyst bracelet, early 19th century, hand-wrought cannetille work surrounding six graduated amethysts, three at 7.45 carats and two at 9.12 carats, 18k, with later fitted case by Garrard & Co., with appraisal, minor bends to some of the outer loops in cannetille work, minute wear to crown surfaces of amethysts, missing safety chain, 25 to 28 mm wide x 7" long, 41.7 grams. **$9,300**

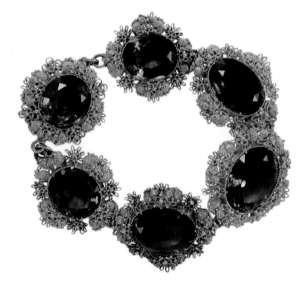

BROOCHES, PINS & CLIPS

Courtesy of Heritage Auctions, ha.com
Diamond and tri-color gold brooch with mine-cut diamonds weighing approximately 0.20 carat, set in 14k pink, yellow, and white gold, gross weight 18.30 grams, very good condition, can be separated into two brooches, 3" x 2 9/16". **$400**

Courtesy of Heritage Auctions, ha.com
Coral cameo, seed pearl, and gold pendant-brooch with oval-shaped coral cameo measuring 38.00 mm x 31.00 mm x 8.20 mm, with seed pearls set in 14k gold, 2" x 1 5/8", gross weight 17.40 grams. **$350**

Courtesy of Heritage Auctions, ha.com
Emerald, ruby, and gold brooch with emerald-cut emeralds and round and cushion-shaped rubies, set in 18k gold, very good condition, 2 3/8" x 1 5/8", gross weight 12.30 grams. **$688**

Courtesy of Heritage Auctions, ha.com

Blue topaz and gold pin, 14k gold, three stones, very good condition, 12 mm x 40 mm, 4.5 grams. **$263**

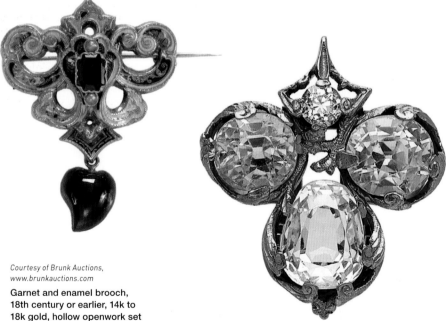

Courtesy of Brunk Auctions, www.brunkauctions.com

Garnet and enamel brooch, 18th century or earlier, 14k to 18k gold, hollow openwork set with one emerald-cut red garnet weighing 0.60 to 0.70 carats, two 1.5 mm seed pearls, and enamel decoration, later 12.5 mm x 10 mm heart-shaped cabochon red garnet drop, 30.7 mm x 28.3 mm, enamel losses, chips and scratches to garnets, 5.2 grams. **$806**

Courtesy of Heritage Auctions, ha.com

Sapphire, diamond, and gold clip with cushion-cut yellow sapphire measuring 11.11 mm x 8.95 mm x 6.18 mm and weighing approximately 5.75 carats, with oval-shaped yellow sapphires weighing approximately 9.20 carats, with European-cut diamond weighing approximately 0.35 carat, set in 14k gold, very good condition, 1 1/8" x 1", gross weight 11.20 grams. **$1,563**

Platinum brooch with 14k yellow gold findings with one medium blue 7 mm x 5 mm oval faceted sapphire, four 2 mm round cultured pearls, and 10 round European-cut diamonds weighing approximately 0.40 carats, 2" long, 3.5 dwt. **$500-$800**

Oval cameo brooch/pendant with diamond in woman's necklace, approximately 0.12 carats, 14k gold mount, reticulated design with three marquise-cut emeralds weighing approximately 0.30 carats, circa first half of 20th century, marked "COS/14K" to verso of mount, 2 3/8" long x 1 7/8" wide, total weight approximately 11.1 dwt. **$272**

Blister pearl, diamond, ruby, emerald, and gold bird-shaped pendant-brooch, pearl measuring 23.00 mm x 14.00 mm, with rose-cut yellow and colorless diamonds weighing approximately 0.95 carat, with marquise and round-cut rubies weighing approximately 0.25 carat, with triangle-shaped emerald, set in 14k gold, very good condition, 2" x 7/8", gross weight 10.20 grams. **$1,250**

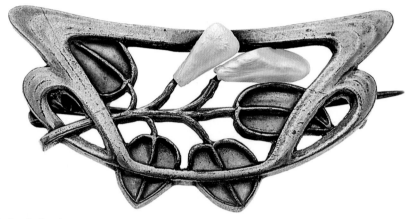

Courtesy of Heritage Auctions, ha.com

Art Nouveau cultured pearl, plique-a-jour enamel, and gilt sterling silver brooch, baroque freshwater pearls measuring 9.00 mm x 3.10 mm and 6.50 mm x 3.40 mm, plique-a-jour enamel in blue, set in gilt sterling silver, very good condition, 1 17/16" x 11/16", gross weight 4.30 grams. **$275**

Courtesy of Elite Decorative Arts, www.eliteauction.com

Trifari sterling silver designer figural crown brooch pin, fully hallmarked "TRIFARI STERLING" and numbered 137542 to verso, approximately 1 3/4" high x 2" wide, total weight approximately 22.6 grams. **$158**

EARRINGS

Courtesy of Heritage Auctions, ha.com

Diamond and silver-topped gold earrings with European- and mine-cut diamonds weighing approximately 1.70 carats, with rose-cut diamonds weighing approximately 0.30 carat, set in silver-topped 14k gold, good condition, 1 3/4" x 3/16", gross weight 4.70 grams. **$1,375**

Courtesy of Heritage Auctions, ha.com

Emerald, diamond, gold, and silver earrings with emerald-cut emeralds weighing approximately 1.50 carats, with rose-cut diamonds weighing approximately 2.40 carats, set in 14k gold and silver, 14k gold clip backs, very good condition, 11/16" x 11/16", gross weight 7.80 grams. **$2,125**

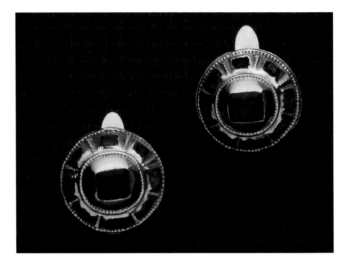

Courtesy of Heritage Auctions, ha.com

Emerald and 18k gold Mallorcan button earrings, unmarked, buttons converted to earrings, some emeralds with rough edges or small chips, lever backs for pierced ears, good condition, 14 mm x 11 mm, 7.0 grams. **$813**

Courtesy of Heritage Auctions, ha.com

Sapphire, diamond, and silver-topped gold earrings with cushion-cut sapphires measuring 7.35 mm x 6.20 mm x 3.90 mm and weighing approximately 2.25 carats, with European- and rose-cut diamonds weighing approximately 1.25 carats, set in silver-topped 18k gold, good condition, 1 7/8" x 1/2", gross weight 7.00 grams. **$1,250**

Courtesy of Heritage Auctions, ha.com

Opal and gold screwback earrings with opal cabochons measuring 4.50 mm, set in 14k gold, good condition, 1 1/2" x 1/2", gross weight 3.35 grams. **$325**

EARRINGS

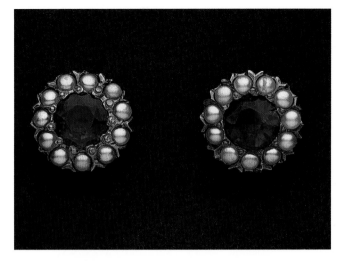

Courtesy of Heritage Auctions, ha.com

Ruby and pearl earrings, screwback posts, 14k gold, half pearls and central rubies, fair condition, one ruby crooked in setting, 10 mm diameter. **$200**

Courtesy of Brunk Auctions, www.brunkauctions.com

Cartier Art Deco platinum and gemstone ear or dress clips set with hand-carved green chrysoprase flowers, with rose-cut and single-cut diamonds weighing approximately 0.25 carats, and square-cut blue sapphires weighing approximately 2.0 carats, platinum and 18k white gold mounts, marked "Cartier 3519897" on each clip, with appraisal and Cartier box, good condition, very light wear, 19.6 mm x 16.5 mm, 12.5 grams. **$44,640**

Courtesy of Brunk Auctions, www.brunkauctions.com

Enamel and pearl dangle-style earrings, each with 6 mm and 4.6 mm cultured pearls and seven 1.0 mm seed pearls, opaque dark blue enamel accents on 14k gold mounts, threaded posts, bellows clutch backs, light wear, 35.5 mm long, gross weight 7.6 grams. **$620**

*Courtesy of Doyle New York,
www.doylenewyork.com*

**Cultured pearl, diamond,
sapphire, coral, emerald, and
aquamarine ear clips, Italy
hallmark, 3/4" x 1". $2,000**

Courtesy of Elite Decorative Arts, www.eliteauction.com

**Kenneth Jay Lane stamped clip-on costume jewelry earrings with pink and clear rhinestones,
3 1/2" high, 58.9 grams. $91**

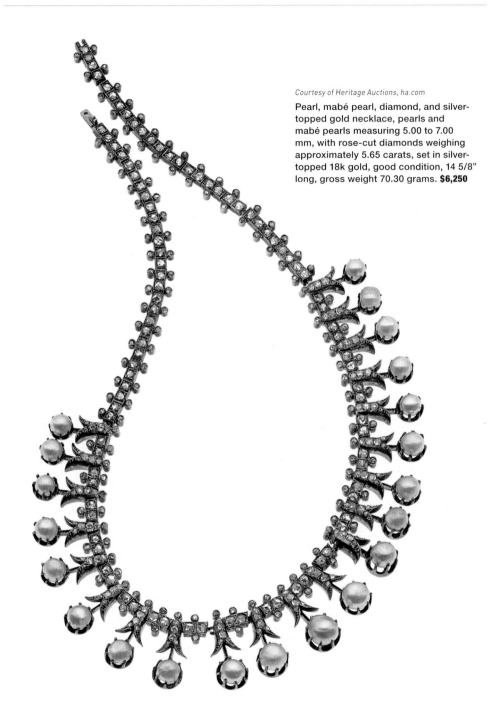

Courtesy of Heritage Auctions, ha.com

Pearl, mabé pearl, diamond, and silver-topped gold necklace, pearls and mabé pearls measuring 5.00 to 7.00 mm, with rose-cut diamonds weighing approximately 5.65 carats, set in silver-topped 18k gold, good condition, 14 5/8" long, gross weight 70.30 grams. **$6,250**

Courtesy of Heritage Auctions, ha.com

Architectural Revival-themed necklace with micromosaics in malachite frames, set in 18k gold, good condition, 14" long, gross weight 44.30 grams. $5,313

NECKLACES & PENDANTS

Courtesy of Heritage Auctions, ha.com

Necklace with oval-shaped garnet cabochon measuring 21.14 mm x 17.91 mm x 7.10 mm and weighing approximately 27.40 carats, with rose- and cabochon-cut garnets weighing approximately 134.75 carats, set in gilt metal, 14k gold spring ring clasp, very good condition, 15" long, gross weight 69.00 grams. $1,500

Courtesy of Heritage Auctions, ha.com

Pendant necklace with round-cut peridot measuring 6.20 to 6.30 mm x 2.84 mm and weighing approximately 0.65 carat, and round-, square-, cushion- and pear-shaped peridot, ruby, spinel, garnet, and sapphire, with round pearls measuring 4.00 to 5.50 mm, set in silver, pendant 4 1/2" x 2 5/16", chain 29 1/2" long, gross weight 90.20 grams. **$275**

NECKLACES & PENDANTS

Courtesy of Heritage Auctions, ha.com

Kunzite, pearl, diamond, platinum, and gold necklace, Tiffany & Co., pear-shaped kunzite measuring 14.20 mm x 9.70 mm x 8.22 mm and weighing approximately 7.20 carats, with round-cut kunzites weighing approximately 18.55 carats, pearls, European-, mine-, and rose-cut diamonds weighing approximately 0.75 carat, set in 18k gold, marked Tiffany & Co., 21" long, gross weight 32.70 grams. **$27,500**

Courtesy of Heritage Auctions, ha.com

▲ Ruby, diamond, and platinum-topped gold ring with oval-shaped ruby measuring 8.60 mm x 6.90 mm x 4.45 mm and weighing approximately 2.20 carats, European- and single-cut diamonds weighing approximately 2.60 carats, set in platinum-topped 14k gold, very good condition, size 6 1/4, gross weight 9.00 grams. **$3,750**

Courtesy of Heritage Auctions, ha.com

◄ Emerald and gold ring with carved oval-shaped emerald cabochon measuring 13.72 mm x 11.18 mm x 9.29 mm and weighing approximately 7.40 carats, set in 18k gold, very good condition, size 7 1/4, gross weight 10.80 grams. **$3,750**

Courtesy of Heritage Auctions, ha.com

Carved onyx and gold filigree ring, 14k gold, carved black onyx with small center diamond, very good condition, size 4 1/2, 22 mm from top to bottom, 4.3 grams. **$250**

Courtesy of Heritage Auctions, ha.com

Aquamarine and diamond ring, 14k filigree gold, four aquamarines with small center diamond, very good condition, size 7, 15 mm from top to bottom, 3.5 grams. **$425**

Courtesy of Elite Decorative Arts, www.eliteauction.com

Platinum, diamond, and sapphire ring, circa 1930s, with approximately 3.0 carat synthetic sapphire, size 5, 3.5 dwt. **$363**

Lamps & Lighting

By Martin Willis

MARTIN WILLIS is the Director of the Decorative Arts at James D. Julia, Inc., one of the nation's premier auction galleries. Formerly of New Hampshire, Willis comes from a family of auctioneers: His father, Morgan Willis, developed and ran the Seaboard Auction Gallery in Eliot, Maine, which Martin eventually took over. He has 40 years of experience in the antique auction business with companies in Maine, New Hampshire, Massachusetts, Colorado and California. He spent six years with Clars Auction Gallery of Oakland, California, as senior appraiser, cataloger and auctioneer, handling the estate of TV mogul Merv Griffin as well as talk show host Tom Snyder. In 2009, Martin launched Antique Auction Forum, a biweekly podcast on the art and antiques trade with followers across North America and throughout the world.

A fine lamp provides illumination as well as a decorative focal point for a room. This dual-purpose trend had its origins in the mid-to-late 1800s with American lighting. As with most game-changing style movements, timing was key in this evolution.

Arguably, the vanguard name of decorative lighting was Louis Comfort Tiffany (1848-1933) of New York City. Urban homes became electrified on a wide scale near the end of the 19th century; it was then that Tiffany was becoming recognized as a designer as well as a commercial success.

Tiffany's first stained glass shade for an electric lamp was designed by Clara Driscoll around 1895. Since their introduction over a century ago, Tiffany's shades have always had a unique, glowing quality to them due to their masterful designs and chemically compounded stained glass colors. Today, Tiffany Studios lamps remain collectors' favorites. Rare and unusual designs – including the Hanging Head Dragonfly, Peony, Apple Blossom, and Wisteria patterns – generate the most interest and dollars; outstanding examples have commanded up to $2 million. More common items such as Acorn, Tulip, or Favrile art glass shade lamps have experienced falling prices relative to a decade ago.

Tiffany's commercial success catalyzed the creation of many new stained glass lamp companies. Contemporaries included Duffner & Kimberly, Suess, Chicago Mosaic, and Wilkinson. See *Mosaic Shades II* by Paul Crist for more information.

There were several other companies in the United States making fine glass lamps at the turn of last century. These included Handel, from Meriden, Connecticut, and Pairpoint, from New Bedford, Massachusetts. Handel was known primarily for its reverse painted shades. Fine examples of the company's landscape, aquarium, and other unusual motifs have garnered prices up to $85,000. Pairpoint opened in 1880 and soon merged with Mt. Washington Glass of Boston. They created reverse painted shades as well, the most

Courtesy of Heritage Auctions, ha.com

Duffner & Kimberly hanging leaded glass lamp, circa 1905, domed leaded shade with floral decoration and hanging hardware, missing piece to one tile, some cracked tiles, 15" high, 26" diameter. $3,500

popular being their "Puffy" shade. Prices for Pairpoint lamps start around $1,000 and peak at about $25,000 for top examples.

Perhaps the most notable European glass lamp manufacturer from the late 19th century was Daum, founded by Jean Daum in France in 1878. The company is still in business today, manufacturing crystal art glass. Daum's lamps were made of cameo glass, produced through a proprietary technique of using acid to cut through layers of fused glass. This creates dramatic color reliefs. During the heyday, 1895-1914, Daum produced beautiful cameo glass lamp bases and shades. Today, early examples can be purchased starting at $1,000. Exceptional pieces may garner up to $80,000.

It is important to note that when it comes to vintage lamps, reproductions and fakes dominate the secondary market. If a price seems too good to be true, it probably is. It is imperative to buy from a reputable dealer or an auction house that will stand behind an item's authenticity. If a piece has the word "style" as part of its description, i.e., a "Tiffany style" lamp, this indicates that it is either a reproduction or that the seller is uncertain of its origins. Always ask plenty of questions before investing in a fine art lamp.

As always, anything is worth whatever someone will pay, and there are often good buys available – even from top manufacturers. With the exception of the very rarest examples, enthusiasts should be able to find and afford a nice authentic vintage lamp to admire and enjoy.

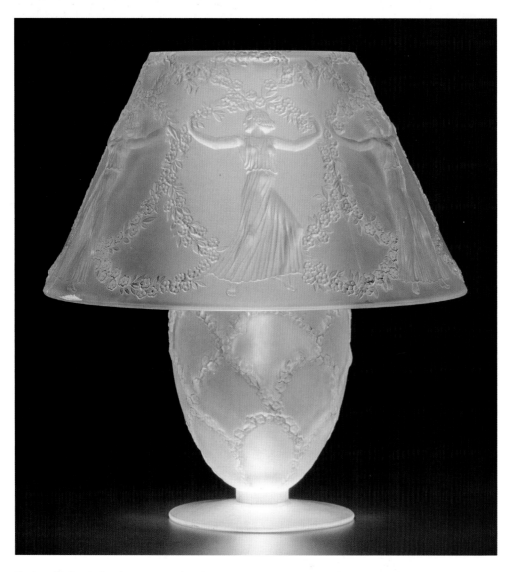

Courtesy of Heritage Auctions, ha.com

R. Lalique clear and frosted glass Six Danseuses lamp, circa 1931, stenciled R. LALIQUE to base, overall good condition, needs rewiring and to be fitted for lighting, missing flake along lip of base and loss of frosted finish, 10 1/4" high. **$17,500**

Courtesy of Morphy Auctions, www.morphyauctions.com

Cameo art glass lamp signed "Galle" on shade, very good condition, chips to bottom and top of base, rewired, 14" high, shade 6" diameter. **$1,200**

Courtesy of Heritage Auctions, ha.com

French Art Deco silvered metal and glass table lamp, circa 1925, surmounted by domed frosted glass shade with molded geometric and floral decoration, hexagonal geometric stepped standard with single light, very fine original condition, surface wear commensurate with age, 22" high. **$438**

Courtesy of Morphy Auctions, www.morphyauctions.com

◄ Pairpoint metal lamp No. 3059 with embossed floral design and metal shade, very good condition, 15" high. **$480**

Courtesy of Heritage Auctions, ha.com

Kerosene lamp possibly from *Gone With the Wind*, Metro-Goldwyn-Mayer, 1939; glass in 1860s-era style, two parts, bottom interior painted gold, top portion with metal holder at base, hurricane portion hand-painted with brown floral design, metal part with patina due to age, some floral design smudged, middle metal part possibly replaced later, 19" high, base 5 1/2" x 5 1/2". This lamp is possibly the one seen to the far right in the scene from *Gone With the Wind* where Vivien Leigh as Scarlett O'Hara and Olivia De Havilland as Melanie Hamilton Wilkes nurse a wounded Confederate soldier. The former owner obtained the lamp from the owner of the bar directly opposite the SIP, Inc./Metro-Goldwyn-Mayer studios on Washington Boulevard in Culver City, California where, years before, the bar owner obtained the lamp as payment for an $8,000 tab racked up by the prop master. **$11,875**

Courtesy of Heritage Auctions, ha.com

Pair of Murano mushroom striped glass lamps, circa 1960s, glass, steel, cord, 22" x 13" x 13". **$6,250**

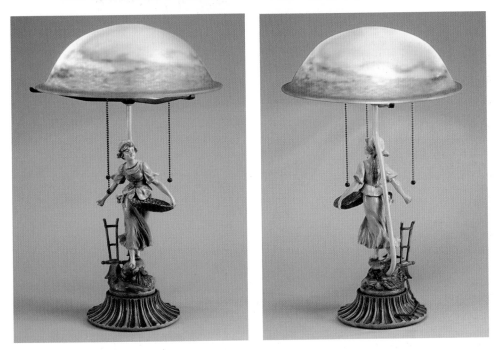

Courtesy of Great Gatsby's Antiques and Auctions, www.greatgatsbys.com

French art glass lamp by Muller Freres, polychrome figural base of young maiden carrying harvest basket with art glass dome-shaped shade, 24" high, 15" diameter. $1,331

Courtesy of Heritage Auctions, ha.com

Daum etched and enameled glass lamp with trees in rain, circa 1900, enameled DAUM, NANCY, with cross of Lorraine, good condition, 14 1/4" high. **$43,750**

◀ Bronze base slag glass lamp in bamboo pattern bronze casing, Wilkinson Co., stamped to base: Wilkinson Co Brooklyn New York, shade 14 1/2" diameter, original base 21" high. **$726**

▲ Slag glass lamp with brass trim and bronze base attributed to Pittsburgh Glass Co., Arts & Crafts period, tan slag glass, floral-style trim around base of shade, no signature but similar to works of Pittsburgh Glass Co., shade 18" diameter, bronze base 19" high. **$424**

◀ Pairpoint red poppy lamp, signed Pairpoint base, very good-plus condition, 22 1/2" high, shade 12" diameter. **$7,800**

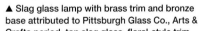

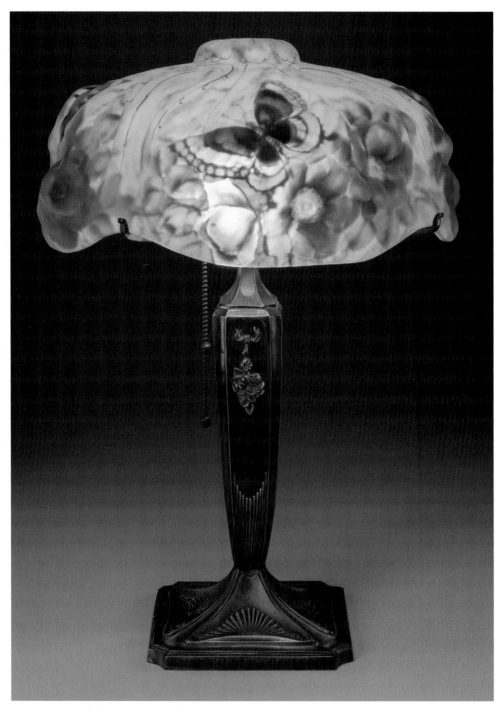

Courtesy of Heritage Auctions, ha.com

Pairpoint glass and bronzed metal butterfly puffy lamp, circa 1900, two-light lamp surmounted by domed reverse-painted shade with butterflies and roses, raised on patinated metal, canted standard and base with cast floral and gadrooned decoration, marks: PAIRPOINT MFG. CO., P (within diamond), 3099, expected loss of gilt detail, 22 1/2" high, 14 1/2" diameter. **$3,438**

Courtesy of Neal Auction Co., www.nealauction.com

Rare pair of gilt bronze Argand lamps, early 19th century, probably English, each with Classical amphora font, navette-shaped acanthine bowl, on bed of acanthus with scrolled feet, etched and frosted shades, with antique presentation cases, 13 1/2" high x 11" wide. **$15,625**

Courtesy of Heritage Auctions, ha.com

Tiffany Studios gilt leaded glass Roman lamp on gilt bronze stick base, circa 1910, marks to shade: TIFFANY STUDIOS, NEW YORK, 1594, marks to base: TIFFANY STUDIOS, NEW YORK, 531, hairline crack to one tile near outer edge, light scuffing to base, 30" high. **$32,500**

Courtesy of Morphy Auctions, www.morphyauctions.com

Tiffany Favrile candle lamp, base marked L.C.T. – Favrile, excellent condition, 12 1/8" high. **$1,140**

Courtesy of Heritage Auctions, ha.com

François Raoul Larche Art Nouveau gilt bronze lamp, circa 1900, four wheat-formed shades surmounted by seated putto, pair of putti embracing between wheat to front, marks: RAOUL LARCHE, 189E, SIOT PARIS, rare Larche model with fine original patina and condition, 23 1/2" x 15" x 15". **$6,000**

Courtesy of Heritage Auctions, ha.com

Chinese porcelain vase mounted as lamp, Qing Dynasty, bottle-form with dragon and phoenix medallions painted between horizontal bands of polychrome leaf and floral designs, marks: 557, surface wear commensurate with age, 35" high. **$1,188**

Courtesy of Heritage Auctions, ha.com

Tiffany Studios leaded glass peony border bronze floor lamp, circa 1910, marks to shade: TIFFANY STUDIOS, NEW YORK, 1374, overall fine condition, no evidence of damage to shade or base, 74 1/2" high, 24" diameter. **$131,000**

Courtesy of Heritage Auctions, ha.com

Tiffany Studios leaded glass and turtleback tile bronze floor lamp, circa 1910, tapering standard issued from squat base supporting shade in mottled green glass and turtleback tile border, marks to lamp base: Tiffany Studios, NEW YORK, 377, marks to shade: TIFFANY STUDIOS, NEW YORK, 1511-2, overall very fine and original condition, pigtail finial appears original, 72" high, 21 1/4" diameter. **$106,250**

 For more Tiffany lamps, please see the "Tiffany Studios" section.

*Courtesy of Morphy Auctions,
www.morphyauctions.com*

**Tiffany Favrile candle lamp, base
marked L.C.T. – Favrile, excellent
condition, 12 1/8" high. $1,140**

Courtesy of Heritage Auctions, ha.com

**Egyptian Revival bronze and iridescent glass figural two-light
lamp, circa 1900, light fleabites to socket rim of shades, light
surface wear commensurate with age, 23 1/2" high. $1,625**

Courtesy of Elite Decorative Arts, www.eliteauction.com

**Bradley & Hubbard table lamp, circa early
20th century, hand-painted panels
inserted into shade in chipped
ice design, six panels
decorated with lake scene,
signed B & H, 16" long,
23" base. $369**

Courtesy of Morphy Auctions,
www.morphyauctions.com

Coca-Cola bottle lamp, 1930s, with original embossed bronze-colored iron base and metal display cap with wear and patch, excellent condition, small touched rubs or paint nicks, light soiling, factory paint irregularities, 20 1/4" high. **$4,200**

Courtesy of Heritage Auctions, ha.com

▲ Peter Tereszczuk bronze table lamp, circa 1920, boy and girl with cold-painted faces standing beneath hooded tree, marks to base: P. Tereszczuk, surface wear commensurate with age, some missing cold-painted finish to figure's faces, 12 1/2" high. **$1,000**

Courtesy of Dirk Soulis Auctions, www.dirksoulisauctions.com

◄ Floral leaded glass shade handmade by Richard A. Bennett Jr. on circa 1920s base attributed as being Carnelian pattern Roseville art pottery, good condition, no damage or repairs, 20 1/2" high. **$580**

Mantiques

By Eric Bradley

ERIC BRADLEY is one of the young guns of the antiques and collectibles field. Bradley, who works for Heritage Auctions, is a former editor of *Antique Trader* magazine and an award-winning investigative journalist with a degree in economics. His work has received press from *The New York Times* and *The Wall Street Journal*. He also served as a featured guest speaker on investing with antiques. He has written several books, including the critically acclaimed *Mantiques: A Manly Guide to Cool Stuff.*

Men tend to think of "antiques" as a euphemism for stuffy, musty, dainty, shatter-prone headaches with no practical purpose in today's modern world. Mantiques, on the other hand, are complete opposites.

If you think about the premise of most of the "found money" collecting television shows dominating every channel, it's easy to see why they all star men. Mantiques are fun and, as it turns out, pretty lucrative. The trend isn't limited to American television; dealers and collectors in Europe are also celebrating the renewed attention to items that appeal to men. U.S. auction houses are developing the trend as well, with Heritage Auctions, the world's largest collectibles auctioneer, now holding a Gentleman Collector auction every year.

Although the name "mantiques" to describe items appealing to guys has existed for about 30 years, the concept of the mantique is ancient. When they weren't chasing mammoths off cliffs, our ancestors were saving interesting stones, carving ivory tusks, or trading with other tribes. Why go through the trouble? The dude with the coolest stuff was seen as better able to care for offspring or lead the tribe to greatness. From Alibaba's lamp to Luke Skywalker's lightsaber (it is a hand-me-down, remember), mantiques are in our DNA.

Fast forward to the 21st century and we've got television shows devoted to them. The mantiques movement is big and chances are you're already a part of it.

For more information on mantiques, see *Mantiques: A Manly Guide to Cool Stuff* by Eric Bradley.

Courtesy of Heritage Auctions, ha.com
1914 Tacoma Road Race event display with pennant and mechanics photograph of Billy Carlson, Huey Hughes, Teddy Tetzlaff, Billy Parsons, Earl Coopers, and others, 25" x 38", with letter of provenance. **$837**

Courtesy of Heritage Auctions, ha.com
Victorian oval painted porcelain snuff box, circa 1890, box lid, bottom, and exterior frieze painted with ducks in landscape, inside lid painted with interior genre scene, surface scratches commensurate with age, 1" x 3" x 2". **$275**

Courtesy of Heritage Auctions, ha.com

Elgin 18 size multicolor gold hunters case with antique watch stand, circa 1895; case: 55mm, four body, 14k gold, large rose crest on front with multicolor flowers and leaves, back with flowers and two horses and rose gold water trough, ornate vermicelli on edges and scallop rim; dial: double sunk, Roman numerals, red five minutes, blue spade hands; movement: No. 6348807, nickel full plate, 21 jewels, adjusted, gold jewel settings, private label signed "Geo. W. Hickox & Fox, Albuquerque N.M."; case signed "Roy," 157.7 grams, together with 7 1/2" high brass display stand. **$6,875**

Gold Stanhope retractable pencil, 10k gold-filled with banded agate seal on top and Stanhope showing microphotograph of Lord Lawson, Mayor of Edinburgh, very good condition, 21.60 grams, 4" x 1/2". **$250**

"Garrett's XXXX Baker Rye" pocket mirror, "Oldest Brand in Baltimore," circa 1910, with woman with bow, 98% silvering, 99% mint condition, pinpoint dots on upper side edge, darker mark on top edge, celluloid with little surface wear, 2 13/16" high. **$411**

Lalique clear and frosted glass Femmes Antiques decanter and 10 whiskey tumblers, post 1945, engraved Lalique, France, good condition overall, flea bite to rim of one tumbler and to foot of another, chips to bottom of stopper of decanter and flea bite to base, decanter 9 3/8" high. **$3,125**

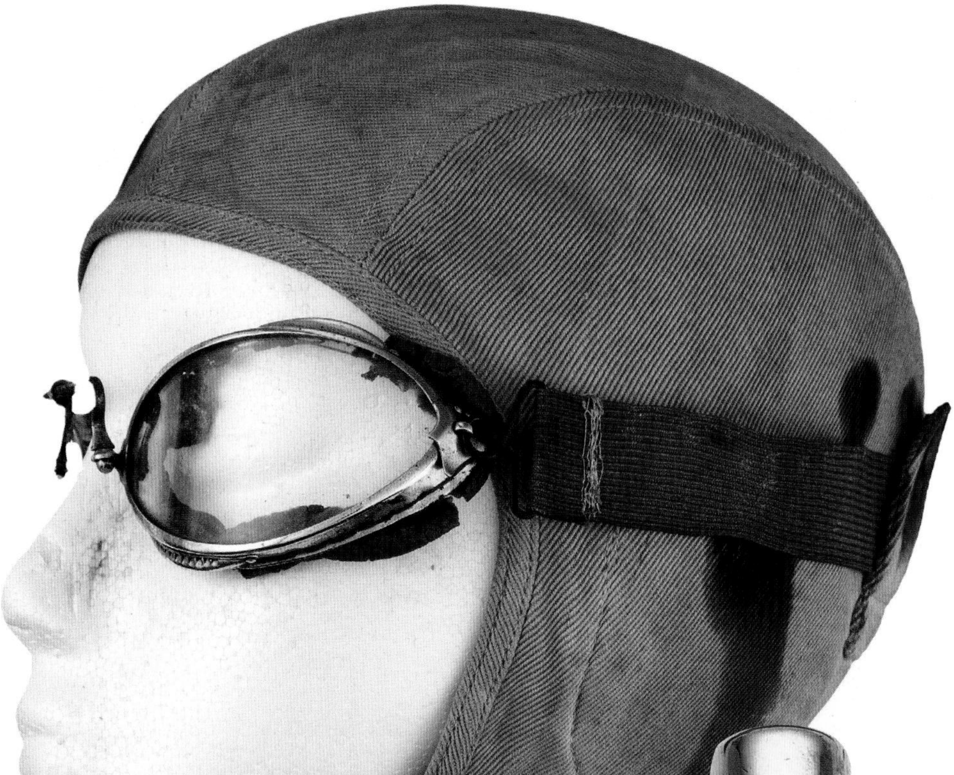

Goggles and race cap worn by 1933 Indianapolis 500 winner Bill Cummings, right lens missing, with letter of provenance. $1,673

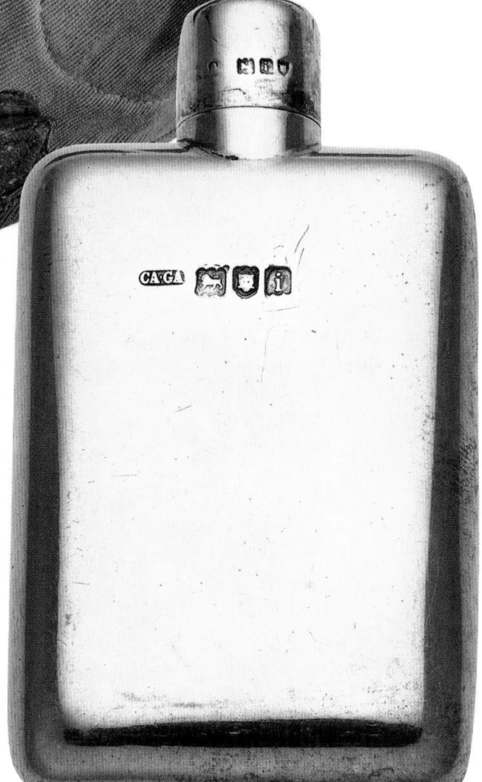

Gold pocket flask designed by Asprey, marked with English hallmarks indicating 22k gold, London, 1904, and maker's mark "CA GA," Asprey, London, holds 2 oz., scratches commensurate with normal use and age, does not leak, 3 5/8" x 2 1/16", 73.00 grams. $3,250

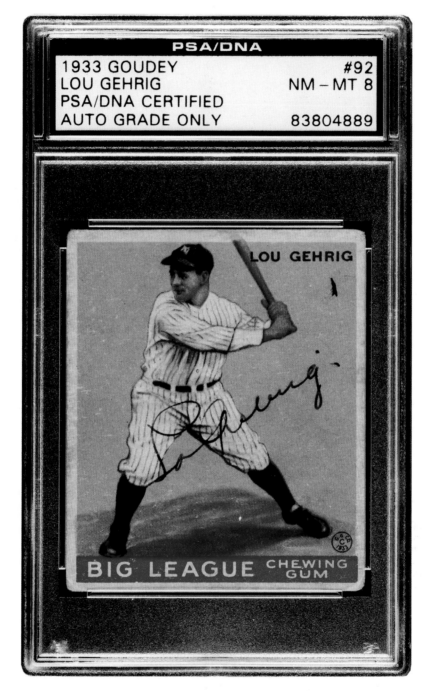

Courtesy of Heritage Auctions, ha.com

1933 Goudey Lou Gehrig #92 baseball card, signed, PSA/DNA NM-MT 8, rare specimen from the year Gehrig broke Everett Scott's streak record. **$37,045**

"Hogan's Heroes" metal dome lunchbox with Thermos, Aladdin Industries, Inc. ©1966, Bing Crosby Productions, Inc., prison barracks with character illustrations on all sides and additional scene on underside, fine overall condition, scattered edge/rim wear and metal "feet" down to bare metal, metal latches and handle attachments with scattered light oxidation, front bottom edge of box with shallow dent, 6 1/2" high metal Thermos and plastic cap with wraparound illustration of cast. **$278**

Royal Doulton porcelain tobacco jar with lid, circa 1910, Kingsware series, men playing golf. **$387**

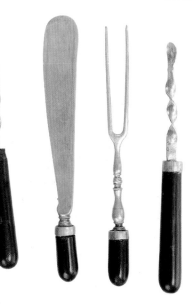

Brunk Auctions, www.brunkauctions.com

Necessaire, French or English, first half 19th century, vertical mother-of-pearl panels and hinged cap, large oval carnelian mounted on cap, with four tiny tools with ebony handles, silver push piece, unmarked, silver test .800 fine or better, good condition, significant wear to silver. **$806**

Showtime Auction Services, showtimeauctions.com

Ruder Beer Vitrolite sign, Wausau, Wisconsin, original copper flashed frame, excellent condition, 12 3/4" x 18 1/2". **$11,400**

Morphy Auctions, www.morphyauctions.com

Shaving mug with steam-driven farm tractor, very good condition, moderate gold loss, 3 1/4" high. **$1,320**

DuMouchelles, www.dumouchelle.com

Six-drawer antique tool chest with marble top, each drawer labeled and with two pull knobs, 23" high x 15" wide x 12" deep. **$431**

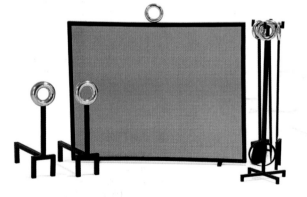

Rago Arts and Auctions, www.ragoarts.com

Four fireplace tools on stand, Michael Aram, 1970s, scissoring tongs, fire screen, and pair of andirons, chromed and patinated metal, signed Aram with copyright symbol, very good overall condition, light rust to frames, screen in good condition, screen 31" x 34". **$1,280**

Courtesy of Heritage Auctions, ha.com

Silver cigar cutter and pipe tool, George W. Shiebler & Co., New York, 1895, marks: (winged S), STERLING, 2872, 4520, surface wear commensurate with age, 2.92 troy ounces, cigar cutter 4 3/4" long. **$238**

Hake's Americana & Collectibles, www.hakes.com

"Superman" metal lunchbox, Adco-Liberty Mfg. Corp. ©1954, National Comics Publications, Inc., Superman with giant robot on front, back panels with yellow Superman symbol, "Superman" comic book title and images on red band, left side of band with slot for name and "Superman's Friend Is ..." text (unused), fine overall condition, rim edges with scattered wear and streaks of bare metal, small hairline scratches on edges on back side, metal latch and handle attachments with trace oxidation. **$1,426**

Morphy Auctions, www.morphyauctions.com

Shaving mug with C.A. Girard, pitcher for Philadelphia Phillies in 1910, and other early baseball players, marked "Limoges" on bottom, excellent condition, no damage. **$5,100**

Maps & Globes

Courtesy of Heritage Auctions, ha.com

"Americae Sive Novi Orbis, No Va Descriptio" [N.p., circa 1580] map of North and South America, engraved and hand-colored, color bleeding through onto verso, very good condition, vertical repair through center of verso, attaching two separate pages together, text in Latin on right half of verso, light biopredation on lower corners and on image, some brown stains on image, approximately 21 3/4" x 16". **$3,250**

Throughout the ages, pictorial maps have been used to show the industries of a city, the attractions of a tourist town, the history of a region, or its holy shrines. Ancient artifacts suggest that pictorial mapping has been around since recorded history began. "Here be dragons" is a mapping phrase used to denote dangerous or unexplored territories, in imitation of the medieval practice of putting sea serpents and other mythological creatures in blank areas of maps.

"SEPTENTRIONALIUM
REGIONUM DESCRIP,"
(Northern Region
Described), Abraham
Ortelius, Antwerp, circa
1570-1587, hand-colored
with sea monster and
sailing ship vignettes,
originally engraved by
Frans Hogenberg, very
good condition, 19" x 14",
framed and matted under
glass 26" x 21 1/2". **$1,250**

▲ Italian globe-form cave a liqueur, 20th
century, on carved oak Black Forest-style
putto, opening to cut-glass decanter and 10
glasses, yellowing to globe, missing flake to
stand, heavy rubbing to putto's nose, surface
wear commensurate with age, 46" high. **$2,000**

◄ Large Replogle world floor model globe,
circa 1951, marks: REPLOGLE 32 INCH
LIBRARY GLOBE, with booklet, yellowing of
lacquered finish with light craquelure, nicks to
stand, wear commensurate with age, 51 1/2"
high. **$2,375**

"Globular Projection of the Map of the World on the Plans of the Equator" schoolgirl world map, watercolor and pen and ink, Miss H.W. Lyon, Rye Academy, 1831, inscribed world in northern and southern hemispheres, highlighted in watercolor, with countries, cities, and bodies of water named, tears, 22 1/4" x 33". **$2,706**

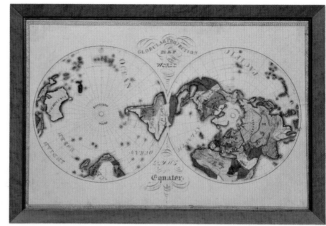

H.B. Nims & Co. 16" terrestrial library globe, Troy, New York, last quarter 19th century, with 12 printed gores, calibrated brass meridian ring with hour circle, printed horizon ring on molded mahogany band with Gregorian and zodiacal calendars, on rococo cast iron stand with acanthus leaf-decorated central baluster and inverted trumpet flower tri-foot base, 41" high. **$1,353**

Texas, Thomas G. Bradford, Boston: Charles D. Strong, 1842, G.W. Boynton engraved, hand-colored map of Texas Republic with land grants shown in lieu of counties in addition to settlements and roads, relief shown in hachures, light staining at lower edge, 13 1/2" x 17 1/2". **$2,250**

Courtesy of Heritage Auctions, ha.com

"America Sive Novi Orbis, No Va Descriptio" copper-engraved map of North America with hand-coloring, Abraham Ortelius, cartographer (1527-1598), Antwerp: 1587, double-leaf plate with descriptive text in French on verso, very good condition, minor wrinkling and foxing, minor rubbing and edge wear to wooden frame, framed (double-sided) to approximately 18" x 24". **$2,750**

Courtesy of Heritage Auctions, ha.com

"ASIAE I TAB:" [Turkey and Cyprus], Gerhard Mercator, Duisburg, circa 1578 or Amsterdam circa 1584, very good condition, 18" x 13 1/2", framed and matted under glass 24" x 19". **$625**

Courtesy of Skinner, Inc., www.skinnerinc.com

China, "Descriptio Chorographica Regni Chinae," Theodor de Bry (1528-1598), Paris, 1628, small folio map on paper, Chinese title: Huang Ming yi tong fang yu bei lan, vignettes in corners depict Matteo Ricci and Chinese couple, matted and framed, 13 3/4" x 12" (sight). **$10,455**

Courtesy of Skinner, Inc., www.skinnerinc.com

Near pair of Philip's 6" globes, George Philip & Son, London, first quarter 20th century, each with 12 colored printed gores, uncalibrated lacquered brass half meridian ring, on turned bulbous stems and molded circular base, terrestrial globe with cartouche reading in part, "Philip's 6 inch Terrestrial Globe London Geographical Institute," celestial cartouche reading "Philip's Popular Celestial Globe Magnitudes," 11 1/2" high. **$738**

Holbrook's Apparatus Mfg. Co. hinged terrestrial pocket globe, Wethersfield, Connecticut, mid-19th century, marks: HOLBROOK'S APPARATUS Mfg. Co., WETHERSFIELD, CT, foxing throughout, minor loss of paper to edges, slight buckling of paper to interior, 2 7/8" diameter. **$1,625**

Near pair of Philip's 6" globes, George Philip & Son, London, first quarter 20th century, each with 12 colored printed gores, uncalibrated lacquered brass half meridian ring, on squat ring-turned base, terrestrial globe with cartouche reading in part, "Philip's 6 inch Terrestrial Globe London Geographical Institute," celestial cartouche reading "Philip's Popular Celestial Globe Magnitudes," 9" high. **$1,722**

Schoolboy map of United Kingdom, Saxton B. Little, Columbia, Connecticut, circa 1828, watercolor and pen and ink hand-drawn map with watercolor borders depicting England, Scotland and Ireland, selected towns, islands, and bodies of water identified, inscribed in upper right with maker's name, location, and date "March 5, 1828," 18" x 17 1/4" (sight), in molded frame with gilt liner. **$1,968**

Weber Costello Co. 18" terrestrial library globe, circa 1930, with calibrated meridian ring and printed horizon ring with Gregorian and zodiacal calendars, in bronzed white metal frame with three glass-inset ball feet, approximately 44" high. **$1,169**

J. Forest 2" terrestrial globe, Paris, early 20th century, 12 chromolithographed paper gores with cartouche reading "Globe Terrestre Dresse par J. Forest 17 rue de Buci Paris," continents identified in French, on black-painted and turned base, 5" high. **$369**

Maritime Art & Artifacts

By Martin Willis

MARTIN WILLIS is the Director of the Decorative Arts at James D. Julia, Inc., one of the nation's premier auction galleries. Formerly of New Hampshire, Willis comes from a family of auctioneers: His father, Morgan Willis, developed and ran the Seaboard Auction Gallery in Eliot, Maine, which Martin eventually took over. He has 40 years of experience in the antique auction business with companies in Maine, New Hampshire, Massachusetts, Colorado, and California. He spent six years with Clars Auction Gallery of Oakland, California, as senior appraiser, cataloger and auctioneer, handling the estate of TV mogul Merv Griffin as well as talk show host Tom Snyder. In 2009, Martin launched Antique Auction Forum, a biweekly podcast on the art and antiques trade with followers across North America and throughout the world.

For extended periods, sometimes even years, a sailor was at sea on a whaling expedition. But little of that time was spent doing actual whaling work. Often months would pass between whale sightings. Sailors had hours of idle time, and some filled that time creating trinkets and art.

Sailors' artwork includes scrimshawed whale's teeth and bone; fancy rope knot work; wood and ivory carvings, such as whimsies, cane heads, pie crimpers, pipe tampers, fids (made for splicing rope); and more. There were valentines made with seashells, swifts (yarn winders), corset busks, and many more interesting and beautiful pieces.

The art of scrimshaw began in the early 1800s and is still practiced today. A scrimshaw artist is called a scrimshander. Starting with a raw tooth in its natural state with ridges, a scrimshander would spend hours polishing it to a smooth surface. He would then begin his design using a sharp needle and India ink. Most of the time black ink was used, but sometimes other colors were also used, mostly red.

I have been lucky enough to see some fabulous whale's tooth scrimshaw work. In the 1980s, I spent several days with collector Barbara Johnson in Princeton, New Jersey. Her entire collection was a premier selection of some of the finest pieces known, considered the foremost in the world.

Scrimshaw can tell a story, often with a design of the captured whale on the verso side. The work may be valued as primitive or folk art. In general, most collectors want extensive detail and a great subject, including beautiful maidens, couples, portraits, whaling ships, American eagles and political designs, whaling scenes, and home ports or ports visited. Sometimes a tooth is completely covered with art telling intricate stories, some with named places and dates. Surprisingly, most scrimshaw work is not signed by the scrimshander.

French silver pocket sundial, late 17th century, oval silver plate with outer hour scale engraved IIII-XII-VIII, divided into quarter-hour subdivisions around central rosette with radial hour-lines between, glazed four-point compass with adjacent inscription, used by naval crews, 2". $2,720

An original period scrimshaw tooth is very desirable and can sell from several hundred dollars to $50,000. In rare cases a few have sold for as much as $100,000, including one called Susan's Tooth from the whaling ship "Susan," by scrimshander Frederick Myrick.

However, the record goes to the scrimshander known only as "The Pagoda Artist." An unsigned and attributed tooth sold several years ago in Portsmouth, New Hampshire, for $303,000.

Before purchasing a vintage scrimshawed tooth, seek an expert's opinion. An old tooth should have a mellow patina, and the ink should be somewhat faded. Resin fakes can fool a novice, and antique whale's teeth can be recently scrimshawed. The ink is usually very dark on these pieces.

Whale's teeth are hollow on the underside, unless cut. Later teeth usually look very white. Sometimes people confuse walrus or elephant ivory with whale ivory. Walrus tusks are scrimshawed as well but are worth a fraction of the value of whale's teeth.

Collecting scrimshaw fell out of favor for many years until President John F. Kennedy was elected. He was an avid collector, and this spawned a renewed interest in the hobby. Today there are many collectors all around the world.

Fine examples of scrimshaw are exhibited at the New Bedford Whaling Museum (www.whalingmuseum.org) and the Peabody Essex Museum (www.pem.org) in Salem, Massachusetts.

Naval photographic archive CDV album of Lt. Dabney Scales of CSS Shenandoah, uniformed and non-uniformed Confederate naval officers from CSS Shenandoah, CSS Florida, and CSS Alabama, quarter-inch plate ambrotype of Scales in uniform, with extracts from log of CSS Shenandoah from Aug. 2-5, 1865, detailing encounter with British ship and learning of overthrow of Confederate government. **$24,760**

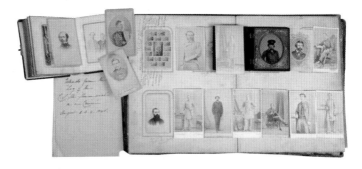

"Steamboat #2 on the Mississippi River," August Norieri, oil on canvas, late 19th century, signed lower right, cove-molded giltwood frame, 18" x 26". Artist specialized in maritime scenes documenting the culture centering around the waterways of Louisiana, Mississippi River, and Lake Pontchartrain. **$22,140**

Portrait of packet ship Emerald off Liverpool, oil on canvas, unsigned, early 19th century, painting shows ship in two views with display of flags, 28" x 39"; Emerald once held record for fastest passage from Liverpool to Boston Light: 16 days, 21 hours. **$40,848**

Engraved sea map of Antwerp, circa 1583, by Lucas Janszoon Waghenaer (1534-1606), example of second state of Waghenaer's general sea chart of Europe, considered to be earliest printed sea chart of Europe, 22" x 15 1/2". **$22,500**

Pair of copper and brass marine beacons with brass maker's badges from "The Patent Lighting Company, Limited. Hayes England," with cut crystal Fresnel lens prisms set into bronze frames, hinged and vented tops, with hoisting rings and gas fitting, 20" wide x 50" high. **$27,675**

Courtesy of Heritage Auctions, ha.com

International Maritime Exposition travel poster, Bordeaux, France, Minot, Paris, 1907, for six-month expo launched by an institution to develop and promote France's military and merchant shipping industry, linen trimmed to border, with tears in top border into background, staining in lower right border and corner, touch-up applied to folds, 29 1/4" x 41 3/4". **$1,015**

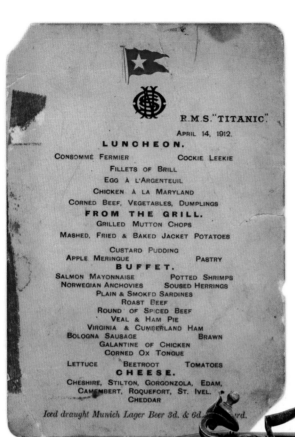

◀ Menu from last lunch served aboard R.M.S. Titanic, just hours before the ship hit an iceberg, 8vo, dated April 14, 1912, formerly belonging to first-class passenger Abraham Lincoln Salomon, who was a wholesale stationer with offices in New York and Philadelphia; he carried the menu with him on board lifeboat No. 1 when being rescued; signed on verso by another first-class passenger, Isaac Gerald Frauenthal, who also survived by leaping from Titanic's deck onto lifeboat No. 5. **$88,000**

▼ English flintlock blunderbuss, early 19th century maritime pistol, flared brass, 7 1/2" barrel with 1 1/4" diameter muzzle, ribbed and in two stages with fine floral engraving, panoply of arms and marked both London and Seagalls, top of muzzle embellished with vine and flower figure, fine condition, small patch of powder fouling at breech, minor hairline cracks near muzzle and front of lock. **$2,437**

Early Barbotine plaque with ocean scene, attributed to Mary Keenan, stamped ROOKWOOD 1883, 6 1/4" x 11". **$17,920**

Courtesy of Ahlers & Ogletree Auction Gallery, www.aandoauctions.com

"Three Ships," in manner of Henry Moore, oil on canvas, 19th century, central steam-powered boat with two figures, flanked on either side by abandoned tall ships with colorful sails, with white-capped waves in foreground and cloudy blue skies above, 35 1/4" x 51 1/4". **$5,856**

Courtesy of Lion Heart Autographs, www.lionheartautographs.com

Ship's passport for the Mary Augusta of New York and its commander, William Hall, for President James Madison, mid-19th century, countersigned by then-Secretary of State and future president James Monroe, "Jas Monroe," and David Gelston, a New York delegate to Continental Congress. **$1,500**

Courtesy of Auctionata, www.auctionata.com

Atlas Maritime (Atlas Maritime ou Cartes reduites de toutes les Côtes de France avec des Cartes particulierres des Isles Voisines des plus considerable, suivies des Plans des principals Villes Maritimes) by French cartographer Rigobert Bonne, 1778, hand-colored title page and 38 tipped-in hand-colored plates of maps, published by Lattré in Paris, some wear to gilt edges, minor rubbing and gilt losses to exterior, and cracking to upper front spine hinge, 48" x 31 1/2". **$2,160**

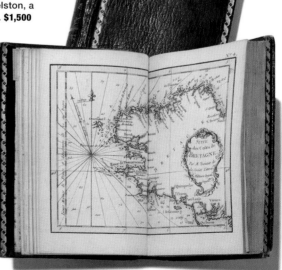

Courtesy of Heritage Auctions, ha.com

U.S. Navy brass ship's compass, manufactured by C.G. Conn Ltd., Elkhart, Indiana. **$625**

"Sailing at Sunset," Hermann Ottomar Herzog, oil on canvas, late 19th century, signed lower right: H. Herzog, unlined canvas loose on stretcher with creases along all four edges, craquelure throughout, light surface grime, 16" x 20". **$2,250**

Automaton clock with maritime theme, circa 19th century, in ormolu-mounted case with lighthouse and castle flanking realistic crushed silk sea, tall-masted ship rising and falling and pitching side to side over rockwork surrounded by winding harbor, and marked with sea serpents, shells, foliate, scrollwork and wreath, with Roman dial and two-train movement with silk suspension, 14 1/2" wide x 17 1/2" high. **$4,869**

Powder horn with scrimshaw decoration, barque in full sail above inscription "Louis M.E. Govin, Maker, AD1868, Cadargah, Queensland," with Masonic insignia beneath scroll inscribed "Friendship and Truth," some damage. $2,358

Letter from Earnest Hemingway to screenwriter Peter Viertel about fishing sequences in adaptation of his novel *The Old Man and the Sea*, "But all I give a shit about is making a good picture; truly good," 20th century, three-line holograph postscript signed in pencil ("E.H"), circa 1955. $4,750

American silver and enamel match safe with maritime signal flag alphabet in enamel on front, circa 1899, monogrammed and dated 99, ED to verso, minor nicking to sides, 2 1/4" high, .82 oz. $812

Movie Posters

By Noah Fleisher

NOAH FLEISHER received his Bachelor of Fine Arts degree from New York University and brings more than a decade of newspaper, magazine, book, antiques and art experience to his position as Public Relations Director of Heritage Auctions, one of the country's foremost auction houses. He is the former editor of *Antique Trader*, *New England Antiques Journal* and *Northeast Antiques Journal*, is the author of *Warman's Modern Furniture* and co-author of *Collecting Children's Books*, and has been a longtime contributor to *Warman's Antiques & Collectibles*.

There is magic in old movie posters; the best directly channel the era from which they came. The totality of movie poster art, the oldest and rarest going back more than a century, taken as a whole, is no less than a complete graphic survey of the evolution of graphic design and taste in Western culture.

The broad appeal of movie posters stems from that nostalgia and from the fact that so many pieces can be had at very fair prices. This makes it an attractive place for younger collectors, many of whom don't even realize they are starting on the incredible journey that collecting can be. Most are simply looking to fill space on a wall or give a gift, and they fill it with art from a movie they loved when they were kids, or one that meant something to them at a specific point in their lives.

"There's a natural evolution with many of them," said Grey Smith, director of movie posters at Heritage Auctions. "As they progress in their lives, they tend to progress as collectors, trading up as they go. When it's all said and done, you see accomplished, broad-based collections."

Movie posters can rightly be called a gateway collectible for that very reason. Very few true collectors just collect one thing and, for more than a few, the first taste comes in the form of movie posters.

So where, exactly, is the top of the market and how has it fared in the last few years?

"As always, universal horror is the top of the market," said Smith. "Top examples of any great film – the older the better – will always bring respectable prices. As a whole, though, the market is off from five and 10 years ago when top posters were bringing $250,000 and $350,000, but it's been steady at the bottom of the high end and in the middle."

What does this mean to today's collectors? It means that a cooled market constitutes incredible opportunity to the trained eye. The untrained eye can benefit by association with reputable dealers and auction houses, by keeping a steady eye on prices in various auctions and on eBay, and by learning what they like, where to get it and when to buy.

Courtesy of Heritage Auctions, ha.com

The Day the Earth Stood Still (20th Century Fox, 1951) autographed one-sheet, very fine condition-plus, on linen, 27" x 41". **$11,353**

Courtesy of Heritage Auctions, ha.com

London After Midnight (MGM, 1927) three-sheet,
top panel mounted on linen, excellent condition,
missing bottom panel, 41" x 81". A "holy grail"
of lost cinema, the last known copy of the
classic silent horror film starring Lon Chaney
was destroyed in a fire in an MGM studio vault in
1965, and movie posters have been as elusive as
the film itself. **$71,700**

Courtesy of Heritage Auctions, ha.com

The Maltese Falcon (Warner Brothers, 1941) six-
sheet, folded, very fine-minus condition, 80 1/2" x
80". **$191,200**

Courtesy of Heritage Auctions, ha.com

Cat People (RKO, 1942) one-sheet, fine-plus
condition, on linen, 27" x 41". **$14,340**

Any dealer or auction house worth its salt is going to spend some time with you – if you want – at whatever level you are collecting, to help you figure out what you can get within your budget. From $100 to $1,000 and up into five and six figures, there are relative bargains to be had right now and, to go back to the top of this discussion, the artwork just can't be beat.

"Ultimately, I would tell anyone looking to buy a movie poster to buy it because they like it," said Smith, echoing the first rule of the business across all categories. "It's all about individual taste. Never get into something for the money because you'll be disappointed."

Besides buying online or from auction houses – at least a few of which, like Heritage, have weekly offerings online to complement its larger thrice yearly events – good posters can be found, for the intrepid explorer, in country auctions, flea markets and antiques shows across the country.

The movies are universal and every town had a movie house. The result is that posters were distributed everywhere and, while not meant for display purposes in the long-term, many found second lives as insulation in walls or as a single layer in a thick, glued board of movie posters, as theater owners would wallpaper the posters over each other from week to week. The erudite eye can pick out the corners of one of these constructs, or can recognize the quality of paper and the neat folds of a quietly stashed one-sheet. The result can often be a treasure, financially and artistically.

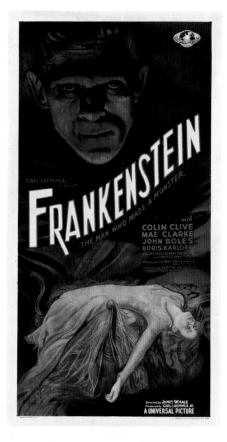

Courtesy of Heritage Auctions, ha.com

Frankenstein (Universal, 1931) Style C three-sheet, only known copy of either of two style three-sheets created for debut of film, fair/good condition on linen, 41" x 78 1/2". **$358,500**

Two aspects of movie poster collecting that get much attention and much misinformation are restorations versus forgeries and fakes.

Every collector should be wary of fakes and forgeries: If it seems too good to be true, ask questions and consult reputable sources. There are always unscrupulous people looking to take advantage of the unsuspecting. A pro will know, based on a variety of factors, whether you have a once-in-a-lifetime find or if you're looking at a clever reprint.

This should never be confused, however, with respectable restoration. Older posters often come with the damage of age – they were not printed on the highest quality paper, as they were not meant to be lasting mementos. Movies played for a few weeks and were replaced, as were the posters. If a poster is linen-backed or framed, there has likely been restoration work on it, and a good dealer or auctioneer will be very up front about this.

"Oftentimes a poster would not have been saved had it not been for quality restoration," said Smith. "Good restoration work is respectful of the original and will enhance the value of a piece, not hurt it. A fake is a fake, no matter what, and should never be portrayed as an original. Educate yourself, check your sources and you should do just fine."

Courtesy of Heritage Auctions, ha.com

Gone With the Wind (Metro-Goldwyn-Mayer, 1939) one-sheet, style DP, "Atlanta Bazaar" scene, by illustrator Armando Seguso, who was responsible for most of the artwork for the film's original 1939 posters as well as other advertising materials; rarest of all *Gone With the Wind* one-sheets, poster 41" x 27", 46" x 32" matted and framed. **$20,000**

Courtesy of Heritage Auctions, ha.com

The War of the Worlds (Paramount, 1953) half-sheet, style B, very fine-minus condition, on paper, 22" x 28". **$14,340**

Courtesy of Heritage Auctions, ha.com

The Wizard of Oz (MGM, 1939) one-sheet, style D, fine-plus condition, on linen, 27" x 41". **$65,725**

Courtesy of Heritage Auctions, ha.com

Breakfast at Tiffany's (Paramount, 1962) Italian 2-Foglio, rare, very fine condition, on linen, 39" x 54 1/2". **$13,145**

Courtesy of Heritage Auctions, ha.com

The Adventures of Robin Hood (Warner Brothers, R-1953) Italian 2-Foglio, folded, very fine condition-minus, 39" x 55". **$5,975**

Courtesy of Dan Morphy Auctions, www.morphyauctions.com

Creature from the Black Lagoon, 1954, one-sheet poster matted and framed under glass, very good condition, poster 27" x 41", 47" x 33 1/2" framed. **$6,000**

Courtesy of Budapest Poster Gallery, budapestposter.com

Star Wars Episode V: The Empire Strikes Back, 1980, Hungarian, two-sheet, 46" x 33". **$4,000**

Courtesy of Dan Morphy Auctions, www.morphyauctions.com

The Pride of the Yankees, 1940, excellent condition, 46 1/2" x 33 1/2" framed. **$1,700**

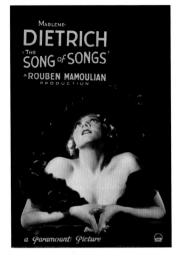

Courtesy of Heritage Auctions, ha.com

The Song of Songs (Paramount, 1933) full-bleed one-sheet, style A, very fine condition, on linen, 26" x 40". **$35,850**

Courtesy of Heritage Auctions, ha.com

Godzilla (Toho, 1956), Japanese B2, very fine condition, on linen, 20" x 28 1/2". This movie was inspired by several real events: the atomic bombing of Japan at Hiroshima and Nagasaki at the end of World War II, the hydrogen bomb explosion at the Bikini Atoll in March 1954, and the subsequent irradiation of the fishing boat Daigo Fukuryu Maru. **$13,145**

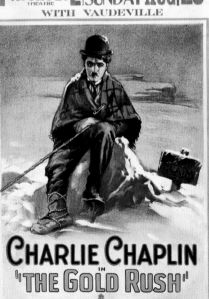

Courtesy of Heritage Auctions, ha.com

The Gold Rush (United Artists, 1925) window card, fine-minus condition, on linen, 13 3/4" x 21 3/4". **$8,365**

Love Before Breakfast (Universal, 1936) one-sheet, very fine condition, on linen, 27 1/2" x 41". **$33,460**

The Dawn Patrol (Warner Brothers, 1938) three-sheet, remake of Howard Hawks' homage to British pilots who suffered heavy losses during World War I, fine/very fine condition, on linen, 41" x 79". **$15,535**

It's a Mad, Mad, Mad, Mad World (United Artists, 1963) Cinerama 24-sheet, folded, very fine condition-plus, 104" x 232". **$8,365**

Music Memorabilia

By Susan Sliwicki

SUSAN SLIWICKI is the former editor of *Goldmine* magazine, which she joined in 2007. Her favorite childhood memories are of hours spent with her oldest brother, listening to his collection of albums, including Pink Floyd's "Dark Side of the Moon" and Deep Purple's "Machine Head."

The state of the hobby for those who collect music and related memorabilia is healthy, according to Jacques van Gool of Backstage Auctions. Based in Houston, the boutique online auction house specializes in authentic rock memorabilia consigned directly by legendary musicians and entertainment professionals.

"I have not seen a massive exodus or departure from collecting music memorabilia as a hobby," van Gool said. "I think the number of collectors and buyers is just as high as it was three or five years ago. But there is definitely a bigger interest for lower- to mid-range items."

Before the economy went south in 2008, multiple buyers might be in the market for a pricey item, such as a fully signed photo of The Beatles. The resulting bidding battle could drive that lot's price up to $10,000. These days, fewer people are looking for that type of lot to begin with, and those who are interested likely would pay less for it, too. Instead, buyers are gravitating toward low- to mid-price lots that previously might not have been considered for auction, van Gool said. And, the acts that buyers are interested in aren't necessarily your parents' favorites.

"There is definitely a new generation of collectors, which is people that currently age-wise are between 35 and 55, who didn't grow up listening to '60s music," van Gool said.

Artists from the late 1970s and 1980s, especially hard rock, heavy metal and pop acts, are poised to be the next generation of headlining acts for collectors, van Gool said. He listed Guns N' Roses, Motley Crüe, Bon Jovi, U2, Prince and Madonna as prime examples.

And just as the desired artists are changing, so, too, are some of the items that are being collected.

"Obviously, concert posters are becoming more and more

Glossy photo of singer Billie Holiday standing behind the counter of a record store with five other people, pointing to Okeh 78 RPM record in sleeve marked 35¢, same label Holiday recorded on in 1941, photo signed by Holliday with message "To too [sic] fine and Mellow / people Bernie an Bill / stay on it / Billie Holiday," good condition, 10" x 8". **$1,250**

extinct because there hardly is a need to do concert posters anymore," van Gool said. "Back in the '60s, it was almost the only way to communicate that hey, there's a concert coming, and you would see these posters staple-gunned to phone poles. These days, you announce concerts via e-mail and websites and text messages and Facebook and Twitter and all of that."

Also on the endangered species list: ticket stubs, printed magazines, handbills, and promotional materials. The sharp decline of many record companies and the rise of CD and digital formats have combined to reduce the production of promotional items, van Gool said.

And those reports you've heard about the pending demise of vinyl records in the wake of digital formats? Don't believe 'em.

"Vinyl is far from dead. Vinyl is alive and kicking," van Gool said. "Of '60s artists, vinyl is a prime collectible. But the same holds true for collectors of '80s bands or artists. They are just as intrigued and as interested in vinyl as the previous generation."

Whatever your interest in music and memorabilia, van Gool offers one key piece of advice.

"I have never looked at collecting music memorabilia as an investment," he said. Instead, he recommends building a collection around your passion, be it punk music, concert posters or all things Neil Diamond.

"If you just collect for the sheer and simple fact of pleasure and passion, then the money part, the investment part, becomes, at best, secondary," van Gool said. "In a way, collecting represents pieces of history. Whether it's an old handbill or a ticket stub or a T-shirt, every picture tells a story. When you buy that 1978 Blue Öyster Cult Wichita, Kansas, T-shirt, you've bought a piece of history."

Collecting Tips

There are a few things you should consider as you invest in your hobby, according to van Gool.

• **Condition, condition, condition.** Strive to acquire items that are in the best condition possible, and keep them that way.

"One universal truth will always be condition," van Gool said. "Obviously, the more mint an item, the more it'll hold its value. That was true back then, it's true today, and it'll be true 40 years from now."

From poster frames to ticket albums to record storage sleeves, bags and boxes, there are ways to preserve basically every collectible you might seek. "It's money well spent to make sure you preserve your items well," van Gool said.

• **Put a priority on provenance.** Some collectors feel that personal items, like an artist's jewelry, stage-worn clothing or even a car, have more value than other pieces. But the personal nature of a piece doesn't matter if you can't prove its pedigree.

"Personal items are considered valuable, but you'd better have the provenance to back it up, and provenance is harder to come by than the actual item," van Gool said.

Working with reputable auctioneers and dealers is a great way to boost the likelihood that an item is everything you want. But even if you acquire a personal item with an impeccable provenance, keep in mind that doesn't necessarily make it more valuable than something of a less personal nature.

"What I've seen is that a fully signed Beatles

Courtesy of Gotta Have Rock and Roll, www.gottahaverockandroll.com

Elvis Presley's stage and personally worn black velvet jacket with high collar, matching cape with red lining and IC Costume label, and matching bell bottom pants, with two letters of provenance including note confirming Elvis wore outfit in 1970-1971, with black and white photograph of Elvis with Engelbert Humperdink, very good condition. $15,568

Uncashed bank check from shared account of Bruce Springsteen and his road manager, Robert E. Chirmside, from Colonial First National Bank, dated Sept. 20, 1979 and made out for $35 for "Strings," filled out and signed by Springsteen, near mint condition, 2 3/4" x 6". **$1,669**

item may be worth $10,000. But there's an enormous amount of non-personal items that are worth more. We've seen certain concert posters sell for $20,000, $50,000, even $100,000," van Gool said.

• **Weigh quantity and rarity.** "You always want to collect those types of items that there are the fewest of – promotional items or items that are local, for instance," van Gool said. "Anything that is made in smaller quantities or made for promotional purposes or a local purpose, like a concert, eventually will be more collectible."

• **Take advantage of opportunities geared toward collectors.** "Record Store Day is once a year, and I really think that it pays off to go to your local record store and buy the releases that will be unique for Record Store Day only," van Gool said. "The vinyl that is going to be offered is typically limited to 1,000 or 3,000 or 5,000 copies, and those limited editions will always become more valuable as time goes by."

Today, some bands release limited-edition vinyl LPs or singles in addition to CDs and MP3s. Van Gool recommends music lovers buy one format to enjoy (be it CD, vinyl or MP3) and buy a copy of the vinyl record to keep – still sealed, of course – in your collection.

"Because there are fewer records pressed, if you keep yours sealed, 20, 30 years from now, there's a good chance that you'll be happy you did that," he said.

• **Refine the focus of your collection.** The hottest acts tend to have the most collectors and, by extension, the most items you can collect, van Gool said. If you try to collect everything that is available, you'll need a lot of time to chase pieces down and a lot of money to acquire them.

"Figure out what really excites you as a collector," van Gool said. "If you do that, you make the hobby a lot more fun for yourself. You set some parameters so you protect yourself from spending an enormous amount of money."

• **Think before you toss.** Good-condition, once-common items that date back before World War II – like advertising posters, Coca-Cola bottles, 78 RPM records and hand tools – today are cherished by collectors.

"Nothing saddens me more than people going through their basements, garages, storage facilities, attics, etc., with big plastic bags and just putting it out for the trash," van Gool said. "Eventually, true historic treasures are just being thrown away. Why keep that concert poster? Well, you can pitch it, but that might be the only piece of evidence for that particular venue, and now it's gone."

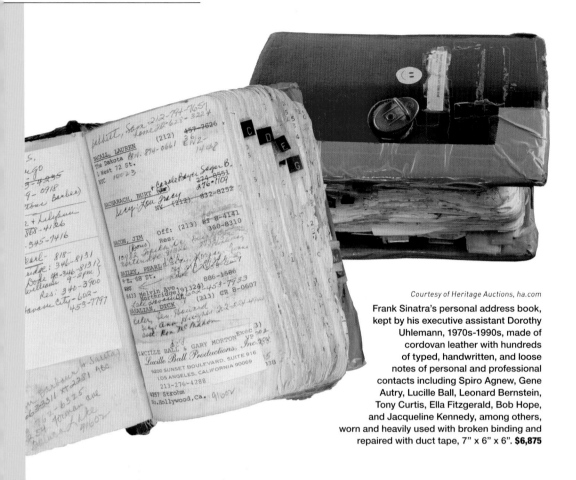

Courtesy of Heritage Auctions, ha.com

Frank Sinatra's personal address book, kept by his executive assistant Dorothy Uhlemann, 1970s-1990s, made of cordovan leather with hundreds of typed, handwritten, and loose notes of personal and professional contacts including Spiro Agnew, Gene Autry, Lucille Ball, Leonard Bernstein, Tony Curtis, Ella Fitzgerald, Bob Hope, and Jacqueline Kennedy, among others, worn and heavily used with broken binding and repaired with duct tape, 7" x 6" x 6". **$6,875**

Courtesy of Backstage Auctions, Inc., www.backstageauctions.com

Ludwig drum kit, circa 1973, first kit played by Peter Criss with KISS, glitter logo bass drum, snare, two floor toms, four tom-toms varying in size, five original cymbals, two high hats, Criss' cow bell, drum pedal and drum stool, hardware with stenciled KISS logo on all sides, all drums with original skins, used by Criss between December 1973 through end of 1974. **$34,552**

Courtesy of Omega Auctions,
www.omegaauctioncorp.com

Six Ero Saarinen tulip chairs, circa 1960s, from John Lennon's Kenwood home in Weybridge Surrey, chairs were used in Lennon's sunroom and were given to his housekeeper, Dot Jarlett, in 1967-1968. **$6,627**

Courtesy of Heritage Auctions, ha.com

Steppenwolf/Santana/Grateful Dead Fillmore West concert poster, circa 1968, first-printing poster with artist Lee Conklin's "Lion/Human" design, opening act, Santana commissioned Conklin to do second version of this design for their first album cover, two sets of shows held in August and September, uncoated stock, near mint-minus condition, 14 1/2" x 21". **$2,875**

Courtesy of Hake's Americana & Collectibles,
www.hakes.com

Thin cardboard poster promoting The Beach Boys' Sept. 18, 1965 concert at Convention Hall in Philadelphia, with photo of band and "The Beach Boys" and notes about sponsors and accompanying acts; very fine condition with minor margin handling wear, tape stain near ticket price information, 14" x 22". **$2,783**

Courtesy of Julien's Auctions, www.juliensauctions.com

Four framed photographs of musicians Ann and Nancy Wilson of rock band Heart, taken during same sitting, one of Ann and one of Nancy, and two of sisters together, photographer unknown, each 16" x 14". **$1,920**

Courtesy of Gotta Have Rock and Roll, www.gottahaverockandroll.com

◀ Michael Jackson's "Billie Jean" black fedora worn on stage during "Bad" world tour and signed in gold pen, with copy of letter from Jackson on MJ Productions letterhead, very good condition. **$2,925**

Courtesy of Heritage Auctions, ha.com

Evening gown worn by singer Whitney Houston, circa 1990s, silver nylon top, long sleeves, black velvet mock turtleneck, back zip-up closure, label reads "Marc Bouwer," favorite designer of Houston. **$1,125**

Courtesy of Heritage Auctions, ha.com

Handwritten and signed letter by Patsy Cline with set list and photographs, circa 1956, written to club owner confirming date and time of performance at Poplar Tavern before Cline became famous, with two photos of Cline and band on stage and another of Cline and friends; letter in excellent condition, envelope and photo of Cline and friends in very good condition, group photo is later reprint, photos 8" x 10", letter 8 1/2" x 11". **$2,250**

Courtesy of Heritage Auctions, ha.com

Oil painting on canvas by Frank Sinatra, mountains set against orange sky, signed in lower right corner "FAS '85," signed in blue felt-tip ink on back lower right corner "Frank Sinatra '85," with handwritten note that reads, "Dot – / Here is your picture! / Now stop hollering at me! / the Artist / Who????," gifted to Dorothy Uhlemann, Sinatra's assistant of 30 years, painting 23" x 19". **$10,625**

Courtesy of Heritage Auctions, ha.com

Custom-made shirt-jacket worn by Jimi Hendrix, circa 1969, red, white and blue suede with appliqué on front, back, and cuffs, with color photograph of Hendrix backstage with friends, very good condition, some bleed of red suede onto white and some overall wear. **$12,500**

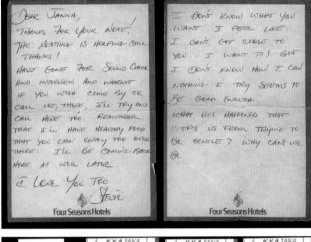

◄ Handwritten letter by Stevie Ray Vaughn to his fiancé, Janna Lapidus, in blue ballpoint pen on Four Seasons Hotel stationary; on first page Vaughn writes about Lapidus joining him on tour, on second page he discusses their relationship and problems they are having; very good condition. **$1,774**

▲ Fifteen unused tickets for The Beatles 1966 concert at Candlestick Park, with business card for concert producer Tom Donahue, Autumn Records; concert was last one The Beatles did before formally disbanding and it did not sell out; mint condition, tickets 2 1/2" x 5 3/4". **$10,000**

Gibson hollow-bodied electric guitar, circa 1960, with original "Gibson Byrdland, Number A34663, guaranteed Gibson Inc." label intact inside body, neck inlaid with mother-of-pearl, in original hard-shell case, with guitar pick engraved with owner's name "Ken Raymond," with promotional photograph of Chet Atkins hand-signed by Atkins in blue ink, 40 1/2" long x 17" wide. **$8,400**

Gibson Explorer guitar used by Motley Crue's Mick Mars during recording of "Theatre of Pain" in 1985, one of several guitars Mars brought into studio, excellent condition with pick marks on front and buckle marks on back. **$68,513**

North American Indian Artifacts

By Russell E. Lewis

RUSSELL E. LEWIS is a university professor, anthropologist, collector and author of several books, including *Warman's North American Indian Artifacts Identification and Price Guide.*

Our interest in Native American material cultural artifacts has been long-lived, as was the Indians' interest in many of our material cultural items from an early period.

During recent years, it has become commonplace to have major sales of these artifacts by at least four major auction houses, in addition to the private trading, local auctions, and Internet sales of these items.

Anthropologists have written millions of words on American Indian cultures and societies and have standardized various regions of the country when discussing these cultures.

We have been fascinated with the material culture of Native Americans from the beginning of our contact with their societies. The majority of these valuable items are in repositories of museums, universities, and colleges, but many items that were traded to private citizens are now being sold to collectors of Native American material culture.

Native American artifacts are now acquired by collectors in the same fashion as any material cultural item. Individuals interested in antiques and collectibles find items at farm auction sales (an especially good place for farm family collections to be dispersed), yard sales, estate sales, specialized auctions, and from private collectors trading or selling items.

Native American artifacts are much more difficult to locate for a variety of reasons: scarcity of items; legal protection of items being traded; more vigorous collecting of artifacts by numerous

"The White Gate," Victor Higgins (American, 1884-1949), oil on canvas, 1919, signed lower right "Victor Higgins," 18 1/8" x 20 1/4". Many of Higgins' early Taos paintings, including this one, feature the landmark pueblo as a backdrop for scenes of everyday Native American life. **$461,000**

international, national, state, regional, and local museums and historical societies; frailties of the items themselves, as most were made of organic materials; and a more limited distribution network through legitimate secondary sales.

However, it is still possible to find some types of Native American items through the traditional sources of online auctions, auction houses in local communities, antique stores and malls, flea markets, trading meetings, estate sales, and similar venues. The most likely items to find in the above ways would be items made of stone, chert, flint, obsidian, and copper. Most organic materials will not have survived the rigors of a marketplace unless they were recently released from an estate or collection and their values were unknown to the previous owner.

For more information on Native American collectibles, see *Warman's North American Indian Artifacts Identification and Price Guide* by Russell E. Lewis.

Sioux spontoon tomahawk, circa 1860, with beaded buffalo hide drop, ash wood, buffalo hide, glass beads, dyed porcupine quills, sinew, and hand-forged iron, 23" long excluding attachment. **$87,500**

Forty-eight full-color portraits of Native Americans, Thomas L. McKenney and James Hall, *History of the Indian Tribes of North America with Biographical Sketches and Anecdotes of the Principal Chiefs*, Vol. II, Philadelphia: Daniel Rice and James G. Clark, 1842, 20th century half-brown Levant Morocco over brown cloth boards. **$11,875**

McKenney, Thomas (1785-1859) and James Hall (1793-1868), *History of the Indian Tribes of North America with Biographical Sketches of the Principal Chiefs, Embellished with One Hundred and Twenty Portraits from the Indian Gallery in the Department of War, at Washington*, Philadelphia: Biddle, 1837; Philadelphia: Greenough, 1838; Vol. I and part of Vol. II bound as one, folio, illustrated with 71 of 72 full-page hand-colored lithographs, lacking plate of Se-Quo-Yah in first volume, second volume ending with portrait of Ahyouwaighs, the 77nd plate, 19 1/2" x 14 1/4". **$17,200**

Sioux beaded hide dress, circa 1900, with glass beads, brass beads, metal beads, sinew, and cotton thread, 49" long. **$15,000**

Courtesy of Heritage Auctions, ha.com

Zuni polychrome painted clay canteen, circa 1880, overall very good condition, surface with wear commensurate with age, including loss to slip and soiling, 4" high. **$625**

Courtesy of Thomaston Place Auction Galleries, www.thomastonauction.com

Sioux beadwork saddle blanket, circa 1880, geometric designs in red, pink, Prussian and aqua blue, silver on white background, on native tanned hide with old canvas backing and center, fringe at ends, set with trade bells, worn from use, some bead and bell loss, 62" (excluding 8" fringe) x 29". **$1,500**

Courtesy of Skinner Inc.; www.skinnerinc.com

Native American with rifle statue, bronze with gold/brown patina, signed "C. Kauba" in bronze on back edge of blanket, stamped and numbered "GESCHÜTZT / 5305" on drapery on back, inscribed "694" on underside, 9" high. **$1,476**

Courtesy of Heritage Auctions, ha.com

Southwest painted rawhide dance shield, circa 1880, red with concentric orb flanked by two geometric elements, dots along perimeter, 17 1/2" diameter. **$1,063**

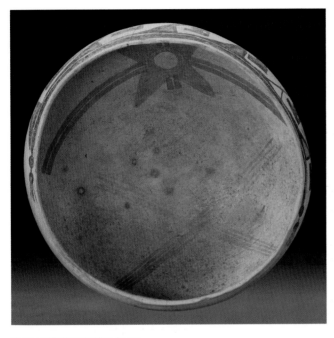

Courtesy of Heritage Auctions, ha.com

Sityaki polychrome bowl, circa 1300-1400 AD, clay, paint, overall good condition, one crack descending from rim, shallow chips on rim, surface wear, some fading of painted design on interior, some discoloration to painted design on exterior, 10 1/2" diameter. **$1,750**

Courtesy of Rich Penn Auctions, www.richpennauctions.com

Ceremonial beaded relic of otter skin and sinew, metallic eyes resembling coins, dark blue, green, red, white, and yellow beads alongside mother-of-pearl with small metallic bells and other adornments, excellent condition with no signs of use, 48" long. **$250**

Courtesy of Skinner Inc.; www.skinnerinc.com

Paint-decorated wood and iron tavern sign, American, early 19th century, double-sided with turned stiles and wrought iron hangers joining shaped cresting above rectangular panel of Native American in feathered headdress with bow and arrow, lettered "JOHNSON" below, reverse painted with landscape and lettered "JOHNSON," 58 1/2" high to top of hangers x 25" wide. **$15,990**

Courtesy of Thomaston Place Auction Galleries, www.thomastonauction.com

◄ Story-telling staff, Wabanaki tradition, 19th century, carved from alder root, eagle head top from one root, crown with star in relief-cut bark at top of shaft, bark symbols of canoe, tomahawk, and snake over length, terminating in naked female form from torso down, good condition, 37 1/2" long. **$800**

Courtesy of Heritage Auctions, ha.com

"Land of Navaho (Young Indian Goat Herder)," William Robinson Leigh (American, 1866-1955), oil on canvas, 1948, signed and dated lower left "W.R. Leigh 1948 ©," titled on labels verso, artist's stamps on original frame verso, 45" x 60". **$575,000**

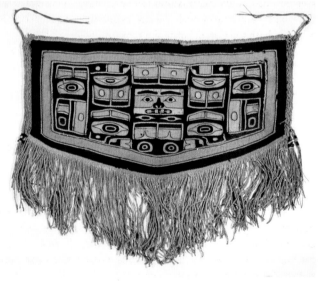

Courtesy of Jeffrey S. Evans & Associates, www.jeffreysevans.com

Northwest Coast child's ceremonial Chilkat blanket, circa 1890, woven panel dyed yellow, blue-green, and black, with central mask surrounded by clan symbols and stylized natural forms, original applied border and fringe, 24" x 33". **$9,000**

Perfume Bottles

By Kyle Husfloen

Although the human sense of smell isn't nearly as acute as that of many other mammals, we have long been affected by the odors in the world around us. Science has shown that scents or smells can directly affect our mood or behavior.

No one knows for certain when humans first rubbed themselves with some plant or herb to improve their appeal to other humans, usually of the opposite sex. However, it is clear that the use of unguents and scented materials was widely practiced as far back as Ancient Egypt.

Some of the first objects made of glass, in fact, were small cast vials used for storing such mixtures. By the age of the Roman Empire, scented waters and other mixtures were even more important and were widely available in small glass flasks or bottles. Since that time glass has been the material of choice for storing scented concoctions, and during the past 200 years some of the most exquisite glass objects produced were designed for that purpose.

It wasn't until around the middle of the 19th century that specialized bottles and vials were produced to hold commercially manufactured scents. Some aromatic mixtures were worn on special occasions, while many others were splashed on to help mask body odor. For centuries it had been common practice for "sophisticated" people to carry on their person a scented pouch or similar accoutrement, since daily bathing was unheard of and laundering methods were primitive.

Commercially produced and brand name perfumes and colognes have really only been common since the late 19th and early 20th centuries. The French started the ball rolling during the first half of the 19th century when D'Orsay and Guerlain began producing special scents. The first American entrepreneur to step into this field was Richard Hudnut, whose firm was established in 1880. During the second half of the 19th century most scents carried simple labels and were sold in simple, fairly generic glass bottles. Only in the early 20th

KYLE HUSFLOEN, Southern California representative for Kaminski Auctions, is a well-respected expert on antiques and collectibles. He was with *Antique Trader* publications for more than 30 years.

century did parfumeurs introduce specially designed labels and bottles to hold their most popular perfumes. Coty, founded in 1904, was one of the first to do this, and they turned to Rene Lalique for a special bottle design around 1908. Other French firms, such as Bourjois (1903), Caron (1903), and D'Orsay (1904) were soon following this trend.

People collect two kinds of perfume bottles – decorative and commercial. Decorative bottles include any bottles sold empty and meant to be filled with your choice of scent. Commercial bottles are any that were sold filled with scent and usually have the label of the perfume company.

The rules of value for perfume bottles are the same as for any other kind of glass – rarity, condition, age, and quality of glass.

The record price for perfume bottle at auction is something over $200,000, and those little sample bottles of scent that we used to get for free at perfume counters in the 1960s can now bring as much as $300 or $400.

For more information on perfume bottles, see *Antique Trader Perfume Bottles Price Guide* by Kyle Husfloen.

Courtesy of Rago Arts and Auctions, www.ragoarts.com

Lepage perfume bottle, Lalique, frosted and clear glass with amber patina, France, circa 1920, molded R. Lalique, 4 5/8" x 1 1/2" x 3/4". **$7,500**

Courtesy of Perfume Bottle Auctions, www.perfumebottlesauction.com

Parera Varon Dandy clear glass perfume bottle, painted glass stopper, ribbon bowtie, leather coat exterior, stained paper label, 5". **$9,840**

Courtesy of Perfume Bottle Auctions, www.perfumebottlesauction.com

Langlois perfume bottle and stopper, Depinoix, circa 1925, black crystal, raised red enameled detail imitating eggshell lacquer, 4 1/4". **$4,305**

Courtesy of Perfume Bottle Auctions, www.perfumebottlesauction.com

French atomizer, Jean Sala, circa 1880, aqua blue crystal, applied amber feet, and lion head medallions, enameled overall, worn gilt metal hardware and replacement hose and ball, 7 1/8". **$2,583**

Courtesy of Authenticated Internet Auctions, www.authenticatedinternetauctions.com

Boxed perfume set, circa 1760, fully fitted with four perfume bottles, two agate caged in gold, two crystal gold mounted, gold patch box, Lapis seal, gold knife writing slip. **$31,318**

Courtesy of Brunk Auctions, www.brunkauctions.com

Cameo glass swan's-head perfume bottle, English, late 19th century, Thomas Webb & Sons, carved opal over blue crystal, gilded mount by Paris firm Keller, locking hinge mechanism decorated with band of fleur-de-lis and hallmarks for Gustave Keller, very good condition, minor repair to tip of bill, 9". **$10,540**

Courtesy of Perfume Bottle Auctions,
www.perfumebottlesauction.com

Vienna enamel perfume dispenser in shape of wine barrel, circa 1880s, enameled overall in allegorical tableaus with gilt metal fittings, figural stopper with English import marks, gilt metal dwarf supports, 5 1/2". $14,760

Courtesy of Royal Crest Auctioneers, Gardena, California

Rare Femme de Paris Ybry pour perfume bottle flacon by Baccarat, circa 1925, Art Deco-style with jade glass, white crystal interior, truncated angle, original clear and frosted glass stopper, emerald enamel on gilt brass lid, signed under bottle "YBRY PARIS," believed to be only one of three in existence, exceptional condition, chip to top of glass stopper, 7 3/4". $16,470

Czechoslovakian perfume bottle, Hoffmann, circa 1930s, pink crystal blown as tubular reservoir, crackle finish, openwork frost stopper, gilt metal foot, jeweled metalwork collar and central medallion with crystal cameo Medusa head, molded Hoffmann mark visible, 10". **$10,445**

Czechoslovakian perfume bottle and stopper/dauber, circa 1920s, polished and frosted ruby crystal, jeweled gilt metal filigree, Bakelite roses, missing one jewel, metal marked Austria, 7 1/2". **$8,610**

Art Deco atomizer, Czechoslovakian, circa 1930s, black crystal, enameled silver gilt metal work, marked Austria, replacement hose and ball, 4 5/8". **$5,223**

Palais Royal automated perfume carousel, Baccarat, circa 1860s, brass-trimmed rotating tray set with mother-of-pearl segments holding 10 hand-cut crystal perfume bottles atop wooden pedestal with pearl-handled brass crank, 8 1/2". **$8,610**

Colmy C'est Un Secret perfume bottle, J. Viard, circa 1920s, clear glass, sepia patina, blue-enameled glass stopper, two paper labels, molded Viard mark, with original box, 4 1/8". **$18,450**

Seldom-seen green Bouchon Cassis perfume bottle, France, circa 1920, base etched "172 R. Lalique No. 494" with faint molded LALIQUE mark, 4 1/2" x 3 1/2" x 1 1/2". $25,000

Petroliana

Petroliana covers a broad range of gas station collectibles from containers and globes to signs and pumps and everything in between.

The items featured in this section are organized by type and have been selected at the high end of the market. The focus is on the top price items, not to skew the values, but to emphasize the brands and types that are the most desirable. Some less valuable items have been included to help keep values in perspective.

As with all advertising items, factors such as brand name, intricacy of design, color, age, condition, and rarity drastically affect value.

Beware of reproduction and fantasy pieces. For collectors of vintage gas and oil items, the only way to avoid reproductions is experience: making mistakes and learning from them; talking with other collectors and dealers; finding reputable resources (including books and websites), and learning to invest wisely, buying the best examples one can afford.

Marks can be deceiving, paper labels and tags are often missing, and those that remain may be spurious. Adding to the confusion are "fantasy" pieces, globes that have no vintage counterpart, and that are often made more for visual impact than deception.

How does one know whether a given piece is authentic? Does it look old, and to what degree can age be simulated? What is the difference between high-quality vintage advertising and modern mass-produced examples? Even experts are fooled when trying to assess qualities that have subtle distinctions.

There is another important factor to consider. A contemporary maker may create a "reproduction" sign or

Courtesy of RM Auctions, Blenheim, Ontario, Canada

Phillips 66 neon sign, porcelain, die-cut, embossed lettering, 48" x 48". $5,700

**Signal Gas porcelain sign,
72" diameter. $6,000**

**Rare Record Motor Oil can, half-
gallon, fine condition. $660**

gas globe in tribute of the original, and sell it for what it is: a legitimate copy. Many of these are dated and signed by the artist or manufacturer, and these legitimate copies are highly collectible today. Such items are not intended to be frauds.

But a contemporary piece may pass through many hands between the time it leaves the maker and wind up in a collection. When profit is the only motive of a reseller, details about origin, ownership, and age can become a slippery slope of guesses, attribution, and – unfortunately—fabrication.

As the collector's eye sharpens, and the approach to inspecting and assessing petroliana improves, it will become easier to buy with confidence. And a knowledgeable collecting public should be the goal of all sellers, if for no other reason than the willingness to invest in quality.

For more information about petroliana, consult *Warman's Gas Station Collectibles Identification and Price Guide* by Mark Moran.

Wadhams Ethyl Gasoline Corp. globe, New York, metal body with curved glass inserts, 18 1/2" high x 16 1/2" wide. $660

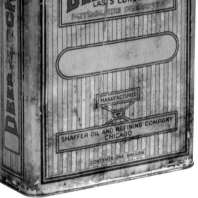

Deep-Rock Petroleum Products can, Shaffer Oil and Refining Co., Chicago, gallon, 11 1/4" high. $162

Set of eight motor oil bottles in wire carrier, all bottles embossed with Mass. 0-11-B Seal, five have Masters tops, carrier 13" high x 17" wide x 8 1/2" deep. $270

Courtesy of Rich Penn Auctions, www.richpennauctions.com
Phillips 66 Buddy Lee plastic doll, 13" high. $420

Courtesy of Rich Penn Auctions,
www.richpennauctions.com

▲ Gasoline price calculator,
Christopher Computing Co.,
porcelain, metal, and glass,
24" x 8". **$600**

Courtesy of Rich Penn Auctions,
www.richpennauctions.com

◄ Mobilgas station attendant's
hat, average wear, size medium.
$180

*Courtesy of Rich Penn Auctions,
www.richpennauctions.com*

▲ Fleet-Wing Ethyl Gasoline
porcelain sign, two-sided,
30" diameter. **$1,920**

*Courtesy of Rich Penn Auctions,
www.richpennauctions.com*

◄ Mutual Oil Co. Liberty Air-O
Oil can with spout, half-gallon,
biplane graphic, 10" high x 8"
wide. **$5,100**

Courtesy of RM Auctions, Blenheim, Ontario, Canada

DeSoto dealership sign, circa 1960, last year for model, enamel on metal, 16" x 36". **$1,800**

Ford two-sided pierced metal oval sign with hanger, lights up, 42" high x 71" wide. **$8,400**

Eco Tireflator, manufactured by John Wood Co., Bennett Pump Division, Muskegon, Michigan, original red paint, mounted on newer stand, 51" x 10 1/2". **$2,700**

En-Ar-Co Motor Oil and White Rose Gasoline curb sign, boy with blackboard, double-sided die-cut metal on cast iron base, boy marked Mathews Industries Inc.- Detroit, Copyrighted 1917, 46" high x 28" wide. **$5,100**

Courtesy of Rich Penn Auctions, www.richpennauctions.com

Sinclair Gasoline two-sided die-cut metal flange sign manufactured by Ellwood Myers Co., Springfield, 17 1/2" x 18 3/4". **$2,040**

Courtesy of Rich Penn Auctions, www.richpennauctions.com

Studebaker Authorized Service / Genuine Parts hanging two-sided die-cut porcelain sign, 26" high x 48 1/2" wide. **$5,400**

Perfect Circle piston rings embossed tin sign with Perfect Circle Oil Hog, 19" x 25". **$4,680**

Manhattan Gasoline double-sided porcelain sidewalk sign with base, 30" diameter. **$1,920**

Red Crown gasoline globe, three-dimensional with red details. **$2,640**

Photography

By Noah Fleisher

NOAH FLEISHER received his Bachelor of Fine Arts degree from New York University and brings more than a decade of newspaper, magazine, book, antiques and art experience to his position as Public Relations Director of Heritage Auctions, one of the country's foremost auction houses. He is the former editor of *Antique Trader, New England Antiques Journal* and *Northeast Antiques Journal,* is the author of *Warman's Modern Furniture* and co-author of *Collecting Children's Books,* and has been a longtime contributor to *Warman's Antiques & Collectibles.*

Fine art in general took it in the gut when the economy, and the art market, tanked in 2008. Of the various markets that fell within the umbrella of fine art, few saw its fortunes fade faster than vintage and contemporary photography. Unless the name on your pictures was Mapplethorpe, Avedon, Weston, Sherman – or among the handful of photographers who transcended – then the value of your pieces fell, precipitously in some cases.

Burt Finger is the owner of Photographs Do Not Bend (PDNB) Gallery on Dragon Street in Dallas (PDNB.com), the center of the city's Design District, and is a longtime recognized expert from his 20 years in his gallery championing both individual artists and collectors.

"Photography, like the other disciplines, has been a struggle since the recession," he said. "Good pieces between $1,000 and $50,000 are selling again. People have some new-gained confidence from what's been going on and there's a new-found equilibrium between buyer and seller."

That's good news for collectors and dealers alike, though the market still favors buyers at auction a little more, with a large concentration of offerings all at once giving collectors a chance to get good buys on a great many pieces in the middle range. Unless you really know your stuff, though, buying photographs at auction can be a daunting world to just jump into.

That is where dealers like Finger come in. While he's in the business of selling photography, like the best of his ilk, he does not approach it from the financial standpoint. His is an artist's eye, and he curates from inspiration; he educates from a love of the imagery and its meaning. He's the sort of dealer who embodies the ethics you want when you are looking for guidance starting or propping up a collection.

In fact, a few weeks after talking with Finger and visiting him at his Dallas gallery, I found myself in conversation with a longtime client (and now friend) of Finger's – a lawyer from Dallas – who related the following assessment of Finger:

"When I first started thinking about collecting, back in the mid-1990s, I wandered into Burt's gallery. I didn't have much

"Marilyn Monroe, Here's to You (from the Last Sitting)" chromogenic print, Bert Stern, circa 1962, signed in ink lower right margin, with "232/250" notation in ink and artist's stamp verso, overall toning, small handling crimp, 19" high x 19" wide. **$10,000**

discretionary income back then, but he took the time and talked with me and soon was sending me home with books and catalogs, pointing me to shows and specific artists and galleries. He was more like a teacher than a dealer. Soon I was ready to start buying."

He noted that he recently purchased his first William Eggleston. That would be music to any good dealer's ears, and business.

Where does Finger see the market right now, besides on the rebound? He casts a philosophic glance on where it stands.

"Collectors and collections have to move forward," he said, "and there's definitely a shift forward right now as a new generation ages in and the previous generation moves up. While the 1940s and 1950s were very popular a decade ago, right now vintage pieces from 1960s and 1970s are very attractive to collectors – the '70s in particular."

Another element that the world of photography has had to

Courtesy of Heritage Auctions, ha.com

Original news photograph of Mickey Mantle used for 1951 Bowman rookie baseball card, one of the most recognizable Mantle images ever rendered, believed to be taken by Bob Olen, 1951, adhesive removal along one edge on verso, handwritten notations and team stamping, PSA/DNA Type 1, 8" high x 10" wide. $71,700

contend with is the lightning quick progress of technology.

How does photography keep up and stay relevant in a world where iPhones and applications can imbue any photograph with any range of effect that photographers used to have to study years to master?

"A good camera does not make someone an artist," Finger points out. "I'm not concerned with it being 'digital photography,' I'm concerned with the finished product. I think the bar has been changed, it's risen. We have photographers now that are thinkers, that buy into a whole concept."

Finger cautions against getting too stuck on a particular era or artist, however, as you'll miss opportunities to learn, and to collect, in a variety of venues. A good relationship with a dealer prepares you for gallery buying, but it will also get you set to enter the auction market and to look for hidden gems in the corners of markets, shops and shows all over the country, if not the world.

"It's a thrill to be expansive rather than reductive," he said. "Find out what your interests are individually, not what someone tells you. When it comes to photography it has to be something you really love, not an investment. You are going to live with this image."

Courtesy of RR Auction, www.rrauction.com

Samples of 27 unpublished photographs of John F. and Jacqueline Kennedy, taken during a visit to Cape Cod by Katharine Graham, *Washington Post* heiress, circa 1961, varying sizes. **$32,500**

"Route 66, Albuquerque, New Mexio" chromogenic print, Ernst Haas, circa 1969, with Haas Studio label and Alexander Haas' signature, title, dates, printing notation, and edition notation 2/50 in ink, 17 1/4" high x 26" wide. **$5,250**

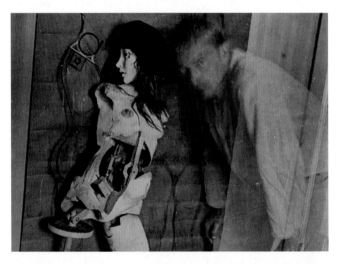

Black and white photograph by Hans Bellmer, published as part of "Die Puppe," Germany, 1934, one of 10 photographs, collaged on yellow paper, bound in marbled boards, signed in pencil, very good condition with minor signs of age and use, 12 1/3" high x 10 1/8" wide. **$41,839**

"White Sands" portfolio of 12 silver prints documenting New Mexico landscape, by Brett Weston, 1946-1947, photographer's signature and date in pencil on each print, folio is gilt-lettered gray cloth case with flaps, 1975, desert image 9 1/2" high x 7 3/4" wide. **$35,000**

"Maya Angelou" silver print by Jeanne Moutoussamy-Ashe, circa 1993, extensive hand-coloring, signed and dated 11/93 in ink, lower margin, with artist's ink stamp verso, 10" high x 10 1/2" wide. **$17,500**

"Alert Soldier, Saipan" silver print of Angelo S. Klonis by W. Eugene Smith, circa 1944, with notation, "This authenticated photograph by W. Eugene Smith was in his private collection at his death – October 15, 1978," 13" high x 10 5/8" wide. Klonis joined the Army in order to gain citizenship and became one of the faces of World War II; the photo appeared in books and magazines and on a postage stamp. **$13,750**

Samples of 92 gelatin silver prints by Osvaldo Salas, printed in 1980s, all signed by photographer in ink on reverse, most dated and annotated by photographer, 15 3/4" high x 11 1/3" wide. **$27,713**

Silver contact print of still life with peacock feathers, wooden shoe, and conch shell by Josef Sudek, circa 1956, photographer's signature and date in pencil on recto and his inscription and another date in pencil on verso, 9" high x 11 1/2" wide. **$9,375**

"The Dream" albumen print by Julia Margaret Cameron, flush-mounted on contemporary card, circa 1869, signed, dated, and annotated "From Life Registered Copyright" in brown ink, titled in pencil by photographer, with G. F. Watts' printed inscription ("quite divine") on mount recto, 11 7/8" high x 9 3/8" wide. **$21,122**

Courtesy of Swann Auction Galleries, www.swanngalleries.com

"Woman in a Bird Mask, N.Y.C." silver print by Diane Arbus/ Neil Selkirk, circa 1968, with Arbus' signature and edition notation 7/75, with estate and copyright hand stamp on verso, 14 1/4" high x 14 1/2" wide. **$6,250**

Courtesy of Swann Auction Galleries, www.swanngalleries.com

"In Wildness" portfolio with 10 dye-transfer prints of nature scenes across United States by Eliot Porter, 1953-1981, photographer's signature in pencil on mount recto, in clamshell box with gilt-lettered brown leather title label, colophon with his signature and edition number 180 (of 300) in ink, 1981, 16" high x 12 1/2" wide. **$6,750**

Courtesy of Heritage Auctions, ha.com

"Shoeless Joe" Jackson" black and white photograph by Frank W. Smith, circa 1911, with Jackson's signature and inscription, "Alexandria, Mar. 1911" added by Smith, graded PSA/DNA, Mint 9, 8" wide x 10" high. Photograph was taken just 30 games into Jackson's Major League Baseball career, on the cusp of becoming the first and only rookie to hit .400, and eight years away from the abrupt end of that career due to the Black Sox scandal. **$179,250**

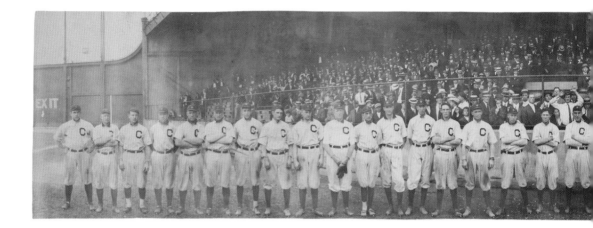

▲ Addie Joss Benefit Game panoramic photograph from July 24, 1911; Cleveland Naps took on players from American League in first All-Star Game, which came about in response to the unexpected death of Hall of Fame pitcher Addie Joss from meningitis; 37 uniformed baseball players with coaches, including nine Hall of Famers: Cy Young, Napoleon Lajoie, Walter Johnson, Bobby Wallace, Frank "Home Run" Baker, Sam Crawford, Tris Speaker, Eddie Collins, Ty Cobb, and "Shoeless Joe" Jackson. **$23,302**

Untitled gelatin silver print by Brassai, circa 1932, Brassai copyright stamp verso, 9 1/2" high x 7" wide. **$4,270**

Courtesy of Clars Auction Gallery, www.clars.com

"Aboard the Cressida, South Pacific" gelatin silver print by Walker Evans, 1932, artist stamp verso, 6 1/4" high x 8" wide. **$4,130**

Courtesy of Swann Auction Galleries, www.swanngalleries.com

▲ "Premiere at La Scala, Milan" silver print by Alfred Eisenstaedt, circa 1933, photographer's signature and edition notation 21/50 in ink on recto, Eisenstaedt and *Time* copyright hand stamps with title and dates on verso, 1979, 12 1/2" high x 9" wide. **$5,460**

Courtesy of Swann Auction Galleries, www.swanngalleries.com

◄ "Portrait of Elephant in Dust, Amboseli" (from "Across the Ravaged Land, Part I") by Nick Brandt, archival pigment print, 2011, signed by photographer, dated and edition notation 9/12 in pencil on recto, framed, 40" high x 44 1/2" wide. **$46,800**

Political Memorabilia

By Noah Fleisher

NOAH FLEISHER received his Bachelor of Fine Arts degree from New York University and brings more than a decade of newspaper, magazine, book, antiques and art experience to his position as Public Relations Director of Heritage Auctions, one of the country's foremost auction houses. He is the former editor of *Antique Trader, New England Antiques Journal* and *Northeast Antiques Journal,* is the author of *Warman's Modern Furniture* and co-author of *Collecting Children's Books,* and has been a longtime contributor to *Warman's Antiques & Collectibles.*

The great American historian Arthur M. Schlesinger (1917-2007) described the American political system as working on a pendulum, swinging back and forth on the spectrum from liberal to conservative and through the middle of both extremes. It's hard to argue with his logic, especially as it is playing right now in a presidential election year. (This book was published in 2016.)

While I enjoy nothing more than spirited political debate, the purpose of this section is concerned with more concrete pursuits; namely, the pursuit of the best of political memorabilia. I contend here and now that Schlesinger's theory is also perfectly applicable when it comes to the fortunes of political memorabilia (buttons, autographs, posters, ephemera, and gifts), especially as relating to the American presidency.

The political memorabilia pendulum – representing a market that could not boast of particularly good health a few years ago – seems to have swung back upward in the last two years. Marsha Dixey, Expert Generalist and Consignment Director at Heritage Auctions, is well-positioned to have witnessed this upswing. Dixey has been front and center for Heritage's Political and Americana Auctions of the recent past and can testify to the new availability of a core grouping of large, deep political collections. She also sees historical trends playing out in expected ways.

"We've sold several great collections in the past few years that have brought exceptional prices," Dixey said. "I expect the values on rare items to be steady for the coming year and to bring a surge of interest due to the most recent presidential election. Every four years we see this trend."

So politics and political memorabilia both move on a pendulum. They also can be traced in cycles. As far as our purposes here are concerned, the cycles in memorabilia are driven, ultimately, by rarity, name, and generation.

Certain truisms will always hold: Lincoln sells, JFK sells,

Flag banner from Abraham Lincoln 1864 election, "Lincoln and Johnson / Liberty and Union." No category of political campaign memorabilia is more highly prized than 1860 and 1864 flags supporting Lincoln's candidacy; portrait varieties are particularly sought-after. $106,250

popular modern presidents sell, quality "Founding Father" material sells. Within all of these wrinkles are variations in price. In all of them, however, the most important aspect is rarity.

"No question, rarity is the key driving factor," said Dixey. "Examples never seen or rarely seen are bringing very strong prices."

We should not, however, overlook the generational aspect of collecting. Civil War material is still popular and will always be to a certain extent, but the market is not as strong as it once was. This is not because the war itself has diminished in importance or influence, but because the majority of the once-active collecting base for the material has aged out and, in most cases, sold their collections. This is exactly what we're seeing in straight political memorabilia as it relates to presidents, wars, and the era in which the respective wars were fought and presidents served.

"What we see is that younger collectors are turning toward items they can relate to from World War II or the political campaigns of the 1940s and 1950s," said Dixey. "We're not seeing 20-year-olds pursuing political items, but we *are* seeing a new group of 40- and 50-year-old collectors picking up political items as a sideline to their other collections."

The Confederate flag controversy of 2015 has a direct relationship to both politics and political memorabilia collecting. In the wake of the terrible summer 2015 hate crimes in South Carolina, in which the perpetrator openly venerated the Confederate flag, most states that used it

Lyndon B. Johnson picture pin with portrait reading, "Ladies For Johnson," clean, well-centered example with no defects, 3". $188

Courtesy of Heritage Auctions, ha.com

Lock of Abraham Lincoln's hair (30+ strands) removed from his head by Surgeon General Joseph K. Barnes at Peterson House, shortly after Lincoln was shot; hair is dark brown with silver strands, contained in original tissue paper enclosure, as sent by Barnes to Mrs. Edwards Pierrepont of New York, with original transmittal envelope addressed in Barnes' hand, along with his letter. Barnes writes, "Hair removed from head of President Lincoln April 14th 65 in examination of wound." **$25,000**

removed it from state offices, and many retailers stopped selling it altogether.

From our perspective at *Warman's*, the Confederate flag represents a (failed) political system in America that came about at a crucial political time: the Civil War. Confederate flags from that time period are direct, important political and historical relics that have upfront meaning to the time they came from and the people they represented. Any historical piece should never be confused with the $10 cloth flag your neighbor bought online and flies from his truck. The two simply are not the same and have nothing whatsoever to do with one another.

"The Confederate flag was a battle flag and was a signal to begin the fight," said Dixey. "A flag from the 1860s is a part of our shared history and should remain so. Confederate flags that have sold to collectors or museums have significant provenance, which helps to tell the story of the Civil War and its part in our history. The current use of the flag on cars or license plates appears to me to be a statement of opinion and does not incorporate the history lesson provided by the Civil War."

What we collect in this hobby, especially in political memorabilia, is historic materialism – items with a direct link to our past and a direct influence on our presence via their provenance – not historic opinion, however much an opinion may be wrapped up in a piece. Opinion should never be mistaken for provenance, especially when it comes to controversy.

Courtesy of Heritage Auctions, ha.com

Scarce large-sized John F. Kennedy/Lyndon B. Johnson 1960 presidential campaign poster with images of candidates over background of red, white, and blue, "Kennedy for President" in red field, "Johnson for Vice President" in blue field, exceptional condition, paper loss in upper left corner, 26 3/4" x 41 1/2". **$3,500**

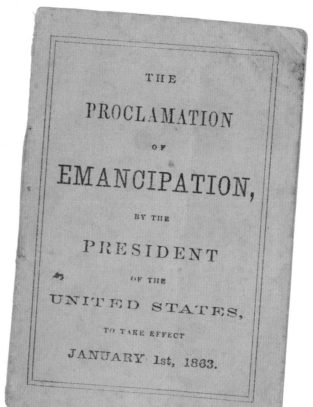

Courtesy of Heritage Auctions, ha.com

Rare printing of preliminary Emancipation Proclamation, from first version made public on Sept. 22, 1862, booklet intended for distribution to troops who, in turn, could distribute copies to slaves in regions of South occupied by Union forces; original thread binding and quote about slavery by Confederate Vice President Alexander Stephens on back cover. **$13,750**

Courtesy of Heritage Auctions, ha.com

Franklin D. Roosevelt and Horner, two scarce Illinois coattail jugates, fine condition, 7/8" and 1 1/4", respectively. **$213**

Frank Sinatra-gifted Ronald Reagan inauguration silver-plated cigarette box, 1981, rectangular, top lid engraved with same text as on original invitation for presidential inauguration on Jan. 20, 1981, further engraved "Thank you / F.S.," inside lined in cedar, bottom with partially worn maker's sticker, commissioned by Sinatra to give to VIPs who attended event, this one gifted to his executive assistant of 30+ years, Dorothy Uhlemann, who went to Reagan/Bush inauguration with her boss. **$1,750**

▼ John F. Kennedy popular slogan button reading, "High Office Demands High Principle / Elect Kennedy President," issued by Andrew P. Quigley and Winthrop Transcript, Inc., mint condition, 2 1/4". **$450**

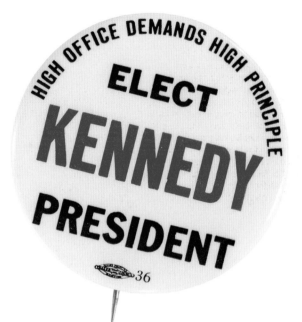

William Jennings Bryan and Arthur Sewall jugate bicycle brooch, silvered brass with paper photos of 1896 nominees on each wheel, fine example, uncommon, 1 1/4". **$813**

Bill Clinton White House china, part of collection commissioned for 200th anniversary of White House in 2000, produced by Lenox, excellent condition, 5" saucer and 2 3/4" x 3 1/4" cup. **$2,125**

A BEAUTIFUL GOBLET OF WHITE-HOUSE CHAMPAGNE.

Matching Abraham Lincoln and Stephen A. Douglas tokens. **$375**

William Henry Harrison, anti-Van Buren metamorphic card by Davis Claypoole Johnston showing how Van Buren's countenance changes when he switches from "Goblet of White-House Champagne" to "An Ugly Mug of Log-Cabin Hard Cider," excellent condition, fully operational, 3" x 5". **$250**

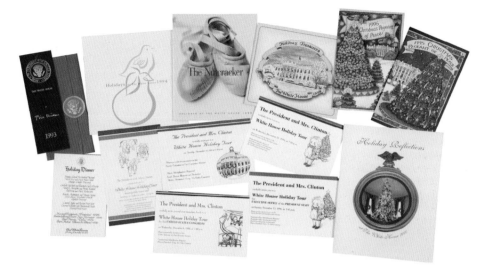

Courtesy of Heritage Auctions, ha.com

Bill Clinton, large assortment of White House Christmas cards from 1993, 1995, 1996, 1998, 1999, and 2000, with original envelopes. $227

Courtesy of Heritage Auctions, ha.com

Presidential photograph signed by Richard Nixon, Gerald Ford, Jimmy Carter, and Ronald Reagan, circa 1980s, undated, with four living presidents standing side by side in front of American flag and presidential flag, signed by each man under his respective image, 8" x 10". **$1,750**

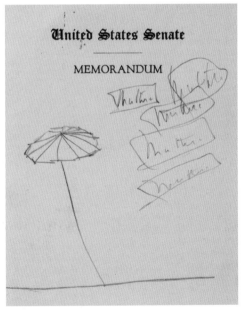

Courtesy of Heritage Auctions, ha.com

John F. Kennedy doodle on United States Senate stationery, umbrella beside which Kennedy wrote "Multer" five times, light foxing at lower edge with paper clip rust stain at upper edge, 5 1/4" x 8". **$500**

Abraham Lincoln brass pinback shell pin with period provenance from 1860 presidential campaign, original pin on verso, affixed with original thread on card, penned in 19th century, reading: "Worn by the Union men in Richmond during the Rebellion under their coats and shown to each other when they met. Presented by H. (?) Crofts." **$4,250**

Rare George W. Bush large pinback button given to GOP members and former members of Congress at 2000 Republican National Convention, numbered 038/300, pristine condition, 3 7/8". **$837**

John F. Kennedy Texas Welcome Dinner press ticket for evening of Nov. 22, 1963 in Austin, for "Press Section," new condition, as issued, 2 1/2" x 6". **$475**

Rare John F. Kennedy 1958 U.S. Senate campaign poster, scarcer smaller cardboard version, minor light wrinkles, 14" x 22", 22" x 30" framed. **$3,000**

Barack Obama, 1996 state senate button issued for his first attempt at political office for 13th district of Illinois (part of Chicago), which he won with 82% of vote; most desirable Obama button produced for first Obama fund-raiser, 2 1/4". **$750**

Thomas Dewey anti-Truman slogan pin reading, "The Issue is Truman's Record / Nothing Else!," issued as response to Truman's criticism of so-called "Do Nothing" 80th Congress, 1 1/2". **$250**

Courtesy of Heritage Auctions, ha.com

Ronald Reagan, Gerald Ford, and Jimmy Carter cartoon plates, hand-painted porcelain, produced in 1976 when Reagan challenged Ford for Republican nomination with Carter and Ford in general election, Reagan and Ford in tug-of-war over "nomination line," GOP elephant pondering choice of Reagan or Ford, convention of pro-Carter delegates, and Carter as peanut-man hitching ride to Washington, D.C., excellent condition, 10" diameter. **$50**

Courtesy of Heritage Auctions, ha.com

William McKinley "McKinley at Home" button with candidate seated on his porch reading newspaper with anti-silver quote, Novelty Button Co. of Canton back paper, excellent condition, scarce, 1 1/2". **$425**

Courtesy of Heritage Auctions, ha.com

Ronald Reagan consent for use of name as second choice for presidency form, signed, one page, 8 1/2" x 14", [Ohio], March 23, 1976, authorizing "the following persons to use my name in their Declarations of Candidacies as Delegates and Alternates to the Republican National Convention for the Presidency of the United States by said National Convention to be held in the year 1976," countersigned by Reagan campaign manager, John P. Sears. **$938**

Barack Obama signed 2008 campaign flag with "Yes We Can" slogan and dated '08 in black felt tip, perfect condition, 15" x 11". **$1,625**

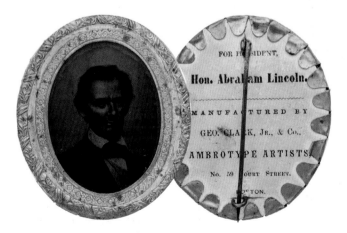

George Clark brooch, pin-back with ambrotype version of Mathew Brady "Cooper Union" Abraham Lincoln photo, near mint condition, 2 1/8" x 2 5/8". **$16,250**

Porcelain
Signs & Others

By Noah Fleisher

NOAH FLEISHER received his Bachelor of Fine Arts degree from New York University and brings more than a decade of newspaper, magazine, book, antiques and art experience to his position as Public Relations Director of Heritage Auctions, one of the country's foremost auction houses. He is the former editor of *Antique Trader, New England Antiques Journal* and *Northeast Antiques Journal,* is the author of *Warman's Modern Furniture* and co-author of *Collecting Children's Books,* and has been a longtime contributor to *Warman's Antiques & Collectibles.*

Dale Fenton, the department director of Porcelain Signs at Manifest Auctions in Greenville, South Carolina, is quick to point to the health of his market right now.

"Porcelain has really taken off," he said. "Right now the sky is really the limit."

This should surprise no one who has followed this segment of the market. The popularity of oil and gas signs – petroliana, as we all commonly think of it – has been soaring for years. What Fenton is talking about, though, is not those wonderful early petroliana pieces. What he's referring to is the rising tide of everything else in the world of porcelain signs.

Is it safe to say that porcelain signs, in general, are a market that has reached maturity? We'd have to say yes. As would Fenton, from his perch at Manifest.

"As far as areas in the market that still have room for growth, there's really not a whole lot left that hasn't been pretty well scouted out," he said. "Perhaps there's a bit of room in certain food store signs or food brands. We all know how popular oil and gas [are], but beer signs are also popular right now, as are traditional country store signs, good brand names like Coca-Cola and Lifesavers, too. People always take notice of a good brand."

Digging through the photo archives of Manifest bears this out. The diversity of product advertised on these signs is as varied as the people and places to which they were marketed. At this point, any kind of genre you can think of is collected: Santa Claus, barber shops, cleaning products, clothing brands, drugstores, dairies, candy, and so on. Think of a product and there is a niche.

If the momentum behind porcelain signs has been building for the last decade, the last three years have seen that pace quicken even more. The best examples of non-petroliana signs can easily bring strong four- and low five-figure prices – signs made by makers like Walker and Ingram-Richardson, in

Double-sided porcelain flange sign for Taylor clothing, "Let Taylor Tailor You," light bend halfway along flange, some crazing in porcelain, 18" x 9". **$200**

Coca-Cola single-sided porcelain sign from French Canada, translates to "Drink Coca-Cola Sold Here Iced," edge chipping at mounting holes and nickel-sized chip in field, 12" x 31". **$150**

particular. "Finding a piece with an Ing-Rich mark on it is a very good thing," said Fenton. The middle market is routinely in the $500-$1,000 range.

It is possible to get interesting signs at just a few hundred dollars, but at that level, these days, you pay for what you get or, as it goes in so many of the strongest markets, condition is absolutely everything.

"That's always going to be the biggest thing," Fenton said. "Are the graphics good? Period. Is it something more than just a logo? Do the colors stand out? Do they really pop? Even relatively common signs with fairly plain graphics in sharp condition will bring a significant premium because of the condition."

Porcelain signs have an added brilliance in their appeal to neophyte and experienced collectors alike. To the latter, signs double as art, as statements of character and value. Someone with no experience whatsoever in the market can walk into an auction, a shop, or a show and fall head over heels in love even if they've never considered signs before. There is a feeling inherent in the form that appeals to our simplest, humblest, and most American of sensibilities: Nostalgia for our shared past. What can possibly say it better?

"Most of these pieces were mass-produced and not made to

Courtesy of Manifest Auctions,
www.manifestauctions.com

**Rare single-sided
porcelain sign for Anchor
Stoves and Ranges,
established 1865, late
1800s/early 1900s, five-
color porcelain with
flame graphics, damage
to edges and field, 21" x
23". $750**

survive as long as they have," said Fenton. "It's not a total fine
art mentality, it's almost more of an archeological mentality
of preservation that we find with collectors. They just have
a passion for it and would rather put their money in these
signs than anything else."

Getting into the market is not hard, just buy the best you
can afford and ask questions of experts like Fenton (www.
manifestauctions.com). The hard part is stopping at just one
sign. Ours is a business of acquisition, and few groups of
collectors enjoy the process more than those who love signs.

Courtesy of Manifest Auctions, www.manifestauctions.com

Single-sided porcelain sign for Ferguson Tractor System, originally neon but only mounting holes remain, chips to porcelain, 60" x 48". **$2,000**

Courtesy of Manifest Auctions, www.manifestauctions.com

Double-sided porcelain sign for Carnation Ice Cream with illustration of ice cream sundae, good gloss and colors, small chips around edge, 30" x 30". **$1,000**

Courtesy of Manifest Auctions, www.manifestauctions.com

▲ Single-sided Coca-Cola bottle die-cut porcelain sign, chips in field and at right of bottle's neck, 5" x 16 1/2". **$150**

Courtesy of Manifest Auctions, www.manifestauctions.com

▶ Rare single-sided porcelain sign for Indianapolis Beer by Indianapolis Brewing Co., image of Winged Victory with tagline "The World's Standard of Perfection," original manufacturer's label on reverse from National Enameling Co. of Cincinnati, brewery dates to around 1910, 18" diameter. **$1,450**

Single-sided porcelain sign for Velvet Pipe Tobacco with image of tobacco tin and Velvet name in trademark smoke logo, fading across top, 40" x 12". **$325**

▲ Single-sided die-cut porcelain sign for Goblin Orangeade with trademark goblin character, excellent condition, some fleabite edge chips, 12" x 18". **$950**

► Red Seal Dry Battery double-sided die-cut flange porcelain sign, hard to find, colors faded, two field chips and some edge chipping, 13" x 24". **$292**

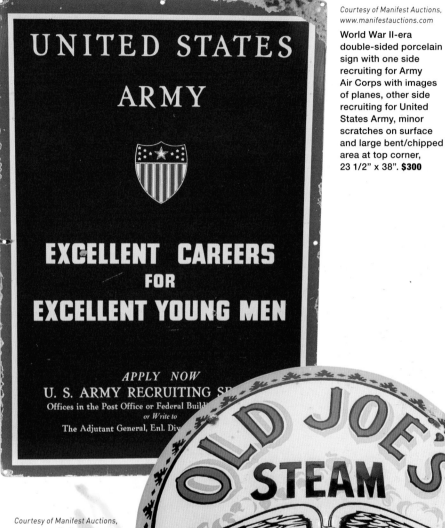

World War II-era double-sided porcelain sign with one side recruiting for Army Air Corps with images of planes, other side recruiting for United States Army, minor scratches on surface and large bent/chipped area at top corner, 23 1/2" x 38". **$300**

Single-sided curved porcelain sign for Old Joe's Steam Beer with corner mounting bracket and image of eagle, small chips at upper left and upper right, 18" diameter. **$6,500**

Courtesy of Manifest Auctions, www.manifestauctions.com

Double-sided porcelain sign for Mansfield's Ice Cream in ivory and green color scheme, good overall condition with minor edge chips, 36" x 14". **$200**

Courtesy of Manifest Auctions, www.manifestauctions.com

Porcelain door push sign for Pepsi-Cola, advertising in French reads "Merci Au-Revoir" on back and "Buvez Pepsi-Cola Glacé" on front, minor chips at mounting grommets, 32" x 3 1/4". **$125**

Courtesy of Manifest Auctions, www.manifestauctions.com

▲ Single-sided porcelain strip sign for Bell System Public Telephone, black paint around edges, small chip at top right and bottom left covered by paint, 19" x 5 1/2". **$125**

Courtesy of Manifest Auctions, www.manifestauctions.com

► Single-sided porcelain sign for *Los Angeles Evening Herald-Express*, excellent condition, 14" x 6". **$225**

Double-sided hanging sign for Kodak Developing, Printing, and Enlarging with original mounting bracket, excellent condition, no bends, sign 17" x 17", bracket 20" x 14". **$600**

▲ Porcelain sign for H.E. Butt Grocery Co., which became H.E.B., now the largest grocery store in Texas, gold lettering with red Texas silhouette, edge chips, die-cut ribbon on one side has been bent, 36" x 40". **$1,800**

◄ Single-sided porcelain sign for H.P. Hood & Sons Milk, rare, near mint condition with all original grommets, tiny flaws around edge, tiny chip over right eye, 30" diameter. **$8,000**

▲ Double-sided heavy porcelain sign for Acme Beer & Ale by California Brewing Association of San Francisco and Los Angeles, yellow, red, and black color scheme, gunshot chips on both sides, 42" diameter. **$1,100**

◄ Single-sided porcelain badge from City of Beverly Hills in die-cut shape with seal, excellent condition, etched faintly on back "BHFD," likely originally for fire department, probably NOS with no wear or damage around mounting holes, 8 1/2" x 8 1/2". **$550**

Single-sided die-cut porcelain sign for Nectar Tea in shape of cup and saucer, surface with minor wear, edge chips, 21" x 12". **$200**

Courtesy of Manifest Auctions, www.manifestauctions.com

Rare double-sided porcelain die-cut sign for Martin-Senour Paints, excellent graphics of hand with paintbrush, 18" x 22". **$1,700**

Courtesy of Manifest Auctions, www.manifestauctions.com

Heavy single-sided porcelain sign advertising Kirk's Flake Soap with red graphics and image of namesake soap package, few large chips, 40" x 15". **$200**

Courtesy of Manifest Auctions, www.manifestauctions.com

Single-sided self-framed porcelain sign advertising "Equipped With Murray Combing Lint Cleaners," used at cotton gin or processing facilities that had Murray Combing Lint Cleaner equipment, surface and main field of sign in good shape with some small chips, mounting points at top corners and top middle bent and damaged from what appears to be its original mounting, 72" x 22". **$300**

Courtesy of Manifest Auctions, www.manifestauctions.com

▲ Double-sided sign for Polk's Milk with image of cow's head, field in excellent condition, edge nearly completely chipped with some rusting, 22" diameter. **$900**

Courtesy of Manifest Auctions, www.manifestauctions.com

▶ Die-cut multicolored porcelain sign advertising Poll Parrot Shoes with image of green parrot, tagline reads "For Boys / For Girls," working neon, porcelain in excellent condition, 13" x 26" x 7". Poll Parrot sold shoes starting in 1925 and sponsored the "Howdy Doody" television show in the late 1940s. **$2,750**

Sherwin-Williams Paints die-cut double-sided porcelain sign, bent at top, chipped porcelain and paint splatters, 42" x 57". **$500**

Rare early porcelain strip sign for lime Life Savers with illustration of roll of Life Savers with candies spilling out, reads "Like the fruit itself / Cooling and Refreshing," 22 1/2" x 3 1/4". **$4,750**

OTHER MATERIALS

Courtesy of Manifest Auctions,
www.manifestauctions.com

Self-framed tin embossed sign for Carnation Feed, Milling Division, small scratches, 30" x 30". **$125**

Courtesy of Manifest Auctions,
www.manifestauctions.com

▲ Rare heavy cardboard die-cut sign for Western Shells with hunter and pheasants, diagram of shotgun shell and illustrations of two types of shells: "New Chief" and "Record" sold by Western Shells brand; chunk of sign missing on right side, crease across hunter's face, overall warping from moisture, 26 1/2" x 38". **$650**

Courtesy of Manifest Auctions,
www.manifestauctions.com

▶ Single-sided metal advertising thermometers for Orange Crush soda, both keep roughly accurate temperature and have surface rust, white thermometer reads "Naturally – / It Tastes / Better! / It's That Natural / Fresh Fruit / Flavor" with image of Orange Crush soda bottle, 6" x 14 1/2"; green thermometer reads "Thirsty? / Crush That Thirst!" with image of Orange Crush bottle cap, 6" x 16". **$175**

OTHER MATERIALS

Courtesy of Manifest Auctions, www. manifestauctions.com

Self-framed tin embossed stand-up sign for Moxie-Cola with company's Moxie car and rider on horse on car, marked on back "The Donaldson Art Sign Co. Covington KY" and "M2 – 33," probably dating it to 1933, finish in good condition, bends and dents to tin, 18 1/2" x 13". **$650**

Courtesy of Manifest Auctions, www.manifestauctions.com

▲ Single-sided tin sign for Star Tobacco with pack shown, sign marked ACCo 71-A, light scratches, 24" x 12". **$125**

Courtesy of Manifest Auctions, www.manifestauctions.com

▶ Double-sided die-cut painted metal sign for National Keys, in shape of key with company's "Mr. Key" character, scratches and bend in middle of key shape, 32" x 12". **$150**

Quilts

Each generation made quilts, comforters and coverlets, all intended to be used. Many were used into oblivion and rest in quilt heaven, but for myriad reasons, some have survived. Many of them remain because they were not used but stored, often forgotten, in trunks and linen cabinets.

A quilt is made up of three layers: the top, which can be a solid piece of fabric, appliquéd, pieced, or a combination; the back, which can be another solid piece of fabric or pieced; and the batting, which is the center layer, which can be cotton, wool, polyester, a blend of poly and cotton, or even silk. Many vintage quilts are batted with an old blanket or even another old, worn quilt.

The fabrics are usually cotton or wool, or fine fancy fabrics like silk, velvet, satin, and taffeta. The layers of a true quilt are held together by the stitching, or quilting, that goes through all three layers and is usually worked in a design or pattern that enhances the piece overall.

Quilts made from a seemingly single solid piece of fabric are known as wholecloth quilts, or if they are white, as whitework quilts. Usually such quilts are constructed from two or more pieces of the same fabric joined to make up the necessary width. They are often quilted quite elaborately, and the seams virtually disappear within the decorative stitching. Most wholecloth quilts are solid-colored, but prints were also used. Whitework quilts were often made as bridal quilts and many were kept for "best," which means that they have survived in reasonable numbers.

Wholecloth quilts were among the earliest type of quilted bedcovers made in Britain, and the colonists brought examples with them

Courtesy of Hyde Park Country Auctions, www.hpcountryauctions.com

Chintz crib quilt in Compass pattern, circa 19th century, original printed fabric backing with flowers and birds, discovered in old farm in New Kingston, New York, 50" x 50". $660

according to inventory lists that exist from Colonial times. American quiltmakers used the patterns early in the nation's history, and some were carried with settlers moving west across the Appalachians.

Appliqué quilts are made from shapes cut from fabric and applied, or appliquéd, to a background, usually solid-colored on vintage quilts, to make a design. Early appliqué quilts dating back to the 18th century were often worked in a technique called broderie perse, or Persian embroidery, in which printed motifs were cut from a piece of fabric, such as costly chintz, and applied to a plain, less expensive background cloth.

Appliqué was popular in the 1800s, and there are thousands of examples, from exquisite, brightly colored Baltimore Album quilts made in and around Baltimore between circa 1840 and 1860, to elegant four-block quilts made later in the century. Many appliqué quilts are pictorial—with floral designs the predominant motif. In the 20th century, appliqué again enjoyed an upswing, especially during the Colonial Revival period, and thousands were made from patterns or appliqué kits that were marketed and sold from 1900 through the 1950s.

Pieced or patchwork quilts are made by cutting fabric into

Courtesy of Case Antiques Auctions & Appraisals, caseantiques.com

East Tennessee pieced and appliqué quilt in variant Rose of Sharon pattern, 19th century, white ground with red, pink, orange, and green with red binding, diamond and circular stitching, scattered light stains, 81 1/2" x 65". $744

Courtesy of Keystone Auctions, LLC

Appliqué-style quilt, varied floral motif with multiple fruits and vegetables with grapevine border, stitch signed "Ann B. Payne / Feb 1861," loss of color and staining, 83" x 70". **$1,353**

shapes and sewing them together to make a larger piece of cloth. The patterns are usually geometric, and their effectiveness depends heavily on the contrast of not just the colors themselves, but of color value as well. Patchwork became popular in the United States in the early 1800s.

Colonial clothing was almost always made using cloth cut into squares or rectangles, but after the Revolutionary War, when fabric became more widely available, shaped garments were made, and these garments left scraps. Frugal housewives, especially among the westward-bound pioneers, began to use these cutoffs to put together blocks that could then be made into quilts. Patchwork quilts are by far the most numerous of all vintage-quilt categories, and the diversity of style, construction and effect that can be found is a study all its own.

Dating a quilt is tricky unless the maker included the date on the finished item, and unfortunately for historians and collectors, few did. The value of a particular example is affected by its age, of course, and educating yourself about dating methods is invaluable. There are several aspects that can offer guidelines for establishing a date. These include fabrics; patterns; technique; borders; binding; batting; backing; quilting method; and colors and dyes.

For more information on quilts, see *Warman's Vintage Quilts Identification and Price Guide* by Maggi McCormick Gordon.

*Courtesy of Jeffrey S. Evans & Associates,
www.jeffreysevans.com*

Appliqué quilt in Friendship Album pattern, signed and dated 1853, Mid-Atlantic region, 16 half-inch square blocks with floral-patterned sprig or wreath in print fabric and one chintz example, signed by 11 people, sawtooth border with double bands of hand stitching, very good condition overall, 83" x 85". **$2,880**

*Courtesy of Case Antiques
Auctions & Appraisals, caseantiques.com*

Tennessee pieced quilt in star variant pattern, early 20th century, primarily of satin and velvet, dark green background with peach, rust, and black; blue prize ribbon attached to quilt reading "First Premium Women's Dept., Tenn. State Fair, Nashville, 1909," overall very good condition, some loses to border, 70" x 84 1/2". **$3,198**

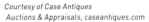

*Courtesy of Mroczek
Brothers Seattle Auction House,
mbaauction.com*

**American silk embroidered crazy
quilt, 19th/20th century, with
horseshoes, parasols, spider
webs, flowers, butterflies, rings,
half moons, and vessels, excellent
condition, 76" x 76". $1,180**

Courtesy of A-1 Auction, a-1auction.net

**Hand-stitched Peonies pattern
appliqué quilt in red and green,
circa 1860, Ohio origin, cotton seed
batting, good condition with minor
wear, 92" x 80". $1,298**

Courtesy of Briggs Auction, Inc., www.briggsauction.com

Bowmansville Star quilt, circa 1910, Lancaster County, Pennsylvania, with plain and printed fabrics on cream-colored background, shades and patterns in red, blue, and yellow, deaccession from Pennsylvania Quilt and Textile Museum, excellent condition, 81" sq. **$1,694**

Courtesy of Case Antiques Auctions & Appraisals, caseantiques.com

▲ Lone Star or Star of Texas pattern pieced and appliqué quilt, circa 1900, hand-stitched in pastel shades on purple background with pink backing, good condition, scattered stains to front and back, 88" x 72". **$310**

Courtesy of Hyde Park Country Auctions, www.hpcountryauctions.com

▶ Patchwork quilt, 19th century, with pheasants and stars on chintz background, found in early Salt Point, New York, farmhouse, sewn label with inscription "Museum of American Folk Art NY, NY – The NY Quilt Project 1988-1991 – 11-11-89 - WPF65," 79" x 87". **$900**

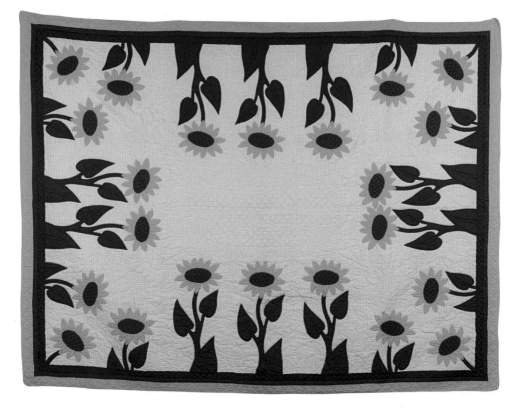

▲ American Southern hand-stitched cotton appliqué sunflower quilt, circa early 20th century, sunflowers around perimeter growing toward center of quilt, brown and yellow border, very good condition, tight stitches repeat theme throughout, slight fading to colors, 83" x 72". **$744**

◄ Appliqué Album summer quilt, 19th century, red and green with floral embroidered center, signed by girls from Cowell family, Museum Street, Schenectady, New York, 1863, cloth label affixed to back reads, "...professionally restored by Rocky Mountain Quilts...Betsey Tilford, York Village, Maine," minor staining on edge, 66" x 76". **$1,298**

Records

By Susan Sliwicki

Values for records – much like those for other collectibles – depend on a mix of factors, including condition, rarity, overall demand, market trends, and past sales results. Here are some key points to remember as you buy, sell, and value your records.

Discern the record's quality, which is not the same thing as condition. Quality relates to the materials that were used in the first place. When 78 RPM blues records were pressed in the 1920s to 1930s, manufacturers used either stock shellac or laminated discs. Stock shellac discs had a lower-quality playing surface, which made them prone to more noise at playback, while laminated discs (which were used by labels including Columbia and OKeh) featured a higher quality playing surface.

Likewise, quality can vary for vinyl records. For 12" records, the low end of the scale is 120-gram vinyl (4.23 ounces), with 150 grams (5.29 ounces) considered a "heavy" weight, and anything pressed on 180 grams (6.35 grams) or more deemed audiophile grade. The higher the weight, the higher the quality and durability.

Be ruthless when you assess condition. Goldmine magazine established (and continues to follow) the Goldmine Grading Standard, which determines how well a record, cover, or sleeve has survived since its creation. These are high standards, and they are not on a sliding scale. A record or sleeve from the 1950s must meet the same standards as one pressed today.

Rarity does not guarantee value. You thought you bought a copy of Lynyrd Skynyrd's "Street Survivors" album; the cover and labels were correct, after all. But when you put it on the turntable, you discovered the A-side was actually Steely Dan's "Aja." Or maybe the labels were wrong, but the music was what you thought you bought. Or perhaps you bought a still-sealed record that advertised one group on the cover and contained a completely different artist's album inside. These types of scenarios happened more often than you might think at a record pressing plant. While these records are snowflakes, they don't possess the types of errors that draw big bucks from collectors;

SUSAN SLIWICKI is the former editor of *Goldmine* magazine, which she joined in 2007. Her favorite childhood memories are of hours spent with her oldest brother, listening to his collection of albums, including Pink Floyd's "Dark Side of the Moon" and Deep Purple's "Machine Head."

NEW IMPROVED FULL DIMENSIONAL STEREO

File Under: The Beatles ST 2553

YESTERDAY · DR. ROBERT
I'M ONLY SLEEPING · AND YOUR BIRD CAN SING
WE CAN WORK IT OUT · DAY TRIPPER
NOWHERE MAN · WHAT GOES ON?
DRIVE MY CAR · IF I NEEDED SOMEONE
ACT NATURALLY

The Beatles
Yesterday
And Today

if anything, they negatively impact value. Depending on the music fan, these errors may only be a source of frustration, because the listener was anticipating "What's Your Name" and got "Black Cow" instead.

A record can be old without being valuable, and vice versa. Head to a garage sale, a thrift store or a relative's attic, and chances are good you'll find some old records. We're not saying you'll never find a beauty or two in the mix, but you're far more likely to find copies of Frankie Yankovic's "40 Hits I Almost Missed," Tom Jones' "Live In Las Vegas," and Glenn Miller's "The Carnegie Hall Concert" (worth $5 or less apiece) than a rare 78 RPM of Charley Patton's "High Water Everywhere" Parts 1 and 2 on the Paramount label, which sold for $5,000 in March 2012. Condition, quality, demand and rarity are far

Courtesy of Heritage Auctions, ha.com

The Beatles, "Yesterday And Today" (Capitol ST-2553, 1966), factory-sealed "first state" stereo record with "Butcher Cover," more rare than mono release. When first seen by DJs and record stores, there was an immediate negative reaction to album's graphic nature. Capitol recalled all "Butcher Cover" albums and, in many cases, glued what's generally called the "Trunk Cover" over it (known as a "second state"). **$75,000**

more important than age when determining value.

The laws of supply and demand rule. Meat Loaf's claim that "Two Out of Three Ain't Bad" doesn't count if the missing No. 3 is demand. No demand means no value; it doesn't matter how fine or rare the record is unless others want to buy it and own it. Supply figures in, too. A quality record in great condition that also is in great supply means buyers deem what the market is worth.

Trying to sell a record but not getting the price you seek? *Get a second, third or more opinion* on the record in question. Has your record gotten a better grade than it deserves? Is it a first pressing? Or is it a reissue or a counterfeit? Are similar-condition copies selling for wildly different amounts on the Internet or with other dealers? This will give you a better picture of what you have, what it's worth, and how in-demand it really is.

If you feel a dealer is offering an unfair price, make a counter offer. If the dealer shows no interest in negotiating, ask why he or she arrived at the price offered. Keep in mind that reputable dealers offer what they feel are fair prices, based on the costs and risks they assume for the items they acquire.

Collect what you love and what you can afford. Don't raid your 401(k) account to buy a too-good-to-be-true rarity under the guise that it is an investment. Enjoy the thrill of the chase within your budget, buy the best that you can afford, and always take time to appreciate what you have, from super-cool sleeves and covers to great-sounding music.

Goldmine's Record Grading Guide

Record grading uses both objective and subjective factors. Our advice: Look at everything about a record – its playing surface, the label, the record's edges, the cover and/or sleeve – under a strong light. If you're in doubt, assign the record a lower grade. Many dealers grade records, sleeves, or covers and sometimes even labels separately. The grades listed below are common to vinyl records, including EPs, 45s, LPs and 12" singles.

MINT (M): Perfect in every way. Often rumored, but rarely seen. Never played, and often still factory sealed. Never use Mint as a grade unless more than one person agrees that a record or sleeve truly is in this condition. Mint price is best negotiated between buyer and seller.

NEAR MINT (NM OR M-): Nearly perfect. Looks and sounds like it just came from a retail store and was opened for the first time. Jackets and sleeves are free of creases, folds, markings, or seam splits. Records are glossy and free of imperfections. Many dealers won't use a grade higher than NM, implying that no record or sleeve is ever truly perfect.

VERY GOOD-PLUS (VG+) or EXCELLENT (E): Except for a few minor things – slight warps, scuffs, or scratches that don't affect playback, ring wear on the labels, a turned up corner, cut-out hole, or seam split on the sleeve or cover – this record would be NM. Most collectors, especially those who want to play their records, are happy with a VG+ record, especially if it's toward the high end of the grade (VG++ or E+). Worth 50 percent of NM value.

◄ Jimi Hendrix, "Are You Experienced" (Reprise R-6261), mint condition, 1967 original U.S. pressing, first edition, mono, three-tone label. **$500**

▲ The Mothers of Invention, "Freak Out!" (Verve V6-5005-2), mint condition record, NM condition sleeve, light corner wear, rare, sealed, stereo 1966 2xLP gatefold U.S. release. **$225**

VERY GOOD (VG): Many of the imperfections found on a VG+ record are more obvious on a VG record. Surface noise, groove wear, and light scratches can be found on VG records. You may find stickers, tape or writing on labels, sleeves, and covers, but no more than two of those three problems. VG records are among the biggest bargains in record collecting. Worth 25 percent of a NM record.

GOOD (G), GOOD-PLUS (G+), or VERY GOOD-MINUS (VG-): Expect a lot of surface noise, visible groove wear and scratches on the vinyl, as well as more defects and repairs to labels, sleeves, and covers. Unless the record is unusually rare, G/G+ or VG- records are worth 10 to 15 percent of the NM value.

POOR (P) and FAIR (F): Records are cracked, impossibly warped, or skip and/or repeat when an attempt is made to play them. Covers and sleeves are heavily damaged, if they even exist. Unless they are incredibly rare, P and F records sell for 0 to 5 percent of the NM value (if they sell at all).

LPS

Courtesy of Heritage Auctions, ha.com

Velvet Underground – "And Nico" acetate LP, VG- condition, only two known copies of "Scepter Acetate," this version was purchased at a street sale for 75 cents. $18,750

Paul Revere and the Raiders, "Like, Long Hair" (Gardena Records LP G1000), 1962 U.S. release, sealed, original pressing. $204

LPS

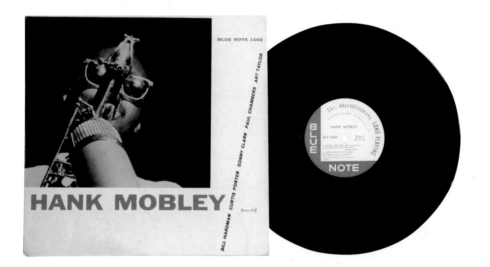

Hank Mobley, "Hank Mobley" (Blue Note BLP 1568), VG++ condition record, G+ condition sleeve, mono, 1957 original pressing. **$4,719**

Alice Cooper, "Pretties For You" (Straight Records STS-1051), NM condition, original white label promo, stereo. **$152**

The Beach Boys, "Pet Sounds" (Capitol Records DT 2458 STEREO), EX condition, 1966 "Duophonic" LP, first U.S. pressing in original shrinkwrap. **$360**

LPS

Pink Floyd, "Piper At the Gates
of Dawn" (Tower ST-5093), mint
condition, 1967 U.S. pressing,
stereo, sealed, first pressing
(1967). **$662**

Marvin Gaye, "The
Soulful Moods
of Marvin Gaye"
(Tamla TM-221), NM
condition, original
mono pressing,
yellow label. **$485**

LPS

Rolling Stones, "Big Hits (High Tide and Green Grass)" (London NPS-1), EX condition, sealed LP, stereo, 1966 U.S. compilation release. **$120**

▲ Small Faces, "From the Beginning" (Decca LK 4879), NM condition record, VG+ condition cover sleeve, mono, 1967 UK unboxed red Decca labels. **$140**

Courtesy of Julien's Auctions, www.juliensauctions.com

◄ The Jacksons, "Victory" (Epic 8E8-39576) Picture Disc 1984, autographed, signed on front cover in black marker "Michael Jackson." **$448**

Moby Grape, "Moby Grape" (Columbia CL-2698), mint condition, sealed, original 1967 first pressing, mono, uncensored cover and poster. **$1,225**

The Zombies, "Odessey and Oracle" (Date TES-4013), VG++ condition, green label, stereo, 1968 original U.S. pressing. **$260**

LPS

JAMES BROWN
and the Famous Flames

THINK!

THINK
SO LONG
BEWILDERED
I'LL GO CRAZY
IF YOU WANT ME
I KNOW IT'S TRUE
GOOD GOOD LOVIN'
BABY, YOU'RE RIGHT
YOU'VE GOT THE POWER
I'LL NEVER NEVER LET YOU GO
NDER WHEN YOU'RE COMING HOME

INCLUDES
THE HIT SINGLE
SUMMERTIME
BLUES
DL 79175

THE WHO LIVE AT LEEDS
DECCA DL 79175

James Brown, "Think!" King (LP 683), VG+ condition, 1959 mono, first U.S. pressing, 1st edition, rare baby face cover. **$113**

The Who, "Live At Leeds" (Decca DL-79175), mint condition, factory sealed, 1970 U.S. first pressing, rare gatefold with inserts and poster. **$989**

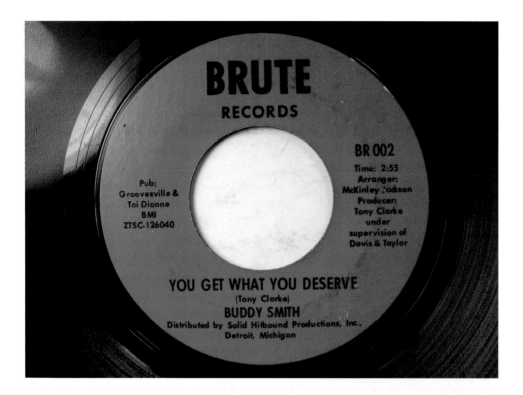

Buddy Smith, "When You Lose the One You Love" / "You Get What You Deserve" (Brute BR 002), NM condition, "Northern Soul" genre, 7" 45. **$4,303**

The Channels, "Yo Yo" / "Instrumental" (Mas-Ter w3477), VG condition, 7" 45, 1966 "Northern Soul." **$599**

Courtesy of Julien's Auctions, www.juliensauctions.com

Davy Jones, "Theme for a New Love" (Colpix Records CP-789), Davy Jones' personal copy of his pre-Monkees 7" single "Theme for a New Love" and "The Girl From Chelsea," released by Colpix Records in 1965, songs appear on Jones' first solo album, "David Jones." Provenance: From the estate of Davy Jones. **$192**

The Grateful Dead, "Don't Ease Me In" / "Stealin'" (Scorpio Records, Inc. 201), mint condition, 7", 45 RPM, single, 1966 unofficial release promo. **$3,999**

The High Numbers, "Zoot Suit" (Fontana TF-480), NM condition, 7" 45 RPM, 1964 UK original pressing of the band that would become The Who. **$2,099**

Courtesy of Heritage Auctions, ha.com

The Beatles, "P.S. I Love You" / "Love Me Do," Parlophone (4949), VG-/EX condition, autographed first pressing, 7" 45, 1962 UK release; one of the first-ever signed Beatles records, in matted display, with certificate of authenticity. Provenance: From the Uwe Blaschke Beatles Collection. **$25,000**

MISCELLANEOUS

Robert Johnson, "Me and the Devil Blues" / "Queen of Spades" (Vocalion 04108), G condition, 78 RPM, 10", 1938. **$4,071**

Courtesy of Hake's Americana & Collectibles, www.hakes.com

"Golden Age Radio Three Record Set," original 8" x 8 1/2" illustrated sleeve with images of Superman, Flash Gordon, Green Hornet's Black Beauty car, Mandrake the Magician, The Shadow, and The Lone Ranger, with 8" x 8" square thin vinyl flexi-disc 16-2/3 RPM records, issued in 1970s by Eva-Tone Soundsheets for $3; each record double-sided, includes "The Shadow" (1937), "Superman" (1945), "Captain Midnight" (1947), "Flash Gordon" (1935), "The Avenger" (1941), "Mandrake" (1939), "The Blue Beetle" (1943) and theme songs from "The Green Hornet," "The Lone Ranger," "Dick Tracy" and "Hop Harrigan"; sleeve with scattered wear and even, light aging, records appear unused and in mint condition. **$115**

Science and Technology

By Eric Bradley

ERIC BRADLEY is one of the young guns of the antiques and collectibles field. Bradley, who works for Heritage Auctions, is a former editor of *Antique Trader* magazine and an award-winning investigative journalist with a degree in economics. His work has received press from *The New York Times* and *The Wall Street Journal*. He also served as a featured guest speaker on investing with antiques. He has written several books, including the critically acclaimed *Mantiques: A Manly Guide to Cool Stuff.*

Scientific models, diagrams, and lab equipment are now hot collectibles, thanks to a boost in the Steampunk design movement and the rise of "geek chic."

It's cool to be smart, and it's a cool collector who has at least a few fascinating objects devoted to mankind's pursuit to knowing more about the world we live in. From books to microscopes to calculators and even quack medical devices, this collecting category spans several object classes.

Increasingly, auction houses are pursuing this trend with specialty-themed sales. Bonhams, Heritage, Skinner, and even Sotheby's have all offered major technological auctions, many with strong results. However, the undisputed leader in this

Courtesy of Skinner, Inc., www.skinnerinc.com

Heath & Co. boxed sextant, New Eltham, London, no. P46, model Hezzanith with pierced frame, quick release index arm, inset silvered scale calibrated 0-130, vernier knob calibrated 0-55 for fine adjustment, sun shades, and horizon mirror in fitted mahogany box with certificate of examination reading "Hezzanith," Instrument works, with additional eyepieces. **$215**

Courtesy of Skinner, Inc., www.skinnerinc.com

Ebony octant, H. Duran, New York, 19th century, brass index arm with bone vernier scale from 0-20 with thumbscrew lock, bone arc reading "0-100," cross-arm bone boss reading "Joseph Liverpool H. Duren New York," sighting pinnula, horizon mirror, and sunshades, 10". $338

category is based in Germany. Auction Team Breker, located in Cologne, offers several sales each year on office antiques, photographica, and film. The sales are just one more example of how auction houses are seeking to cater not only to what collectors collect, but how collectors collect.

Trends in this area are likely to be centered on the dawn of personal computing. The first personal computer sold to the public was Simon, a hulk of wire and cabinetry holding a simple mechanical brain. It debuted in 1950 for $600 ($5,723 in today's dollars) and was able to perform addition, negation, greater than, and selection. It's rare for these early computers to come to market, and when they do, collectors and investors take notice.

A rare 1976 Apple I computer brought $374,500 at a June 2012 auction. Similar models don't sell for nearly as much money, with provenance, condition, and exposure key to an object's auction value.

Rare examples aside, collecting scientific and technology collectibles is a very affordable hobby and one that stands an excellent chance to grow as today's tech-savvy youth become the nostalgic collectors of the future.

Courtesy of Farmer Auctions, farmer-auctions.com

Mercury stick barometer by G. Davis, optician, mahogany case, missing finial, mercury in tube intact, good condition, 39" x 5 1/2". Gabriel Davis of Leeds, England was an optician and scientific instrument maker working in the 1830s and 1840s (d. 1851). $720

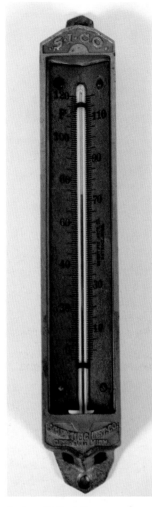

Cast aluminum wall thermometer, circa 1920, Scientific Instrument Co., Detroit, inscribed "S. I. CO" on top of frame, "Scientific Inst. Co. Detroit, Mich." on bottom of frame, pitting to temperature scale, glass thermometer intact, 12" high x 2" wide. **$98**

Swiss mini vertical milling machine with 12" solid column, rotary table, spring-assisted head return, assortment of collets, run by two-horsepower D.C. motor, mounted on wooden base, 23" high. **$1,599**

Schaublin-Villeneuve 70mm clock and watchmaker's lathe, Bevilard, Switzerland, mid-20th century, reportedly used in Bulova Watch Co. Research and Development department; steel bed with cast maker's mark and CH Schaublin-Villeneuve/Bevilard (Suisse), steel plate inscribed "Brevet 81805," head stock with three-speed flat belting with minor index or locking plate and removable 6" index plate, tail stock, tool rest, V rest, bed to center, 70mm, lathe 23 1/2" long; Schaublin motor No. 5659 with three-step pulley on exit end, overhead drive rods and pulleys for cross slide attachments, and manufacturer's spec plate, Roto-Phase Generator or phase converter, electrical box and forward-reverse switch, Schaublin accessories: milling attachment powered by overhead drive, approximately 55 collets, tailstock centering tools, grinding attachment, and 3" Pratt Burnerd International three-jaw chuck with inside/outside jaws and Schaublin mounting. **$2,706**

Courtesy of Skinner, Inc., www.skinnerinc.com

Multi-tooth wheel cutters, various makers, sizes for various size wheels and pinions, makers: Bergeon, A Musitilli & Cie, L. Carpano, and others, total of approximately 75 pieces. **$2,337**

Courtesy of Guernsey's, www.guernseys.com

Christian Becker Chainomatic analytical scale, circa 1920, nickel and iron, covered by glass case, base and single drawer of mahogany with Bakelite pull, 25" high x 20" wide x 10" deep. **$375**

Courtesy of Skinner, Inc., www.skinnerinc.com

James Condliff field regulator movement and dial, Liverpool, circa 1820, 4 5/8" silvered brass dial engraved "Ja(m) Condliff/Liverpool" with three subsidiary dials, upper for seconds, object lower left for minutes, object lower right for hours, four-pillar, brass chain fusee, time only-movement with cut corners, duplex escapement, rise and fall gearing, approximately 9" pendulum, movement 7" high. **$5,228**

Courtesy of Skinner, Inc., www.skinnerinc.com

◀ Gimbaled brass compass, Star, Boston, no. 33421, dry compass card with cardinal and intercardinal points, and 0-360 azimuth scale, mounted in finger-jointed mahogany box with painting of whale on top by "Richard Sparre," 4". **$308**

Courtesy of Skinner, Inc., www.skinnerinc.com

◀ Kaleidoscope attributed to designer Charles Bush, C.G. Bush & Co., manufacturer, Providence, Rhode Island, circa 1870s, pebbled paper-covered cardboard cylinder with brass ship's wheel-form movable fitting, on turned walnut base, circular chamber box containing multicolored glass segments and liquid-filled ampules (patented in 1873), producing geometric patterns in viewing lens, 12" high. **$400**

Courtesy of Skinner, Inc., www.skinnerinc.com

Rochester Optical "New Model View" camera, Rochester, New York, circa 1895, cherry body with square brown leather bellows, white name plate mounted above lens, fitted with lens marked "R.O. Co., 2," with cast iron tripod mount, camera 5" x 8". **$215**

Courtesy of Skinner, Inc., www.skinnerinc.com

Henry Browne & Son Ltd. "Sestrel" compass, London, 19th/20th century, brass case engraved in part "Henry Browne & Son Ltd. Barking & London no. 9349/B" along top edge, wet card compass with cardinal points, sighting prism and turned wood handle, in fitted hinged case with "Sestrel" Henry Browne & Son Ltd celluloid plaque attached to door panel, instrument 9 1/2" high. **$369**

Leica IIIF camera with three Nikon lenses, Germany and Japan, circa 1952, chrome body with serial number 546293, lenses: Nikkor C 3.5cm f/3.5, Nikkor SC 5cm f/1.4, and Nikkor QC 13.5cm f/3.5, Nikon 3.5 to 13.5cm variable viewfinder and Weston Master II light meter. **$738**

◄ Armillary sphere, Italy, 20th century, composite model with 2 1/4" terrestrial globe surrounded by calibrated and adjustable equatorial and meridian rings, large equatorial ring inscribed with signs of zodiac, on turned wooden stand, 18 1/2" high. **$369**

▼ Keuffel & Esser Co. lacquered brass pantograph, no. 1127, serial No. 42508, instrument with calibrated arm with vernier dial and marked Keuffel & Esser New York 42508, fitted oak box with knurled brass and wood tie-downs, instruction label, and celluloid plaque with serial and model numbers. **$123**

Silver

Silver has been known since ancient times and has long been valued as a precious metal, used to make ornaments, jewelry, tableware and utensils, and coins.

Pure silver is too soft to be fashioned into strong, durable, and serviceable utensils. Adding alloys of copper and nickel to silver gives it the required degree of hardness. Silversmithing in America goes back to the early 17th century in Boston and New York and the early 18th century in Philadelphia. Boston artisans were influenced by the English styles; New Yorkers by the Dutch.

Silver-plated items are made from a base metal coated with a thin layer of silver.

For more information on sterling silverware, see *Warman's Sterling Silver Flatware*, 2nd edition, by Phil Dreis.

Courtesy of Leslie Hindman Auctioneers, www.lesliehindman.com

Silver-plate jewelry casket, French, circa late 19th century, octagonal shape, four paw feet, panels of landscapes and flowering urns on body, oval cartouches and floral garlands and running bellflowers throughout, interior lined with silk, 16 1/2" long including handles. $1,500

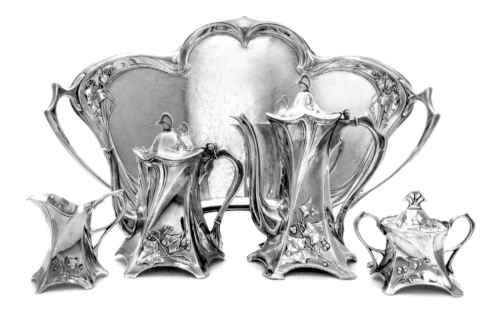

Courtesy of Leslie Hindman Auctioneers,
www.lesliehindman.com

Silver-plate four-piece tea and coffee service, Wurttembergische Metallwarenfabrik, Germany, circa 1905, teapot, coffee pot, creamer, covered sugar bowl and tray, each with sloping panels and domed covers with applied branches of berried ivy, bases with retailer's mark and WMF supplementary marks, tray 24 3/4" long including handles. **$2,250**

Courtesy of Leslie Hindman Auctioneers,
www.lesliehindman.com

George III silver coffee pot, circa 1777, Daniel Smith & Robert Sharp, London, baluster form with hinged lid, urn finial, and beaded border, C-scroll handle, engraved with tied ribbon suspending floral garlands, fully marked on underside, lid with lion passant, 28 oz., 11" high. **$2,250**

Courtesy of Leslie Hindman Auctioneers, www.lesliehindman.com

▲ Chrysanthemum pattern silver flatware service, Tiffany & Co., New York, 480 pieces including knives, forks, spoons, ladles, spreaders, servers, and tongs, 654 ozt., 10 dwt. **$40,000**

Courtesy of Rago Arts and Auctions, www.ragoarts.com

▶ Silver monogrammed cup gifted from General Lafayette to Nathanael Green, circa 1780, 3 1/2" x 3 1/2", 5.1 ozt. **$16,250**

Courtesy of Clars Auction Gallery, www.clars.com

◀ Chinese Export repoussé silver trophy tankard by Luen Wo, Shanghai, circa late 19th/early 20th century, molded with band set over hammered ground with figures in landscape surrounding festive interior, sculpted dragon handle, polished reserve inscribed "Shangai, Springs Meeting 1896 Mr. Toeg's CLYDE Winner Of THE JOCKEY CUP Ridden By W.W. COX," 15.17 ozt., 6" high. **$5,937**

Courtesy of Pook and Pook, Inc.,
www.pookandpook.com

William Wilson & Son coin silver presentation flask with chased frog and trailing vine, inscribed "David W. Sellers / FROM HIS FRIEND / Henry C. Terry / Philadelphia / May 11th 1883," 5 3/4" high. $861

Courtesy of Clars Auction Gallery, www.clars.com

Faberge-style jeweled, silvered, and enamel-decorated troika, possibly Russian or Austrian, with amethyst cabochons, large seed and cultured pearls, and garnets, with enamel-decorated floral sprays, three horses with purple enamel-decorated saddles and with two attendants, interior of sleigh with enamel finish, on black lacquered wood base, 6" high x 14" wide x 7 1/2" deep. **$3,125**

Courtesy of Pook and Pook, Inc., www.pookandpook.com

Set of 12 Stieff repoussé sterling silver plates, 48 ozt., 6 1/8" diameter. **$836**

Courtesy of Rago Arts and Auctions,
www.ragoarts.com

Sterling silver cocktail shaker in lighthouse design, circa 1930, stamped Meriden S.P. Co. Internationals Co., 20" x 7 1/4", 150 ozt. $5,937

Courtesy of Rago Arts and Auctions,
www.ragoarts.com

English sterling silver figural centerpiece, woman holding cornucopia, London, circa 1834, with dedication to Rev. Frederick Blunt, 18 3/4" x 9", 54.19 ozt. $2,625

Royal Danish pattern silver flatware service, International Silver Co., 189 pieces total, 256 ozt. $4,250

Pair of covered serving dishes, Georg Jensen and Wendel, sterling silver and ebony, mid-20th century, 5 1/2" x 11", 57.6 ozt. $13,750

Courtesy of Clars Auction Gallery, www.clars.com

"Cupid et Psyche" silver gilt and enamel bronze sculpture on red marble base, Mathurin Moreau, circa late 19th century, signed lower left, 26 1/2" high x 11 1/2" wide x 19 1/2" deep. **$5,937**

Courtesy of Rago Arts and Auctions, www.ragoarts.com

Set of 12 sterling silver open cups and saucers, Tiffany and Co., circa early 20th century, marked for John C. Moore II, director of Tiffany and Co. from 1907-1947, 2 1/2" x 6", 94.18 ozt. **$1,875**

Courtesy of Rago Arts and Antiques, www.ragoarts.com

Silver Sails coffee and tea set, sterling silver pot, teapot, creamer, sugar and tray by Michael and Maureen Banner, rosewood base, 97.8 ozt., coffee pot 14" x 9 1/4". **$33,750**

Pair of Italian three-light silver candelabra, circa mid-20th century, Buccellati, each with baluster standard issuing scroll arms, marked on bases, 90 ozt., 2 dwt, 15" high. **$3,250**

Georg Jensen sterling silver mini ice bucket with tongs, designed by Sigvard Bernadotte, tongs in Bernadotte pattern, Copenhagen, 1945-1952, both marked, 18.9 ozt., bucket 5" x 4 3/4". **$2,125**

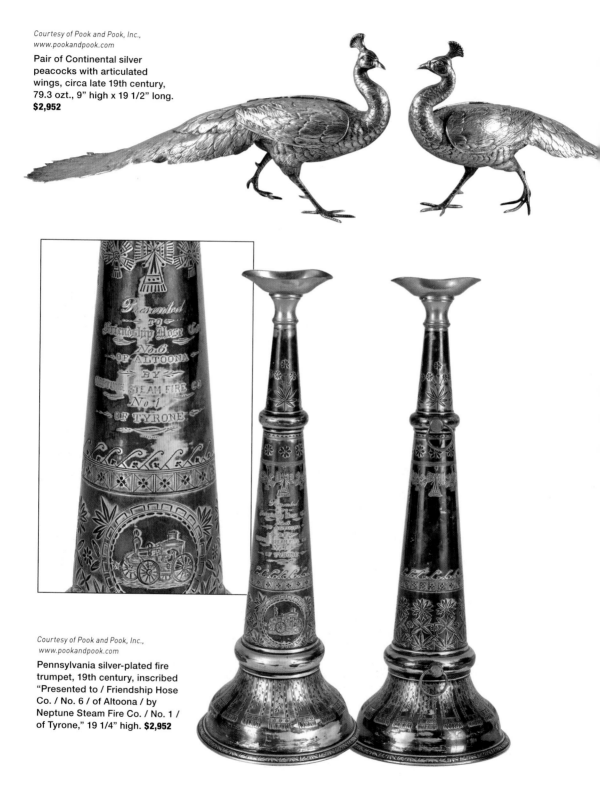

Courtesy of Pook and Pook, Inc.,
www.pookandpook.com

**Pair of Continental silver
peacocks with articulated
wings, circa late 19th century,
79.3 ozt., 9" high x 19 1/2" long.
$2,952**

Courtesy of Pook and Pook, Inc.,
www.pookandpook.com

**Pennsylvania silver-plated fire
trumpet, 19th century, inscribed
"Presented to / Friendship Hose
Co. / No. 6 / of Altoona / by
Neptune Steam Fire Co. / No. 1 /
of Tyrone," 19 1/4" high. $2,952**

Courtesy of Rago Arts and Antiques,
www.ragoarts.com

Avanti pattern sterling
silver flatware service for
12, CELSA, 74 pieces, circa
1950s, stamped "Sterling
by Celsa Mexio," 87.84 ozt.
$4,375

Courtesy of Clars Auction Gallery,
www.clars.com

Georg Jensen Art Nouveau
sterling silver service in 80
pattern, 1945-present, coffee
pot, covered sugar bowl, and
cream pitcher, each with ebony
mounts, with Georg Jensen
Blossom-pattern circular tray,
each base with engraved
inscription "Annette and Allison
September 13, 1969," 47.89 ozt.
$4,750

Sports

Sports and sports memorabilia are eternally intertwined. Since sports began, there have been mementoes to draw in audiences, attract attention to the games or invite future fans to the stadiums. And because the games evoke fond memories, many times those mementoes are kept for a long time. Sports memorabilia is our connection to sporting events we remember and the players we loved to watch.

Today, sports memorabilia is used for more than simply waking up the memory bank or providing a connection to the past. These items are also increasingly used for home or office décor, as well as investments. Sports collectibles are more accessible than ever before through online auctions, with several auction houses that dedicate themselves solely to that segment of the hobby. Provenance and third-party authentication is extremely important when investing in high-ticket sports collectibles. In today's market, high-quality and rare items are in most demand, with a heavy nod toward stars and Hall of Famers. Condition is everything – keep an eye toward temperature, humidity and exposure to sunlight with pieces in your collection.

Courtesy of Goldin Auctions, goldinauctions.com

▼ O.J. Simpson's "Most Touchdowns in a Single Season" record-breaking game football, 1975. Simpson broke the mark in a 34-14 win over the New England Patriots on Dec. 14, 1975. **$4,463**

Courtesy of Lelands, lelands.com

▲ Actual game ball used in the National Football League's American Football Conference Championship Game on Jan. 18, 2015, at Gillette Stadium in Foxboro, Massachusetts. This game evolved into "Deflategate," where the New England Patriots used under-inflated footballs. **$43,740**

Courtesy of Robert Edward Auctions,
www.robertedwardsauctions.com
Brooklyn Dodgers usher's cap,
circa 1950s, with original button,
size 7 1/4. **$10,200**

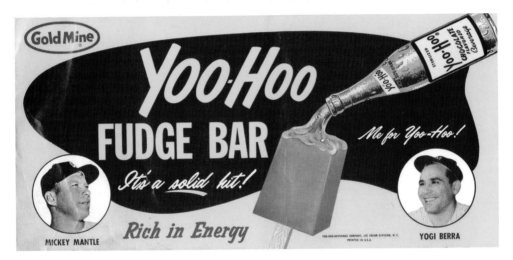

Courtesy of SCP Auctions, scpauctions.com
▲ 1960s Yoo-Hoo Fudge Bar
advertising sign with Mickey Mantle
and Yogi Berra, 6 3/4" x 14". **$581**

Courtesy of Lelands, lelands.com
◄ Actual racing horseshoe
from legendary thoroughbred
Secretariat, 1973, acquired
from Buck Peters, official
photographer for Phillip Morris
assigned to cover 1973 Marlboro
Cup at Belmont Park in New York.
$36,543

Courtesy of Lelands, lelands.com
◄ U.S. passport originally issued
to Muhammad Ali in 1972 for fight
with boxer Al Lewis, issued by
U.S. embassy in Dublin, Ireland,
likely a replacement. **$18,752**

"Union Prisoners at Salisbury, N.C., Drawn from Nature by Act. Major Otto Boeticcher" Civil War baseball lithograph, 1863, one of earliest color representations of baseball, 25" x 42". $8,365

1916 Army vs. Navy football game committee medal, Dieges & Clust, 3 1/2" long. $240

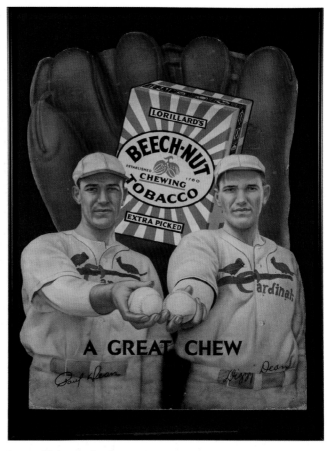

1934 Beech-Nut Tobacco oversized die-cut advertising sign with Paul and Dizzy Dean, 28" x 42". $14,340

Brooklyn Atlantics CDV, circa 1860, only known pre-Civil War baseball team card, SGC Authentic, Atlantic Base Ball Club of Brooklyn, produced by Farach & Lalumia Studio. **$179,250**

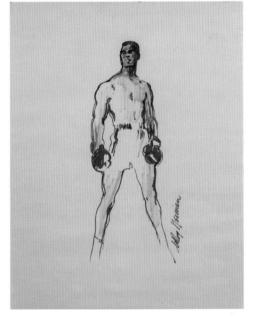

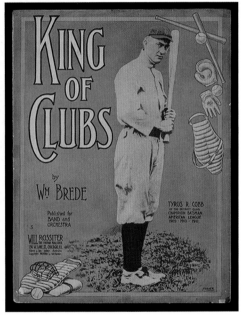

LeRoy Neiman signed original Muhammad Ali artwork, 1960s, 18" x 24" from Bert Sugar Collection. **$10,710**

1912 Ty Cobb "King of Clubs" sheet music written by William Brede and published by Will Rossiter, Chicago, 10 1/2" x 14". **$420**

Pair of 14k gold 1958 New York Yankees World Championship cuff links, given to scout Raymond Garland, 7/8" diameter, 14 grams. **$4,680**

**1897 Home Base Ball Game,
manufactured by McLoughlin Bros.,
10 1/2" x 19 1/2" x 1". $1,320**

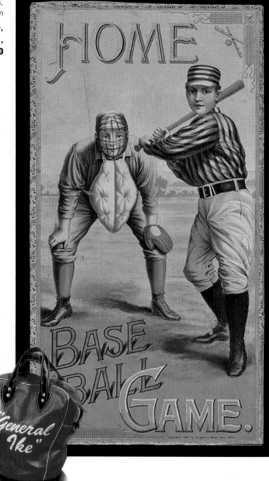

▲ Dwight D. Eisenhower's
custom golf bag and full
set of Spalding clubs,
engraved "General Ike,"
1960s, from Newport
Sports Museum. **$121,122**

▶ Kareem Abdul-Jabbar
basketball game-worn
goggles, 1980s. **$8,963**

Courtesy of Goldin Auctions, goldinauctions.com

1992 Barcelona Summer Olympics Gold Medal (unissued), "XXV Olympiada Barcelona" engraved on front, 2" x 2 1/2". **$3,645**

Courtesy of Lelands, lelands.com

▲ Poster of *The Umpire* silent film, 1917, only specimen known, marked by Morgan Lithograph Co. of Cleveland, Ohio, mounted on linen, 27" x 41". **$8,843**

Courtesy of SCP Auctions, scpauctions.com

◄ 1938 New York Yankees World Championship Hamilton gold pocket watch presented to Johnny Murphy, 19" long. **$33,378**

Tiffany Studios

By Noah Fleisher

NOAH FLEISHER received his Bachelor of Fine Arts degree from New York University and brings more than a decade of newspaper, magazine, book, antiques and art experience to his position as Public Relations Director of Heritage Auctions, one of the country's foremost auction houses. He is the former editor of *Antique Trader, New England Antiques Journal* and *Northeast Antiques Journal,* is the author of *Warman's Modern Furniture* and co-author of *Collecting Children's Books,* and has been a longtime contributor to *Warman's Antiques & Collectibles.*

If there was a dictionary of antiques and collectibles, the listing under the word "quality" would surely feature the work of Tiffany Studios. If the world of antiques and collectibles were a horse race, certainly Tiffany Studios would be considered a sure bet. If antiques and collectibles were bought and sold in the same fashion as the stock market, Tiffany Studios would be a blue chip.

Louis Comfort Tiffany (1848-1933) was the son of Charles Lewis Tiffany, the namesake of Tiffany and Co. Though he started as a painter, Tiffany was a prodigious glassmaker, a fantastic designer and, at heart, always an artist. These things all show in glassware and ceramics that came out of his design collective in New York City in the late 19th century and the first quarter or so of the 20th century. His work in large part defined both the Art Nouveau and Aesthetic movements.

In the world of antiques and collectibles, his name is ubiquitous – even those who do not collect Tiffany Studios items know who he is and what his work looks like. Every appraiser in the nation can identify his trademark. One of the first things any writer in this business ever learns about or covers is, inevitably, Tiffany glass.

This enduring fame has translated into enduring value. At whatever level of the market in Tiffany Studios you may be looking to buy – $100 to $100,000+, from humble inkwells and ashtrays to exquisite high-end peony lamps – there is a pretty good bet that whatever you put into it you will always be able to get out of it. As with every market, there are troughs and crests, but Tiffany always recovers.

Part of the appeal of Tiffany is in its sheer variety: Opalescent, Favrile, Steamer, Fracture, Fracture-Steamer, Ripple, Ring Mottle, Drapery, bronze work, silver, brass, and those famous lamps of all kinds. This just scratches the surface, so to speak. What are your tastes? Fancy? Formal? Abstract? Representational? Start looking at any shop, auction, or show and you'll find something that appeals to you.

Take away the world of fine art and I'm hard-pressed to think

of any form that is more widely enshrined in institutions. There are permanent collections of Tiffany Studios work in more than 50 institutions across 20 different states.

What do collectors look for in Tiffany Studios glass, ceramics, and other decorative works? The first thing, as it is with any antique or collectible, is quality. Does it have the Tiffany Studios stamp? Are the surface or edges chipped? Your eyes will tell you what you need to know at first blush.

It's important to keep in mind, however, that just as Tiffany Studios' work is so widely loved and collected, so is there a significant market in fakes, especially as it concerns the higher end of the Tiffany spectrum, most specifically in lamps. This makes verification the most important thing to look for when it comes to Tiffany Studios. If you come across a Tiffany lamp and it seems too good to be true, chances are it is. In some cases it may even be an unwitting fake that was never intended to be passed off as a real Tiffany piece, but is simply glasswork with bars in it, or a Tiffany knockoff made by an imitator in the popular style.

A qualified expert will be able to tell you right away. Ask a dealer, an auctioneer, or a museum. Send them images, details of condition, and descriptions of any markings on the piece. Auction houses like Fontaine's Auctions, Cottone Auctions, Sotheby's, Heritage Auctions, and Rago Arts all have experts dedicated to the form on staff. Check with dealers in your area or attend antiques shows. Any expert worth his salt is going to take the time to help you discover what is real and what is not. The payoff, especially if a lamp in particular is real, can end up being significant.

Most of all, when it comes to Tiffany Studios, whatever area of the name appeals to you, enjoy the ride and buy only what you love because you're going to be living with it. It should make you happy every time you look at it.

Courtesy of Heritage Auctions, ha.com
Favrile glass bowl, circa 1900, marked "L.C.T. Favrile," 1 1/4" high x 3 3/4" wide. $213

GLASS ITEMS

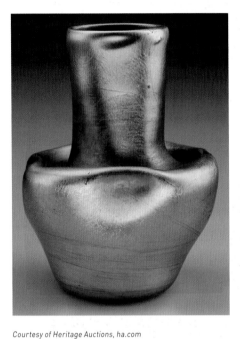

Courtesy of Heritage Auctions, ha.com
Favrile glass cabinet vase, Corona, New York, circa 1900, marked "L.C.T., N1535," original label over pontil, 4 1/2" high. **$550**

Courtesy of Heritage Auctions, ha.com
Favrile glass vase, circa 1904, marked "L.C.T., U6150," 5" high. **$688**

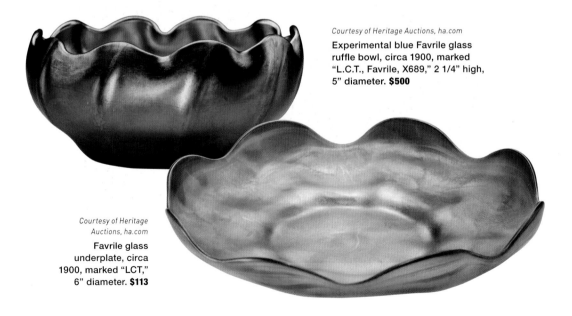

Courtesy of Heritage Auctions, ha.com
Experimental blue Favrile glass ruffle bowl, circa 1900, marked "L.C.T., Favrile, X689," 2 1/4" high, 5" diameter. **$500**

Courtesy of Heritage Auctions, ha.com
Favrile glass underplate, circa 1900, marked "LCT," 6" diameter. **$113**

GLASS ITEMS

Courtesy of Heritage Auctions, ha.com

Favrile glass Tel-El-Amarna vase, circa 1910, engraved "L. C. Tiffany – Favrile, 9990 E," 8 5/8" high. **$7,500**

GLASS ITEMS

Courtesy of Heritage Auctions, ha.com

Monumental paperweight glass vase, circa 1902, engraved "Louis C. Tiffany, R2367," 13 1/2" high.
$35,000

GLASS ITEMS

Courtesy of Heritage Auctions, ha.com

Favrile glass compote, Tiffany Studios, Corona, New York, circa 1900, iridescent green glass to interior, underside with white leaves and vertical ribbing, baluster stem set on circular foot, marked "LCT, FAVRILE, 5-1701," 5" high, 6" diameter. **$406**

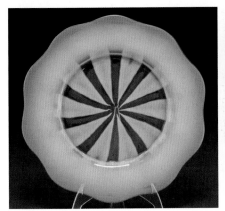

Courtesy of Heritage Auctions, ha.com

Pastille glass plate, circa 1910, engraved "L.C.T., Favrile," 10" diameter. **$375**

Courtesy of Heritage Auctions, ha.com

Gold Favrile glass floriform footed bowl, circa 1905, engraved "L.C.T., Y6680," 4 1/2" high. **$625**

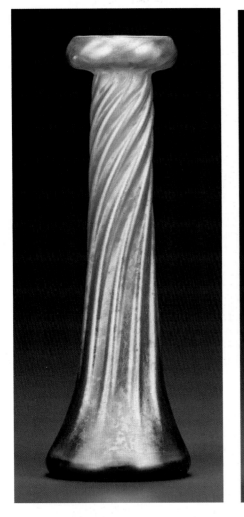

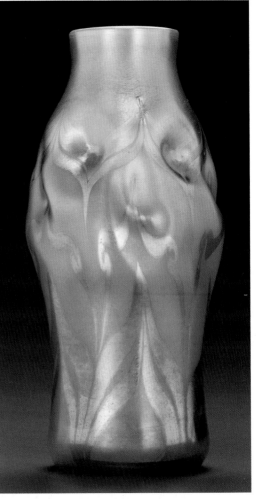

Courtesy of Heritage Auctions, ha.com

Favrile glass candlestick vase, circa 1900, engraved "L.C.T., II, 8518," 7 1/8" high. **$1,063**

Courtesy of Heritage Auctions, ha.com

Green Favrile glass dimpled vase, circa 1910, enameled "L.C. Tiffany, Favrile, 04871," 11 5/8" high. **$1,375**

GLASS ITEMS

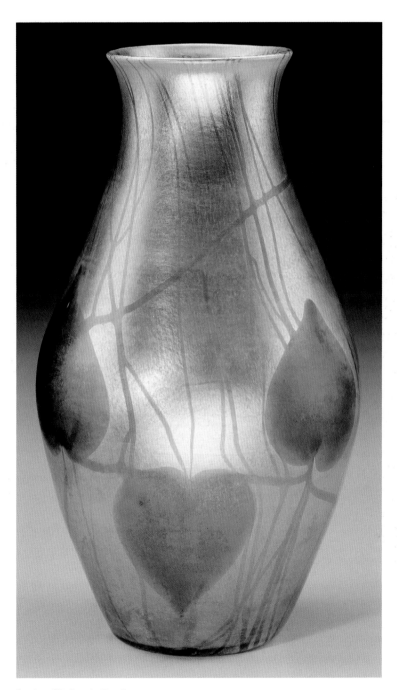

Courtesy of Heritage Auctions, ha.com
Gold Favrile foliate vase, circa 1917, marked "L.C. Tiffany, Favrile, 710L," 8 1/2" high.
$1,125

GLASS ITEMS

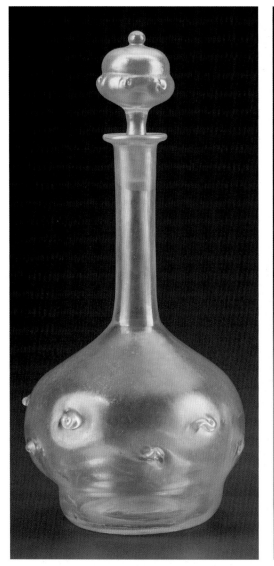

Courtesy of Heritage Auctions, ha.com
Favrile glass pigtails prunt decanter with stopper, circa 1900, marked "LCT, 6338," stopper marked "38," 10 1/4" high x 5" wide. **$500**

Courtesy of Heritage Auctions, ha.com
Gold Favrile glass trumpet vase with gilt bronze base, Corona, New York, circa 1910, marked to base "TIFFANY STUDIOS, NEW YORK, 1043," marked to glass "L.C.T.," 14 3/4" high. **$1,688**

Courtesy of Heritage Auctions, ha.com
Favrile paperweight glass morning glory vase, circa 1900, engraved "L.C.T., Y 3147," 8 1/8" high.
$30,000

DESK ACCESSORIES

Courtesy of Heritage Auctions, ha.com

Pair of bronze Chinese bookends, Corona, New York, circa 1910, marked "TIFFANY STUDIOS, NEW YORK, 1025," 6" x 4 7/8" x 5 3/4". **$750**

Courtesy of Heritage Auctions, ha.com

Two gilt bronze bookmark pattern desk items, Corona, New York, circa 1900, marked to all "TIFFANY STUDIOS, NEW YORK, 967, 973," inkwell 2 1/4" x 3 1/8" x 3 1/8". **$406**

DESK ACCESSORIES

Courtesy of Heritage Auctions, ha.com

Glass and bronze grapevine pattern folding book stand, circa 1915, stamped "TIFFANY STUDIOS, NEW YORK, 1027," 6" x 14" x 6 3/8". **$1,625**

Courtesy of Heritage Auctions, ha.com

Rare bronze Chinese pattern desk scissors and paper knife in original leather sheath, circa 1910, both fully marked "TIFFANY STUDIOS, NEW YORK" with design number. **$906**

DESK ACCESSORIES

Bronze zodiac master inkwell, Corona, New York, circa 1910, marked "TIFFANY STUDIOS, NEW YORK, 1072," 3 1/2" high, 7" diameter. **$300**

Rare glass and bronze grapevine pattern adjustable desk lamp, circa 1915, stamped "TIFFANY STUDIOS, NEW YORK, 552," 9" high. **$5,313**

DESK ACCESSORIES

Courtesy of Heritage Auctions, ha.com

Glass and bronze grapevine pattern card case, circa 1915, stamped "TIFFANY STUDIOS, NEW YORK," 4" high. $875

Courtesy of Heritage Auctions, ha.com

Rare square glass and gilt bronze pine needle pattern desk box, circa 1920, stamped "TIFFANY STUDIOS, NEW YORK, 824," 2 5/8" x 8 1/4" x 8 1/4". $1,188

Courtesy of Heritage Auctions, ha.com

Bronze and enamel zodiac pattern letter rack, circa 1900, stamped to base "TIFFANY STUDIOS, NEW YORK, 1009," 6 1/4" x 9 3/8' x 2 1/4". **$938**

Courtesy of Heritage Auctions, ha.com

Rare glass and gilt bronze pine needle pattern seal, circa 1920, stamped "TIFFANY STUDIOS," 3" high. **$875**

LAMPS

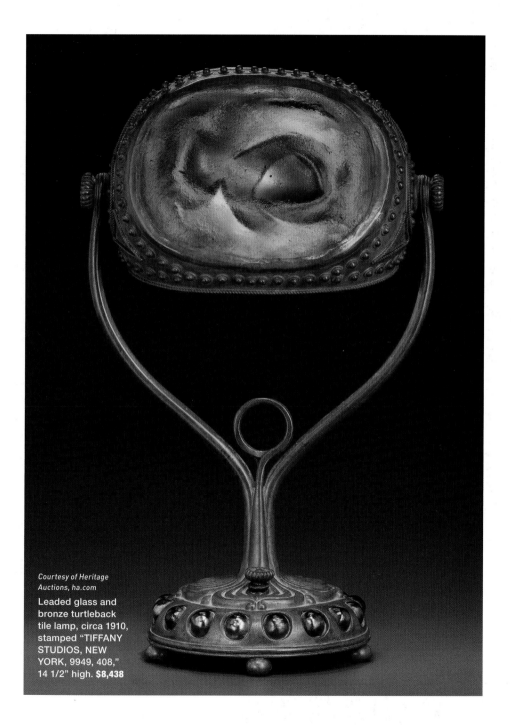

Courtesy of Heritage Auctions, ha.com

Leaded glass and bronze turtleback tile lamp, circa 1910, stamped "TIFFANY STUDIOS, NEW YORK, 9949, 408," 14 1/2" high. $8,438

LAMPS

Courtesy of Heritage Auctions, ha.com

▲ Bronze single student lamp with Damascene glass shade, circa 1903, iridescent green shade with silver and gold decoration, patinated bronze base with adjustable oil canister with applied beaded and rope borders, marked to shade "L.C.T., S115556," 24 3/4" x 17" x 10 1/2". **$3,750**

Courtesy of Heritage Auctions, ha.com

◄ Leaded glass and bronze border peony floor lamp, circa 1920, stamped "TIFFANY STUDIOS, N.Y.," 78" high. **$143,000**

i *For more Tiffany lamps, please see the "Lamps & Lighting" section.*

LAMPS

Courtesy of Heritage Auctions, ha.com
Pair of gilt bronze and Favrile glass five-light lily lamps, circa 1925, marked to bases (miss stamp), "TIFFANY STUDIOS, NEW YORK, A7736," marked to shades "L.C.T. Favrile," 15" high. **$16,250**

MISCELLANEOUS

Courtesy of Heritage Auctions, ha.com
◀ Bronze smoking stand, circa 1905, stamped "TIFFANY STUDIOS, NEW YORK, 1651," 25 1/4" high. **$1,062**

Courtesy of Heritage Auctions, ha.com
▲ Patinated bronze six-light candelabrum and snuffer, New York, circa 1900, marked "TIFFANY STUDIOS, NEW YORK, 1290, 948A," 21" long. **$1,563**

Toys

Toy collecting has gone through dramatic changes over the years, but the premise of collecting remains the same – holding onto something from childhood that brings a smile to your face every time you see it.

Toys are fun. There are no hidden messages when it comes to toys. They are produced for entertainment, and while they can also be quite valuable, that is not the driving force behind collecting toys.

If you collect now, you're doing it as a passion. And that's what toys are all about, a piece of nostalgia that can grow into a fascination that fills rooms in houses and provides endless stories for relatives and friends.

Over the past few years, one aspect of the hobby is becoming apparent: More people are becoming acquainted with toys and their values than at any other point in American history, thanks to the exposure the hobby has garnered from the collectible-based reality programs broadcast on television.

The best weapon in the battle for equitable prices for toys is acquiring knowledge: Education is power. Learn about the toy and its backstory, know its manufacturer and date of production as well as its importance in the realm of popular culture.

When estimating the value of a toy, you must first evaluate its condition. Mint toys in mint packaging command higher prices than well-played-with toys whose boxes disappeared with the wrapping paper on Christmas day. Mint is a rare condition indeed as toys were meant to be played with by children. Realistic evaluation of condition is essential, as grading standards vary from class to class. Ultimately, the market is driven by buyers, and the bottom line final value of a toy is often the last price at which it is sold.

For more information on toys, see *Toys & Prices,* 20th edition, by Mark Bellomo.

Courtesy of Sotheby's, www.sothebys.com

English silver toy tea service by Francis Higgins, London, 1936, teapot, kettle on stand, creamer, sugar bowl, and tray, with corner chair (not shown), Birmingham, 1910, tray 4 1/2" diameter (stemmed glasses shown for scale purposes).
$4,063

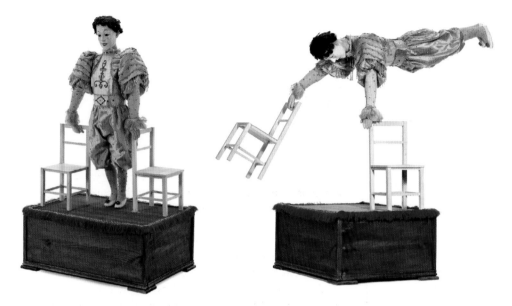

Courtesy of Auction Team Breker, www.breker.com

Musical automaton gymnast by Vichy-Triboulet, circa 1910, plaster-composition head, fixed brown glass eyes, open smiling mouth with two rows of modeled teeth, curly mohair wig, papier-mâché body, gold silk circus costume trimmed with glass beads and sequins, two painted wood chairs, and wood base with large going-barrel motor driving five cams and four-air cartel cylinder movement, gymnast 35" high, base 13 1/4" x 19 1/2" x 8 1/4". Gymnast stands between two chairs, raises chair in right hand and flexes wrist, then lowers chair and elevates body into handstand position; in mid-air, he raises chair a second time, flexes wrist, lowers head, and lowers body slowly back to standing position. **$22,474**

Courtesy of Bertoia Auctions, www.bertoiaauctions.com

Stutz auto pressed steel pull toy by Gendron, circa 1926, tan body, red fenders and running boards, nickeled grille, bumper, and dummy lights, mesh grille panel, hood ornament, hardtop model with mounted covered spare tire on side, rubber tires, disc wheels, finest known example, excellent condition, 28 1/2" long. Provenance: Don Kaufman Collection. **$19,000**

Courtesy of Sotheby's, www.sothebys.com

Batman and Batmobile tin toys, battery-operated, 1966, based on Japanese TV series, in original carton boxes, Batman 12" x 5 1/4" x 3 3/8", Batmobile 11 3/4" x 4 3/4" x 2". **$2,901**

Courtesy of RSL Auction Co., www.rslauctions.com

Ten Pins game with figural baseball players, wood and paper litho, probably by Selchow & Righter, American, circa 1880s, with three original wooden balls used to knock down figures, chromo-lithographed label on lid of box shows ballgame in progress, second label on side of box reads, "One Piece Base Ball, S & R [Selchow & Righter] Ten Pins," rare set in mint condition. **$35,000**

Courtesy of Morphy Auctions, www.morphyauctions.com

German tin litho Distler racecar, large size, original lithographed driver, marked "Dunlop Cord" on tin wheels, battery-operated headlights, "No. 85" on front hood and "J.D.N." on front and rear, near mint condition, 20" long. **$17,500**

Courtesy of Bertoia Auctions, www.bertoiaauctions.com

Flying artillery toy by Pratt & Letchworth, rare, polychromed, four varying colored horses drawing caisson, two mounted soldiers and four seated figures, museum quality, only known example to have these specific details, 33 1/2" long; this example considered finest horse-drawn artillery toy ever made. **$48,000**

Courtesy of Heritage Auctions, ha.com

Beatles toy banjo by Mastro Industries, New York, 1964, four-stringed toy instrument originally manufactured with instruction manual and packaged on colorful cardboard backing, early Mastro box of same vintage, very fine condition. **$1,375**

Courtesy of Bertoia Auctions, www.bertoiaauctions.com

Goat bell toy by Althof Bergmann, hand-painted tin with clockwork mechanism, open gig drawn by black and white goats, bell between goats rings when toy is pushed, wheel causes galloping motion, seated driver dressed in full cloth outfit, gig with fully railed backrest and luggage rack on tail of cart, 18" long. **$20,000**

Shirley Temple collectibles sold at auction on July 14, 2015. Clockwise: toy trumpet marching costume from film "Rebecca of Sunnybrook Farm," $15,000; "In Our Little Wooden Shoes" costume from film "Heidi," $27,000; composition doll of Shirley Temple in dress from film "Stand Up and Cheer," $14,000; Shirley Temple's monogrammed accordion gifted to her by fan, $4,250; "Pinkie" prop doll from 1934 film "Bright Eyes," $14,000; red and white polka dot dress worn by Shirley Temple in "Stand Up and Cheer," $75,000.

Collectors Love Shirley Temple Auction

Theriault's "Love, Shirley Temple" auction, featuring nearly 600 costumes, memorabilia, and dolls from Temple's personal archives, began with a record price of $11,500 for her Raggedy Ann play doll and continued that way for 13 hours in Kansas City, Missouri, on July 14, 2015.

Thousands of people worldwide came to the auction, bid absentee, or bid live on the Internet via Proxibid, who provided a live streaming view of the entire proceedings.

The UFDC Museum in Kansas City now owns the 13" doll of Shirley Temple in her Texas Centennial costume, which sold for $4,500; the 27" Shirley Temple doll dressed in her Texas Centennial costume, which sold for $8,500, will make its eventual home at the Dallas Historical Society.

The famous Lenci doll known as "Pinkie," which appeared in a rivalry scene between Temple and Jane Withers in the 1934 film "Bright Eyes," sold for $14,000. A private Illinois collector took home nine Raggedy Ann books with amusing inscriptions to Shirley from Raggedy Ann creator Johnny Gruelle (hammer price $12,500) and a Shirley Temple doll in a unique Fox Studio-made costume (hammer price $19,000).

Sponsored by Theriault's, the collection toured museums around the United States for two months prior to its auction on July 14, followed by an auction of antique dolls on July 15. The two days of auctions totaled more than $4.2 million, a new record for the Annapolis, Maryland-based firm.

Courtesy of Morphy Auctions, www.morphyauctions.com

Snow White set by Chad Valley, all-cloth Snow White with mask face, molded and painted features, all original with black mohair wig and dress in original box labeled "Chad Valley Hygienic Textile Toys Made in England 1572 Snow White," with all original Seven Dwarfs in good color in original labeled boxes with each dwarf's name, "Sleepy" with Walt Disney wrist tag, excellent condition, tallest 15" high. **$6,500**

Courtesy of Sotheby's, www.sothebys.com

George III silver and glass toy cruet set by John Cann, London, circa 1740, marked on frame and casters, maker's mark only, 3 1/2" long. **$3,438**

Courtesy of Morphy Auctions, www.morphyauctions.com

Japanese tin litho Gang of Five Target Robot by Masudaya, battery-operated with original gun and darts, robot in near mint condition, original box in excellent condition, some creasing to top and bottom of lid, robot 15" high. **$12,000**

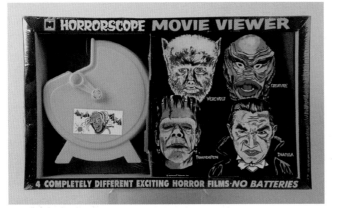

Courtesy of Morphy Auctions, www.morphyauctions.com

Horrorscope Movie Viewer by Multiple Toy Makers, plastic movie viewer with decal, original box with Werewolf, Creature from Black Lagoon, Frankenstein, and Dracula, marked "1964 Multiple Products, Inc." and "Universal Pictures, Inc.," resealed in plastic, excellent condition, 20" x 12". **$1,900**

Courtesy of Heritage Auctions, ha.com

Hydrid bull moose teddy bear in homage to Teddy Roosevelt, who ran as Progressive Bull Moose candidate in 1912; jointed arms and legs of fuzzy brown cloth over composition parts, head of plaster-like composition material, back of head with raised letters "E I H C[opyright] 1912," stuffed with excelsior material, 13" high. **$750**

Courtesy of Shapiro Auctions, www.shapiroauctions.com

Soviet Agitlak travel chess set, 1929, hinged cover with detailed rural domestic scene of young players winning chess game against adult, made of Karelian birch with gold floral pattern on body, inside hinged cover with motto "Smena-Smene-Idyot [A Change Goes for a Change]," red flag with hammer and sickle below, set of red and white chess figures (some missing) and folding board with checkered pattern of red stars on black ground and gilt flowers on unpainted ground, signed on cover "N. Zinoviev" lower left, inscribed and dated "Palekh 1929" lower right, unfolded board 3 1/8" x 3 3/8", box 3" x 3 7/8". **$14,000**

Courtesy of RSL Auction Co., www.rslauctions.com

▲ Packard cast iron eight-cylinder sedan by Hubley Mfg. Co., Pennsylvania, early 1930s, Art Deco silhouette and folding hood flaps, fine condition. **$21,000**

Courtesy of Bertoia Auctions, www.bertoiaauctions.com

◄ Carpenter burning building, cast iron and wood, molded flames, balcony, and fireman climbing ladder, considered one of the great casting effects of early toys, 16 1/2" high. **$9,000**

Courtesy of Bertoia Auctions, www.bertoiaauctions.com

Tin hoop toy by George Brown, circa 1890s, scarce, William Goodwin girl in cloth dress, hand-painted composition head, suffragette figure at center, clockwork mechanism at center axle, varying size hoops for circular motion, 11 1/4" high x 12" long. **$24,000**

Courtesy of Morphy Auctions, www.morphyauctions.com

German tin litho Tippco Santa Claus automobile, full-figured lithographed Santa driver, original tree in rear, dry-cell makes tree light up, marked "Dunlop Cord" on tin litho tires, excellent-near mint condition, 12 1/4" long x 10 1/4" high. **$25,000**

Courtesy of Morphy Auctions, www.morphyauctions.com

Japanese tin litho Friction Super Cycle, original hard rubber driver and original front antenna, marked "Space Patrol" and "Super Cycle" on both sides of toy and "B – 557" on right side of gas tank, compass between antenna and handlebars, with rare box with graphics and Japanese writing, friction works but needs flint to spark, excellent condition, box 12 1/2" long. **$17,500**

Courtesy of Clars Auction Gallery, clars.com

French Bru Bebe Jne No. 10 bisque socket head and shoulder plate doll, hand-painted face with feathered eyebrows, blue paperweight eyes, painted eyelashes, closed mouth, and pierced ears with earrings and matching pearl necklace, on kid body with bisque arms, dressed in period clothes, 28" high. **$16,000**

◄ French Bru circle/dot model with rare painted teeth, circa 1880, marks: circle and dot, Bru Jne 8 (on head), Bru Jne 8 (shoulder plate), bisque swivel head on fully modeled bisque breastplate, blue paperweight eyes, painted lashes, eyeliner, mauve-blushed eyelids, feathered and brush-stroked brows, closed mouth with space and painted teeth between shaded lips, plump lower cheeks, blushing on cheeks and chin, pierced ears, blonde mohair wig over cork pate, original kid body with gusset jointing at hips and knees, unarticulated kid arms with sculpted bisque forearms, antique white dotted Swiss dress with pink silk ribbon, lace bonnet, pink stockings, white leather high-top shoes, pristine condition, 24" high. **$14,000**

Rare Popeye Olive Oyl Tank by Linemar, battery operated, Olive Oyl pops out of top turret, Popeye holds back and lifts tank, mostly original condition, replaced plastic pins holding Popeye's legs, excellent condition, rare original box with some tearing and creasing, 11 1/2" long. **$14,000**

Japanese tin litho wind-up The King of Jungle toy by Nomura, tin litho body with hard vinyl head, toy makes roaring noise, original box with some creasing throughout, toy in excellent condition, box in very good condition, 10 1/2" high. **$11,000**

Vintage Fashion
and Accessories

The history of fashion is a mirror to the future. Nearly every style has already been done in some form and is reproduced with variations today. The popularity and demand for vintage pieces are growing because clothing and accessories are great collectibles that are also a good investment.

Many factors come into play when assessing value. When shopping vintage fashion, keep the following in mind:

Popularity: How well known the designer is affects the price.

Condition: Collectors tend to want the original design condition with no modifications or repairs.

Relevance: The piece should be a meaningful representation of a designer's work.

When you're hot you're hot: As a trend develops, it is shown in fashion magazines, and the original vintage pieces go up in value (and plummet when it goes out of favor).

Location: Prices fluctuate from one geographic region to another.

Value: The appeal of vintage fashion items has greatly increased over the last few years. Our rule of thumb is to buy quality.

For more information on vintage fashion, see *Warman's Handbags Field Guide* by Abigail Rutherford, *Vintage Fashion Accessories* by Stacy LoAlbo, and *Warman's Shoes Field Guide* by Caroline Ashleigh.

Courtesy of Heritage Auctions, ha.com

Christian Dior black cannage leather Lady Dior MM tote bag with gold hardware, two top handles, zip closure, and Dior charm on one handle, interior in red fabric with one zip pocket, very good condition, 9 1/2" wide x 8" high x 4" deep. **$1,500**

Courtesy of Heritage Auctions, ha.com

Christian Dior beige perforated leather lace Lady Dior MM tote bag, perforated lace exterior over leather with silver hardware, two leather handles, Dior hang charms, and zip top closure, interior in beige Diormisso lining with one zip pocket, good to very good condition, 9 1/2" wide x 8" high x 4" deep. **$1,500**

Courtesy of Heritage Auctions, ha.com

Christian Dior brown crocodile and suede Lady Dior bag with shoulder strap, cannage pattern, sides, handles, and optional shoulder strap in brown crocodile, brass hardware, zip top closure and Dior charm on one handle, interior in brown monogrammed fabric lining with one zip pocket, excellent condition, 9" wide x 7 1/2" high x 5" deep. **$2,500**

Courtesy of Heritage Auctions, ha.com

Hermès 40cm shiny miel crocodile Sellier Kelly bag with gold hardware, one top handle, flap top with turnlock closure, interior in miel chevre leather with one large slip pocket and two smaller slip pockets, with shiny bordeaux crocodile clochette, two keys, and lock, fair condition, 15 1/2" wide x 13" high x 5 1/2" deep. **$13,750**

Courtesy of Heritage Auctions, ha.com

Hermès shiny miel alligator Collier de Chien belt with gold hardware, good condition, 2" wide x 27 1/2" long. **$2,125**

Courtesy of Heritage Auctions, ha.com

Judith Leiber full-bead crystal horse minaudiere evening bag with black, silver, gold, red, green, and blue crystals, multicolored enamel stones throughout exterior, base exterior in brushed gold-tone finish, gold-tone pushlock closure at side exterior, interior of gold metallic leather and one slip pocket, excellent condition, 6" wide x 4" high x 2" deep. **$1,375**

Judith Leiber full-bead multicolor crystal minaudiere evening bag in shape of partridge, with silver crystals and multicolored stones in floral patterns throughout, red enamel stone eyes, beak of gold-tone hardware, side of exterior with gold-tone snap, exterior base of gold metallic leather to support bag upright, interior gold metallic leather, one slip pocket to one interior wall, gold chain shoulder strap, with mirror and comb with tassel attached, excellent condition, 4" wide x 4" high x 1 1/2" deep. $844

Louis Vuitton monogram canvas umbrella with wooden handle, brass hardware, and button eye closure, good to very good condition, 36" high, 40" diameter. $406

Hermès red "Les Mythologies des Hommes Rouges" silk scarf by Kermit Oliver, depicting Native American motifs from mythology and legends, excellent condition, no signs of wear, with Hermès box, 36" wide x 36" long. $325

Courtesy of Augusta Auctions, www.augusta-auction.com

Silk brocade at-home gown, circa 1890, one-piece port satin with pink boteh design, trained, excellent condition. $330

Courtesy of Augusta Auctions, www.augusta-auction.com

Silk brocade reception gown, 1890s, cream silk satin with striped pink and blue floral brocade, olive green velvet sleeves, very good condition. $660

Courtesy of Charles A. Whitaker Auction Co.,
www.whitakerauction.com

Beaded velvet dinner dress,
1920s, brown silk with bronze
iridill beads, shaped neckline and
hem with shaped points, excellent
condition. **$300-$500**

Courtesy of Augusta Auctions,
www.augusta-auction.com

Red velvet ball gown, 1850s,
pointed waist bodice,
trained full skirt, excellent
condition. **$540**

Courtesy of Augusta Auctions,
www.augusta-auction.com

Figured silk afternoon
gown, 1860s, two-piece
pale lavender ombre
stripe, peplum bodice, fair
condition. **$1,680**

Courtesy of Augusta Auctions, www.augusta-auction.com

ABOVE LEFT **Silk and velvet bustle dress**, late 1880s, pink and green floral print on cream silk, olive green velvet trim, excellent condition. **$540**

ABOVE MIDDLE **Tea gown**, circa 1914, heavy linen with cutwork and embroidery, excellent condition. **$240**

ABOVE RIGHT **Velvet redingote**, 1888-1890, garnet-colored velvet lined in burgundy satin, knotted fringe trim, bodice with hook and eye closure to waist, open front skirt, bustle, excellent condition. **$330**

Courtesy of Charles A. Whitaker Auction Co., www.whitakerauction.com

◀ **Men's French metallic embroidered court coat, waistcoat, and cape**, late 18th/early 19th century, cobalt velvet coat with high stand collar, wide cuff and faux pockets, foliate pattern in metallic gold braid, cord, and sequins, reproduced white satin waistcoat using trim from original, velvet cape with white satin front borders with matching foliate decoration and appliquéd with stylized gold owls, Viette and Gourdin Paris coronet and eagle buttons, Paris labels likely conservator, vest fair condition, coat and cape very good condition. **$3,000-$4,000**

◄ Printed lamé cocoon coat, circa 1912, green, purple, and yellow print with gold lamé brocade, fur-trimmed collar and sleeves, very good condition. **$900**

Sarmi evening ensemble, early 1960s, unlabeled, strapless chiffon, beaded top, together with Sophie of Sax pink beaded evening ensemble (not shown), excellent condition. **$420**

◄ Metallic brocade cocktail dress, 1960s, pale gold chiffon printed with ribbon floral in brown, metallic brocade vines, long cuffed sleeve, A-line skirt with inverted pleats, crepe under-dress, very good condition. **$100-$200**

▲ Scassi ball gown, circa 1960s, unlabeled, one shoulder, lavender and mint chiffon with shawl, very good condition, together with two 1950s party gowns (not shown), one ivory damask with gold meandering stripe and one yellow tulle, excellent condition. **$180**

Courtesy of
Charles A. Whitaker Auction Co.,
www.whitakerauction.com

**Lady's English Hudson's Bay
blanket coat,** 1960s, mod-style
double-breasted orange wool
with wide darker orange stripe
above hem, black vinyl buttons,
side panels with pockets, and
back belt with gold plastic
rectangle details, black silk
lining, garment labeled and
blanket label, very good
condition. **$200-$300**

Courtesy of Charles A. Whitaker Auction Co.,
www.whitakerauction.com

**Christian Dior Paris numbered wool skirt
suit,** mid-20th century, black boucle
princess line cropped jacket with front
hem cutout and button detail, matching
pencil skirt, fully lined in silk, boutique label
stamped 72802, excellent condition. **$250-
$350**

Courtesy of
Charles A. Whitaker Auction Co.,
www.whitakerauction.com

**Sequined chiffon evening
dress,** 1920s, blue silk
with copper and blue
sequins and faceted blue
glass drops, blouson
bodice, hip sash and side
streamers over crepe
under-dress with sequin-
decorated neckline, good
condition. **$250-$350**

Courtesy of Charles A. Whitaker Auction Co., www.whitakerauction.com

Courtesy of Charles A. Whitaker Auction Co., www.whitakerauction.com

Courtesy of Charles A. Whitaker Auction Co., www.whitakerauction.com

Beaded and fringed flapper dress, 1920s, cream silk with allover floral pattern in gold bugle beads and rhinestones, neckline and armhole decorated with rhinestones, silver beads, and pearls, back with rhinestone ornament, and lower skirt with three asymmetrical tiers of chenille fringe over silver sequined bands, good condition. **$400-$600**

Edwardian beaded silk gown, black silk with short bell sleeves, V-neck blouson bodice over black satin with stylized floral in white and crystal beads, satin sash with beaded tassels, good condition. **$300-$400**

Men's Edwardian three-piece lounge suit, black and charcoal-striped wool tweed with horizontal stripe in widely spaced pairs and herringbone weave, three-button jacket with three pockets and unusual cuff detail, wool twill lining, waistcoat with four pockets and striped cotton lining, both pieces with gutta percha buttons, button fly trousers with waistband pocket, side seam and back welt pockets, suspender buttons and side waistband adjustment with buckle, striped cotton facings, leather suspender loops attached to buttons, excellent condition. **$400-$600**

World War II Collectibles

During the seven decades since the end of World War II, veterans, collectors, and nostalgia-seekers have eagerly bought, sold, and traded the "spoils of war." Actually, souvenir collecting began as soon as troops set foot on foreign soil. Whether Tommies from Great Britain, Doughboys from the United States, or Fritzies from Germany, soldiers eagerly looked for trinkets and remembrances that would guarantee their place in the historic events that unfolded before them. Helmets, medals, Lugers, field gear, daggers, and other pieces of war material filled parcels and duffel bags on the way back home.

As soon as hostilities ended in 1945, the populations of defeated Germany and Japan quickly realized they could make money selling souvenirs to the occupation forces. The flow of war material increased. Values became well established. A Luger was worth several packs of cigarettes, a helmet, just one. A Japanese sword was worth two boxes of K-rations, an Arisaka bayonet was worth a Hershey's chocolate bar.

Over the years these values have remained proportionally consistent. Today, that "two-pack" Luger might be worth $5,000 and that one-pack helmet, $1,500. The Japanese sword might fetch $1,200 and the Arisaka bayonet $95. Though values have increased dramatically, demand has not dropped off a bit. In fact, World War II collecting is the largest segment of the militaria hobby.

For more information on World War II collectibles, see *Warman's World War II Collectibles Identification and Price Guide*, 3rd edition, by John Adams-Graf.

Courtesy of Morphy Auctions, www.morphyauctions.com

Large World War II airplane propeller, wood with brass tips, marked "No. 1901 9' x 5'9," very good condition, 9' 1" x 14 1/2". **$720**

Gen. Mark Clark two- and four-star general overseas caps: beige fabric cap with gold piping and two separate stars attached to one side, interior tag from Quarter Master Purchasing Office in Hawaii indicates size 7, dated July 28, 1943, small scattered holes and reddish-brown residue stains; dark khaki cap with bar of four stars attached on one side, brown and black piping, interior stamp indicates size 9, inspected by U. S. Army Inspector No. 76, ink inscription on lining reads "1985.3.22," excellent condition. **$1,875**

▲ Gen. Mark Clark U.S. Army three-star general's flag, wool, with three U.S. Army Lt. General's white stars on red field, minor wear and staining, light mothing from storage. 3' x 5'. **$1,875**

General Clark held the rank of lieutenant general from Nov. 11, 1942, until March 10, 1945. This flag would have flown and traveled with him as he commanded the U.S. 5th Army during its landing at Salerno and Anzio, Italy, as well as the battle of Monte Cassino and fall of Rome. By December 1944, Clark assumed command of all Allied forces in Italy as Commanding General of the 15th Army Group. This flag would have flown over his headquarters in Italy.

American World War II folding military chair along with early 20th century folding stool, Michigan, chair 19" wide x 34 1/2" high, stool 28 1/4" high. **$209**

Courtesy of Heritage Auctions, ha.com

"UNITED we are strong" propaganda poster, No. 64, U.S. Government Printing Office, 1943, issued by Office of War Information, near fine condition, folding creases, 28 1/2" x 40". **$188**

Courtesy of Heritage Auctions, ha.com

▲ Welcome home pennant, Chicago, B.P. Bonter, 1945, very good condition, some wrinkling and closed tears to edges, 34" x 15". **$94**

Courtesy of Heritage Auctions, ha.com

▶ Miniature New Testament Bible presented to unidentified acquaintance named "Ed" by Joseph P. Kennedy, Jr., killed in action in World War II, "Remember, Ed, / Jesus is always / ready to walk / with you – be the / road smooth or / rough – if you'll only ask Him – / Jos P. Kennedy Jr. / October 1941." **$4,250**

Courtesy of Heritage Auctions, ha.com

Field Marshall Bernard Law Montgomery autograph letter signed and dated September 28 [circa 1943], reads "September 28th / Eighth Army / Italy / Thank you so much for / the drawing you sent me of myself. / I think it is excellent and am / most pleased with it. / B. L. Montgomery / General / Eighth Army," single leaf, folded, approximately 7" x 5 1/2" and tipped onto larger card backing, good or better condition, separated at center vertical crease, repaired with tape on verso, some toning, creasing and chipping, minor tearing and loss at corners. **$200**

Courtesy of Elite Decorative Arts, www.eliteauction.com

World War II spent military shell decorated with floral design, 12" high, approximately 911 grams. **$90**

Courtesy of Heritage Auctions, ha.com

◄ Cased Colt Model 1911A1 1970 WWII Series Pacific Theater semi-automatic pistol, serial no. 4313PTO, .45 caliber, 5" barrel, nickel-plated finish with hardwood grips with gold Colt medallions, standard markings and features, light engraving throughout, with original light tan wooden case with plaque, key, and seven nickel-plated dummy rounds, very good to excellent condition, light scuffs to muzzle area, case with minor scuffs and wear, dummy rounds with some wear and handling, action crisp, bore good. **$1,063**

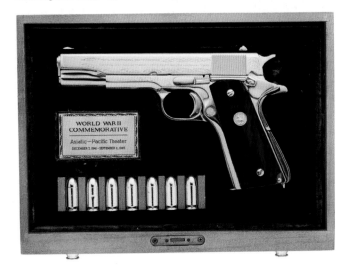

Courtesy of Morphy Auctions, www.morphyauctions.com

German Army officer's brigade belt and buckle, marks on buckle, with German Red Cross officer's belt and buckle. **$660**

Courtesy of Heritage Auctions, ha.com

▲ Italian Fascist youth dagger/knife, gilded brass hilt with eagle head and capstan, red stones for eagle's eyes, lacquered black leather grip, original brass wire, mint condition, missing original scabbard, with custom-made reproduction scabbard identical to original, 11" overall with 6 1/2" blade. **$238**

Courtesy of Heritage Auctions, ha.com

▶ World War II Soviet SSH39 steel helmet shell with painted decoration, recovered in Dukla Pass, 1" x 3" preprinted label affixed to inside crown, "Soviet SSH39 Stalshyem / Found In The Carpathian / Mountains, Dukla Pass," entire helmet painted olive drab green with hand-painted scene on front of confrontation between German tiger and Russian T-34 tanks, in large red letters on back "Dukla Pass / 1944" and below in Russian "Valley of Death," top of helmet with 40mm hole from projectile strike, good condition, paint in excellent condition, showing some age. **$250**

Courtesy of Morphy Auctions, www.morphyauctions.com

▼ Nazi souvenir ladle/serving spoon, stainless steel, marked "MDA Sch.dA" with swastika and cog wheel on back ("Modell des Amtes Schönheit der Arbeit" or "Model approved by the office for pleasant work"), marked "RKW Kantinen DR RBD Augsburg" with crude eagle on front (likely from military canteen in Augsburg, Germany), marked "Rostfrei" (German rust-free stainless steel) on handle, very good condition, 10 1/2" long. **$120**

Louis J. Dianni Antiques Auctions, louisjdianni.com

▲ German Luftwaffe paratrooper single-decal helmet shell with eagle gripping swastika, painted decal on one side of helmet. **$685**

Courtesy of Morphy Auctions, www.morphyauctions.com

1933-1945 Nazi officer's sword with lion head handle, manufactured in Eichorn, Germany, excellent condition, 38" long. **$900**

Courtesy of Morphy Auctions, www.morphyauctions.com

Japanese officer's dress sword, minor overall wear, very good-plus condition, 36" long. **$210**

Index

A

Abraham Lincoln, *122, 124, 290, 294, 527, 586-588, 592, 594, 597*
Action Comics, *44, 322*
Advertising, *20, 22, 54-62, 102, 108, 178, 306, 311, 402, 536, 545, 566, 604, 607-608, 610, 653-654*
Alcock & Co., Samuel, *238*
Amazing Fantasy, *322, 329*
American Art, *64-81*
American Bisque, *336-337*
American Ceramics, *148-199*
Americana, *11, 55, 306, 358-364, 586*
Amphora, *200-201*
Animation Art, *49*
Apollo, *122*
Arcade, *314, 320*
Art, *62-111*
Art Deco, *9, 149, 155, 200, 205, 239, 314, 320, 375, 393, 396, 422, 473-474, 476, 483, 495, 562, 564, 683*
Art Glass, *398-401, 404, 406, 438-440, 449, 454, 492-493, 495, 497*
Art Nouveau, *176, 200, 205, 314, 373, 400, 472, 480, 502, 651, 658*
Arts & Crafts, *172, 374, 382, 384-385, 472, 499*
Asian, *9, 112-121*
Atomizer, *561, 564*
Autographs, *122-125, 133, 137, 342-343, 350, 533, 586, 627, 632, 699*

B

Babe Ruth, *122*
Baccarat, *398, 562, 564*
Bailey Alloa Pottery, W. & J.A., *238*
Bakelite, *473, 563, 637*
Banks, *5, 9, 126-131*
Baseball, *27, 30, 62, 70, 318, 364, 511, 515, 576, 583-584, 654-655, 678*
Batman, *42, 124, 678*
Beatles, The, *22-23, 32, 542, 544, 551, 621, 632, 679*
Belleek, *200-201*
Bevington, *238*
Boats/Ships, *88, 128, 257, 416, 430, 522-531, 540*

Bohemian Glass, *399-400*
Books, *132-139, 276-289, 292, 351, 680*
Bottles, *140-147, 559-565*
Bradbury, Ray, *133*
Bronze, *71, 85, 114, 120-121, 128, 258, 260, 264, 266, 293, 299-301, 382, 387-389, 472, 499, 501-505, 525, 556, 647, 658, 666, 668-675*
Brown Westhead, Moore & Co., T.C., *238*

C

Caille, *316*
Camera, *576, 638-639*
Cars, *25, 36, 43, 53, 57*
Capo-di-Monte, *202*
Carnival Glass, *402-408, 438-439, 443*
Cartier, *46, 444, 483*
Cash, Johnny, *34*
Ceramics, *147-275*
Chanel, *473*
Charbonnier, Robert, *239*
Children's Books, *276-289*
Chippendale, *304, 367, 375, 386*
Civil War, *6, 122, 142, 290-297, 587-588, 654-655*
Clocks, *298-305*
Cloisonné, *112, 114, 119*
Clothing, *292, 295, 544, 599, 614, 686, 689-695, 697, 700-701*
Coca-Cola, *9, 54-55, 57, 103, 142, 306-313, 505, 545, 598-599, 601*
Coin, *423*
Coin-Operated Devices, *314-321*
Colt, *699*
Comic Books, *17, 20, 22, 42, 44, 102, 132, 322-335, 515*
Confederate, *291, 294, 496, 524, 587-588, 590*
Contemporary Art, *82-93*
Cookie Jars, *336-341*
Copeland, *202-203, 238*
Costume Jewelry, *472, 484*
Creamware, *203, 206-207, 209, 217, 267*

Cunha, Jose A., *238*

D

Daum, Nancy, *398, 402, 409-419, 498*
DC Comics, *42, 44, 327*
Delftware, *204*
Depression Glass, *5, 402, 420-437*
Detective Comics, *327*
Disney, *342-357, 681*
Disneyana, *342-357*
Dr. Seuss, *277, 284-285*
Dresden, *246*
Dressler, Julius, *238*

E

E.B. White, *281*
Eames, *376, 393*
Edwardian, *381, 471, 695*
Elvgren, Gil, *40, 65, 68, 72, 74, 102, 306*
Elvis Presley, *34, 544*
Etruscan, *245*
European Ceramics, *200-275*

F

Favrile, *402, 492, 501, 504, 658-661, 663-667, 675*
Fenton, *267, 398, 404, 406, 438-443*
Fielding, *239*
Fiesta, *148-154*
Fine Art, *94-101*
Flagg, James Montgomery, *102*
Flags, *587*
Folk Art, *8-9, 358-364, 467, 522*
Football, *315, 652, 654*
Frank Sinatra, *550, 591*
Frederic Remington, *64, 68, 71*
Frederick Hurten Rhead, *149, 182*
Fulper, *155-161*
Furniture, *36, 39, 48, 365-396*
Furniture Styles, *366-381*

G

Gas Station Collectibles, *566-573*
Gehrig, Lou, *122, 511*
George Jones & Sons, Ltd., *239*

George Washington, *56*
Georgian, *422, 470*
Gibson, *461, 551*
Glass, *397-458*
Globes, *516-521*
Gorham, *177*
Gouda, *205*
Grueby, *162-169*
Gruelle, Johnny, *680*
Guitar, *32, 551*

H

Halloween, *459-468*
Handbag, *686-689*
Handel, *492*
Hanna-Barbera, *49*
Harry Potter, *132, 278*
Haviland, *206, 233, 235*
Hendrix, Jimi, *123, 550, 623*
Hermès, *235-236, 687-689*
Holdcroft, Joseph, *239*
Homer Laughlin China Co., *148, 150*
Hooked Rugs, *359*
Hubley, *683*

I

Illustration Art, *102-111*
Indian, *56, 58, 552-558*

J

J. & E. Stevens Co., *126-127, 129-131*
Jackson, Michael, *548, 627*
Jade, *112, 121*
Jadite, *440*
James MacIntyre & Co., *210*
Jewelry, *46, 444, 469-491, 640*
Jimi Hendrix, *123, 550, 623*
John Adams & Co., *238*
John F. Kennedy, *124, 523, 577, 589, 591, 593-595*
John Lennon, *23*
Johnny Cash, *34*
Jones, George, & Sons, Ltd., *239*

K

Kennedy, John F., *124, 523, 577, 589, 591, 593-595*
Kenton, *127-128*
KPM, *219-231*
Kyser & Rex, *127, 130*

L

Lalique, *398, 444-453, 494, 509, 560, 565*

Lamps, *48, 306, 410, 492-505, 659, 670, 673-674*
Lear, Samuel, *239*
Leeds Pottery, *206-207*
Lennon, John, *23*
Lenox, *200, 592*
Leyendecker, Joseph Christian, *64, 80, 102*
Lighting, *492-505*
Limoges, *206, 232-236, 515*
Lincoln, Abraham, *122, 124, 290, 294, 527, 586-588, 592, 594, 597*
Liverpool Potteries, *207*
Loetz, *398-402*
Lonitz, Hugo, *239*
Lunéville, *239-240*

M

Majolica, *198, 208, 237-245, 269, 271, 275*
Mantle, Mickey, *26, 31, 576, 653*
Mantiques, *506-515*
Maps, *70, 292, 516-521, 525*
Marilyn Monroe, *6, 575*
Maritime, *522-531*
Marvel Comics, *42, 329, 331, 333*
Massier, *239-240*
Maurice, François, *239*
McCartney, Paul, *23*
McCoy Pottery, *192, 338*
Mechanical Bank, *126-127, 130-131*
Meissen, *246-257*
MGM, *52, 124, 534, 537*
Michael Jackson, *548, 627*
Mickey Mantle, *26, 31, 576, 653*
Mickey Mouse, *343, 350*
Mid-Century Modern, *22, 25, 36, 39, 48, 376, 390-396, 473*
Military, *697, 699, 701*
Millersburg, *438*
Milne, A.A., *134, 138-139*
Minton, *208, 237-238, 242-243*
Mocha, *209*
Modernism, *22, 25, 36, 39, 48, 64, 314*
Moonstone, *430, 472*
Moorcroft, *210*
Moser, *10, 398-401*
Movie Posters, *32, 342-343, 345, 347, 349, 352-353, 355-356, 532-541, 657*

Mt. Washington, *398, 492*
Music Memorabilia, *23, 32-35, 542-551*

N

Nelson, George, *48, 303, 376*
Norman Rockwell, *64-65, 70, 72, 80, 102, 105, 108, 125, 306*
North American, *552-558*
Northwood, *403-408*

O

Orchies, *240*
Oriental (see "Asian")

P

Pairpoint, *492-493, 495, 499-500*
Palissy, *237-241*
Parian, *208, 238*
Pattern Glass, *5, 9, 402, 441*
Paul McCartney, *23*
Peanuts, *50, 325*
Perfume Bottles, *212, 448, 451-452, 457, 559-565*
Petroliana, *566-573*
Photography, *123, 292, 507, 544, 550-551, 574-585, 593*
Picasso, Pablo, *22*
Political Memorabilia, *586-597*
Pop Culture, *17-18, 20-22, 57, 102, 122*
Porcelain Signs, *310, 567, 570, 572, 598-611*
Pornic, *240*
Posters, *22-23, 32, 133, 343, 345, 347, 349, 352-353, 355-356, 526, 532-541, 545, 547, 589, 595, 628-629, 657, 698*
Presley, Elvis, *34, 544*
Purse (see "Handbag")

Q

Quezal, *398, 454-458*
Quilt, *612-619*
Quimper, *240*

R

Railway Pottery, *239*
Ray Bradbury, *133*
Records, *620-633*
Redware, *206*
Remington, Frederic, *64, 68, 71*
Revere, Paul, *624*
Rhead, Frederick Hurten, *149, 182*
Rhinestones, *473, 695*

Rockwell, Norman, *64-65, 70, 72, 80, 102, 105, 108, 125, 306*
Rolling Stones, The, *627*
Rookwood, *170-181, 192, 197, 527*
Roosevelt, Franklin, *590*
Roosevelt, Theodore, *682*
Rörstrand, *240*
Roseville Pottery, *149, 182-192, 337, 339, 505*
Royal Bayreuth, *211*
Royal Crown Derby, *212*
Royal Doulton, *213, 215, 512*
Royal Worcester, *203, 215-217, 238*
Ruth, Babe, *122*

S

Salins, *240*
Sampler, *361*
Samuel Alcock & Co., *238*
Sandwich Glass, *420, 427*
Scientific Instruments, *634-639*
Scrimshaw, *522-523, 531*
Sendak, Maurice, *279, 289*
Sergent, Thomas Victor, *240-241*
Sèvres, *208, 258-266*
Sheraton, *368*
Ships/Boats, *88, 128, 257, 416, 430, 522-531, 540*
Sicard, *194-197*
Signs, *55, 57, 59-62, 178, 311, 566-567, 570-573, 598-611, 653-654*
Silver, *46, 146, 176-177, 300, 303, 309, 399-401, 455, 458, 470, 472-473, 475, 480-482, 488, 513-514, 523, 531, 564, 591, 640-651, 658, 674, 676, 681, 687*
Sinatra, Frank, *550, 591*
Sioux, *554-556*
Slot Machine, *316*
Space, *49, 122, 348, 684*
Spatterware, *217*
Spider-Man, *322, 329*
Spode, *202-203, 238*
Sports, *17, 26-31, 122, 652-657*
Springsteen, Bruce, *545*
St. Clement, *240*
St. Jean de Bretagne, *240*
Sterling, *146, 176-177, 399, 401, 473, 480, 514, 640, 644-646, 648-649, 651*

Steuben, *398*
Stevens Co., J. & E., *126-127, 129-131*
Still Bank, *127-129*
Stoneware, *129, 155, 182, 209, 213, 215, 363*
Superman, *44, 57, 326-327, 515, 633*
Sword, *292, 696, 701*

T

Technology, *634-639*
Theodore Roosevelt, *682*
Thomas-Victor Sergent, *240-241*
Thompson, Maggie, *102*
Tiffany, *214, 312, 454, 472, 489, 501, 503-504, 642, 648, 658-675*
Tiffany Glass, *454, 501, 503-504, 658-675*
Tiffany Studios, *501, 503, 658-675*
Toys, *41, 462, 465, 676-685*
Trade Stimulator, *315, 317*

V

Vallauris, *239-240*
Vargas, Alberto, *102*
Vending Machine, *61, 312, 315, 319*
Victoria Pottery Co., *240*
Victorian, *237, 314, 369, 370-373, 381, 461, 470-471, 507*
Vintage Fashion, *686-695*
Vuitton, *689*

W

Walt Disney, *342-346, 350-351, 353, 355, 357, 681*
Warhol, Andy, *85*
Wardle & Co., *240*
Washington, George, *56*
Weathervane, *360*
Webb, *561*
Wedgwood, *170, 203, 206, 239-240, 267-275*
Weller Pottery, *149, 182, 183, 192-199, 341*
White, E.B., *281*
Wilhelm Schiller and Sons, *240, 245*
Worcester Porcelain, *215, 217*
World Series, *364*
World War II, *16-17, 183, 233, 438, 473, 540, 545, 579, 587, 603, 696-701*
Wyeth, Andrew, *306*

Z

Zanesville, *182-183, 192*
Zsolnay, *5, 218*

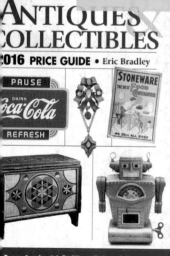
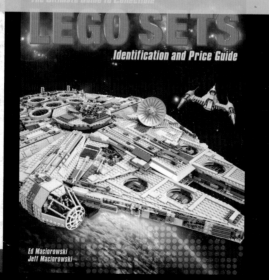